Harry's Farewell

Harry's Farewell

Interpreting and Teaching the Truman Presidency

Edited with an Introduction by
Richard S. Kirkendall

University of Missouri Press   Columbia and London

Copyright © 2004 by
The Curators of the University of Missouri
University of Missouri Press, Columbia, Missouri 65201
Printed and bound in the United States of America
5 4 3 2 1   08 07 06 05 04

Library of Congress Cataloging-in-Publication Data

Harry's farewell : interpreting and teaching the Truman presidency / edited with an introduction by Richard S. Kirkendall.
    p. cm.
    Includes index.
    ISBN 0-8262-1552-1 (alk. paper)
  1. United States—Politics and government—1945–1953.
2. Truman, Harry S., 1884–1972—Political and social views.
3. Truman, Harry S., 1884–1972—Influence.   I. Kirkendall,
Richard Stewart, 1928–
    E813.H369 2004
    973.918—dc22

                                              2004013431

♾ This paper meets the requirements of the
American National Standard for Permanence of Paper
for Printed Library Materials, Z39.48, 1984.

Designer: Kristie Lee
Typesetter: Crane Composition, Inc.
Printer and binder: Thomson-Shore, Inc.
Typefaces: Adobe Caslon and Romana

The University of Missouri Press offers its grateful acknowledgment to the Howard and Frances Keller Endowed Fund
in History at the University of Washington for a generous
contribution in support of the publication of this volume.

To the Great People
Of the Truman Library and Institute,
Past and Present,
For their Many Contributions
To Research-Based Education

Contents

List of Documents

Preface

In the hot midsummer of 2003, researchers, teachers, and staff members gathered in the Truman Library to explore how to interpret and teach the Truman presidency. A group of about fifty people, we came together for four full days (July 15–18). Papers had been circulated and read in advance, enabling us to devote the sessions to discussion. Taking breaks and eating most of our meals together, we had many opportunities for informal conversation. Enthusiasm ran high throughout the four days. In the end, the teachers rated the conference a 5 on a 5-point scale, and many said they had never attended a better conference. It was "a model that others should follow," one teacher proposed. Another called it "a real gift." The participants who had prepared the papers and the staff members from the Truman Library and the Truman Library Institute felt equally good about the event and were "pumped up" by the teachers' responses to our work.

The idea for the conference originated in the institute's Committee on Research, Scholarship, and Academic Relations. At first, the institute's Board of Directors declined to endorse it because of budgetary difficulties, but after a time, the group voted to sponsor it, and the fund-raisers found the money. The financial support came from the Ewing Marion Kauffman Foundation of Kansas City, a group eager to strengthen the educational system.

The institute had sponsored a number of conferences, beginning in 1960, but this one was unlike any other in its history. The early ones (1960–1972) were designed to promote research on the Truman presidency and brought scholars together to discuss the topic—what had already been done on it and what more should be done. For several years after that, the institute brought scholars together with people who had worked with Truman. One purpose of this second series of conferences was enrichment of the research base by recording the memories of participants in the Truman story. Like two of the earlier conferences, these produced books. More recently, the institute contributed financially to several other conferences that were held away from the Truman Library and emphasized the presentation and discussion of scholarly papers.

What was new about the conference in 2003 was its focus on the high school history classroom. This was in line with efforts underway in the historical profession at large to bridge gaps between research-oriented historians and history teachers in the schools. It harmonized as well with the significant enlargement of education in the offerings of the Truman Library and its institute. This development can be seen in the modernization of the museum and the creation of a White House Decision Center. The library has become a "Classroom for Democracy" as well as a research center. Now that Truman historiography has reached an advanced stage, the Truman Library is able to fulfill its original promise. It now offers "research-based education."

President Truman provided the basic text for the conference. He did so in his "Farewell Address," delivered on January 15, 1953. For many years, I had talked about this address, for it offered a bold interpretation of his presidency and struck me as a most interesting and meaningful document, worthy of serious discussion, much more than it had so far received.

The Committee on Research, Scholarship, and Academic Relations based its plan for the conference on the document. Analyzing it, we decided the conference needed papers on the address itself and on each of its main topics: the president and the people, the economy, civil rights, the bomb, foreign policy, Korea, and the prediction as to how the Cold War would end. Because of the conference's main aim, we also agreed that there should be a paper on teaching that would draw upon the discussions. All of this, however, did not seem to be enough. What about important matters that Truman did not discuss? We agreed that we must also have papers on four of them: the Red Scare, women's rights, immigration and ethnicity, and the environment. Several members of the committee accepted invitations to write some of these papers, and we called upon other scholars for the other papers. We also invited the leading Truman biographers to make presentations in a public event connected with the conference.

At this juncture, the education-oriented people on the staff took over and made the conference much richer than it would have been without their contributions. They designed the teaching sessions, selected documents that teachers might find useful, developed a list of resources available on the Internet, planned tours of the archives, museum, decision centers, and the Truman home, and invited a Truman impersonator to visit with the group. Also very important, they recruited the teachers!

During the conference, all participants made contributions. Staff members presided over the sessions and did much teaching. The authors of the papers summarized their work and responded to questions. The teachers discussed how the topics might be taught, and in the last hour of the last day, two of us summarized what had been said during four idea-packed days.

The conference is the basis of the book that follows, which includes the papers and presentations. It also offers documents that teachers might use in their classes. The book should spread the benefits of the conference to teachers far beyond Jackson County, Missouri.

I have referred to the many people and groups that contributed to the conference and the book. You will find many of the names in the appendixes. I am deeply grateful to every contributor, to Beverly Jarrett and the University of Missouri Press for their willingness to make the benefits of a great gathering widely available, and to Jane Lago for her excellent editing of the manuscript. I wish also thank John Findlay, chair of the University of Washington History Department, and the Howard and Frances Keller Endowed Fund in History for their support.

Harry's Farewell

Harry's Farewell Address and the Historical Significance of the Truman Presidency

Richard S. Kirkendall

At the end of his years in office, Harry Truman felt confident that he had been a great president. He said so in his "Farewell Address" to the American people, delivered on January 15, 1953. A bold statement, it challenged widely held views in his time and anticipated what has become the dominant view of him in the United States in our time. The address portrayed the man who gave it as a president of large historical significance, highly important for the American economy and American race relations but even more so for the American role in the world. This address—why and how it was written, what it said, how it was received at the time, and how it compares in its definition of Truman's historical significance with the reigning interpretation of his presidency in our day—is the subject of what follows.

Those who wrote the speech rejected what most Americans then believed about Truman. Most believed he had failed. In July 1950, 46 percent of the

Dennis Bilger, Liz Safly, Carol Briley, and Scott Roley, members of the excellent staff at the Truman Library, made essential contributions to this essay. Colleagues in the History Research Group at the University of Washington—Stephanie Camp, Patricia Ebrey, Thomas Hankins, Alexandra Harmon, Karl Hufbauer, Richard Johnson, Moon-Ho Jung, Otis Pease, Thomas Pressly, William Rorabaugh, and Nikhil Singh—also contributed, as did Robert Ferrell, Jeffrey Gall, Alonzo Hamby, Susan Hartmann, Kenneth Hechler, Mary Ann Heiss, David McCullough, Tracy McKenzie, and James Sundquist.

people had believed he was doing a good job and only 37 percent disagreed, but by the beginning of 1952 his approval rating had dropped to 25 while 62 percent of the polled population voted no. The numbers improved slightly later that year, but only after he had announced that he would not run again, and the disapproval rating remained well above 50 percent. Many Americans regarded Truman as weak and ineffective, not big enough for the job, and preferred other possibilities, above all Dwight Eisenhower.[1]

The frustrating course of the Korean War had driven down Truman's rating.[2] At first, his decision to intervene was widely supported and gave him a boost in the polls. Even before the Chinese entered the war, however, he had begun to slip, and after they moved in late in 1950, forcing American troops into a humiliating retreat, he fell rapidly. By June 1951, following his clash with Gen. Douglas MacArthur over how to fight the war, his approval rating had dropped to 24 percent, far below his disapproval number of 61. Half the people then believed that American intervention had been a mistake. A year later, only a small percentage of the population favored Truman's policies of limited war and negotiation, and most Americans wanted the United States to end the war by hitting the Communists harder.[3]

Other factors contributed to Truman's decline. They included the rising cost of living, charges of corruption and Communists in the federal government, and the expansion of presidential power.[4]

Emphasizing Korea, corruption, and Communism, the Republicans in 1952

1. *Public Opinion Quarterly* 14 (Winter 1950–1951): 815; *Dallas Morning News,* November 8, 1951, February 8, June 23, 1952; Elmo Roper, *You and Your Leaders: Their Actions and Your Reactions, 1936–1956* (New York: William Morrow and Co., 1957), 162–64.

2. *Dallas Morning News,* October 12, 1951, March 8, 1952; *New York Herald Tribune,* May 15, 1952; Robert J. Donovan, *Tumultuous Years: The Presidency of Harry S Truman, 1949–1953* (1982; rpt. Columbia: University of Missouri Press, 1996), chap. 34; Donald R. McCoy, *The Presidency of Harry S. Truman* (Lawrence: University Press of Kansas, 1984), 261–63, 265–66, 288, 294.

3. Alonzo L. Hamby, *Beyond the New Deal: Harry S. Truman and American Liberalism* (New York: Columbia University Press, 1973), 507, 511, and *Man of the People: A Life of Harry S. Truman* (New York: Oxford University Press, 1995), 534, 547–48, 550–52, 557–58, 560–62, 564, 569, 583; David McCullough, *Truman* (New York: Simon and Schuster, 1992), 815–26, 831, 841, 843–55; *Public Opinion Quarterly* 14 (Winter 1950–1951): 815, 15 (Spring 1951): 170, 177–78, (Summer 1951): 387, 395–96; *Dallas Morning News,* June 14, 1951, April 3, 1952; McCoy, *Truman,* 260, 297; *New York Herald Tribune,* September 15, October 27, 1952; Louis Harris, *Is There a Republican Majority? Political Trends, 1950–1956* (New York: Harper, 1954).

4. *Dallas Morning News,* October 12, 1951, February 8, May 13, 1952; *New York Herald Tribune,* May 15, October 27, 30, November 3, 1952; Harris, *Republican Majority?* 35–37, 131–35; Donovan, *Tumultuous Years,* chaps. 35–36; McCoy, *Truman,* 250–51, 257, 259, 273–80, 288–93, 297, 299; Robert H. Ferrell, *Harry S. Truman: A Life* (Columbia: University of Missouri Press, 1994), 358–75; Hamby, *Man of the People,* 575–98.

ran against Truman much as Democrats for years had run against Herbert Hoover. Near the end, the party's popular candidate, Eisenhower, promised to go to Korea. The promise implied that he could end the war, something Truman had failed to accomplish, and helped the general win by a wide margin in a high-turnout election.[5]

Two themes dominated the criticism of Truman during these late years of his presidency. He was, according to his critics, most of them to his right on the political spectrum, both corrupt and weak. They often suggested that he had become corrupt under the tutelage of Boss Tom Pendergast of Kansas City during the early years of his political career and had remained so after he entered the White House. In addition, they frequently characterized his foreign policy, especially his responses to the Communists in the Soviet Union, China, and North Korea, as a policy of weakness.

Confident that his critics were wrong, Harry had struggled throughout 1952 to prevent them from enjoying a great victory. Early on, he tried to select his own successor, hoping to find someone who would continue his policies. Discussing the matter with Chief Justice Fred Vinson, General Eisenhower, and Governor Adlai Stevenson of Illinois, he failed to persuade any of them to run as his choice. After the Democratic national convention chose Stevenson, Truman advised him to run on the Democratic record of the past twenty years, but the candidate, determined to be his own man, distanced himself from the unpopular president, infuriating him by doing so. Nevertheless, Truman campaigned strenuously for the party's candidate, emphasizing his own record while doing so.[6] After Eisenhower triumphed, Truman felt a need to do more to improve his reputation and increase the possibility that his policies would survive.

---

5. Roper, *Leaders,* 239–40, 244, 250–54, 257–58; Herbert H. Hyman and Paul B. Sheatsley, "The Political Appeal of President Eisenhower," *Public Opinion Quarterly* 17 (Winter 1953–1954): 443–60; *New York Herald Tribune,* March 3, April 21, October 27, November 3; 1952; Harris, *Republican Majority?* 33, 49–57, 112–16, 124–31; Angus Campbell, Gerald Gurin, and Warren E. Miller, *The Voter Decides* (Evanston: Row, Peterson and Co., 1954), 56–68, 175–76; Donovan, *Tumultuous Years,* 399, 401, 407; Ken Hechler, *Working with Truman: A Personal Memoir of the White House Years* (1982; rpt. Columbia: University of Missouri Press, 1996), 192–95, 201–2, 211, 273; McCoy, *Truman,* 299, 300, 305; McCullough, *Truman,* 813–14, 840, 860–73, 876, 899–901, 909, 911–13; Ferrell, *Truman,* 377–79; Hamby, *Man of the People,* 547–48, 550–51, 558–60, 564–66, 568, 587, 590, 592, 612.

6. Hamby, *Beyond the New Deal,* 483–84, 487, 500–502; Donovan, *Tumultuous Years,* 399–401; McCoy, *Truman,* 305; McCullough, *Truman,* 887–93, 903, 906–9; Ferrell, *Truman,* 375–77; Hamby, *Man of the People,* 600–614; Robert H. Ferrell, ed., *Off the Record: The Private Papers of Harry S. Truman* (1980; rpt. Columbia: University of Missouri Press, 1997), 266–69, 272; Monte Poen, ed., *Strictly Personal and Confidential: The Letters Harry Truman Never Mailed* (1982; rpt. Columbia: University of Missouri Press, 1999), 118, 122.

The president was proud of his record and concerned about his place in history, and as criticism of him had mounted, so had his frustration and anger. Feeling robbed by his critics of the admiration he had earned, he focused much of his anger on elements of the media and expressed his frustrations privately in letters he did not mail and memorandums to himself. Among the newspapers, his targets included the Hearst, Pulitizer, Scripps-Howard, and McCormick-Patterson chains. He protested against the *Chicago Tribune*, *New York Daily News, Washington Times-Herald, Washington Post, St. Louis Post-Dispatch, Kansas City Star, Los Angeles Times,* and *Dallas News* and also Henry Luce, Roy Howard, Walter Winchell, Drew Pearson, and Fulton Lewis, among others. He called these institutions and individuals the "sabotage press," "character assassins," "the kept press," the "dirty press," and "liars," among other equally unflattering names, and labeled the columnist Westbrook Pegler "a louse." He complained that in 1952 only one metropolitan paper "was editorially favorable to the continuance of the most prosperous administration in the history of the United States" and proposed that the "so-called 'free press'" was "about as free as Stalin's press."[7]

Two thoughts comforted the president. He assured himself that "thinking readers" recognized that the newspapers he so disliked did not tell the truth and thus their "political influence" was "not what they'd like to have it." He also drew upon his knowledge and sense of history to predict that future historians would vote for him. In the historians' accounts, his foes in the media would "be the sons of bitches," not he. "If you will study the history of our country you'll find that our greatest presidents and congressional leaders have been the ones who have been vilified most by the current press," he wrote to himself. "But history justifies the honorable politician when he works for the welfare of the country."[8]

7. Ferrell, ed., *Off the Record,* 226, 228–34, 237–39, 249–50, 259, 268, 270–72; Poen, ed., *Strictly Personal,* 9–10, 56, 83, 108, 118, 122, 127; Monte M. Poen, ed., *Letters Home by Harry Truman* (1984; rpt. Columbia: University of Missouri Press, 2003), 257; Longhand Personal Memos, November 15, 18, 28, December 1, 4, 6, 1952, Box 333, President's Secretary's Files, Truman Papers, Truman Library; McCoy, *Truman,* 297–99, 302, 304, 306–9; Hamby, *Man of the People,* 557–58, 574. The *St. Louis Post-Dispatch* supported Stevenson. For a full account of Truman's relations with the newspapers and other media, see Franklin D. Mitchell, *Harry S. Truman and the News Media* (Columbia: University of Missouri Press, 1998). Mitchell devotes pages 235–45 to the efforts Truman made in 1952–1953 "to secure for himself and his presidency an honored place in American history." In addition to the Farewell Address, these efforts included his participation in the political campaign, the State of the Union Message, and a series of one-on-one interviews with members of the White House press corps.

8. Poen, ed., *Strictly Personal,* 10; Longhand Personal Memos, December 6, 1952, and undated.

Truman's anger extended to the Republicans and included Eisenhower, whom earlier he had liked and admired and with whom he had worked harmoniously. During the campaign, he advised a cousin that "Ike has taken up with [Sen. Joseph] McCarthy and [Sen. William] Jenner, the proponents of the Big Lie, and has himself completely distorted the truth on Korea, R.R. strikes and the European Foreign Policy." After the election returns came in, he asked his staff for an analysis of the Republican campaign. He believed it had been "made up of lies[,] misrepresentation and bald demigogery [*sic*] mixed with a holy approach in a long faced Cotton Mather manner" and "[m]ilitary hero glamour, character assassination (McCarthyism) and promises of world peace (which are impossible of fulfillment)."[9]

The president regarded the press and the Republicans rather than Stevenson's blunders as chiefly responsible for the damage that had been done to the Democratic cause and to his own reputation, and he believed the press contributed to the mistakes made by the Democratic candidate. He explained— to himself—that the man from Illinois read Republican newspapers that overlooked the evils of Republican machines and portrayed the members of Democratic machines as "crooks." Thus, Stevenson could not believe that "a life long politician" could be "an honest man." He had "read Bertie McCormick's awful Tribune and Hearst's Chicago sewer sheet," "more than half believed what they had to say," and consequently suffered during the campaign from a "half hearted approach" and a "lack of faith" in the Truman administration.[10]

On the day after Christmas, Truman openly challenged the negative views of his presidency. He conducted a series of half-hour, one-on-one interviews in the Oval Office with journalists who had covered the White House since the beginning of his presidency. The group included Ernest B. (Tony) Vacarro of the Associated Press, Edward T. Folliard of the *Washington Post*, Joseph A. Fox of the *Washington Evening Star*, Anthony Leviero of the *New York Times*, and Robert G. Nixon of the *Washington Times Herald*. The journalists regarded the event as unprecedented and reported on the interviews the following day.

---

9. Ferrell, ed., *Off the Record*, 272; Poen, ed., *Letters Home*, 257–58; Longhand Personal Memo, December 22, 1952. Truman and Eisenhower had worked together while the general served as the army chief of staff (1946–1948) and supreme commander of NATO forces (1951–1952), and more than once Harry had offered to support Ike for the presidency. Steve Neal, *Harry and Ike: The Partnership That Remade the Postwar World* (New York: Scribner, 2001).

10. Longhand Personal Memo, December 22, 1952.

Expressing pride in his record and confidence that future historians would give him a high rank, Truman emphasized two areas of accomplishment: the economy and foreign affairs. Vacarro reported that the president told him "history" would "credit his Administration with success" for "we've got here at home an economic situation without equal in the history of the world." According to Folliard, Truman believed he had "put the United States in a position of economic prosperity such as no other country has ever known." "We are the most prosperous nation in the world," Truman said to Nixon. "But the voters shot Santa Claus just the same." They did so, Truman insisted and Leviero reported, even though the national income was now distributed fairly to farmers, workers, and businesses—big and little.

The president boasted even more of his handling of international matters. He defended his use of the atomic bombs against Japan, insisting it had saved thousands of lives, but did not regard that decision as his most difficult or important. He saved that ranking for his decision to send troops into Korea. It may have saved the United Nations from destruction and humanity from World War III by demonstrating that the "peace-loving nations" were willing to use force to protect a nation against an invader. To have "allowed Soviet Russia's puppets unrestrained sway in that peninsula," as Leviero described Truman's point, "would have been interpreted as a sign of weakness of the free world." To avoid war with the Soviet Union, he urged, the United States must continue its Korean War policies of strength and international cooperation.

Truman went beyond the bomb and Korea to applaud the whole of his foreign policy. Brushing aside the argument that it was weak, he portrayed it as strong and effective. He advised Folliard that he had "kept the country out of a third world war that would mean the destruction of civilization." He told Leviero that he had been "working more than seven-and-one-half years, walking a tight rope, keeping us out of war—keeping communism from overrunning the free world" and had "succeeded." Fox concluded that the president derived "most satisfaction" from his program "for building world peace, and checking the sweep of Soviet imperialism" and continued to believe that the only way to deal with Russia was "to meet force with force." The *Evening Star* reporter added that the president believed he had established a "permanent" foreign policy that the incoming administration could not change.

More than his colleagues, Robert Nixon discussed Truman's reading of the lessons of history. "If the free world makes itself so strong that the Russians will know that they cannot gain by war, they will probably not resort to war," the journalist reported, capturing one of the president's biggest ideas. "If we do what we did after World War I, when we scuttled the League of Nations, all our efforts for peace will be knocked in the head." Defining the United Nations as "our real hope for peace," Truman had insisted that he had "made it a going concern and it must remain so."

In addition, Nixon had much to say about Truman as prophet. According to this account, the president predicted that the Russian people would refuse "to be ground under an iron heel forever" and would "bring about a gradual change in their government." The prediction would enable him to leave office a confident man, certain that the United States and its allies would "in due time triumph over the forces of Communist aggression." His prediction implied that a combination of forces, not one alone, would end the Cold War. They included pressure from the people of the Soviet Union, eager for freedom, as well as pressure from American policy. This combination would prevent the Soviet state from controlling its people forever.

The president also dealt with the puzzle of his party's loss of power. His explanation ignored his own contribution and the fact that no party had won six consecutive elections since the Civil War era. Instead, he emphasized Stevenson's shortcomings, Eisenhower's status as a military hero, his promise to go to Korea, McCarthyism, and the press. "We had a candidate who did not have long-time political experience," he explained to Leviero, "and he was up against glamour, character assassination, and the most vicious political campaign of misrepresentation in American history." He informed Nixon that there were three reasons the Republicans won: "(1) Glamour and hero worship. (2) McCarthyism and the effect of wholesale character assassination deliberately applied over a long period. . . . And (3) just plain demagoguery: the promising of things that can't be performed: the raising of hopes of mothers and wives and loved ones that their men can soon come home from Korea; fooling people into believing there is an easy solution."

Truman also touched on other matters. He expressed his bitterness toward several newspaper chains and journalists, claiming that their false propaganda had, among other results, prevented him from giving the American people a true picture of the Korean War. He also maintained that large advertisers influenced news coverage, praised members of his administration, and attacked his critics' handling of the "corruption-in-government issue." Still further, he discussed the presidency and his relations with the Congress, endorsed his vigorous use of the veto power, expressed continued support for his stands on civil rights and national health insurance, and spoke of his plans for a presidential library.

Truman indicated clearly and forcefully that he regarded his critics as seriously mistaken. "If a President makes decisions that are right and for the welfare of the people, it does not make any difference what is said about him while he is alive," he advised Leviero. "The Presidents who have done things, who were not afraid to act, have been the most abused." Comparing himself with Washington, Jefferson, Jackson, Lincoln, Cleveland, Wilson, and Franklin Roosevelt, he insisted that he had "topped them all in the amount of abuse I have received." Leviero, who gave his interview especially full and friendly treatment, added that the president "said this with a smile."

These were the subjects and ideas that occupied large places in Truman's thinking as his administration moved toward its end. Looking back, one surprising feature is how little he said about civil rights. It was a highly controversial feature of his presidency that won him praise for boldness, included the desegregation of the armed forces, and began the breakup of the "Solid South." Perhaps, however, his opponents in Congress, most of them southern Democrats, had prevented him from deriving a sense of great satisfaction from his efforts to promote change in race relations. What seems clear is that he was not nearly as pleased with what he had accomplished in this area as he was with what he had done in international relations.

Truman could have converted these interviews into a farewell address, and according to some journalists at the time and some historians more recently, he did write his own Farewell Address. It was, Paul P. Kennedy of the *New York Times* reported the day after the president spoke, "perhaps the most personal speech the President had made" and was based "on a first draft he himself wrote Sunday night [January 11] in his study in the White House." Although "reorganized somewhat in conferences with the White House staff," the newsman added, "essentially it remained, in tone and mood, the type of a talk the President was accustomed to making to little groups in the White House Rose Garden." "The President wrote most of the speech himself in longhand on 15 pages of White House stationery in his study last Sunday," Robert J. Donovan of the *New York Herald Tribune* maintained. "While his staff subsequently worked on detail and expansion, his aides said the speech was more a personal product of Mr. Truman's than any of his previous addresses." After he switched from journalism to history in the 1970s and published a highly regarded two-volume book on Truman's presidency, Donovan continued to believe the president had drafted the speech. More recently, David McCullough, Truman's most popular biographer, endorsed this version, flatly stating that the president "insisted on writing his farewell speech himself."[11]

11. Kennedy's and Donovan's reports were published on Friday, January 16, 1953; Donovan, *Tumultuous Years*, 407; McCullough, *Truman*, 916.

This story of the writing of the speech appears to have originated with the White House press secretaries. They were the staff members with whom the press corps worked most closely, and they told the story in this way, perhaps in response to the talk at the time about Stevenson writing his own speeches. "This was an address, which to a very large extent, he wrote out in long hand in the privacy of his study without any help from speechwriters or staff," Irving Perlmeter, the assistant press secretary, recalled a decade after the event. "Of course, after his preliminary draft was ready, his staff went over it and assisted him in filling in little spots here and there, but basically, it was a personal message which is exactly what all of us hoped he would give." McCullough, in his discussion of the address, relied on Perlmeter's boss, Roger Tubby, drawing upon his diary and "a number of fascinating hours talking" with him.[12]

The story suffers from three weaknesses. First, the press secretaries were not the best source on this matter, for they were not heavily involved in the speechwriting process, usually not participating until the final or "freezing session."[13] Second, speechwriting in the Truman White House tended to be a cooperative enterprise. Furthermore, drafts of the speech and related documents challenge the story.

Truman did regularly participate in the speechwriting process. At the staff conferences he held each morning, the members working on speeches discussed them with their colleagues, and he interjected "his thoughts, his directives, and his philosophy." He also came in and out of "roundtable" discussions conducted by the people working on his speeches. At various points in the process, he offered advice on timing, length, and content and asked for evidence on audience reactions to earlier speeches so as to find ways of improving his performance.[14]

Truman would not deliver a speech that he had not given a critical reading. Not to do so would have been "utterly foreign, and alien" to his "personality," one adviser insisted. "He was no puppet"; he was his "own man." After a speech had reached an advanced stage, he would take a copy to the family's

12. Perlmeter, Oral History, 10, Truman Library; McCullough, *Truman*, 916, 1053; McCullough to author, March 28, 2003. Advised that Tubby's papers, deposited at Yale University, have been closed until 2050(!), I have been denied access to them.

13. Francis H. Heller, ed., *The Truman White House: The Administration of the Presidency, 1945–1953* (Lawrence: Regents Press of Kansas, 1980), 108–9, 148; Hechler, *Working with Truman*, 238–39.

14. Heller, ed., *White House*, 43–44, 89, 149, 151; Hechler, *Working with Truman*, 133, 213–15; Murphy, "Some Aspects of the Preparation of President Truman's Speeches for the 1948 Campaign," 4, 44, 82, 84, 87, 90–92, Box 14, Murphy Papers, Truman Library.

living quarters in the evening, work over it, and read it to Mrs. Truman. He regarded her as his "best critic."[15]

The White House also drew representatives of the departments and agencies into the speechwriting process. The president and his staff sometimes asked them for a first draft, usually turned to them for advice, and often called upon them for comments on drafts developed elsewhere. Marshall Shulman, a special assistant and top speechwriter for Secretary of State Dean Acheson, and James L. Sundquist from the Bureau of the Budget and then the Office of Defense Mobilization, frequently worked closely with the White House staff on the president's speeches.[16]

It was the White House staff, however, that had most of the responsibility for the development of the speeches. Charles Murphy played the leading role in this small group. A forty-three-year-old North Carolinian and lawyer, he had gone to work in Washington in 1934 following graduation from the Duke University law school. After serving in the Senate's Office of the Legislative Counsel for thirteen years, he had joined the president's staff as an administrative assistant in 1947 and moved up to special counsel in 1950. By the end of Truman's presidency, Murphy had acquired rich experience as a speechwriter, but he doubted his talents as a writer and relied heavily on drafting teams that he organized. White House staff members, including David Lloyd, David Bell, Richard Neustadt, and Kenneth Hechler, served regularly on these teams. Individuals worked alone on the drafts, but the teams met frequently to discuss what should be said, work over drafts, and seek consensus. Murphy usually presided over these meetings, participated in the discussions, sometimes rewrote the drafts, and decided when a speech was ready for the president's "preliminary reactions." After taking a draft to the president, he reported back to the team members, who then exchanged ideas once again and moved the speech forward. This "progressive roundtable system," Neustadt recalled, enabled the participants "to exchange views," "make recommendations," and "gauge the president's feelings, mood and attitudes." Murphy had confidence that the process turned out good speeches.[17]

15. George Elsey, Oral History, 190, Truman Library; Heller, ed., *White House,* 133.

16. Heller, ed., *White House,* 60, 89, 129, 132, 140, 151–52, 201, 202; Murphy, "Some Aspects," 2; Hechler, *Working with Truman,* 233, 235, 236, 237; Elsey, Oral History, 153; Sundquist, Oral History, 36, Truman Library.

17. Neustadt, "Notes on the White House Staff under President Truman," June 1953, pp. 14–16, Box 10, Neustadt Papers, Truman Library; Heller, ed., *White House,* xv, 59, 60, 70, 91, 99, 100, 115, 131, 132, 149, 151, 152, 201, 202; Elsey, Oral History, 137, 153, 179; Murphy, "Some Aspects"; Murphy to President, September 13, 1950, Murphy Papers; Hechler, *Working with Truman,* 49–52, 232–39, 253–54, 262; James Sundquist to author, February 15, 2003.

The speechwriters knew what kind of speeches Truman wanted and tried to produce them. They knew him well, for the staff was small and they saw him frequently—in daily staff meetings, frequent roundtable sessions, one-on-one sessions in his office, and informal contacts as he moved about the White House or vacationed with them in Key West. They knew that "his idea of a speech was 'a direct statement of the facts without trimmings and without oratory.'" They tried to "catch the spirit and style of the President's extemporaneous remarks" and to have "the speeches ready far enough ahead of time" so that the president could "work at length with his reading copy." As one speechwriter recalled, he tried to absorb Truman's "manner of expressing himself, his sentence style, his approach to things" and to make a speech "sound as much like Harry Truman" as he could. This meant simple sentence structure and the avoidance of fancy, complicated, and foreign words and of efforts to make Truman sound like someone he was not, such as Franklin Roosevelt. Truman's writers felt obligated to get a subject "on paper in a fashion that would reflect the Truman language and personality." Murphy and his team were good at that.[18]

When a drafting team was satisfied with what it had, it held a "freezing session," usually in the Cabinet Room. In addition to the members of the team, those in attendance sometimes included representatives of the departments and agencies interested in the topic and always included the White House press secretary and the president. Truman dominated the session, reading the speech aloud "so that he would get the feel and flavor of it" and the others could detect "awkward phraseology or overlong sentences or even words that just didn't sound right coming out of Harry Truman's mouth." On one occasion, an adviser called attention to "an unusually large number of *s* sounds," and the president responded that the sound no longer caused trouble "since the dentist fixed my teeth." Although these sessions tended to be "dress rehearsals," he often suggested revisions before putting his "final stamp of approval on the speech." Sometimes he took a speech back to the living quarters for further work.[19]

The staff members enjoyed working with the president and found him warm, generous, kindly, and considerate. He did not place himself far above them; he entertained them with his sense of humor. They liked his impact on

18. Heller, ed., *White House,* 119, 151; Neustadt, "Notes," 46–48; Murphy to President, September 13, 1950, Murphy Papers; Elsey, Oral History, 137, 168–70, 175; Hechler, *Working with Truman,* 223–24.

19. Heller, ed., *White House,* 133–34, 148, 202; Hechler, *Working with Truman,* 237–40; Elsey, Oral History, 154–55, 169, 189.

the people working in the White House, convinced that he had raised morale to a high level and inspired hard work. He impressed them as a good man, wise and compassionate, courageous and calm in difficult circumstances. They admired his understanding of history, his decisiveness, and the quality of his decisions and policies. They also admired his work habits, administrative ability, and loyal support for his subordinates. Although he often moved too slowly, they applauded his firmness when he did fire men, such as General MacArthur, who let him down.[20]

As chief of staff, Murphy was especially eager to challenge the negative view of the Truman presidency. Although he had encouraged Truman not to run again, Murphy believed his boss had become a great president, a man of wisdom and good judgment who mobilized intelligent people and made great decisions. Badly disappointed by the election outcome, Murphy blamed the press for the fact that many people did not share his opinion and was confident that eventually the general estimation of the presidency would move higher. It had been "a revelation," he told Truman on January 14, "to see how one man could do so much to guide the course of history and to improve the lot of so many millions of people throughout the world."[21]

In working on the Farewell Address, Murphy and his colleagues hoped to influence both public opinion in their day and what historians might say later on. Developed by a team, the address was a "labor of love," one of the writers, James Sundquist, recalled in his oral history interview. Working on it for more than a month, the writers, Sundquist remembered, "agreed that this had to be a masterpiece" that would express "in a sensitive way" their "feeling about . . . the Truman administration" and suggest "that the American people had made a mistake in repudiating it."

For the speechwriters, one document in the history of farewell addresses stood out. "The model of Washington's Farewell Address was not far from our minds," Sundquist remembered recently. "[W]hile we had no delusions we could write anything with as much . . . impact as his [Washington's] words have had over the centuries, we wanted to strike the same tone and come as close as we could to profundity, Harry Truman style." Although the writers

---

20. Hechler, *Working with Truman*, chap. 1; Neustadt, "Notes," 17, 43, 46–48; Heller, ed., *White House*, 114, 120, 141; Tubby, Oral History, 110, 118–21, 126–44, Truman Library.

21. Hechler, *Working with Truman*, 246–47; McCullough, *Truman*, 892; Ferrell, *Truman*, 376; Hamby, *Man of the People*, 604–5; Heller, ed., *White House*, 118, 123, 126; Murphy to Frank V. Keesling Jr., November 5, 1952, Murphy to Dr. G. W. Murphy, November 7, 1952, Murphy to Truman, January 14, 1953, Box 1, Chronological File, and Box 13, Truman File, Murphy Papers.

wished to emphasize Truman's accomplishments, they intended also to offer advice, as the first president had.

Truman wanted to speak positively to the American people. He spent a couple of hours with his writers nearly every day in enjoyable conversation. He talked thoughtfully and confidently about his record, spoke often of Jackson County, his home area, cracked jokes, and challenged the incoming president's prediction that he could do the job on a forty-hour week. He avoided the anger he had expressed in the letters he did not mail and the memorandums to himself. "Even when he showed irritation at some events, or personalities, he did so without bitterness, and often almost light-heartedly," Sundquist advised me. Perhaps he had freed himself from anger by pouring it into those documents. Whatever the explanation, it was obvious to his writers that, as Neustadt has written, he wanted his regime "to wind up its affairs in a posture of dignity and good will, bowing out gracefully, neither cringing nor rancorous," and wanted the address to be a part of that effort.[22]

After some days of group discussion, Murphy called upon his assistant, Neustadt, for the first draft. Thirty-three, a veteran of World War II, and a political scientist with a recently acquired Harvard Ph.D., Neustadt had worked for the Bureau of the Budget from 1946 to 1950 before becoming a special assistant in the White House. In that post, he frequently wrote the first drafts of major speeches and then moved the process along. Several weeks after the election, Murphy had asked him to produce the initial version of the State of the Union Message. A month later, Neustadt saw the final product as "a less complete—perhaps less coherent—document than it was in the first draft" but regarded that as "inevitable," given "the way we have to do these things—lots of cooks and much patchwork." Aware that Truman was concerned about his place in history and wanted to target historians in the message, Neustadt expected that the Republicans would try to revise the historical record of the past twenty years, the years of dominance by the Democrats, and would get help from the press and "a lot of professors." He was determined to counter that in advance. His speechwriting responsibilities offered opportunities to do so.[23]

22. Sundquist, Oral History, 15; Sundquist to author, February 15, 2003; Neustadt, "Notes," 50, 54. See also John Mason Brown, "The Trumans Leave the White House," *Saturday Review*, February 7, 1953, 10–11.

23. Sundquist, Oral History, 15; Heller, ed., *White House*, xv, 115; Hechler, *Working with Truman*, 249, 275; Neustadt to Murphy, January 7, 1953, Neustadt to Harold Stein, December 1, 1952, Neustadt to Peter Odegard, January 7, 1953, Neustadt to David Lloyd, November 14, 1952, Boxes 2–3, Chronological Files, Neustadt Papers.

For help in drafting the address, Neustadt had several documents on his desk. One was a speech, "Our Foreign Policy in Perspective," recently delivered by W. Averell Harriman, the director of the Mutual Security Agency. The stack also included a letter from Charles Brannan, the secretary of agriculture, and Truman's State of the Union Message of January 7. All the documents, even the letter from the secretary of agriculture, emphasized international relations. The message devoted well over half its space to this side of the Truman presidency, an allocation that reflected the way the men of the Truman White House evaluated their challenges and accomplishments.[24]

Drawing heavily on the State of the Union Message, Neustadt had completed a draft of the Farewell Address by January 10.[25] It noted Truman's major renovation of the White House and the transition that lay ahead from Truman to Eisenhower and offered an extended discussion of the president's job. It featured a lengthy presentation of the global struggle between the United States and the Soviet Union, responded to critics of American foreign policy, and contrasted the response in Korea to the invasion from the north with the handling of similar "tests" in the 1930s. It also predicted a favorable outcome of the Cold War. The draft ignored such domestic matters as the economy and race relations but did include two pages on the Red Scare. It ended with several paragraphs on the relations between the president and the people.

On that January day, the president met with his speechwriters, presumably to discuss Neustadt's draft, and then contributed an eighteen-page document written in his own hand.[26] It began with a brief reference to what lay ahead for him, quickly summarized his political career, described more fully the evening he became president, and offered four paragraphs on his first four months as president and a sentence on the atomic bombing of Japan. Next, six short paragraphs surveyed the foreign policies, and four sentences dealt proudly with the progress of the American economy. Strongly critical of the Soviet Union, the pages on foreign policies dealt at greatest length with the

24. Box 8, Farewell Address Folder, Neustadt Papers.

25. Murphy's files in the Truman Papers contain a preliminary version, dated January 10 and largely in Neustadt's hand. The Truman Library also houses fully typed versions of the draft.

26. Copies in Box 42, Speech File, President's Secretary's Files, Truman Papers, and Box 8, Farewell Address Folder, Neustadt Papers. Truman's calendar indicates that he met with his "speechwriters" at 10:30 a.m. on January 10. This may have been the only scheduled meeting with them that month. President's Secretary's Files, Truman Papers.

"Point Four" program of technical assistance to poor countries and predicted that it would be "our greatest contribution to world peace." Then the document moved on to the near-collapse of the White House, the political campaigns, and Truman's travels. At two spots, he pointed out how hard he had worked. After applauding the handling of the transition, the president concluded that the rebuilt White House would "stand for centuries," as would "the country itself," and that he and his wife believed they had "made a contribution to the stability of the U.S.A. and the peace of the world."

Although not dated, this was the document Truman wrote on Sunday, January 11. It was not the draft of a speech. Written in a large hand on small pages, it was quite short and merely suggested topics that should be covered in the address. "Tell about them," the president instructed his writers. He had said much more in his conversations with the journalists and given them a much more impressive interpretation of the historical significance of his presidency.

The document influenced the second draft, largely written by Hechler and dated January 12. What the new draft said about Truman's move into the presidency, his first months there, the defense pacts, and the Trumans' sense of accomplishment came from what the president had written.[27] That manuscript, it seems, also encouraged the writers to add a paragraph on Point 4 and another on the American economy and to keep in two paragraphs on the size of the president's job. It also appears likely that the description of the decision to go to war in Korea drew upon the conversations between the president and his staff.

The second draft differed from the first in other ways. It did not make such heavy use of the State of the Union Message, cut much regarding the tasks of the president, and dropped the Red Scare. It also dropped much of the response to the critics of the administration's foreign policy but kept in the contrast between Truman's foreign-policy decisions and policies and those of the interwar years and the prediction as to how the Cold War would end. They were big themes.

The staff produced a third draft by January 13.[28] It restored pieces that had been in the first version but dropped from the second, including a paragraph about the life of the Trumans in Blair House during the renovation of the White House. The draft more explicitly recognized the president's

27. Hechler, *Working with Truman*, 276–78; rough draft in Murphy Files, Truman Papers; final version in Bell Files, Box 1, Farewell Address, Truman Papers.
28. Copies in Neustadt's Papers and Bell's Files, Truman Papers.

enthusiasm for Point Four and indicated more clearly and forcefully that Truman opposed the dropping of atomic bombs as a way of dealing with Communism. Several other changes made use of the president's memo. One praised the handling of the transition from Truman to Eisenhower; a second exclaimed about the extent of the president's travels; a third dealt enthusiastically with the performance of the economy.

Charlie Murphy contributed to the fourth draft in his own hand.[29] Many of his changes were small, mainly stylistic, and improvements upon what his colleagues, including his boss, had done. He also added an explanation of the decision to use the bomb to a section that originated in Truman's memo, deleted six paragraphs from the discussion of the Cold War, improving the flow by doing so, and strengthened the paragraph on the Korea decision. Still further, he enlarged the discussion of a first-strike use of atomic bombs, deleted a paragraph on how "long and hard and costly" the Cold War "struggle" would be, and cut out others on Point Four and the ways in which the United States was "meeting the world-wide communist challenge." In their place, he wrote of "a wonderful new golden age" that would follow the Cold War, picked up examples Truman had offered in his memo, and inserted paragraphs on "the things we could do to enrich the lives of people everywhere." Following more contributions to this draft by other staff members, he reworked the prediction about the ending of the Cold War.

On January 13, the date of delivery was close at hand, and the writers devoted much attention to the address, moving it from the third to the fifth draft and encouraging the president to "mark it up a lot." He marked it up, but not a lot. To a reference to his desk in the Oval Office, he added: "This has been the desk of many Presidents and will be the desk of many more." He pointed out that living in Blair House "was not as convenient" as living in the White House. "I had to get in a car in the morning to cross the street to the White House office, again at noon to go to the Blair House for lunch, again to go to the office and finally take an automobile at night to return to the Blair House." Obviously amused by a situation created by his major renovation of the White House, he added: "Fantastic isn't it? But necessary so my guards thought—and they are the ones exposed to danger." To the discussion of the night he became president and a passage that read "I walked over to the office of the Speaker of the House, Mr. Rayburn," he inserted "to discuss pending legislation." Perhaps he did not want anyone to believe he had come

29. Copy in Murphy Files, Truman Papers.

only for bourbon! Revising only slightly, the speechwriters incorporated his suggestions into the sixth draft.[30]

In that draft, dated January 14, the writers also made other changes, some of them worthy of attention. The draft enlarged the discussions of Iran in 1945–1946 and Greece and Turkey in 1947, deleted most of the paragraph on the Marshall Plan, and added brief references to the Berlin airlift and the military aid programs. It also inserted two paragraphs on the complexities of the decision to enter the Korean War and another on the valiant way in which Americans were now fighting. It referred to those who would "drop the atomic bomb" as "impatient" and to the Soviet Union as "a godless system." Reducing somewhat the discussion as to how the Cold War would end, the draftsmen revised Murphy's insertion about the "golden age." Turning to domestic matters, the writers improved a paragraph on "spreading the blessings of American life to all our people."[31]

Time was running out, and the speech was ready for a reading by the president. David McCullough has described the reading, which must have taken place on the fourteenth:

> [A]t the big table in the Cabinet Room one evening, the staff gathered, he read it aloud, stopping at the end of each page for their comments. Recounting the decision on Korea, he described how he had flown from Independence to Washington, the fateful Sunday in June 1950. "Flying back over the flatlands of the Middle West," he read, "I had a lot of time to think." Roger Tubby [the press secretary] suggested he make it "*rich* flatlands"—"rich flatlands" would sound better, Tubby said. "The parts of southern Illinois, Indiana, and Ohio that I flew over are not rich, Roger," Truman replied. Plain "flatlands" it remained.[32]

The president gave the address the next evening, January 15. It came at the end of a busy day, dominated by conversations with individuals and small groups, including Secretary Acheson and representatives of the Reserve Officers Association. He met with his staff at ten in the morning and again for picture taking at three and then held his last press conference, his 324th, at four.[33]

---

30. Murphy to President, January 13, 1953, Box 42, Speech File, President's Secretary's Files, Truman Papers.

31. Box 8, Farewell Address Folder, Neustadt Papers.

32. McCullough, *Truman*, 916.

33. Box 84, Appointments, President's Secretary's Files, Truman Papers; Folliard, *Washington Post*, January 16; "The News of the Week in Review," *New York Times*, January 18,

Much later, beginning at 10:30 that evening, the president spoke from the Oval Office to the nation by radio and television. Several features of the address stand out. One was how little it contained about domestic policies, only five sentences on the economy and two on civil rights. These passages boldly proclaimed that Americans had "learned how to attain real prosperity for our people" and there had been "a tremendous awakening of the American conscience" on civil rights. He spoke at greater length on the presidency, emphasizing the president's role as the ultimate decision maker and his dependence on support from the people. "The greatest part of the President's job is to make decisions," he maintained. "He needs the understanding and help of every citizen."

The president devoted most of the speech to international relations. Here, he defended his use of the atomic bomb against Japan, suggesting that it had saved many more lives than it had destroyed. He also challenged those who would rely upon that bomb now to end the Cold War. Americans were "not made that way," he insisted, a declaration that assumed they adhered to a high moral code. Furthermore, the United States was not the only nation that was "learning to unleash the power of the atom." In these circumstances, starting an atomic war was "totally unthinkable for rational men." This argument suggested that he regarded Soviet as well as American leaders as rational.

In a major part of the speech, Truman suggested that the nation had learned the lessons taught by the history of the 1920s and 1930s and had not repeated the mistakes of that past. In sharp contrast with those earlier years of "weakness and indecision," the nation had moved with "speed and courage and decisiveness . . . against the Communist threat since World War II." That war had been the "evil result" of the mistakes. The new and very different policies of his presidency—"positive policies, policies of world leadership, policies that express faith in other free people"—had "averted World War III up to now" and may have established conditions that would "keep that war from happening as far ahead as man can see." The address contained less than a sentence on the Marshall Plan and more than two dozen on the Korean War. The decision to go to war in Korea, Truman proposed, as he had to the journalists three weeks before, was the "most important" of his presidency.

From our angle of vision, Truman's prophecy about the outcome of the Cold War may be the most impressive feature of the address. He boldly predicted that the United States would win the Cold War as a consequence of its own strengths and policies and the oppressive character—that "fatal flaw"—of

---

1953; Hechler, *Working with Truman*, 222. On the press conferences, see Mitchell, *Truman and the Media*, chap. 4.

the Communist regimes. "In the long run," he insisted, "the strength of our free society, and our ideals, will prevail over a system that has respect for neither God nor man." The prophecy implied that the Cold War was a contest between two essentially different systems and would end when the inferior system collapsed.

Although the departing president did not speak of Point Four, he did foresee similar programs that would produce the "golden age" that Murphy had envisioned. It would be based on our "capital, our skills, our science—most of all atomic energy"—once they were "released from the tasks of defense and turned wholly to peaceful purposes all around the world." Offering several illustrations, he concluded that this was "our dream of the future—our picture of the world we hope to have when the communist threat is overcome." To use language from a later generation, he anticipated a "peace dividend" that would be used to raise standards of living around the world.

The president spoke without anger, ignored the press, and praised the people. He insisted that he had "never once doubted" that they had "the will" to do what was "necessary to win this terrible fight against communism." That confidence had enabled him "to make necessary decisions even though they called for sacrifices by all of us." No president, he proposed, could "lead our country" or "sustain the burdens of this office" if he did not have popular support. The American people, he assured them, had given him what he needed "on all our great essential undertakings to build the free world's strength and keep the peace."

The address paid no attention to one of the dominant themes in the critics' interpretation of Truman's presidency and emphasized the other. The president and his writers obviously regarded the charge that he was corrupt as unworthy of their attention, but they responded clearly and forcefully to the claim that he had given the nation and the world a weak foreign policy. Instead, the address asserted, the United States under Truman's leadership had rejected the policy of weakness that had prevailed in the 1920s and 1930s and put in place a policy of strength.

Even though Truman's numbers in the polls were low, much of the commentary on the speech was favorable. Many journalists liked the "friendly," "cheerful," "homey," "temperate and moving," "affectionate and hopeful," "mellow and reflective" spirit—the departure from "the bitterness of the political campaign."[34] The editors of the New York Herald Tribune saw the

34. Garnett D. Horner, *Washington Evening Star,* January 16, 1953; Robert J. Donovan, *New York Herald Tribune,* January 16, 1953; *Newsweek,* January 26, 1953; *Kansas City Times,* January 16, 1953; William V. Shannon, *New York Post,* January 16, 1953.

"affecting, simply written address" as revealing "the side of Mr. Truman
which the people like and which they will want to remember when the battles and controversies of his Administration fade into the background." "In
the manner of his going Mr. Truman has been every inch the President, conscious of the great office and worthy of it," the columnist Walter Lippmann
observed. Another columnist, Thomas L. Stokes, forecast that "what Harry
Truman has said will shine out in history, for it tells again the story of a free
people."[35]

Some journalists also endorsed much of the content of the address. It was
"the testament of a decent, generous and conscientious American who has
blundered often on minor matters but invariably exhibited courage and vision on the great issues," James Wechsler, the editor of the *New York Post*,
proclaimed. What he admired most about Truman was his "unwavering faith
that free men can combat tyranny without surrendering their own liberties or
unleashing the awful weapons of destruction we now command." Worried
about what lay ahead as "the Big Deal" displaced the New Deal and the Fair
Deal, the *Nation* advised "all citizens, including the members of the Eisenhower Administration, to file [the address] but not forget it."[36]

Nearly all of those who wrote to the president praised the address. The
letters contained such phrases as "you rose far above partisanship, and you
made me proud to be an American." Letter writers called the speech "primed
with sincerity and truth," "the best you have ever made," "wonderful," "simple
yet eloquent," "truly inspired," "the greatest piece of Americanism that it has
ever been my pleasure to hear and see," "a fitting climax to a glorious career."
The address, one admirer wrote, "revealed the true qualities of statesmanship
which you have . . . constantly demonstrated."[37]

In their responses to the address, some of the commentators saw greatness
in the man who gave it. One letter writer predicted that he would "go down
in history as one of our great presidents. Like Lincoln, like Roosevelt." A
cautious journalist predicted he would "get a chapter in future histories that
certainly will be lengthy and probably will be respectable," but others proposed that historians would not "mark Harry Truman down as one of the
lesser Presidents, like Millard Fillmore or Benjamin Harrison" and would

35. *New York Herald Tribune*, January 16, 19, 1953; *Washington Evening Star*, January 19,
1953.

36. *New York Post*, January 16, 1953; *Nation*, January 24, 1953, 61.

37. Letters from Arnold J. Zurcher, Charles E. Patterson, Benjamin Sosland, Mrs. M.
Mattos, Irving H. Berkowitz, Catherine A. Andersen, Thomas C. Kyle, Helen S. King, and
Albert Feinberg in Box 354, Farewell Address, President's Personal File, Truman Papers.

"rate him as one of the abler and more important American presidents." The editors of the *New York Times* suggested that although he seemed "anxious about his place in history," he "need not worry much" for he had "guided the nation through tremendous years, sometimes uncertainly, often with a wisdom that will be remembered." He would not be forgotten, the journalist Anne O'Hare McCormick predicted, for he had risen "out of petty politics to great occasions," taken "great steps without hesitation or dismay," and "carried the revolution of [foreign] policy much further than Mr. Roosevelt did."[38]

Much like Truman, some writers blamed the press for his low ranking and predicted that historians would place him much higher. "I doubt if any president has ever had such a hostile press working against him," one letter writer recalled, "yet you didn't let it get you down. You went on working for the little people of this country." According to one prediction: "Those shallow men who have been critical of your decisions will earn a deservedly anonymous niche in our future history books, while . . . your place will grow more secure with each sober reflection." After contrasting praise for him in the British press with harsh attacks by the press at home, one writer called him "the finest and the most courageous person in our time." "We owe you a great debt which will be acknowledged with the passing of time," another writer predicted. "Some day the people of the United States will realize that you are a much greater man than your detractors," another prophet assured him.[39]

The speech did provoke predictably negative responses from some of his critics. One Texan wired only one word: "fooey." Another wrote that the address was "most ridiculous and inappropriate" and asked, "Aren't you big enough to take defeat?" To a Californian, Truman's "latest radio blast" sounded as though he enjoyed the sound of his voice "in a rain barrel," while a couple from Pennsylvania called what he said a "poor vindication effort" and "contemptuous" and exclaimed "Good Riddance." "An American" from New Jersey labeled the speech "disgusting, child-like and immature," advised the departing president to read the Bible now that he would "have some time," and expressed hope that it would "enlighten" him "because our Constitution didn't seem to help any."[40]

Critics in the press had more to say. Some challenged the president's

38. Letter from Dorothy Raphaelson; Richard Frykland, *Washington Evening Star,* January 18, 1953; Royce Brier, *San Francisco Chronicle,* January 23, 1953; J.D.B., *Brockton Daily Enterprise,* January 21, 1953; *New York Times,* January 16, 18, 1953.
39. Letters from Mattos, Berkowitz, Anne Teeman, and Agnes C. Downey.
40. Letters from Edward L. Racey, J. Marshall Huitts, A. C. Lamb, Mr. and Mrs. L. P. Tyler, and James C. D. Pappas.

prediction that the Soviet Union would collapse and his apparent confidence that "history would treat him well." The Hearst press chided him for ignoring "such unhappy memories as the treachery of Alger Hiss" and the mounting national debt. Employing the weakness theme, the editors of the *Washington Evening Star* objected to Truman's "watch-and-wait policy" in Korea and criticized the address for not suggesting how to bring the war to a "successful conclusion." Others emphasized corruption. "The word 'scandal' will be written across the record of the Democratic administration of Harry Truman just as it has been written across the Republican administration of Warren Harding," the columnist David Lawrence concluded. "That's the inexorable fate which befalls men who play petty politics with Presidential power and who are faithless to the public trust." The *Chicago Tribune* challenged Truman's reading of the history of the 1920s and 1930s. The address, the paper editorialized, "rehashed one of his favorite themes—that the United States did the league of nations to death by refusing to enter into it and thereby betrayed the peace of the world and was responsible for all of the calamities that have piled up since 1919." The editors called this "Truman's Pet Myth." Not swayed by the address, the most hostile columnist, Westbrook Pegler, concluded about Truman that the American people hated "him and his war and his traitors and crooks."[41]

Such negative interpretations of Harry Truman no longer have the many endorsements they enjoyed half a century ago. Instead, although some historians write negative books, he has become a national hero, made so by big historical events, including the collapse of the Nixon presidency. "It has been good to think about Harry Truman this spring and summer, . . . the summer of Watergate," Merle Miller began *Plain Speaking*, the first widely popular Truman book, published in 1974. "The memory of him has never been sharper, never brighter than it is now, a time when menacing, shadowy men are everywhere among us."[42] Present-day leaders were corrupt, this interpretation maintained; Truman had been a man of good character, and the nation now

41. Dorothy Thompson column and editorial, *Washington Evening Star*, January 16, 1953; *Los Angeles Times*, January 16, 1953; clipping from a Hearst paper, January 16, 1953, in Box 354, Farewell Address, President's Personal File, Truman Papers; *New York Herald Tribune*, January 18 (or 19?), 1953; *Chicago Tribune*, January 19, 1953; *Washington Times Herald*, January 19, 1953.

42. For major examples of highly critical books by historians, see William E. Pemberton, *Harry S. Truman: Fair Dealer and Cold Warrior* (Boston: Twayne, 1989), and Arnold A. Offner, *Another Such Victory: President Truman and the Cold War, 1945–1953* (Stanford: Stanford University Press, 2002). Merle Miller, *Plain Speaking: An Oral Biography of Harry S. Truman* (New York: G. P. Putnam's Sons, 1974), 15.

needed a leader like him. After the days of Watergate, American presidents and their rivals, including both Gerald Ford and Jimmy Carter and also the first George Bush, Bill Clinton, and Ross Perot, competed with one another in Truman look-alike contests.

In the 1970s and later, enthusiasm for Truman rested in large part on ideas about his personality and character, but the Farewell Address emphasized his policies. First drawn to the address nearly three decades ago as I explored his soaring popularity, I found his claim that he had based his foreign policies on the lessons of history the most impressive feature. Since then, new events—the collapse of the Soviet empire and the Soviet Union and the end of the Cold War—have thrown a spotlight on another part of the address—the prophecy. It rested on confidence in a policy and on an idea about human nature.

Now, the dominant American opinion about Harry Truman, among historians[43] as well as the general public, is much closer to the Farewell Address than to the appraisals by hostile journalists and most Americans in 1953. Recently, book publishers brought three large Truman biographies to market, obviously confident that interest in and enthusiasm for the president ran high, and each biographer, although not uncritical, presented a quite positive interpretation. In *Harry S. Truman: A Life* (1994) Robert Ferrell maintains that he "was the right man for his time, an awkward era in domestic politics and a downright dangerous period in foreign relations." He "took the measure of his responsibilities and made few errors" and "attained a rare balance of qualities that made him . . . one of the best choices fate could have provided when . . . Roosevelt passed on." Much like the interpretation offered in the Farewell Address, Ferrell writes that Truman's "principal accomplishment . . . was to change the foreign policy of the United States, from abstention to participation in the affairs of Europe and the world."

In *Man of the People: A Life of Harry S. Truman* (1995), Alonzo Hamby also gives Truman high marks. This biographer concludes that "Truman was magnificently right on . . . the two most important issues of his time: civil rights and the Soviet challenge." The Farewell Address also dealt positively with both issues but did not give them equal weight. It presented Truman's response to the Soviet challenge as clearly the main feature of his presidency.

Of these three major biographers, only McCullough, in his *Truman* (1992),

43. Steve Neal, "Putting Presidents in Their Place," *Chicago Sun-Times,* November 19, 1995; Arthur M. Schlesinger Jr., "The Ultimate Approval Rating," *New York Times Magazine,* December 15, 1996, 46–51; "C-Span Survey of Presidential Leadership," February 16, 2000, Vertical File, Truman Library.

offers a sizable discussion of the Farewell Address and writes enthusiastically about Truman's powers as a prophet. "Read many years later, in the light of what happened at the end of the Cold War, it [the address] would seem utterly extraordinary in its prescience," the biographer exclaims. "He appeared to know even the essence of what in fact would transpire, and more importantly, why."[44] Truman was not, however, solely or perhaps even mainly responsible for the idea or its appearance in the address. He did make the prediction in his interviews with the White House reporters and may have suggested it in his many conversations with his staff, but he did not include it in his memorandum. Furthermore, it had been an important component of the ideology of the Truman administration for several years. In 1947, George Kennan, the first head of the State Department's Policy Planning Staff, had introduced the idea that containment of the Soviet Union could lead to liberation of the Soviet people, doing so in an article, "The Sources of Soviet Conduct," published in *Foreign Affairs*. In 1950, his successor, Paul Nitze, had developed the idea further in a "Top Secret" document, NSC-68. Members of the president's staff had been interested in the idea for some time and eager to put it in a presidential speech. They did so in the Farewell Address.[45]

The address had been prepared with care, the product of much discussion and six drafts, and contained pieces, large and small, from each of the drafts and from Truman himself. It was his speech. It was his even though he had not written it from beginning to end nor supplied the basic draft. It was his because he had participated heavily in the making of it, he had the final authority, his writers tried to produce a Truman speech, and what they gave him resembled what he had said to the journalists and quite likely said to his team. It was the staff's speech also in that they had done most of the talking about it and most of the writing of it and it said what they, as well as he, wanted to say.[46]

Although the speech did not silence Truman's critics, it did challenge the

44. Ferrell, *Truman*, xi–xii, 246; Hamby, *Man of the People*, 640; McCullough, *Truman*, 919.

45. George Elsey memo for David Lloyd, May 16, 1951, Box 55, 1953, January, Elsey Papers, Truman Library; Heller, ed., *White House*, 129–34. They did so also in the State of the Union Message. *Public Papers of the Presidents of the United States: Harry S. Truman, 1945–1953*, 8 vols. (Washington, D.C.: U.S. Government Printing Office, 1961–1966), 8 (1952–1953): 1127.

46. Sundquist recalls: "in the collective redrafting process each individual's contribution truly gets blended into a group product and is impossible to trace after time has passed. When I listened to the Address, and read the final text, I could identify with pride the words and sentences I could honestly claim originated with me, but I could not do so now after fifty years" (letter to author, February 15, 2003).

dominant view of his presidency at the time and insist strongly that he was a president of large historical significance, worthy of being well remembered. Some Americans agreed in 1953; many more do so now. The portrait of him as the corrupt product of a notorious big-city political machine has been discarded, as has the picture of him as the leader in the development of a weak foreign policy. Instead, many now see him much as the address portrayed him. In addition to admiring his personality and character, they view Harry Truman as a president who established a strong and ultimately successful policy.

CONFIDENTIAL: The following address of the President to be delivered from the White House, is for automatic release at 10:30 p.m., E.S.T., Thursday, January 15, 1953. No portion, synopsis, or intimation may be published or broadcast before that time.

PLEASE GUARD AGAINST PREMATURE PUBLICATION OR ANNOUNCEMENT.

ROGER W. TUBBY
Secretary to the President

I am happy to have this opportunity to talk to you once more before I leave the White House.

Next Tuesday, General Eisenhower will be inaugurated as President of the United States. A short time after the new President takes his oath of office, I will be on the train going back home to Independence, Missouri. I will once again be a plain, private citizen of this Republic.

That is as it should be. Inauguration Day will be a great demonstration of our democratic process. I am glad to be a part of it -- glad to wish General Eisenhower all possible success, as he begins his term -- glad the whole world will have a chance to see how simply and how peacefully our American system transfers the vast power of the Presidency from my hands to his. It is a good object lesson in democracy. I am very proud of it. I know you are, too.

During the last two months, I have done my best to make this transfer an orderly one. I have talked with my successor on the affairs of the country, both foreign and domestic, and my cabinet officers have talked with their successors. I want to say that General Eisenhower and his associates have cooperated fully in this effort. Such an orderly transfer from one party to another has never taken place before in our history. I think a real precedent has been set.

In speaking to you tonight, I have no new revelations to make -- no political statements -- no policy announcements. There are simply a few things in my heart I want to say to you. I want to say "goodbye" and "thanks for your help." And I want to talk with you a little about what has happened since I became your President.

I am speaking to you from the room where I have worked since April 1945. This is the President's office in the West Wing of the White House. And this is the desk where I have signed most of the papers that embodied the decisions I have made as President. It has been the desk of many Presidents, and will be the desk of many more.

Since I became President, I have been to Europe, Mexico, Canada, Brazil, Puerto Rico and the Virgin Islands -- Wake Island and Hawaii. I have visited almost every State in the Union. I have traveled 135,000 miles by air, 77,000 by rail, and 17,000 by ship. But the mail always followed me, and wherever I happened to be, that's where the office of the President was.

The greatest part of the President's job is to make decisions -- big ones and small ones, dozens of them almost every day. The papers may circulate around the Government for a while but they finally reach this desk. And then, there's no place else for them to go. The President -- whoever he is -- has to decide. He can't pass the buck to anybody. No one else can do the deciding for him. That's his job.

That's what I've been doing here in this room, for almost eight years now. And over in the main part of the White House, there's a study on the second floor -- a room much like this one -- where I have worked at night and early in the morning on the papers I couldn't get to at the office.

(OVER)

Of course, for more than three years, Mrs. Truman and I were not living in the White House. We were across the street in the Blair House. That was when the White House almost fell down on us and had to be rebuilt. I had a study over at the Blair House, too, but living in the Blair House was not as convenient as living in the White House. The Secret Service wouldn't let me walk across the street, so I had to get in a car every morning to cross the street to the White House office, again at noon to go to the Blair House for lunch, again to go back to the office after lunch, and finally take an automobile at night to return to the Blair House. Fantastic, isn't it? But necessary, so my guards thought -- and they are the bosses on such matters as that.

Now, of course, we're back in the White House. It is in very good condition, and General Eisenhower will be able to take up his residence in the House and work right here. That will be much more convenient for him, and I'm very glad the renovation job was all completed before his term began.

Your new President is taking office in quite different circumstances than when I became President eight years ago. On April 12, 1945, I had been presiding over the Senate in my capacity as Vice President. When the Senate recessed about five o'clock in the afternoon, I walked over to the office of the Speaker of the House, Mr. Rayburn, to discuss pending legislation. As soon as I arrived, I was told that Mr. Early, one of President Roosevelt's secretaries, wanted me to call. I reached Mr. Early, and he told me to come to the White House as quickly as possible, to enter by way of the Pennsylvania Avenue entrance, and come to Mrs. Roosevelt's study.

When I arrived, Mrs. Roosevelt told me the tragic news, and I felt the shock that all of you felt a little later -- when the word came over the radio and appeared in the newspapers. President Roosevelt had died. I offered to do anything I could for Mrs. Roosevelt, and then I asked the Secretary of State to call the Cabinet together.

At 7:09 p.m., I was sworn in as President by Chief Justice Stone in the Cabinet Room.

Things were happening fast in those days. The San Francisco conference to organize the United Nations had been called for April twenty-fifth. I was asked if that meeting would go forward. I announced that it would.

After attending President Roosevelt's funeral, I went to the Hall of the House of Representatives and told a joint session of the Congress that I would carry on President Roosevelt's policies.

On May seventh, Germany surrendered. The announcement was made on May eighth, my sixty-first birthday.

Mr. Churchill called me shortly after that and wanted a meeting with me and Prime Minister Stalin of Russia. Later on, a meeting was agreed upon, and Churchill, Stalin, and I met at Potsdam in Germany.

Meanwhile, the first atomic explosion took place out in the New Mexico desert.

The war against Japan was still going on. I made the decision that the atomic bomb had to be used to end it. I made that decision in the conviction it would save hundreds of thousands of lives -- Japanese as well as American. Japan surrendered, and we were faced with the huge problems of bringing the troops home and reconverting the economy from war to peace.

All these things happened within just a little over four months -- from April to August 1945. I tell you this to illustrate the tremendous scope of the work your President has to do.

(OVER)

27

All these emergencies and all the developments to meet them have required the President to put in long hours -- usually seventeen hours a day, with no payment for overtime. I sign my name on the average, 600 times a day, see and talk to hundreds of people every month, shake hands with thousands every year, and still carry on the business of the largest going concern in the world. There is no job like it on the face of the earth -- in the power which is concentrated here at this desk, and in the responsibility and difficulty of the decisions.

I want all of you to realize how big a job, how hard a job, it is -- not for my sake, because I am stepping out of it -- but for the sake of my successor. He needs the understanding and the help of every citizen. It is not enough for you to come out once every four years and vote for a candidate, and then go back home and say, "Well, I've done my part, now let the new President do the worrying." He can't do the job alone.

Regardless of your politics, whether you are Republican or Democrat, your fate is tied up with what is done here in this room. The President is President of the whole country. We must all give him our support as citizens of the United States. He will have mine, and I want you to give him yours.

I suppose that history will remember my term in office as the years when the "cold war" began to overshadow our lives. I have had hardly a day in office that has not been dominated by this all-embracing struggle -- this conflict between those who love freedom and those who would lead the world back into slavery and darkness. And always in the background there has been the atomic bomb.

But when history says that my term of office saw the beginning of the cold war, it will also say that in those eight years we have set the course that can win it. We have succeeded in carving out a new set of policies to attain peace -- positive policies, policies of world leadership, policies that express faith in other free people. We have averted World War III up to now, and we may already have succeeded in establishing conditions which can keep that war from happening as far ahead as man can see.

These are great and historic achievements that we can all be proud of. Think of the difference between our course now and our course thirty years ago. After the first World War, we withdrew from world affairs -- we failed to act in concert with other peoples against aggression -- we helped to kill the League of Nations -- and we built up tariff barriers which strangled world trade. This time, we avoided those mistakes. We helped to found and to sustain the United Nations. We have welded alliances that include the greater part of the free world. And we have gone ahead with other free countries to help build their economies and link us all together in a healthy world trade.

Think back for a moment to the 1930's and you will see the difference. The Japanese moved into Manchuria, and free men did not act. The fascists moved into Ethiopia, and we did not act. The nazis marched into the Rhineland, into Austria, into Czechoslovakia, and free men were paralyzed for lack of strength and unity and will.

Think about those years of weakness and indecision, and World War II which was their evil result. Then think about the speed and courage and decisiveness with which we have moved against the communist threat since World War II.

The first crisis came in 1945 and 1946, when the Soviet Union refused to honor its agreement to remove its troops from Iran. Members of my Cabinet came to me and asked if we were ready to take the risk that a firm stand involved. I replied that we were. So we took our stand -- we made it clear to the Soviet Union that we expected them to honor their agreement -- and the Soviet troops were withdrawn.

(OVER)

And then, in early 1947, the Soviet Union threatened Greece and Turkey. The British sent me a message saying they could no longer keep their forces in that area. Something had to be done at once, or the Eastern Mediterranean would be taken over by the communists. On March twelfth, I went before the Congress and stated our determination to help the people of Greece and Turkey maintain their independence. Today, Greece is still free and independent; and Turkey is a bulwark of strength at a strategic corner of the world.

Then came the Marshall Plan which saved Europe, the heroic Berlin airlift, and our military aid programs.

We inaugurated the North Atlantic Pact, the Rio Pact binding the Western Hemisphere together, and the defense pacts with countries of the Far Pacific.

Most important of all, we acted in Korea.

I was in Independence, Missouri, in June 1950, when Secretary Acheson telephoned me and gave me the news about the invasion of Korea. I told the Secretary to lay the matter at once before the United Nations, and I came on back to Washington.

Flying back over the flat lands of the Middle West and over the Appalachians that summer afternoon, I had a lot of time to think. I turned the problem over in my mind in many ways, but my thoughts kept coming back to the 1930's -- to Manchuria -- Ethiopia -- the Rhineland -- Austria -- and finally to Munich.

Here was history repeating itself. Here was another probing action, another testing action. If we let the Republic of Korea go under, some other country would be next, and then another. And all the time, the courage and confidence of the free world would be ebbing away, just as it did in the 1930's. And the United Nations would go the way of the League of Nations.

When I reached Washington, I met immediately with the Secretary of State, the Secretary of Defense, and General Bradley, and the other civilian and military officials who had information and advice to help me decide what to do. We talked about the problems long and hard.

It was not easy to make the decision that sent American boys again into battle. I was a soldier in the first World War, and I know what a soldier goes through. I know well the anguish that mothers and fathers and families go through. So I knew what was ahead if we acted in Korea.

But after all this was said, we realized that the issue was whether there would be fighting in a limited area now or on a much larger scale later on -- whether there would be some casualties now or many more casualties later.

So a decision was reached -- the decision I believe was the most important in my time as President.

In the days that followed, the most heartening fact was that the American people clearly agreed with the decision.

And in Korea, our men are fighting as valiantly as Americans have ever fought -- because they know they are fighting in the same cause of freedom in which Americans have stood ever since the beginning of the Republic.

Where free men had failed the test before, this time we met the test.

We met it firmly. We met it successfully. The aggression has been repelled. The communists have seen their hopes of easy conquest go down the drain. The determination of free people to defend themselves has been made clear to the Kremlin.

As I have thought about our world-wide struggle with the communists these past eight years -- day in and day out -- I have never once doubted that you, the people of our country, have the will to do what is necessary to win this terrible fight against communism. Because I have been sure of that, I have been able to make necessary decisions even though they called for sacrifices by all of us. And I have not been wrong in my judgment of the American people.

That same assurance of our people's determination will be General Eisenhower's greatest source of strength in carrying on this struggle.

Now, once in a while, I get a letter from some impatient person asking, why don't we get it over with? Why don't we issue an ultimatum, make all-out war, drop the atomic bomb?

For most Americans, the answer is quite simple: we are not made that way. We are a moral people. Peace is our goal, and justice and freedom. We cannot, of our own free will, violate the very principles that we are striving to defend. The whole purpose of what we are doing is to prevent World War III. Starting a war is no way to make peace.

But if anyone still thinks that just this once, bad means can bring good ends, then let me remind you of this: We are living in the eighth year of the atomic age. We are not the only nation that is learning to unleash the power of the atom. A third world war might dig the grave not only of our communist opponents but also of our own society, our world as well as theirs.

Starting an atomic war is totally unthinkable for rational men.

Then, some of you may ask, when and how will the cold war ever end? I think I can answer that simply. The communist world has great resources, and it looks strong. But there is a fatal flaw in their society. Theirs is a godless system, a system of slavery; there is no freedom in it, no consent. The iron curtain, the secret police, the constant purges, all these are symptoms of a great basic weakness -- the rulers' fear of their own people.

In the long run, the strength of our free society, and our ideals, will prevail over a system that has respect for neither God nor man.

Last week, in my State of the Union Message to the Congress -- and I hope you will all take the time to read it -- I explained how I think we will finally win through.

As the free world grows stronger, more united, more attractive to men on both sides of the iron curtain -- and as the Soviet hopes for easy expansion are blocked -- then there will have to come a time of change in the Soviet world. Nobody can say for sure when that is going to be, or exactly how it will come about, whether by revolution, or trouble in the satellite states, or by a change inside the Kremlin.

Whether the communist rulers shift their policies of their own free will -- or whether the change comes about in some other way -- I have not a doubt in the world that a change will occur.

I have a deep and abiding faith in the destiny of free men. With patience and courage, we shall some day move on into a new era -- a wonderful golden age -- an age when we can use the peaceful tools that science has forged for us to do away with poverty and human misery everywhere on earth.

Think what can be done, once our capital, our skills, our science -- most of all atomic energy -- can be released from the tasks of defense and turned wholly to peaceful purposes all around the world.

There is no end to what can be done.

The Tigris and Euphrates Valley can be made to bloom as it did in the times of Babylon and Nineveh. Israel can be made the country of milk and honey as it was in the time of Joshua.

There is a plateau in Ethiopia some six to eight thousand feet high, that has sixty-five thousand square miles of land just exactly like the corn belt in northern Illinois. Enough food can be raised there to feed a hundred million people.

There are places in South America -- places in Colombia and Venezuela and Brazil -- just like that plateau in Ethiopia -- places where food could be raised for millions of people.

These things can be done, and they are self-liquidating projects. If we can get peace and safety in the world under the United Nations, the developments will come so fast we will not recognize the world in which we now live.

This is our dream of the future -- our picture of the world we hope to have when the communist threat is overcome.

I've talked a lot tonight about the menace of communism -- and our fight against it -- because that is the overriding issue of our time. But there are some other things we've done that history will record. One of them is that we in America have learned how to attain real prosperity for our people.

We have 62½ million people at work. Businessmen, farmers, laborers, white collar people, all have better incomes and more of the good things of life than ever before in the history of the world.

There hasn't been a failure of an insured bank in nearly nine years. No depositor has lost a cent in that period.

And the income of our people has been fairly distributed, perhaps more so than at any time in recent history.

We have made progress in spreading the blessings of American life to all of our people. There has been a tremendous awakening of the American conscience on the great issues of civil rights -- equal economic opportunities, equal rights of citizenship, and equal educational opportunities for all our people, whatever their race or religion or status of birth.

So, as I empty the drawers of this desk, and as Mrs. Truman and I leave the White House, we have no regret. We feel we have done our best in the public service. I hope and believe we have contributed to the welfare of this Nation and to the peace of the world.

When Franklin Roosevelt died, I felt there must be a million men better qualified than I, to take up the Presidential task. But the work was mine to do, and I had to do it. I have tried to give it everything that was in me.

Through all of it, through all the years that I have worked here in this room, I have been well aware I did not really work alone -- that you were working with me.

No President could ever hope to lead our country, or to sustain the burdens of this office, save as the people helped with their support. I have had that help -- you have given me that support -- on all our great essential undertakings to build the free world's strength and keep the peace.

Those are the big things. Those are the things we have done together.

For that I shall be grateful, always.

And now, the time has come for me to say good night and -- God bless you all.

The Politics of Democracy

Harry S. Truman and the American People

Alonzo L. Hamby

Harry Truman mentioned his relationship with the American people on three separate occasions in the Farewell Address he delivered on January 15, 1953. The presidency, he told them, was a hard, unceasing job that required "the understanding and the help of every citizen." He thanked the people for having "the will and determination" to make the sacrifices essential to the struggle against Soviet Communism. He concluded by declaring, "I have been well aware I did not really work alone—that you were working with me." The presidency and the pursuit of peace were "the things we have done together."

Truman delivered these remarks at the conclusion of an unusually tumultuous presidency and at a time when the country was more than ready to send him off. (In late 1951, the Gallup poll had put his approval rating at 23 percent.) Of course, it is hardly unusual for national leaders to feel that they have the support of "the people" well after they have lost it. A hardheaded, practical politician, Truman understood well at one level that a solid majority of the people perhaps had once supported him but were now ready for a new face. Still, his rhetoric reflected a gauzy sentiment natural to anyone who was leaving the nation's highest office after devoting nearly eight years of his life to coping with its incessant demands and genuinely feeling that he was doing the best he could for the country. Political leadership, even that wielded by many dictators, often demands a sense of popular support. In no society is this truer than in a democracy. Harry Truman's relationship with the American people may in reality have been tenuous, but the way in which he attempted to forge it and the way in which the people responded to him tell us a lot about both him and the society he headed.

Truman's relationship with the American people involved more than Gallup polls. The topic forces us to look at the way in which he understood the nature of politics. Here I will address three questions: What did Truman think of when he heard the term *the people*? How did he think politics, as he practiced it, served them? And how did the people relate to him throughout his career?

It is not very meaningful to talk of "the people" as a large generalization. We need to think of democracy from a pluralist perspective in which political leaders deal with the people as distinct groups, many of them determined by economic function or interest, but others reflecting social, cultural, or philosophical outlooks. The classic early American statement of this idea was made by James Madison in *Federalist No. 10*. Political scientists have elaborated on it endlessly. Among the most important twentieth-century scholars are Arthur F. Bentley, David B. Truman (no relation to Harry!), and Robert A. Dahl.[1]

For most politicians *the people* is also a normative term. "The people" are those clusters in the population that seem most deserving of support against "special interests," perhaps most authentic in terms of their fundamental importance to society, and, cynics might add, ultimately most likely to provide their votes. In any society, those two words are a powerful rhetorical device. In American democracy, they have special resonance.

We need also to think about the nature of political leadership in democratic societies. Madison mentioned as one source of "faction," or group identity, personal attachment to a leader. A relationship of this sort might be a simple patronage transaction, as it frequently was in the eighteenth-century Anglo-American world, but it might also involve the compelling attraction of what we began to call "charismatic leadership" in the twentieth century. All democratic political leaders are forced to one degree or another to deal with the people through the mediating mechanism of interest groups; most are frank about this, some adamantly in denial. The charismatic democratic leader, however, can to some degree transcend group mediation. Truman, we need hardly add, was not charismatic; instead he had the bad fortune to live in an

1. Bentley, *The Process of Government* (Chicago: University of Chicago Press, 1908); Truman, *The Governmental Process* (New York: Alfred A. Knopf, 1951); Dahl, *A Preface to Democratic Theory* (Chicago: University of Chicago Press, 1956) and *Who Governs? Democracy and Power in an American City* (New Haven: Yale University Press, 1961).

age in which charismatic leadership was unusually prominent and to be compared to the likes of Roosevelt, Churchill, and Eisenhower.

Because this essay is about Harry Truman's political conceptualization and his personality, it has to be biographical. We need to turn to his personal history, the social history of the environment in which he grew up, the political concepts he absorbed as a youth, then modified as he grew older, and the actual day-to-day politics that he witnessed, then participated in.

Independence and Grandview: Populism, Democratic Loyalism, and WASP Ascendancy

The first thirty-three years of Harry Truman's life, 1884–1917, were mostly spent in Independence (1892–1902) and on his grandmother's farm near Grandview (1906–1917) in southern Jackson County. Through much of the Grandview period, Truman commuted to Independence regularly to court his beloved Bess Wallace. Town and country were both homogeneous polities with largely similar views of the world. The Independence in which Truman came of age was still a small, if rapidly growing, town best understood as an Upper South county seat. It had the feel of a town that recently had put its frontier past behind it and had progressed on to building the schools and churches. Like much of small-town America it professed a surface egalitarianism. In theory, everyone was equal; in fact, widely understood social distinctions existed, but they were neither as complex nor as extreme as those in large cities. The owner and publisher of the *Independence Examiner*, Col. William Southern, for example, could live in close proximity to the livestock trader Trumans and the marginal Allen family, enjoy a cordial relationship with both, and take an interest in their more talented children. Social or economic distinctions were blurred in part because upward mobility for those who aspired to it was widely assumed. Harry Truman did his part to prove the assumption. The most famous of the Allen children, Forrest, or "Phog," became a legendary basketball coach at the University of Kansas. His older brother, Harry, aka "Pete," was the same age as Harry Truman and a close friend. The two of them served together in World War I as battery commanders. Pete stayed in the army and retired as a colonel on the eve of World War II. Like all generalizations, the assertion that Truman was a product of an egalitarian society is not perfect. Nonetheless, it serves us pretty well.

Independence was not only democratic, it was also "Democratic" in the sense of being a town that normally returned solid majorities for the Democratic Party. In general, those majorities reflected the legacy of the Civil War, still a living memory for many of the town's citizens. Harry's grandparents, in common with many of their friends, had been among a wave of migrants from Kentucky who had settled in Jackson County in the 1840s, owned slaves, supported the Confederacy in the war, and suffered ill treatment from the Unionists. Harry's mother may have been a bit extreme in thinking John Wilkes Booth was a great man and detesting Republicans as a group, but such sentiments were not uncommon in her world.

The Truman loyalty to the Democratic Party may have been forged in the Civil War, but its meaning was redefined by the rise of William Jennings Bryan to party leadership in 1896 and by the "populist" movement that Bryan incarnated—despite never having been a member of the Populist Party. Populism may be defined generically, and a bit crudely, as the general resentment of the lowly ("the people") against the rich and the "special interests" perceived as the controllers of society. Bryan rose to prominence as the advocate of a hard-pressed farm population, whom he depicted as the victims of a greedy northeastern financial elite. He advocated cheap money with a passion and logic that only a straitened debtor class could understand. He coupled this with an equally emotional defense of the values of traditional rural America (mostly old stock and Protestant) against the modernist cosmopolitanism of the cities. The flame of populism never burned as hot in Missouri as it did in Kansas or Nebraska, but it picked up both advocates and fellow travelers. The Trumans, despite their residence in Independence, were farmers who had known hard times. Despite being moderately well off, until Harry's father lost everything in grain futures speculation, they usually owed money to the bank. They worked very hard but had little to show for it. They were Baptists who adhered to a fundamentalist morality. They identified with Bryan and assimilated his message.

Who then were "the people" who were the objects of public policy? In the Independence of young Harry Truman, the definition was quite clear on one point—they were white. Blacks voted in nearby Kansas City, but not in Independence. The racism that existed there appears to have been more benign than malign. Independence blacks were servants and manual laborers; they appear to have sought regular white employers, who generally felt an obligation to take care of them. Still, this was a status that was just a step up from slavery; it assumed dependence and obedience. Most Independence residents appear to have felt they treated "their" Negroes well, at least those who "knew their place," and assumed there was a natural order of things that needed to be observed.

Recent immigrants fared little better in young Harry's world. Letters he wrote to Bess Wallace before World War I display a casual racism shocking to the twenty-first-century sensibility but part of the conventional wisdom in the rural, small-town world of the early twentieth century. For example, the twenty-seven-year-old Truman, on his way to participate in a federal land lottery for would-be homesteaders in South Dakota, wrote: "I bet there'll be more bohunks and 'Rooshans' up there than white men. I think it is a disgrace to the country for those fellows to be in it. If they had only stopped immigration about twenty or thirty years ago, the good Americans could all have had plenty of land."[2]

There was one other important denominator. The Truman of those years was a rural Jeffersonian. Farmers, he remarked, in that same letter to Bess, "are more independent and make better citizens." A country of factories and large cities "soon becomes depressed and makes classes among people." This was more conventional wisdom, especially among Missouri farmers who were also Democrats, touched by the rhetoric of William Jennings Bryan and respectful of the party's patron saint, Thomas Jefferson.

This view of "the people" that Truman had developed by his late twenties seems rather unpromising, to say the least, for the leadership of a party that would appeal heavily to blacks, immigrant-based ethnic groups, and big cities. Did he have a change of mind somewhere along the way? Did he conceal his true feelings? Or did he not really mean the things he wrote in those days? Probably the best answer is "all of the above." Like most people, he did not question the commonly held assumptions of his society and was capable of juggling mutually contradictory propositions in his mind. (Only academics and ideologues have well-worked-out theories of life, politics, or almost anything.) Nor does there appear to have been a lot of intensity in his racial feelings. He was an even-tempered, gregarious young man who got along well with all types of people. As for farming, he may have felt it was virtuous, but he heartily disliked it. After the death of his father in 1914, he would devote his life to making an escape from it.

Businessman, Soldier, Politician, Kansas Citian

Truman's attempts to break away from the farm brought him quickly into the world of speculative business, first as co-lessee of a lead and zinc mine in Commerce, Oklahoma, then as a partner in a wildcat oil and gas exploration company, finally as operator of a haberdashery across from Kansas City's

2. Truman to Bess Wallace, October 16, 1911; see also Truman to Bess Wallace, June 22, 1911, January 25, 1912, July 29, August 22, 1913, April 7, 1914, all in Family, Business, Personal File, Truman Papers, Truman Library.

Muehlebach Hotel. In each instance, he would experience firsthand the difficulties of the typical small business operator, working hard to make a success of underfinanced and poorly conceived ventures, competing unsuccessfully with larger firms that had deep pockets, fighting a business cycle he never fully understood, starting out with high hopes and in the end losing money. Not surprisingly, the small businessman joined his list of those who constituted "the people."

World War I intervened between the oil business and the haberdashery. It surely had the effect of further broadening Truman's sense of "the people." As a lieutenant in training camp at Fort Sill, Oklahoma, he became fast friends with James Pendergast, nephew of Kansas City's notorious Irish-Catholic boss, Tom Pendergast. Appointed to run the regimental canteen, he drew on the services of "a Jew . . . by the name of Jacobson and he is a crackerjack."[3] In France, he received the command of an artillery battery made up mostly of Irish and German Catholics from Kansas City. The respect and affection Truman developed for Jim Pendergast and Eddie Jacobson is undeniable. The sentiment between him and his entire battery was a bit more selective, but a group of loyalists, numbering perhaps half his troops, liked him well enough that a sizable group of them kicked in to buy him a large silver loving cup at the end of the war. Truman himself waxed sentimental about the "Irishmen" who had manned his four seventy-five-millimeter guns, and a lot of them responded by backing his campaigns for public office.

What of the people the populists did not like—bankers, industrialists, fat cats? Here the young Truman seems to have been a bit equivocal. There is no doubt that he felt little empathy for the J. P. Morgans and John D. Rockefellers of the world. But he also wanted to be a successful—that is, wealthy—businessman himself, and he largely accepted the rags-to-riches ideology still prominent in the years before World War I. With hard work— and some luck—one could become a millionaire. Hence the zinc mine, then the oil exploration company. (He came close in the last venture. His oilman partner, David Morgan, ran out of money after drilling down 1,500 feet on a lease near Eureka, Kansas. Morgan sold the lease to a flusher company that went deeper and hit an enormous pool of oil and gas. "Well, Dave," Truman wrote to Morgan years later, "if we had carried that well on down . . . it's a cinch I would not be President today.")[4] It was hard to work up a passion

3. Truman to Bess Wallace, October 28, 1917, Family, Business, Personal File, Truman Papers.

4. Truman quoted in David Morgan, "A Factual Narrative Relating to the Business Activities, etc., of David H. Morgan and Harry S. Truman, 1916–1919," attached to Morgan to Truman, August 5, 1951, President's Secretary's File, Truman Papers.

against the robber barons when one entertained dreams of becoming a member of the club himself. It would be easier when he gave up those ambitions.

Truman's attempts at a business career essentially came to an end when he and Eddie Jacobson shut down their Kansas City haberdashery shop in the fall of 1922. During a two-year period when he was out of office (1925–1926), he supported himself quite successfully as a salesman of auto club memberships and insurance. Over a longer period, he was a partner in an ultimately unsuccessful savings and loan company. But from 1922 on, politics was the ruling preoccupation of his life. His candidacy for Eastern District judge of the county court (essentially the county commission) gave him his first opportunity to make a systematic effort at defining a constituency ("the people") and explaining the ways in which government was supposed to serve it.

The practice of politics also forced him to find ways of reconciling high ideals with far less elevated realities. From the beginning, Truman had to move back and forth between two personas. One was that of the "idealist," as he described it, dedicated to the purest values of public service and pursuing them selflessly in the interests of all the people; this was the way he liked to see himself. The other was that of the pragmatic realist, making one compromise after another to achieve what he could and safeguard his own career, which was his only means of supporting himself and his family. He acknowledged this identity but was invariably defensive about it. It was as the idealist that he presented himself to the people at campaign time, but as the realist that he actually managed his political offices. This was a cause of psychological turmoil for him, as well as a larger problem of public definition vis-à-vis the people.

Truman's first run for significant political office occurred wholly within the world in which he had grown up; the people of Jackson County's Eastern District were white, old-stock, Protestant, and Jeffersonian in the sense of believing in small, frugal government. Politics as practiced was strictly "retail"—meetings with small groups, attendance at local picnics and fairs, face-to-face requests for a vote, one person at a time. Truman was good at it. He had a firm handshake, a ready smile, and an air of sincerity. Such skills could make a difference in a close race, but he already had learned in an unsuccessful and relatively halfhearted contest for township trustee that organization and committed supporters meant more.

The people in Jackson County, as elsewhere, were not simply a homogeneous mass in search of the nicest candidate. A good many of them were also known as "goats" and "rabbits," the popular names for the two leading factions in the local Democratic Party. As the names imply, their political rivalry did not involve a clash of principles. It was about who got the county jobs and contracts and about allegiances based on past preferment or long-standing personal acquaintance. Truman well understood this. His father had been loosely aligned with the goat faction and had been appointed a road overseer when an old family friend was elected to the county court. Truman had inherited the position after his father's death, then lost it when the old friend died and was succeeded by a less congenial figure. The Kansas City anchor of the goat faction was the well-oiled and increasingly powerful machine headed by Tom Pendergast.

Facing the problem of convincing the people that idealism and machine politics could exist side by side, Truman appealed to the people of the Eastern District as a young businessman with Jeffersonian values who would bring runaway county spending under control while improving the county's execrable rural road system. His leading opponent, a small-town banker named E. E. Montgomery, who was allied with the rabbits, did the same. So did the other three contestants in the Democratic primary. The people, as nearly as one could discern, wanted such pledges; all the local newspapers demanded them; so did various civic clubs. Yet in the end the contest was decided by the support of friends and the organization of the machine. Truman had no illusions about this. He did nothing illegal, but he returned favors frankly and openly. The people needed to be served as well as possible, but it was imperative to take care of a special subset, one's "friends." As Truman later wrote, he and H. F. McElroy, a goat loyalist from Kansas City, "ran the county court and took all the jobs."[5] In the end, and to the surprise of almost no one, they proved better at promise than performance, ending their two-year terms with the county budget in deficit and the roads in poor shape. By the standards of the past, however, their service had been better than average. They probably would have been reelected if not for an intense party factionalism that temporarily brought the Republicans to power. The moral would stay with Truman forever: keep the party united. The people were out there to be served as best as one could, but they were not the force that got one elected.

The party reunited under Tom Pendergast's control, Truman won election as presiding judge of the county court in 1926 and reelection in 1930. With Pendergast's powerful support, both elections were easy. The presiding judge was elected by both Kansas City and rural, small-town Jackson County.

5. Truman, Longhand memoir on Pickwick Hotel stationery, May 14, 1934, Family, Business, Personal File, Longhand Notes, Truman Papers.

Truman's new position brought a significant enlargement of his political world and the range of people he served. The most visible aspect of that enlargement was his success in reaching out to Kansas City's business community and civic establishment as an advocate of modern roads, other civic improvements, and administrative efficiency—all within the parameters of patronage politics, which he openly practiced. The businessmen and municipal reformers accepted him as the best presiding judge within memory. By and large he made good on their trust in his administration of bond funds that paid for an excellent county highway system and other improvements with little noticeable waste or corruption. At some risk, he passed over Pendergast's "pet contractors" and let contracts to the lowest bidders. (They, however, would find that they had to buy their cement from a company controlled by Big Tom.) He knew he could not prevent much of the routine waste and graft that accompanied normal county government. But, on this matter, he told the Boss, his honor was at stake. It is no exaggeration to say that he became the pet Democrat of the city's Republican establishment.

His world widened in another way, less visible and hardly discussed at the time. Compared to New York, Cleveland, or Chicago, Kansas City was a relatively homogeneous old-stock town. But compared to eastern Jackson County, it was a seething ethnic cauldron. Irish and Italian Americans were the two largest and most visible ethnic groups. Truman learned to deal with their leaders. Negroes were politically invisible in Truman's old home district. In Kansas City, they constituted a significant pool of votes; the machine worked assiduously to detach them from their traditional Republican allegiance. Truman once had joined in vigorous attacks on a previous county court for lavish spending to construct a Negro boys home. As presiding judge himself, he constructed a parallel facility for Negro girls. Given his southern background, his personal feelings were mixed, but he accepted as a fact that the people now included Negroes. His initiation into ethnic politics and ready adaption paralleled developments that were happening elsewhere in the Democratic Party and would make themselves felt in the emergence of Franklin D. Roosevelt's New Deal coalition.

How had the people of Jackson County reacted to Harry Truman during his fourteen-year political career there? The record seems to show that on the whole they were very positive. He won three of four elections, the last two by large margins. Public comment about him was far more positive than negative. The Republican *Kansas City Star* praised his conduct of the county court. He had few bitter enemies and many friends. Nonetheless, wide approval did not translate into independent political appeal. When he assayed a campaign for governor of Missouri in 1932, it never got off the ground—because Boss Pendergast from the beginning leaned toward another candidate, because Truman was not well known outside Jackson County, and because he lacked the appeal needed to drum up outstate support on his own. In fact, it is likely that, even within Jackson County, Truman could not have won an election without machine support. However satisfying it was to serve the people, the organization remained the indispensable element of advancement.

The U.S. Senate

Truman's elevation to the Senate in 1934 further illustrated the point. Clearly, he won the primary and general elections because he had the strong backing of the Pendergast machine and its close ally, Gov. Guy B. Park. Thousands of "the people" who voted for him in Kansas City were ghosts; state employees, extensively utilized for campaign purposes, rounded up many others. (The tallies of his opponents had similar characteristics, of course, but it was universally conceded that the Pendergast/Park operation was by far the state's most efficient combination of fraud and patronage.) Still struggling with the fundamental inner contradiction of his career, the new senator went off to Washington broadly typed as a boss's puppet while striving to develop an identity as a servant of the public. Just as he had done in Jackson County, he cooperated with Pendergast on issues of patronage and assistance for machine associates, but he seems to have had a free hand in deciding his position on policy issues. On Capitol Hill he began to develop a national identity and further refine his sense of just who "the people" were.

Elected as New Deal liberalism was peaking in 1934 and free to concentrate on large public policy issues rather than the managerial imperatives of local government, surrounded by New Dealers and old-style progressives, he easily and naturally reverted to the neopopulism of his younger days. Most of the problems of America, he believed, had resulted from the misdeeds of Wall Street and the large corporations. He demonstrated this attitude in his support of the Public Utility Holding Company Act of 1935, which broke up the large utility combines. (His personal dealings with Kansas City Power and Light had reinforced his feelings. In private, he referred to it as part of "the power trust.") Investigating the insolvency of the railroads, he emotionally and sincerely bought into the argument that they had been looted by Wall Street bankers and their expensive lawyers. Years later, he wrote bitterly about being kept waiting for an appointment with Winthrop Aldrich, president

of Chase National Bank, and stalking out of the office. At the beginning of
World War II, he would assert that Standard Oil Company had entered into
cartel agreements with the German firm I. G. Farben to block the establishment of a synthetic rubber industry in the United States, and persist in the
charge despite a lack of evidence. Writing to a constituent, he declared: "The
Standard Oil group, of course, are still trying to choke the country to death
and I am trying to keep them from doing it, but I am only one voice in the
wilderness."[6]

"The people" still included small- and medium-sized business owners, a
group with whom Truman felt a special empathy and one he defined very
broadly. They continued to include farmers, another group whose problems
he understood. He added veterans, partly on the basis of shared experience,
partly out of respect for the power of their lobby in Washington. Workers
were an important component, although he was a bit more reserved toward
labor unions than were the most enthusiastic New Dealers. In 1937, he told
an audience at Liberty, Missouri, that "labor" in America needed to be understood as "every man or woman who works with hand or brain for a living."[7]

He, more than ever, accepted Negroes, if with some mental reservations
about their major goal of the 1930s, a federal antilynching act. We know he
thought the bill was an unconstitutional invasion of police powers reserved to
the states; yet he voted for it, probably, as Samuel Lubell has written, out of
respect for the black vote in St. Louis and Kansas City. Throughout his years
in the Senate, he systematically polished his credentials with Missouri blacks.
Privately, he was capable of using the n-word and other disagreeable slang
that had been part of his vernacular since childhood. Publicly, he declared in
a speech appealing for the Negro vote in 1940 that he did not believe in "social equality" (and he clearly did not like aggressive blacks); he also declared
that he believed in the brotherhood of all men and endorsed the idea of equal
opportunity. He never denounced the World War II Fair Employment Practices Committee. It is reasonable to believe that principles were involved in

6. On Kansas City Power and Light, see Pickwick Memo entitled "I have had two wonderful associates. . . ." On the railroads in general, see Alonzo L. Hamby, "'Vultures at the Death
of an Elephant': Harry S. Truman, the Great Train Robbery, and the Transportation Act of
1940," *Railroad History* 165 (Autumn 1991): 6–36. For the encounter with Aldrich, Truman
to Ethel Noland, February 2, 1952, Mary Ethel Noland Papers, Truman Library. For quick
summaries of the larger aspects of the rubber controversy, Richard Polenberg, *War and Society*
(Philadelphia: J. B. Lippincott, 1972), 14–18, and Eliot Janeway, *The Struggle for Survival*, rev.
ed. (New York: Weybright and Talley, 1968), 260–64. For Truman's comment, Truman to
Frank B. Grumbine, June 27, 1942, Truman Senatorial and Vice Presidential Papers, Truman
Library.

7. Speech, Liberty, Mo., October 11, 1937, Truman Senatorial and Vice Presidential Papers.

both judgments, and equally fair to assume that political calculation played a big part in his behavior. Regardless, "the people" included a distinctly black component.[8]

They also included Jews. Here also Truman could seem erratic. When he talked privately about Jews he did not like, he could sound like a confirmed anti-Semite. In fact, from a relatively early age, he had enjoyed good personal relations with Jewish people, most of all his army comrade and business partner Eddie Jacobson and the general counsel on the railroad investigating committee, Max Lowenthal. In the 1930s, he handled numerous requests to facilitate entry into the United States for German Jews. In 1940, his reelection campaign manager in St. Louis, David Berenstein, was not just a Jew but also head of a local Zionist organization. Speaking to a Zionist gathering in Chicago in 1943, Truman endorsed "a haven and place of safety" for European Jews. Writing privately to a St. Louis constituent, he said "when the right time comes I am willing to help make the fight for a Jewish homeland in Palestine."[9]

By then, Truman had made significant progress in his development as a popular politician able to win votes by dint of his own effort. Facing a hard fight for renomination in 1940 against Gov. Lloyd Stark and unable to count on an overwhelming vote tally from the now-defunct Pendergast machine, he had taken charge as never before of his own political destiny. With few fervent supporters, he put together a ragtag organization, got endorsements from more than a dozen fellow senators, lined up important help from the railway unions, appealed to a Negro constituency that Stark had ignored, and campaigned tirelessly throughout the state. Over an eight-week stretch, he spoke in 75 of Missouri's 114 counties. As he showed signs of political life, he made a deal with what had become Missouri's dominant political force, the St. Louis organization managed by Bob Hannegan. Truman's triumph was ultimately made possible by his narrow victory in St. Louis, a machine achievement, but he never would have had organizational support there without a prior demonstration of his viability. It was less important that his win was narrow than that it was predominantly the result of a personal effort.

After winning the general election in November, he returned to Washington

8. See, for example, Truman's correspondence with black leaders such as C. A. Franklin in the Senatorial and Vice Presidential papers. His 1940 speech can be found in 76th Cong., 3d Sess., *Congressional Record* 86: app., 4546–47, 5367–69, for a second, similar effort. For Lubell, see Samuel Lubell, *The Future of American Politics*, 3d ed., rev. (New York: Harper and Row, 1965), 26.

9. Truman, speech to United Rally, Chicago, April 14 [1943]; Truman to Peter Bergson, May 7, 1943, Truman Senatorial and Vice Presidential Papers.

as both a successful political captain and a personality with a stronger identity than ever among Missouri voters. Capitalizing on his success, he initiated an investigation of the rapidly growing defense program. By 1944, he was one of the most important men in Washington and a leader in the Senate. By then also, with Republicans in control of the Missouri statehouse and his Senate colleague Bennett Champ Clark facing repudiation from the electorate, he was the most important Democrat in Missouri.

Still, his success hardly presaged a leap to the vice presidency. For all the attention his war-investigating committee received, his selection for the nomination was an inside job. It rested on the high esteem he enjoyed among his fellow senators and among Democratic party regulars. To a great extent it was engineered by his old Missouri benefactor, Bob Hannegan, whom he had gotten appointed chairman of the Democratic National Committee. Truman had staked out positions on the big domestic issues consistent with his earlier pronouncements, had chaired the most active and arguably most important committee of the U.S. Senate, and had laid out an articulate and realistic foreign policy vision. But his personal style was low-key, his speaking ability and rhetorical skills modest at best. In a manner befitting his background, his career was based on steadiness and hard work; however admirable the ideals, the style invited underestimation. In the tumult of a global war, it did not generate close attention, much less inspire devotion. When Harry Truman was nominated for vice president in July 1944, most Americans had only a vague sense of who he was. That would still be the case when he was sworn in as president of the United States on the evening of April 12, 1945.

President and People

We have seen the way in which Harry Truman defined the people as workers, farmers, small enterprisers, almost anyone other than the wealthy and powerful. We have also seen the way in which the practice of politics assisted him in designating certain groups as key electoral targets. By the time he became president these processes were mature. We also have seen that he established a style of political campaigning in Missouri that emphasized what the analysts would later call retail politics—tireless campaigning that consisted of many personal contacts with relatively small clusters of people. In 1945, he was still uncomfortable with huge audiences and the techniques of mass communications that his predecessor, Franklin Roosevelt, had used so well. What was now important was the reaction the people would have to him.

By 1945, public opinion polling was a standard feature of the American scene. The Roper and Gallup polls give us reasonable snapshots of Truman's standing with the American public at specific intervals, although, then as now, they do not provide the best indicators of intensity of feeling.[10] Clearly the initial reaction to the new president was one of sympathy for an ordinary American who, without warning, found himself forced to assume enormous burdens that had been borne by one of the nation's most popular presidents. Americans knew Truman was ordinary because from the beginning he went out of his way to appear so. He told a group of reporters the next day: "Boys, if you ever pray, pray for me now. I don't know whether you fellows ever had a load of hay fall on you, but when they told me yesterday what had happened, I felt like the moon, the stars and all the planets had fallen on me. I've got the most terribly responsible job a man ever had." His military aide and longtime friend Harry Vaughan not too long afterward contrasted him with Franklin Roosevelt: "After a diet of caviar, you like to get back to ham and eggs."[11] Truman appeared modest and unassuming, yet on top of his job. He told the world he liked it when people called him "Harry." Such democratic posturing was of a piece with his personal history; it could not have come more naturally.

The public seemed to respond at first. In June, the Gallup poll found an 87 percent approval rating for him; in October, a still sky-high 82 percent. In November, Roper confirmed these findings.[12] And why not? Things on the whole had gone well through the year. The United States had won World War II. The United Nations had been launched with great hope. In the flush of victory and the immediate aftermath, the future looked bright.

By 1946, however, things were going badly on numerous fronts. Externally, the world suddenly seemed a more dangerous place as the Cold War began to take shape. The administration appeared to be in serious disarray as

10. Bernard Sternsher, "Harry Truman," in *Popular Images of American Presidents*, ed. William C. Spragens (New York: Greenwood Press, 1988), deftly utilizes public opinion survey data.

11. Harry S. Truman, *Memoirs*, vol. 1, *Year of Decisions* (Garden City: Doubleday, 1955), 19; Robert S. Allen and William V. Shannon, *The Truman Merry Go-Round* (New York: Vanguard, 1950), 49.

12. George H. Gallup, *The Gallup Poll: Public Opinion, 1935–1971*, 3 vols. (New York: Random House, 1972), 1:512, 537; Elmo Roper, *You and Your Leaders: Their Actions and Your Reactions, 1936–1956* (New York: William Morrow and Co., 1957), 127.

two of its leading Cabinet members—Secretary of the Interior Harold Ickes and Secretary of Commerce Henry Wallace—resigned in protest. Worst of all, the inevitable strains of rapid reconversion from a wartime to a peacetime economy threw much of the country into a chaos of labor strikes, housing shortages, and collapsing price controls. Very little of this was Truman's fault. A fair amount of it could be traced to the Roosevelt administration's lack of interest in following up on a recommendation that the Truman committee had made in late 1943 for beginning the economic transition. Most of the rest was the price of a free economy and a long tradition of hostility to restrictive government controls.

Truman's problem was to a great extent one of public relations. As Elmo Roper has put it, "He gave the impression of a man who was being pulled in conflicting directions and did not himself know which way to go."[13] He alienated labor by opposing what he considered to be abusive strikes. In the interest of an orderly economic transition, he angered producers (farmers as well as businessmen) by opposing big price increases and workers by opposing big wage hikes. Consumers, in whose name the struggle was waged, fretted more about shortages than about prices. Worse yet, the president lost most of his struggles. Congress rejected his request for continuation of a strong Office of Price Administration. A federal housing program never got off the ground. Attempts to enforce remaining price controls on meat led to a strike of producers and empty cases at meat counters. In the "beefsteak election" of 1946, Republicans surged back to control on Capitol Hill. No one doubted that the president was the biggest loser, in large measure because of the disappointment or apathy of the workers, farmers, and middle-class consumers who were among the most salient groups in his conception of "the people." A Roper poll taken in January 1947 showed him the probable loser to any of the major Republican possibilities in the 1948 election.[14]

As Truman's popularity crashed in 1946, Americans yearned more and more for his extraordinary predecessor, Franklin Roosevelt.[15] FDR had won four presidential elections, had led the country through depression and war, had been an inspirational presence. His failures and half-successes were forgotten. For a time, a mythology emerged: FDR had mobilized public opinion and got important measures through Congress by making a single radio speech; FDR had been above politics; FDR would have preserved the deteriorating alliance with the Soviet Union; FDR would have handled the eco-

13. Roper, *Leaders,* 127.
14. Ibid., 128–29.
15. Alonzo L. Hamby, "The Liberals, Truman, and FDR as Symbol and Myth," *Journal of American History* 56 (March 1970): 859–67.

nomic mess. The old New Dealers, naturally enough, most fervently bought into and propagated this fantasy, but it had a much wider appeal. And it did have one element of authenticity. Roosevelt surely would have *seemed* more in control. He likely would have been much better at framing issues in ways that deflected at least some of the blame. His charismatic presence would have given him a degree of authority and a substantial hard-core following not available to Truman. It had been much easier for the new president to be an ordinary American democrat as a county executive and a U.S. senator. The popular expectations for a president were different and more difficult. Truman had discovered that it is dangerous for national leaders to invite people to underestimate them; they risk forfeiting authority in those hard times when they most need it.

Truman's first two years in the presidency would establish a pattern. As measured by polls (which despite the embarrassment of 1948 were roughly accurate), his public approval would move up and down with events. When the country seemed on the right track *and* he seemed in command of events, the polls were generally favorable. When things were not going well, however, the public had a way of assuming he was not in control, and his numbers broke downward. Lacking the reserves of charisma possessed by Roosevelt before him or Eisenhower after him, he was in many respects hostage to happenings he could not control. Moreover, he would always be much more vulnerable to personal attack on grounds that ran from incompetence to venality.

In these circumstances, Truman's recovery from repudiation in 1946 to reelection in 1948 was an extraordinary feat. It rested on his skill as, in Robert Donovan's phrase, an instinctive counterpuncher, his ability as president to establish the terms of political debate in the face of a fragmented opposition, and his continuing adherence to his concept of "the people" as objects of public service and the basis for a majority political coalition.

By 1948, most of the strains of reconversion were over. The economy was humming along prosperously. Relatively inexpensive tract housing was beginning to appear in new suburbs; sleek new postwar-design autos were coming onto the market; consumer shortages were mostly a thing of the past. The president had established an anti-Soviet foreign policy that enjoyed majority approval. Moreover, the new opposition Congress, which often seemed excessively cranky and conservative, failed to provide an attractive alternative. Instead, it served him as a whipping boy for the irritations that remained in American life and gave him an ideological focus around which to rally the people in support of the rights and benefits the New Deal and the Democratic Party had given them during and after the Great Depression.

The highlights of this attempt are well known. He brought back labor by vetoing the Taft-Hartley Act, blamed the Republican refusal to bring back price controls for continuing high inflation, brought back a restless Negro vote by becoming the first president ever to advocate a comprehensive civil rights program, and won over Jews by recognizing Israel. Once the presidential campaign actually began, he gave as little attention as possible to his Republican opponent, the moderate and capable Thomas E. Dewey. Instead, he fired away relentlessly at a Congress most often represented on the domestic side by the bluntly conservative Robert A. Taft of Ohio. He was even successful in blaming Congress for falling farm prices in late 1948 because of its refusal to fund adequate surplus grain storage facilities. Dewey foolishly went along with the game by never bothering to establish a centrist program for his prospective administration.

This was a high-risk strategy and not without its speed bumps. The Israel issue was for months caught up in an ugly tug-of-war between national security officials and political operators. It was by no means certain that a civil rights program would be a net political plus for the president. It led to a southern revolt that ultimately manifested itself in the States Rights ("Dixiecrat") Party of 1948. Truman's poll numbers had crept substantially upward in 1947. These two issues sent them into a tailspin in early 1948. But in both cases the president appears to have struggled to reconcile political calculation with the national interest and ultimately to have convinced himself he was doing the right thing. On other issues, the political calculation was pretty raw. It was ludicrous, for example, to blame Congress for failing to reinstitute price controls that had collapsed in 1946 and could not possibly have been brought back.

What one can say with assurance is that, in Truman's mind, it all came together as a campaign to unite "the people," as he had long since defined that term, against the "special interests" that he thought the Republicans represented. It is less amazing that he was successful by a narrow margin than that he was successful at all. Above all, we must understand that it is insufficient to think of his strenuous 1948 campaign as simply a remarkable display of will and endurance. It was that, but it was also a manifestation of the political worldview he had internalized as a young man nearly a half-century earlier and refined thereafter. Whistle-stopping around the country, employing fiery rhetoric, he successfully brought enough of "the people," interest group by interest group, behind him and the Democratic Party by raising the fear that Republican interests would take the good life away from them.

For much of the following year, Truman was a popular, well-regarded president, but even in the best days the base of his popularity was fragile. To poll 49.5 percent of the vote in a race that included two minor parties had been no mean feat; still, slightly more votes had been cast against him than for him. Despite a superficially imposing margin in Congress, the Democratic Party remained sharply divided on many domestic issues and not amenable to presidential control. Much of Truman's Fair Deal domestic program, especially its most visible and original components (civil rights, federal aid to education, the Brannan farm plan, national health insurance), disappeared into the legislative sausage-grinder on Capitol Hill. The few successes either turned out to be failures in practical application (public housing) or unspectacular, if significant, measures that stirred little passion in the larger electorate (social security revision).

Meanwhile the opposition Republicans exploited multiple lacunae of mostly small-bore corruption within the executive branch. In addition, they pounded away at a Communist issue that became more compelling as the tide of the Cold War seemed to turn against the United States with the fall of Nationalist China, the first Soviet A-bomb test, the conviction of Alger Hiss for perjury after Hiss denied that he had engaged in espionage, and the arrests of atomic spies, including Julius and Ethel Rosenberg. Even before the Korean War started, Joe McCarthy had begun his spectacular rampage, effectively cutting off the oxygen supply for many other areas of discussion. Truman, despite his considerable merits, lacked the stature in the popular mind to sway independent-minded congressmen, position himself above foreign policy setbacks, or destroy McCarthy. On June 25, when the North Korean army rampaged across the thirty-eighth parallel, he was already on another downward cycle in public esteem.

Truman's decision to intervene in Korea, popular at first, soon proved damaging beyond rational prediction. War, even a small war, brought with it an initial spurt of inflation, then various economic controls as the United States began a larger rearmament effort to forestall a potential Soviet offensive against Europe. An initial spectacular victory in the early fall at Inchon and an expected quick end to the conflict were transformed into a frustrating reversal and a protracted stalemate after the Chinese intervened. From that point on, the United States had no strategy for winning the war. Rather, the objective was a truce that would stabilize Korea by restoring the approximate prewar boundaries, while building up European defenses. If from a larger perspective the strategy made sense, it was unpalatable to a people who expected to see wars fought to an expeditious victory.

When Truman dismissed Gen. Douglas MacArthur from his command, he touched off a storm of criticism and hit his nadir in the polls. Thereafter especially, the war magnified all the already established irritants in American politics. Although it was being fought to stem a Communist advance, although the rest of a stepped-up defense program was directed toward keeping Soviet power out of Western Europe, the very fact of a frustrating no-win war intensified the power of McCarthy's charges of subversion from within. It also created an atmosphere receptive to other critiques of the president and his administration. It notably made charges of corruption more devastating than they would have been in better times. From the Chinese intervention of November 1950 through the MacArthur dismissal on to the steel seizure debacle of spring 1952, a majority of Americans seemed to feel Harry Truman could do no right. Less than a third approved of his job performance. A good many observers appear to have thought his extensive campaigning for Adlai Stevenson in the fall election did the ticket more harm than good.

Brought down by events, Truman turned over the presidency to a Republican successor elected as much on the basis of personal appeal as for his stand on issues. In the end, the American people—including many from groups Truman placed front and center in his definition of the people—at most felt a certain identification with him. They also felt that a workaday politician who seemed not much different from themselves had not been up to handling the great challenges of the times. His successor, also a man of humble origins, equally possessed a democratic appeal, but added to it a charisma produced by a lifetime of stern self-discipline and the experience of leadership in the greatest of all American military endeavors. Ironically, almost no one had admired him more than did Truman until Eisenhower emerged as a Republican challenger.

Harry Truman continued to be a public figure until a few years before his death. Slowly, his reputation rose back toward its peak of 1945. Especially after he ceased to be a partisan activist in the early 1960s, his widely perceived weaknesses—impulsiveness, hotheadedness, a limited capacity for the demands of the presidency—faded into the background. For the last nine years of his life, he had the good fortune to be compared, not to Franklin Roosevelt and Dwight Eisenhower, but to Lyndon Johnson and Richard Nixon. His blunt honesty and democratic simplicity seemed increasingly attractive. A loving biography by his daughter, Margaret, focused public attention on him, just as his life was ebbing away at the end of 1972. More than a year later, Merle Miller's *Plain Speaking* (1974) portrayed him vividly to a large reading audience. A soft-rock group, Chicago, got into the act with a song named for him. By then, he had achieved the status of a folk hero, winning grudging, even enthusiastic, respect from partisan Republicans who contrasted his foreign policy and moderately liberal domestic programs favorably with the offerings of the leaders of the post–Great Society Democratic Party. All could agree that in the words of a reviewer of *Plain Speaking*, he was "an American original" whose career as president told us something, mostly good, about ourselves.[16]

Leaders and People

Truman suffered a common fate of democratic leaders, his public standing rising and falling with a tide of events for which he frequently could not be held responsible. It is one of the anomalies of democracies that they generally hold the profession of politics in low esteem, treat their leaders with little respect, and dispose of them readily. Millions of Americans readily identified with Truman and thought they knew the type well. For that very reason, however much they might have found him likable, they doubted his capabilities.

The Truman presidency actually was in many ways an extraordinary one. Truman initiated a policy of containment and foreign assistance that very likely prevented Soviet domination of Western Europe and the Middle East. He held a splintering New Deal political coalition together and adapted it programmatically to an era of post-Depression prosperity. Yet it has become customary to remember him for what he did *not* accomplish and to speak of the failures that left him isolated and unpopular during the final year of his presidency. By contrast, Eisenhower essentially carried forth the Truman policies with various tweaks around the edges, deployed exaggerated rhetoric to conceal substantive similarities, and had a spottier record of economic management. Truman's predecessor, Roosevelt, could lay claim to great achievements, but FDR also had great failures on his record. He spent eight years vainly trying to end the American Great Depression; his diplomacy in World War II would have benefited from a clearer-eyed realism toward the Soviet Union. Nonetheless, "the people" elected FDR to the presidency four times— the last time despite abundant, publicly available evidence that he was past his prime; they would have done the same for an unsteady Eisenhower if he had been able to run.

We generally say that the difference was "charisma." FDR and Ike had it; Truman did not. We need to ask ourselves what we mean by this overworked word, which was introduced to political analysis about a century ago by the

16. John P. Roche, "Truman on Tape," *Saturday Review* (February 23, 1974), 20–22.

German political sociologist Max Weber and has made its way disastrously into a popular discourse that today may as easily ascribe it to a brand of perfume as to qualities of leadership.[17] The most precise definition is that of an unusual personal magnetism that places a person beyond the realm of the ordinary and elicits an emotional response from "the crowd." Presumably, charisma is something detached to one degree or another from the issues. To some extent, charisma can be manufactured, at least in totalitarian societies in which a leader has a grip over the means of communication. In all cases, it differs in style from one culture to another. And within cultures, it may differ from one group to another. It elicits intense negative feelings as well as positive ones. With that in mind, perhaps we can understand Truman's relative lack of appeal to the people, compared with the strong attraction of Roosevelt and Eisenhower.

Roosevelt and Eisenhower had charm. They were adept at wielding power. Both combined a common touch with an aura of authority and confidence that came rather naturally to them from the experiences that had brought them to the presidency. Truman wielded power effectively; far more than either Roosevelt or Eisenhower, he made the decisions that shaped the post–World War II world. But he lacked authority. His democratic political style might generate transitory good feelings, but it did not elicit awe. Voters saw Roosevelt and Eisenhower as extraordinary men capable of world leadership. They saw Harry Truman as a little guy who lost his temper too easily and was engaged in one fight after another. Even among many of those who liked him, he did not inspire confidence. In the end, most of the people did not feel the bond he claimed in his Farewell Address. The political damage was heavy. Historians must acknowledge that liability, as they must also acknowledge his considerable achievements.

17. John Patrick Diggins, *Max Weber: Politics and the Spirit of Tragedy* (New York: Basic Books, 1996), is a good introduction to its subject. Perhaps the best starting point for Weber's own musings on leadership and politics is his famous essay "Politics as a Vocation," reprinted in numerous collections, including *From Max Weber: Essays in Sociology,* ed. Hans H. Gerth and C. Wright Mills (New York: Oxford University Press, 1946). See also Reinhard Bendix and Guenther Roth, *Scholarship and Partisanship: Essays on Max Weber* (Berkeley: University of California Press, 1971), chap. 9, for a brief discussion of the concept and its applicability to four major Asian leaders of the 1960s.

REMARKS OF THE PRESIDENT
  At the Victory Celebration
    In Independence, Missouri   #1861d
      November 3, 1948
        In the Evening (around 8:00 p. m.)
          (radio broadcast)

- - - - - - - - - - - - - - - - -

Thank you very much. Thank you.

Mr. Mayor, and my fellow townsmen and citizens of this great County named after Andrew Jackson:

I can't tell you how very much I appreciate this turnout to celebrate a victory -- not my victory, but a victory of the Democratic Party for the people.

I want to inform you, Mr. Mayor, that protocol goes out the window when I am in Independence. I am a citizen of this town, and a taxpayer, and I want to be treated just like the rest of the taxpayers in this community are treated, whether you extend the city limits or not.

And I thank you very much indeed for this celebration, which is not for me. It is for the whole country. It is for the whole world, for the simple reason that you have given me a tremendous responsibility.

Now, since you have given me that responsibility, I want every single one of you to help carry out that responsibility, for the welfare of this great Republic, and for the welfare and peace of the world at large. And I am sure that is what you are going to do.

I can't begin to thank the people who are responsible for the Democratic Party winning this great election. Of course, I am indebted to everybody for that win, and I will have to just say to every single one of you individually that I am going to do the very best I can to carry out the Democratic Platform, as I promised to do in my speeches over this country.

And we have a Congress now, and I am sure we will make some progress in the next four years.

Thank you all very much.

TUESDAY, NOVEMBER 1, 1949

305th
Day

All Saints' Day

60 Days
to come

I have another hell of a day. Look at my appointment list. It is only a sample of the whole year. Trying to make the 81st Congress perform is and has been worse than cussing the 80th. A President never loses prestige fighting Congress. And I can't fight my own Congress. There are some terrible chairmen in the 81st. But so far things have come out fairly well.

I've kissed and petted more consarned S.O.B. so-called Democrats and left wing Republicans than all the Presidents put together. I have very few people fighting my battles in Congress as I fought F.D.R's

Had dinner by myself tonight. Worked in the Lee House office until dinner time. A butler came in very formally and said "Mr President dinner is served." I walk into the diningroom in the Blair House. Barnett in tails and white tie pulls out my chair, pushes me up to the table. John in tails and white tie brings me a fruit cup. Barnett takes away the empty cup. John brings me a plate, Barnett brings me a tenderloin, John brings me asparagus, Barnett brings me carrots and beets. I have to eat alone and in silence in candle lit room

opposite page.

54

MONDAY, OCTOBER 31, 1949

304th
Day

Hallowe'en—Reformation Day

61 Days
to come

from opposite page —

Dining-Barnett takes the plate and butter plates. John comes in with a napkin and silver crumb tray—there are no crumbs but John has to brush them off the table anyway. Barnett bring me a plate with a finger bowl and doyle on it—I remove finger bowl and doyle and John puts a glass saucer and a little bowl on the plate. Barnett brings me some chocolate custard. John bring me me a demitasse (at lunch a little cup of coffee—about two good gulps) and my dinner is over. I take a hand bath in the finger bowl and go back to work.

What a life!

REAR PLATFORM REMARKS OF THE PRESIDENT
AT SAND POINT, IDAHO

October 1, 1952
5.00 p.m., p.s.t.

Thank you very much. That's a good job. You know,
I have never run across so many good young bands as I have
during the last two or three days. You really do a good job
on that -- just as good as the Marine band, and that's saying
a lot.

I am grateful for this wonderful reception here
today. I have had a wonderful day riding through these
mountains in Montana and Idaho. I have seen a lot of mighty
fine people, and I have told them a lot of things that are
good for their souls, if they will just pay attention to
what I am saying.

I am here on one of my five jobs. You see, the
President has five jobs. He is the Chief Executive of the
United States. He is Commander-in-Chief of the armed forces
of the United States. He is the policy-maker for the foreign
policy of the United States, and he is the head of the Democratic Party. And that is the role in which I am working
today. And he is the social head of State when the visiting
firemen like queens and presidents and people like that come
to the country, and he has to entertain them and make them
feel happy so thixx that they will go back and tell what a
nice country it is. But today I am the politician. Iam the
head of the Democratic Party. I am out here to tell you what
the Democratic Party stands for and see if I can't convince
you of what your own best interest is and why it is that
way.

Now I have on the train here with me some of the
Idaho candidates for office. They impress me as being mighty
fine people. Gracie Post is a grand person. I met her in
1948 when I was out here, and I have seen her in Washington,
and I have enjoyed seeing her again. And I hope you will send
her to Congress because she will really represent you down
there. And I will say to you that you need it mighty bad.

I don't want you to forget the national ticket,
either. Adlai Stevenson for President and John Sparkman
for Vice President are two as fine men as have ever been
nominated to those offices; and you can count on them to
look after the interests of the public and the people -- the
plain everyday people, those are the ones that need looking
after.

You know, they have lobbies down there -- the power
trust, and they kx have the real estate lobby, and they have
the China lobby, and theyhave the oil lobbies, and they
have lobbies for this that and the other thing. And the only
lobby that the people have is the man who sits in the White
House. He represents 150 million people who can't afford a
lobby. And when you have a man in that place who looks
after your interests, then you are safe. If you don't,
you are in a terrible fix inxxxxx when the Congress and the
President both go down the lobby road. I never did do it.
That is what caused me so much trouble, and why I had to go
out and make such a xxxxx campaign in 1948. As long as I am
in the White House, I am going to be the lobbyist for 150
million people who haven't anylobby. And that is what Adlai
Stevenson will do if you will put him in there.

He made a great record as Governor of Illinois. He
is the best qualified new leader to come up in this country
since Franklin Roosevelt twenty years ago.

Now I want to tell you something about why I am fond of this part of the world. I like this part of the country, and I want to see it grow and prosper, and I think you will find my actions as President as and as United States Senator from Missouri prove that very statement.

I want to see you people in the Northwest get cheap electric power so that you can build up your industry. I want to see your rivers controled so the water can be used to raise crops and not cause floods. I have been trying to help you get these things for seven years -- all the time I have been President, and all the time I was in the Senate, too. It's 18 years really, altogether. And so has the Democratic Party. We believe in helping you. We believe in helping all the people ax to do things through your Government that you can't do on your own. That is what the Government is for, in my opinion.

But you know, there is another philosophy and theory in this country. You know, the Republican Party doesn't figure it that way. The Republican Party is controlled by the big boys, the power lobby, the big lumber lobby, and the big banks and the rest -- and all the special interests combined in one outfit. And naturally those are the fellows that the Republican politicians serve. And they always have done that ever since I can remember.

I started in politics forty years ago. Started in the precinct, and I went from precinct to President. Amd I have been fighting Republicans ever since that, and I am going to keep on fighting them till I die. Not personally, you xxxxxxx understand. There are many xxx good men who are misled by the Republican doctrine, and Ihave some very wonderful friends who belong to the Republican Party; but they are wrong and I spend a lot of time trying to teach them what they ought to do.

Now, I have been having some fun with the Republicans and I expect to have a lot more before this campaign is over. And their candidate for President has a sign on the back of his train -- as I said something about it the other day in North Dakota -- and on that sign, where my Presidential seal is down there, it said Look Ahead Neighbor. I have been pointing out to the people that it ought to say Look Out Neighbor.

Brother, if you elect that Republican President you had better look out.

Do you want more power, more flood control up here? You'd better look out, neighbor, and vote the Democratic ticket. The great dams we have built so far are the last you are ever likely to see if the Republicans come in. Hell's Canyon xxxxxxxxxxxxxxxx and Libby Dam will be out the window. They have fought Hungry Horse. They fought Bonneville. They fought Grand Coulee. They are fighting Hell's Canyon and Libby. They fought over construction of the TVA. It's just constitutional with them. They don't believe in the development of resources by government in these xx United States. And I can't understand it, because when these resources are properly developed, it increases the land that can be taxed. It increases the wealth of the country, and that is what I am for, and always have been for. As I say, I am going to keep on being for it.

Do you want good education for your kids? More medical care and social security benefits when you are older? Well, look out, now. Don't look ahead, neighbor, as they tell you -- you look out, neighbor.

The Republicans are against these things. The record in Congress proves it. I am talking from the Congressional Record. I helped to make that Congressional Record from 1935 until I became President of the United States. It is a hard document to read. It is full of fine print, and the reason they print it in fine print, they want to be sure that a lot of people won't read it because if you were to read it, you

57

will know the Democratic record, which is good; and you will
find out the Republican record wh is something awful, and
it always has been.

Now the Republicans have tried every way they
possibly can to sabotage REA. The gentlemenax who was
just introduced to you by Miss Post knows the REA picture
out here in this part of the world. He is one of its first
attorneys. But you know, in the 80th Congress -- that
awful Congress that I licked them on in 1948 -- they did one
of the most -- the slickest tricks you ever heard of in your
life. I sent down a request for a certain number for one
hundred million dollars for the REA to make loans to its
cooperatives, so they could build these lines. Well, they
tacked on another 100 million dollars so they could brag
that they had given a hundred million dollars more than I
asked for.

But you know what they did? They took 700 thousand
dollars off the administrative end of the REA and fixed it
so the added 100 million and what I had asked for couldn't
be used. And then they wanted to make you believe
that they were strong for REA. They wouldlike to sabotage
it if they could. If you put them back in there, that is
about what they will do.

And you railroad men and other workers here -- do
you like union recognition and the union shop? Do you like
the accidentprevention work the Government has been doing?
Do you like our minimum wage laws? WXXXXXXXXXXXXXXXXXXXXXXXXXX
Well, if you do, you had better look out on this look ahead
business, because if you don't look out, they will take
all these things away from you, or sabotage them so you
can't use them very much.

The Republicans are out to turn the clock back.
You know most of the policy-maker Republicans are living
in the age of William McKinley in 1896, and they don't
like things that look ahead. That is their intention,
to sabotage all these good things. And the record proves
it. All they have got to do is read that fine print in
that record I am telling you about.

I know you are proud of your scenery out here.
I have heard about the fishing, too.   I hope you will
enjoy these things a long, long time. But let me tell you
this. If the Republicans get control of this country,
scenery and fishing will be about all you will have left.
I think you will probably get tired of having nothing to
do but look at your scenery and eating your fish.

Don't misunderstand me -- I can't promise you that
the Republicans won't try to take those things away from
you too -- as soon as they can figure out how to make a profit
xxxxhxxxxxxxxx out of the deal.

Don't let them fool you with their five-star
xxxxxxxx candidate. He is a good general and I like him.
XXX But as a politician he is no better than the rest of
the Republican Old Guard. Now I know how bad they are,
because I have studied their record in Congress, and I am
telling you you had better study it, too, for your own
welfare and benefit. You had better figure out where your
interests lie. You had better vote for yourselves.

Now, as I said at the beginning, I like this part
of the country. I am told that Paul Bunyan came out here
and stopped from Missouri, and I have been wondering if any
of Paul's descendants are around in this part of the country.
I would like to meet them if they are; because Paul is one
of the tallest tales we have in Missouri. He is as tall a
tale as the Republicans tell you when they tell you they
want to get the government and work for you -- which

they don't want to do. Now, for your own interests, for
the welfare of this great country of ours, for the peace
of the world, I am telling you that on November 4th you
ought to vote for yourselves, because you are the Government, and if you vote for yourselves you will vote the
straight Democratic ticket and keep the country safe and
sound for another four ẍẍẍẍ years.

Thank you very much.

END

Economic Prosperity, Security, and Equality

Harry Truman's Farewell Claims and Presidential Achievements

Robert M. Collins

The presidential farewell address is not a particularly familiar or esteemed art form. Even politically aware citizens would be hard-pressed to call to mind any presidential farewell addresses save George Washington's original (and, perhaps, Dwight D. Eisenhower's farewell warning regarding the modern military-industrial complex). A notably forward-looking people, Americans pay considerably greater attention to presidential inaugural addresses. We care more about where presidents tell us they are going to go in the future than about where they claim in retrospect to have taken us. We strive expectantly to take the measure of our leaders at the beginning of their terms, but we do not particularly trust them to be their own historians as they depart the presidential stage. However, it would be a mistake to dismiss out of hand Harry Truman's 1953 Farewell Address. The speech illuminates the man, his times, and the uses and pitfalls of presidential self-assessment. Despite the fact that Truman devoted surprisingly little of his Farewell Address to his economic achievements, his remarks serve as a useful point of departure for assessing his administration's record in economic affairs.

The economic claims Truman advanced in his farewell speech were simple and few. First, he reported that "we in America have learned how to attain real prosperity for our people." Employed in record numbers, Americans in all walks of life had "better incomes and more of the good things of life than ever before in the history of the world." Second, he observed that such progress had been accompanied by a high degree of institutional security: the bank failures of the 1920s and 1930s had literally disappeared because of federal regulation and deposit insurance. "There hasn't been a failure of an insured bank in nearly nine years. No depositor has lost a cent in that period," he reported. Third and last, he maintained that the nation had achieved the fairest distribution of income in recent history.

The claims themselves tell us something about the man making them. They remind us of Truman's historical-mindedness. The boasts had a clear historical frame of reference, running variously from the immediate past of the preceding decades to the larger frame of "recent [U.S.] history" to the totality of world history. They also revealed a notable analytical ability to gauge relative significance, to see the so-called big picture on such fundamental issues as economic prosperity, security, and equality. Finally, they bespoke a certain humility that we conventionally attribute (perhaps not always accurately) to Truman the man. Note the precise language of the assertions: not "I have" or "my administration has," but rather the more cautious and collective (and undoubtedly more accurate) "we in America have." The language is that of someone who realized presidents do not necessarily create the world-historical waves on which they ride. But the claims, however cautiously advanced, were also demands for recognition and congratulation. Humility in the service of self-promotion was a familiar Truman posture. Alonzo L. Hamby has written insightfully of Truman's "deep need for recognition of his achievements," and that need clearly animated his final presidential address.[1]

Do Truman's claims of achievement in the economic realm hold up under scrutiny? The overall answer is "yes," but establishing the validity of Truman's farewell claims begs the further question of whether the administration actually contributed in unique, purposeful, and concrete ways to those achievements or merely happened to be in power while the developments unfolded. Was Truman, in the terminology made famous by Sidney Hook, an "event-making" hero or merely an "eventful" one?[2] It is this latter line of inquiry that is absent from Truman's Farewell Address and that distinguishes historical reflection from presidential assertion.

1. Hamby, *Man of the People: A Life of Harry S. Truman* (New York: Oxford University Press, 1995), 637.
2. Hook, *The Hero in History: A Study in Limitation and Possibility* (New York: John Day Co., 1943).

Regarding Truman's declaration that over the course of his presidency the American people did indeed achieve "real prosperity," the raw statistical record is instructive and impressive. Between the fiscal years 1946 and 1952 the Gross National Product grew at an average annual rate of 7.4 percent, which compares favorably with the historical rate of 3.4 percent for the period 1870–1973. Year-end unemployment from 1947 to 1952 averaged 3.3 percent, which in an economy with a free labor market constituted something very close to full employment. Between 1946 and 1952 inflation grew at an average annual rate of 6.1 percent, a high rate but one that sinks to a more respectable 3.9 percent if we put aside the obviously unusual year of 1946, which witnessed an extraordinary burst of inflation in connection with the transition from a war economy to a peacetime footing.[3]

Perhaps the most impressive statistical measure of economic progress was the annual rate of productivity increase. Economists are fond of saying that productivity is not everything, but that it is *almost* everything. The reasoning behind their observation is that increased productivity—in other words, increased output per worker—is the most direct way to raise a society's standard of living. For the six-year period 1947–1952, output per hour in the nonfarm business sector, a standard measure of productivity increase, grew by an average of 3.9 percent, which was well above the historical average of 2.3 percent for the period 1900–1970.[4]

The overall record of economic growth and stability under Truman was highly satisfactory, by comparison with either the historical record or the subsequent performance of the U.S. economy. In fact, the Truman years, especially the period beginning in 1948 after the major dislocations of reconversion had been surmounted, are now commonly regarded as having ushered in a quarter-century-long "golden age" of U.S. economic performance that ran up to 1973, when stagflation brought the postwar boom to an end.

Determining the role of federal policy in achieving the postwar prosperity of which Truman was justifiably proud is tricky business. The postwar boom was clearly driven by deep and dynamic economic forces that had little to do

3. A handy summary of relevant economic statistics is provided in Francis H. Heller, ed., *Economics and the Truman Administration* (Lawrence: Regents Press of Kansas, 1981), xvi–xviii; on the GNP see Jeffrey Madrick, *The End of Affluence: The Causes and Consequences of America's Economic Dilemma* (New York: Random House, 1995), 4–5; inflation here is calculated for consumer prices.

4. The figure for productivity growth in the Truman years is calculated from statistics available from the U.S. Department of Labor Bureau of Labor Statistics web site at www.bls.gov. The historical rate is from Paul Krugman, *The Age of Diminished Expectations: U.S. Economic Policy in the 1990s* (Cambridge: MIT Press, 1993), 17.

with whoever occupied the White House. These included the huge pent-up demand from the war years, the additional spur of defense spending for the nascent Cold War (especially in the years following NSC-68 and the outbreak of fighting in Korea), the population spurt known as the baby boom, the exploitation of the new frontiers of the nation's burgeoning suburbs and the emergent Sunbelt, and the postwar routinization of innovation by an academic-military-corporate complex. In truth, these powerful engines of economic growth were neither summoned nor controlled by Truman or his aides and advisers. But the administration did contribute to the success of their interaction in several discernible ways.

One crucial but sometimes overlooked contribution was the decision to return the economy to a peacetime footing by gradually but decisively phasing out the wartime regime of economic controls. The tasks of demobilization and reconversion were not easy. It is difficult to do justice to the flux of the immediate postwar months. The military machine that had helped win a world war against formidable enemies was dismantled so quickly that the U.S. army literally lost track of who was in service and who had been hastily released. In 1946 the Pentagon had to resort to the highly unusual device of a general muster and head count—in effect, having everyone in the army stand in place at an appointed time on a designated date in order to determine who was still in the service and where they were physically located.[5]

Truman added to the postwar welter when, within days of Japan's surrender, he announced a program of gradual yet inexorable economic decontrol. Liberals tended to favor the continuation of controls, conservatives their rapid abolition. Truman soon found himself presiding over a messy scramble as business, labor, and a host of material or ideological special-interest groups maneuvered for maximum advantage in the rapidly changing environment. "Sherman was *wrong*," the president told the annual Gridiron Dinner in December 1945, only half-jokingly. "I'm telling you I find peace is hell." To his mother and sister, he confided that "labor has gone crazy and management isn't far from insane in selfishness."[6] One result was a record year of labor-management strife in 1946—nearly 5,000 strikes involving 4.6 million

---

5. Louis Galambos, ed., *The Papers of Dwight David Eisenhower: The Chief of Staff, Volume VII* (Baltimore: Johns Hopkins University Press, 1978), xvi.

6. Gridiron statement quoted in Robert J. Donovan, *Conflict and Crisis: The Presidency of Harry S Truman, 1945–1948* (1977; rpt. Columbia: University of Missouri Press, 1996), 125; Truman to Martha Ellen and Mary Jane Truman, October 13, 1945, in Robert H. Ferrell, ed., *Off the Record: The Private Papers of Harry S. Truman* (1982; rpt. Columbia: University of Missouri Press, 1997), 72.

workers and costing the economy 116 million person-days of lost production.[7]

The process of reconversion was not pretty. The issue of wage and price controls had become hopelessly entangled with the matter of labor-management conflict, and the combination defied the administration's best efforts. Hamby notes correctly that "Truman's performance was terrible. He appeared to have danced around every side of the issue. He was weak, then strong, then weak again."[8] In November 1946 voters registered their dismay at the polls by giving the Republicans control of both houses of Congress for the first time since 1930; four days after the election, Truman announced the end of price controls, except for rent, sugar, rice, solid fuels, and some heavy consumer durables.

The outcome of the battle over the continuation of wage and price controls, which the head of the Office of Price Administration, Chester Bowles, had labeled "the battle of the century," quickly came to seem to have been predetermined. But the recent scholarship of Lizabeth Cohen argues that the battle over controls could have gone either way: "Whatever reconversion came to mean," she suggests, "it was in no way an inevitability." The struggle over controls was in fact a struggle between competing visions of how best to organize the peacetime political economy. A vigorous liberal coalition of consumer advocates, housewives, veterans, African American activists, and organized labor fought hard for the continuation of controls and, Cohen maintains, nearly won.[9]

Truman's initial inclination in 1945 to gradually phase out controls and his ultimate decision to abolish them in 1946, no matter how wavering or wobbly his performance in between, represented a significant contribution to the economic prosperity that followed. One particularly astute student of the history of wage and price controls in the United States, Hugh Rockoff, has concluded that controls did indeed work effectively during World War II, but he adds: "Such regimentation was appropriate in the war. . . . But when the termination of the war ended the balance of costs and benefits swung against controls, and they were removed. Sometimes democracies (despite their critics) make the right decisions and I believe we did so during and after

7. Donovan, *Conflict and Crisis,* 163.
8. Hamby, *Man of the People,* 381.
9. Cohen, *A Consumers' Republic: The Politics of Mass Consumption in Postwar America* (New York: Alfred A. Knopf, 2003), 102–9. Cohen laments the postwar turn away from controls as a crucial defeat for the progressive forces wishing to use statist micromanagement of the economy to establish a regime of virtuous consumption in the United States.

the war with respect to controls." Controls were "a wasting asset," Rockoff claimed, and to perpetuate them would only have resulted in a nettlesome, bureaucratic regimentation; reduced economic efficiency; and heightened social acrimony.[10] With wage and price controls dead and the most disruptive readjustments over, the wartime *command* economy gave way to the peacetime, consumer-oriented, *market* economy that did indeed achieve the noteworthy prosperity of which Truman boasted in his farewell. That transition was imperative for sustained, and sustainable, prosperity, and it was neither automatic nor predestined.

A second direct contribution to postwar prosperity came through the administration's tentative embrace of modern, or Keynesian, macroeconomics. Truman was no economic theorist, and his approach to taxing and spending policy reflected his own business and governmental experience rather than the direct influence of John Maynard Keynes's ideas. Truman believed, as a general rule, that a balanced budget was both a practical expedient and a moral imperative. "There is nothing sacred about the pay-as-you-go idea so far as I am concerned," he wrote in his memoirs, "except it represents the soundest principle of financing that I know." But he also recognized that fiscal decisions had broader implications. "Government programs," he said in his first budget message, "are of such importance in the development of production and employment opportunities . . . that it has become essential to formulate and consider the federal budget in light of the nation's budget as a whole."[11]

In that light, Truman in September 1945 called for a limited tax reduction in order to bolster consumer demand and forestall the postwar decline that some forecasters feared would come with the return of peace. When the fears of an immediate return to depression proved groundless and an inflationary boom ensued, Truman advocated running a budget surplus not only on bookkeeping grounds but also as a way to moderate the economy's inflationary surge. Twice in 1947 he vetoed Republican-sponsored tax cuts on the grounds that they were inequitable and inflationary—"the wrong tax reduction at the wrong time."[12] When the economy dipped into the first postwar recession from November 1948 to October 1949, the administration adopted a cautious, passive, countercyclical approach, accepting the resultant deficit

10. Rockoff, *Drastic Measures: A History of Wage and Price Controls in the United States* (New York: Cambridge University Press, 1984), 176, 246.
11. Truman, *Memoirs*, vol. 2, *Years of Trial and Hope* (Garden City: Doubleday, 1956), 41; *Public Papers: Truman, 1946*, 37.
12. *Public Papers: Truman, 1947*, 279.

rather than hiking taxes to eliminate it. With the advent of war in Korea in the summer of 1950, inflation returned as the foremost macroeconomic problem, and the administration raised taxes several times to reduce the inflationary pressure. Its action on the fiscal front, together with the imposition of emergency wartime wage and price controls, managed to stabilize the economy at acceptable levels in the last years of the Truman presidency. In all these varied instances, despite occasional ambiguity, political backsliding, and failures in timing, the administration's eclectic but modern fiscal approach had a generally salutary impact on the nation's economic performance.[13] As one of Truman's key economic advisers later put it, "The ultimate test of his policies was that they *worked*."[14]

The Truman administration also contributed (albeit in a less direct way) to the achievement of sustained prosperity by helping to create institutions of economic policy making, notably the Council of Economic Advisers (CEA) and the so-called Monetary Accord of 1951, that would exert a powerful influence on the direction of the U.S. economy for decades. The CEA emerged out of the concerns over full employment at the end of the war. Liberals initially proposed legislation that would have made the federal government the employer of last resort if the private sector proved unable to generate full employment. Their full employment bill of 1945 was not a presidential initiative, but Truman, in the words of one biographer, "took the bill seriously, spoke out vigorously for it, and personally lobbied key legislators." The Employment Act of 1946 as finally passed by Congress was much more conservative than the earlier version Truman had championed, but he signed the measure into law and tried to take some political credit for what he characterized as its "commitment to take any and all measures necessary for a healthy economy."[15]

The Employment Act of 1946 established a three-person Council of Economic Advisers to provide the president with first-rate, professional economic advice on a regular basis. There were some problems early on, as Truman struggled to get a personally and politically congenial council membership in place and as the CEA itself sought to establish just what its advi-

13. See Herbert Stein, *The Fiscal Revolution in America* (Chicago: University of Chicago Press, 1969), 197–240; and Robert M. Collins, "Fiscal and Monetary Policies," in *The Harry S. Truman Encyclopedia,* ed. Richard S. Kirkendall (Boston: G. K. Hall and Co., 1989), 129–31.

14. Leon H. Keyserling, "Truman: The Man and the President," in *Harry S. Truman: The Man from Independence,* ed. William F. Levantrosser (New York: Greenwood Press, 1986), 241.

15. Hamby, *Man of the People,* 366; *Public Papers: Truman, 1946,* 126.

sory role should entail. The council came fully into its own in 1949 with the appointment of Leon H. Keyserling as chairman, and thereafter it enjoyed both a greater unity and a closer working relationship with the White House. The council was an innovation whose impact was felt in both the short term and the long. Its advice contributed—undoubtedly, but to an extent impossible to measure precisely—to the economic well-being Truman trumpeted as he departed Washington. And in the years that followed, at least into the 1980s, the council exerted a significant influence on the making of national economic policy.

The Monetary Accord of 1951 constituted the administration's second great institutional innovation, but it was one that emerged despite, rather than because of, the president. Although ostensibly independent, the Federal Reserve had since 1941 been committed, as a matter of policy but not law, to supporting the price of government securities at predetermined levels in order to ease the federal government's debt burden. The arrangement guaranteed that the Treasury would be able to borrow the huge amounts needed to prosecute a world war at low interest rates, but it also left the Fed unable to use monetary policy to curb inflation. After the war the Fed increasingly chafed under that limitation.

Truman stood foursquare behind the easy-money policy. In this as in other matters, as Keyserling later observed, "the President's policies were shaped by experiences and conditions which entered into the very fiber of his being long before he got to the White House." Truman had grown up idolizing that champion of easy money, William Jennings Bryan. He remembered as a scandalous breach of faith the decline in government bond prices that followed World War I. And he remained convinced that his well-known business fling as a Kansas City haberdasher had been brought low by tight money policies. At a Federal Reserve dinner in 1950, Truman again made clear his position by telling the assembled central bankers: "Now gentlemen, you represent the greatest financial institution in the history of the world, except the Treasury of the United States."[16]

The outbreak of fighting in Korea brought the lingering dispute to a final head, underscoring anew the Treasury's need to finance large deficits at low interest and the Fed's need to avail itself of a flexible monetary policy (that is, varying interest rates for different economic situations) in order to combat

---

16. Keyserling, "The Man and the President," 239; on Truman's attitudes, see Hamby's astute comments in *Man of the People,* 581; for the dinner speech, *Public Papers: Truman, 1950,* 114.

the inflationary pressures war was certain to generate. Finally, after much wrangling, the contending parties in early March 1951 announced: "The Treasury and the Federal Reserve System have reached full accord with respect to debt-management and monetary policies to be pursued in furthering their common purpose to assure the successful financing of the Government's requirements and, at the same time, to minimize monetization of the public debt."[17] The agreement meant that monetary policy was once again available as a tool, alongside fiscal policy, for achieving economic stability. And it initiated the rise over the next half-century of the Federal Reserve as the nation's primary agent of macroeconomic oversight. In the case of the accord, Truman and his administration managed, ironically, to leave a lasting and overwhelmingly positive institutional legacy for economic policy making despite themselves and their best efforts to the contrary.

A final indirect contribution by the administration to the achievement of a genuine postwar prosperity came in the realm of ideas. At Keyserling's urging, the Council of Economic Advisers developed a new, focused, self-conscious, and single-minded emphasis on economic growth as the overriding (but still not sole) national economic goal. Keyserling correctly believed the growth orientation to be a significant departure from what he viewed as Keynes's "really . . . static economics." The council distinguished its growth policy from a compensatory approach, which focused on merely achieving stability by cushioning deflationary declines and damping inflationary booms, without particular heed to whether the level of economic activity thus stabilized was itself wholly satisfactory. Soon Truman himself was adopting Keyserling's approach, telling a Kansas City audience in the fall of 1949 that the United States could achieve a three-hundred-billion-dollar economy and double the income of a typical family. "This is not a pipe dream. It can be done. But it can't happen by itself. And it can't happen if we have a lot of 'pull-backs' at the helm of government."[18]

Keyserling's ideas had a strong influence on Truman, despite the president's occasional backsliding into concern for balancing the budget. As Hamby notes, Keyserling's emphasis on growth was "consciously and enthusiastically accepted by Truman . . . [and] provided a general indication of where the president would take the economy: toward government-stimulated and -managed economic expansion, providing maximum employment and generating bene-

17. Quoted in Stein, *Fiscal Revolution*, 277.
18. Quotes from Robert M. Collins, *More: The Politics of Economic Growth in Postwar America* (New York: Oxford University Press, 2000), 21–22.

fits for all groups in American society."[19] Indeed, the ideas developed by Keyserling and his colleagues constituted the essential core of a growthmanship that would color U.S. economic policy making down to the end of the twentieth century.

"We in America have learned how to attain real prosperity for our people," Truman told his audience at his leave-taking on January 15, 1953. But Truman and his administration did not cause the economic success he applauded. The economic well-being of the Truman years resulted not from public-sector undertakings but primarily from the dynamism of the market economy itself and from the deep-running economic and demographic forces propelling it forward. Still, Truman was more than a passive historical bystander at a particularly yeasty time. He and his administration contributed in concrete ways, both direct and indirect, to the prosperity of the day. Sometimes, as in the case of the Monetary Accord, success came in spite of the president's efforts. Almost always the path was more convoluted and uneven than Truman's brief remarks in his farewell suggested. But, granting these qualifications, he did indeed deserve to be recognized for helping to achieve the "real prosperity" of which he spoke.

Truman's second claim regarding the economy in his Farewell Address concerned the much narrower matter of bank failures. From a remove of more than half a century, Truman's focus on bank losses, in a speech that devoted only five sentences to economic affairs, seems a curious allocation of attention. Perhaps his own less than happy or successful adventures in banking with the Citizens Security Bank and the Community Savings and Loan back home in Missouri in the 1920s left him unusually sensitive to the institutional instability that had plagued American banking in the decades prior to the New Deal's regulation of the financial services sector.[20] But that possible personal dimension notwithstanding, Truman spoke for the large number of Americans who had been scarred by the fear, rumors, and reality of bank failures in the 1920s and 1930s. The popularity of Frank Capra's 1946 movie *It's a Wonderful Life*—the plot of which revolves around the fragility of George Bailey's beleaguered Bedford Falls savings and loan—testified to the continued resonance of such fears in the immediate postwar period.

On the matter of bank failures, Truman's claim was essentially correct, but it oversimplified reality somewhat. Truman overstated when he claimed that there had been no failures of insured banks during his presidency. Figures

19. Hamby, *Man of the People*, 500.
20. Ibid., 137–44.

issued by the Federal Deposit Insurance Corporation in 1957 indicate that during the period 1945–1952 twenty-four banks insured by the FDIC were closed because of financial difficulties.[21] But Truman's larger point stands: because of the protection afforded by federal deposit insurance, depositors suffered no losses in those years, even in the few cases where banks did fail. (Also at work was the fact that wartime pressures had compelled banks to load up on government securities, leaving banks in the immediate postwar period with very conservative, and generally strong and safe, portfolios.)[22] This new institutional stability provided meaningful security for a vast number of American savers.

What is open to question is how much historical credit Truman could rightfully claim for the positive outcomes of policy initiatives—stricter banking regulation and, most specifically, federal deposit insurance—that dated back to the early New Deal. One cannot help but wonder whether Truman was attaching his record to that of his predecessor in this fashion out of calculation or simply because of his own internalized sense of liberal New Deal–Fair Deal continuity. Regardless, the achievement of which Truman boasted was real; but it was hardly one for which he could in any reasonable way claim historical, as opposed to political, credit.

What, finally, of Truman's assertion that "the income of our people has been fairly distributed, perhaps more so than at any other time in recent history"? Here, again, the statistics are clear and compelling, and they illuminate the matter of fairness from a number of different angles. Economists estimate that the U.S. poverty rate dropped from 60.6 percent in 1940 to 27.1 percent in 1945, then rose back to 32 percent in 1947 and stood at 29.3 percent in 1952. Gauging fairness from another direction, scholars have observed that the distribution of U.S. household income became distinctly fairer over the decade of the 1940s and into the early 1950s. Using a standard measure of inequality—the Gini coefficient (named for the Italian statistician Corrado Gini), which establishes a scale running from perfect equality at 0 to perfect inequality at 1.0—the inequality of household income dropped from 0.531 in 1940 to 0.447 in 1945 and 0.415 in 1952.[23]

21. Bureau of the Census, *The Statistical History of the United States from Colonial Times to the Present* (Stamford, Conn.: Fairfield Publishers, 1965), 637.

22. Eugene N. White, "Banking and Finance in the Twentieth Century," in *The Cambridge Economic History of the United States, Volume III, The Twentieth Century,* ed. Stanley L. Engerman and Robert E. Gallman (New York: Cambridge University Press, 2000), 774–78.

23. Robert D. Plotnick et al., "The Twentieth-Century Record of Inequality and Poverty in the United States," in *Cambridge Economic History, Volume III,* ed. Engerman and Gallman, 292–94.

The leveling of household income occurred in part because Americans experienced what economic historians have labeled "the Great Compression," an extraordinary period of wage compression that occurred chiefly in the 1940s and produced a wage structure more equal than the nation had witnessed previously in the twentieth century or has seen since. In the most sophisticated study of the Great Compression phenomenon to date, Claudia Goldin and Robert A. Margo use census data to estimate that the wage spread between wage earners at the ninetieth percentile (near the top of the economic ladder) and those at the tenth percentile (near the bottom) decreased by 35.4 percent between 1940 and 1950. Their findings corroborate the earlier work of Simon Kuznets, who used income tax data to establish that the share of income received by the top 5 percent of taxpayers declined from roughly 30 percent in the 1920s to just below 20 percent in 1946, also a drop of approximately a third.[24] Thus, a variety of statistical measures are in agreement that the United States was indeed a more equal society at the end of Truman's tenure than it had been before, even as recently as 1940.

The matter of growing economic equality was more complicated than Truman's farewell assertion suggested, however, as a closer analysis of the Great Compression in wages discloses.[25] The narrowing of the U.S. wage structure in the 1940s resulted from multiple causes. Primary among those causes were a burgeoning wartime demand for less-skilled labor in mass-production industries that continued into the postwar years and a relative oversupply of educated workers that was exacerbated by the postwar impact of the GI Bill. The strength and numbers of organized labor, which reached new peaks in the mid-1940s, almost certainly worked to compress the nation's wage structure. Government action played a significant role as well, chiefly in the decisions of the powerful National War Labor Board during World War II, which tended clearly to favor wage hikes for those at the lower end of the wage distribution. The further raising of the national minimum wage and continued high tax rates during the Truman years likely contributed to wage compression at the margin.[26] Nevertheless, two key facts stand

24. Goldin and Margo, "The Great Compression: The Wage Structure in the United States at Mid-Century," *Quarterly Journal of Economics* 107 (February 1992): 14; Kuznets, *Shares of Upper Income Groups in Income and Savings* (New York: National Bureau of Economic Research, 1953), 635. The particular measure of income used here is the "economic income variant."

25. The interpretation that follows is based primarily on Goldin and Margo, "The Great Compression."

26. Using Kuznets's data and comparing the economic income variant with the disposable income variant in order to correct for the impact of taxation, it appears that in 1946 the income share of the top 5 percent of the total population was perhaps 2–3 percent lower on an after-tax basis. See Kuznets, *Shares of Upper-Income Groups*, 635, 637.

out: first, among the multiple causes of the greater economic equality of the Truman years were few for which the administration could itself fairly claim credit; and, second, much—indeed the bulk—of the positive change in equality had already taken place before Truman entered the White House. Again, Truman's claim was correct, but it was oversimplified in ways that exaggerated his role in making the positive outcome happen.

There was thus a pattern in the five sentences of Truman's Farewell Address devoted to economic affairs. Truman saw large matters clearly. He made only three claims, and they were big ones. And in each he was essentially correct—the developments he pointed to were real, and they were positive. But in each instance he oversimplified the story, in ways that suggested greater personal credit for his leadership than was his due. To be fair, it was simple human nature to do so; part of Truman's continuing appeal is that he seems to have been more human than most political leaders (or than most people in an increasingly bureaucratized world, for that matter), and we find in that quality the source of both his virtues and his foibles. He was undoubtedly goaded by the occasion of the Farewell Address and the opportunity it afforded finally to offer a corrective to the harsh criticism that had overtaken his leadership. Perhaps the effective leader's tendency to simplify for political advantage and the historian's need for careful qualification and analytical hairsplitting are inevitably in conflict. In any event, Harry Truman's Farewell Address is an instructive, but not conclusive, guide to a pivotal presidency. We neglect it at our peril, not so much because it settles issues as because it opens them up. That is probably all we can rightfully ask of a first draft of history, even—or especially—one written by a president.

STATEMENT BY THE PRESIDENT
ON SIGNING THE EMPLOYMENT ACT OF 1946

I have signed today the Employment Act of 1946. In enacting this legislation the Congress and the President are responding to an overwhelming demand of the people. The legislation gives expression to a deep-seated desire for a conscious and positive attack upon the ever-recurring problems of mass unemployment and ruinous depression.

Within three years after the First World War, we experienced farm foreclosures, business failures, and mass unemployment. In fact, the history of the last several decades has been one of speculative booms alternating with deep depression. The people have found themselves defenseless in the face of economic forces beyond their control.

Democratic government has the responsibility to use all its resources to create and maintain conditions under which free competitive enterprise can operate effectively -- conditions under which there is an abundance of employment opportunity for those who are able, willing, and seeking to work.

It is not the government's duty to supplant the efforts of private enterprise to find markets, or of individuals to find jobs. The people do expect the government, however, to create and maintain conditions in which the individual businessman and the individual job seeker have a chance to succeed by their own efforts. That is the objective of the Employment Act of 1946.

The major provisions of this important legislation can be briefly summarized.

1. The Act declares that it is "the continuing policy and responsibility of the Federal Government . . . to coordinate and utilize all its plans, functions, and resources for the purpose of creating and maintaining . . . conditions under which there will be afforded useful employment opportunities, including self-employment, for those able, willing, and seeking to work . . ." The Congress by this declaration has accepted a great responsibility.

2. The Congress has placed on the President the duty of formulating programs designed to accomplish the purpose of the Act. In signing this Act, I accept this responsibility, which I believe is in line with the responsibility placed on the President by the Constitution. This task is so great that I can perform it only with the full and un-qualified cooperation of all who are sincerely interested in the general welfare inside and outside the government. Making this Act work must become one of the prime objectives of all of us: citizens generally, industry, labor, and agriculture, State and local governments, and the Federal Government.

3. The Act includes a significant provision that will facilitate cooperation between the Executive and the Congress in the formulation of policies and programs to accomplish the objectives of the Act. It establishes a joint Congressional Committee consisting of seven Members of the Senate and seven Members of the House. This com-mittee is given an assignment of great scope and the highest importance.

4. The Act establishes in the Executive Office of the Presi-dent a Council of Economic Advisers, composed of three members to be appointed by the President with the consent of the Senate. The new Council will be an important addition to the facilities available for preparing economic policies and programs. In carrying on this work, I expect the fullest cooperation between the Council, the Cabinet, and the several divisions of the Executive Office.

I am happy that the Senate adopted this legislation unanimously, the House of Representatives by a large majority. The result is not all I had hoped for, but I congratulate Members of both Houses and their leaders upon their constructive and fruitful efforts.

The Employment Act of 1946 is not the end of the road, but rather the beginning. It is a commitment by the government to the people -- a commitment to take any and all of the measures necessary for a healthy economy, one that provides opportunities for those able, willing, and seeking to work. We shall all try to honor that commitment.

Clutching at Civil Rights Straws

A Reappraisal of the Truman Years and the Struggle for African American Citizenship

Carol Anderson

Cowardice asks the question, Is it safe? Expediency asks the question, Is it politic? Vanity asks the question, Is it popular? But conscience asks the question, Is it right? And there comes a time when one must take a position that is neither safe, nor politic, nor popular, but he must take it because his conscience tells him that it is right.

—Martin Luther King Jr.

In many ways President Truman's record on civil rights, in an era of entrenched Jim Crow and lynching, is impressive. Entire books have been dedicated to understanding how a man who emerged from rural roots, in a former slaveholding state, with cities blackened by redlining and educational institutions left ignorant by racial segregation, could have deigned to desegregate the military, ordered the integration of the federal bureaucracy, and commanded his Justice Department to support a series of lawsuits designed to break Jim Crow. Truman's stature is enhanced further when he is compared to his predecessor, Franklin Delano Roosevelt, whose dubious civil rights record left a trail of racial debris strewn from Claude Neal's branded, dismembered body to the internment camps of Manzanar. Truman becomes even more impressive when placed next to his Republican successor, Dwight D. Eisenhower, who "personally wished that the Court had upheld *Plessy v. Ferguson*" and reputedly said that the "biggest damn fool mistake" he had

ever made was "the appointment of that dumb son of a bitch Earl Warren" as
chief justice. Is it any wonder that Truman has emerged in a pantheon occupied by only Abraham Lincoln and maybe Lyndon Johnson?[1]

Yet, is the racially checkered history of Missouri, FDR, and Eisenhower
really the appropriate baseline to use when assessing presidential commitment to safeguarding and protecting the constitutional rights of American
citizens? What happens if the standard is set at a higher and more relevant
level, such as ensuring the protection of constitutional rights and liberties for
all American citizens, even those still bearing the scars of centuries of en-
slavement and more than fifty years of Jim Crow? That is to say, what happens if Truman's courage in the face of southern opposition is viewed, not in
terms of the Dixiecrats' power, but in terms of the federal government wielding its power—the power it was so willing to use in Greece and Turkey—to
ensure that the rights of American citizens, even those in Mississippi and
South Carolina, were also protected? This fundamental assertion about the
federal government's political, legal, and moral obligation to protect the civil
rights of African Americans is not revolutionary or new. There had already
been a long-standing belief among civil rights proponents, stretching back to
antebellum days, that "African Americans had rights as national citizens,
whether their states recognized them as state citizens or not."[2]

1. Michael R. Gardner, *Harry Truman and Civil Rights: Moral Courage and Political Risks*
(Carbondale: Southern Illinois University Press, 2002); William C. Berman, *The Politics of
Civil Rights in the Truman Administration* (Columbus: Ohio State University Press, 1970);
Donald R. McCoy and Richard Ruetten, *Quest and Response: Minority Rights and the Truman
Administration* (Lawrence: University Press of Kansas, 1973); Alonzo L. Hamby, *Man of the
People: A Life of Harry S. Truman* (New York: Oxford University Press, 1995), 364–65; David
McCullough, *Truman* (New York: Simon and Schuster, 1992), 26, 27, 28, 29, 532, 586–89,
629, 634, 638–40, 672, 677; Whittington B. Johnson, "The Vinson Court and Racial Seg-
regation, 1946–1953," *Journal of Negro History* 63:3 (July 1978): 221; Mary L. Dudziak, "De-
segregation as a Cold War Imperative," *Stanford Law Review* 41:1 (November 1988): 61–120;
Grace Elizabeth Hale, *Making Whiteness: The Culture of Segregation in the South, 1890–1940*
(New York: Pantheon, 1998), 222–27; Philip Dray, *At the Hands of Persons Unknown: The
Lynching of Black America* (New York: Random House, 2002), 344–58; Eleanor Roosevelt to
Walter White, May 2, 1934, White to Roosevelt, November 8, 1934, Roosevelt to White,
November 23, 1934, *Papers of Eleanor Roosevelt, 1933–1945* (Frederick, Md.: University
Publications of America, 1986), reel 18; David M. Kennedy, *Freedom from Fear: The American
People in Depression and War, 1929–1945* (New York: Oxford University Press, 1999), 753–59;
Earl Warren, Oral History, Lyndon Baines Johnson Library, Austin, Tex.; Stephen Ambrose,
Eisenhower: The President (New York: Simon and Schuster, 1984), 2:190; Wallace Lynn, Oral
History, Earl Warren Oral History Project, University of California–Berkeley.

2. Michael Les Benedict, *The Blessings of Liberty: A Concise History of the Constitution of the
United States* (1996), quoted in Linda K. Kerber, "The Meanings of Citizenship," *Journal of
American History* 84:3 (December 1997): 835 n. 6.

Of course, by the time Truman had assumed the presidency in April 1945, World War II had already transformed this long-standing belief into a firestorm of discontent within the African American community. Author Pearl S. Buck warned, "The deep patience of colored peoples is at an end. Everywhere among them there is the same resolve for freedom and equality that white Americans . . . have, but it is a grimmer resolve, for it includes the determination to be rid of white rule and exploitation and white race prejudice, and nothing will weaken this will." Buck had only articulated what Philleo Nash, an administrator in the Office of War Information and soon to be minority affairs expert in the Truman White House, reported. "Negroes," he warned, "are in a militant and demanding mood."[3]

Black Americans, already hardened by the false promises of World War I, were not going to be denied. Not this time. They were determined that the Second World War, unlike the First, would result in the total destruction of Jim Crow and the second- and third-class citizenship that came with it. They were determined that, after hundreds of years in the United States, they would finally gain their rightful place as American citizens. They had more than met the "obligation" requirements of citizenship by, at minimum, their service in the military and in the national defense industries. They had also clearly met the "being born on American soil" requirement. Indeed, they could trace their lineage in the United States back much further than could many of the whites who were now receiving the enormous windfall of economic and political rights that the nation had to offer its citizens after World War II. Thus, African Americans' concept of citizenship was not some theoretical, philosophical, epistemological exercise. Even "[p]eople unversed in legal complexity," historian Linda Kerber noted, "understand that they are entitled to free speech, to a right against self-incrimination, to religious freedom, to a jury trial, to the vote." Civil rights advocate Harry T. Moore, who would eventually be killed by the Klan, was even more explicit: "We seek merely the fundamental rights of American citizenship, equality of

3. Carol Anderson, *Eyes Off the Prize: The United Nations and the African American Struggle for Human Rights, 1944–1955* (New York: Cambridge University Press, 2003), 8, 9, 10, 14–16, 19, 25, 82; Mary L. Dudziak, *Cold War Civil Rights: Race and the Image of American Democracy* (Princeton: Princeton University Press, 2000), 7–11; Richard M. Dalfiume, "The 'Forgotten Years' of the Negro Revolution," *Journal of American History* 55:1 (June 1968): 90–106; Buck quoted in Paul Gordon Lauren, *The Evolution of International Human Rights: Visions Seen* (Philadelphia: University of Pennsylvania Press, 1998), 154. Philleo Nash to Jonathan Daniels, memo, December 16, 1943, Box 29, OWI-Files Alphabetical File-Race Tension-Jonathan Daniels File-Memoranda Nash to Daniels: 1942–45; "Attachment No. 1: Factors affecting Negro attitudes towards the war," fragment of report, Box 55, WH Files-Minorities-Negro Attitudes Toward War, Nash Papers, Truman Library.

opportunities, equal protection of the law, justice in the courts, and free participation in the affairs of our government." For black America, these civil rights were essential to the struggle. They were "the attributes of 'citizens', and particularly citizens of the modern state." Most important, as Kerber astutely observed, "'Citizen' is an equalizing word." And African Americans were determined to be equal.[4]

Coming out of World War II, however, black America was anything but equal. A series of lynchings, each seemingly more graphic and gruesome than the one before, bathed the United States in blood. Housing shortages, exacerbated by the mass migration of African Americans into the urban areas, piled one black body on top of the other in tightly segregated, geographically constrained, and decaying inner cities. And then there was the South, where nearly 75 percent of all black Americans still lived but only a small number could even dare to vote.[5]

Truman and his administrative team grasped, and even acknowledged, that there was a problem, a very serious problem. The president said that "we have only recently completed a long and bitter war against intolerance and hatred. . . . Yet, in this country today," he lamented, "there exists disturbing evidence of intolerance and prejudice similar in kind, though perhaps not in degree, to that against which we fought the war." Truman further confessed to former first lady Eleanor Roosevelt that the virulent racism coursing

4. Neil A. Wynn, "The Impact of the Second World War on the American Negro," *Journal of Contemporary History* 6:2 (1971): 44, 49; Thomas J. Sugrue, "Crabgrass-Roots Politics: Race, Rights, and the Reaction against Liberalism in the Urban North, 1940–1964," *Journal of American History* 82:2 (September 1995): 551–78; Kerber, "Meanings of Citizenship," 834–37; Anderson, *Eyes Off the Prize*, 195; Moore quoted in Caroline Emmons, "'Somebody Has Got to Do That Work': Harry T. Moore and the Struggle for African-American Voting Rights in Florida," *Journal of Negro History* 82:2 (Spring 1997): 238; Oliver C. Cox, "The Programs of Negro Civil Rights Organizations," *Journal of Negro Education* 20:3 (Summer 1951): 354; Hale, *Making Whiteness*, 19; Roi Ottley, *New World A-Coming* (1943; rpt. New York: Arno Press, 1968), 306–26.

5. Laura Wexler, *Fire in a Canebrake: The Last Mass Lynching in America* (New York: Scribner, 2002), 86–88, 130–31; Anderson, *Eyes Off the Prize*, 58–59, 100; "Lynching Record for 1946: Chronological Listing," n.d., Box 408, Lynching: Lynching Record, 1946–52 File, Papers of the National Association for the Advancement of Colored People, Library of Congress, Washington, D.C.; Thomas J. Sugrue, *The Origins of the Urban Crisis: Race and Inequality in Postwar Detroit* (Princeton: Princeton University Press, 1996), 17–55; Douglas S. Massey and Nancy A. Denton, *American Apartheid: Segregation and the Making of the Underclass* (Cambridge: Harvard University Press, 1993), 42–57; Earl M. Lewis, "The Negro Voter in Mississippi," *Journal of Negro Education* 26:3 (Summer 1957): 329–50; Allen Lichtman, "The Federal Assault against Voting Discrimination in the Deep South, 1957–1967," *Journal of Negro History* 24:4 (October 1969): 346–67; Emmons, "'Somebody Has Got to Do That Work,'" 232–43.

through the United States reminded him, in so many unsettling ways, of Nazi Germany.[6] He was not alone.

African Americans had earlier made that connection. They looked at Hitler's Germany and saw something distinctly, painfully familiar. In 1941, after reviewing a series of Nazi edicts on such issues as the sterilization of mulatto babies (the so-called Rhineland bastards) and the application of the discriminatory Nuremberg Laws to Germany's black population, *Pittsburgh Courier* journalist George Schuyler remarked that "what struck me . . . was that the Nazi plan for Negroes approximates so closely what seems to be the American plan for Negroes." Although the *Richmond Times-Dispatch* retorted that Schuyler's comparison was "'dangerously misleading' and 'absurd,'" there was nothing misleading or absurd about the charge. As historians Johnpeter Horst Grill and Robert L. Jenkins observed, "An article in the SS *Leithefte,* the official SS indoctrination journal, noted that southern racial laws were similar to the 'progressive' racial legislation of the Third Reich." Thus, Roy Wilkins, assistant secretary of the National Association for the Advancement of Colored People (NAACP), wrote in a nationally published editorial that "the South approaches more nearly than any other section of the United States the Nazi idea of government by a 'master race' without interference from any democratic process." Wilkins further believed that "the major difference between the racism of the two countries was that the national government of the United States did not use its machinery against blacks, it was merely indifferent toward their fate."[7]

With Truman now at the helm, however, that was supposed to change. The president stood before the NAACP at its 1947 annual convention and asserted that the United States had "reached a turning point" in guaranteeing the constitutional rights of "freedom and equality to all its citizens." The impetus for this change was clear. Nazi tyranny followed by the rapid onset of the Cold War and Soviet totalitarianism had made it "more important today than ever before to insure that all Americans enjoy these rights. And," Truman emphasized, "when I say all Americans—I mean all Americans." Truman then insisted that the "extension of civil rights today means, not [only] the protection of the people *against* the Government, but protection of the

6. Truman to Charles G. Bolte, August 28, 1946, Box 543, Official File 93 May–December 1946 [2 of 2], Truman Papers, Truman Library; Truman to Eleanor Roosevelt, December 12, 1945, Box 4560, File Harry S. Truman, 1945–1948, Papers of Eleanor Roosevelt, Franklin Delano Roosevelt Presidential Library, Hyde Park, N.Y.

7. Quoted in Grill and Jenkins, "The Nazis and the American South in the 1930s: A Mirror Image?" *Journal of Southern History* 58:4 (November 1992): 690, 675, 689.

people *by* the government. We must," he concluded, "make the Federal Government a friendly, vigilant defender of the rights and equalities of all Americans. And again I mean all Americans." He reaffirmed that commitment when he told the graduates at Howard University's commencement, "The full force and power of the federal government must stand behind the protection of rights guaranteed by our federal constitution."[8]

This would be no small feat. The federal government was, at its best, a disinterested bystander in the systematic denial of African Americans' constitutional rights. Unfortunately, in far too many instances, it was also a willing accomplice. To compound the problem, the arm of government that seemed the most likely candidate to become the "vigilant defender" that Truman envisioned, the Civil Rights Section of the Department of Justice, was structurally, philosophically, and, to some degree, legally ill-equipped to take on the job.

By 1950, the Civil Rights Section had "only six attorneys," which was the same staffing level it had "at its inception" a decade earlier. Yet these same six "received between 12,000 and 13,000 complaints" in 1950 alone and could easily expect up to 20,000 allegations of civil rights violations in any year. Moreover, the section had no independent investigative wing and, therefore, relied on the Federal Bureau of Investigation (FBI) to determine the veracity of the facts alleged in the complaints. The FBI, however, was the wrong agency, at the wrong time, at the wrong place, for the wrong job. Its director, J. Edgar Hoover, had an intense disdain for civil rights and blacks, and that antipathy shaped the culture and operating code of the bureau for decades. In addition, because the bureau "in most other aspects of its work . . . cooperated closely with local officials and was unwilling to alienate them," the FBI's investigations were often perfunctory and superficial, especially if the sheriff or police were named in the complaint. Finally, because much of the investigation "had to take place within the Negro community . . . the nearly all white FBI" had neither "a good rapport with the Southern black man" nor the necessary "training or experience in conducting" civil rights investigations to be effective. Indeed, in the late 1940s, the FBI "had only three black agents," none of whom were really G-Men, and as late as 1962 there were only ten black special agents out of 6,030. Of the three "agents" in the late 1940s, one was actually Hoover's chauffeur, another was just an office fixture, and the third was a "68 year-old veteran of the Marcus Garvey case."[9]

8. President Truman's Speech before the Annual Convention of the NAACP, press release, June 28, 1947, Box 1235, Official File 413 (1945–49), Truman Papers (emphasis in original); commencement statement quoted in Johnson, "Vinson Court," 221–22.

9. James A. Washington, "The Program of the Civil Rights Section of the Department of Justice," *Journal of Negro Education* 20:3 (Summer 1951): 343, 344; Lichtman, "Federal Assault,"

Adding to the section's structural weakness was its dependence on the apparatus of U.S. attorneys to prosecute cases. Because these lawyers, although officially tied to the Department of Justice, were political appointees chosen from the local areas, they often carried the value system of their community—even if that community was in defiance of the Constitution. Therefore, even when the section could build the type of airtight case that had become its standard for prosecution, the U.S. attorneys would, on far too many occasions, refuse to prosecute. As a result, during Truman's administration, of more than 13,000 complaints received annually, the Civil Rights Section only moved forward on an average of twenty per year.[10]

The section's efficacy was further undermined both by the limits of its statutory authority to protect civil rights and by its decidedly narrow interpretation of that authority. The first part of the problem was that only two statutes, created during Reconstruction, survived a series of Supreme Court decisions in the late nineteenth century. Those court decisions effectively gutted most of the laws Congress had passed to ensure political equality for the freedmen. One surviving statute, section 51, made "it a crime for two or more persons to conspire to 'injure, oppress, threaten, or intimidate any citizen in the free exercise or enjoyment of any right or privilege secured to him by the Constitution or laws of the United States.'" The other, section 52, made "it a crime for anyone, acting under color of law, willfully to subject any inhabitant to a deprivation of 'any rights, privileges, or immunities' secured or protected by the Constitution or laws of the United States or to different punishment, pains or penalties than are prescribed for the punishment of citizens." Section 51 was clearly aimed at a *conspiracy* to deprive citizens of their constitutional rights, and section 52 went after public officials, such as sheriffs and law enforcement officers, who violated the dictates of due process, equal protection, and other rights that all citizens enjoy. The Civil Rights Section staff, however, looked at these two statutes and saw only "'slender reeds upon which to lean' in the enforcement program." Those "slender reeds" were whittled down further when, in June 1948, sections 51 and 52 were replaced by sections 241 and 242. The point of tweaking the civil rights statutes, unfortunately, was not to strengthen these laws but to make them more palatable and acceptable to the South. Thus, one of the "improvements" actually eliminated the clause that forbade anyone convicted of conspiracy from

---

348–49; Kenneth O'Reilly, *Racial Matters: The FBI's Secret File on Black America, 1960–1972* (New York: Free Press, 1989), 29.

10. *To Secure These Rights: The Report of the President's Committee on Civil Rights*, intro. Charles E. Wilson (New York: Simon and Schuster, 1947), 120–22; Washington, "Civil Rights Section," 344–45.

holding public office. Attorney General Tom Clark, therefore, further reinforced the staff's sense of ineffectiveness when he insisted that the federal
government's ability to protect the rights of African Americans "hung on 'a
very thin thread of law.'" One attorney in the section went on to explain why
the results were so limited during the Truman years. We only had these "two
small statutes to work with," she said, and because it was not clear which
rights were protected under the Constitution anyway, the staff determined
that the best way to proceed was with "caution and restraint." To do otherwise could have triggered a Supreme Court decision that would have emas-
culated the civil rights statutes entirely. "[W]e knew we would destroy the
whole thing if we didn't practice caution," she explained. Unpersuaded and,
frankly, outraged, Walter White, secretary of the NAACP, did not see caution and restraint in the Civil Rights Section's actions; he saw downright
timidity. He railed that instead of using the authority it did possess, the "federal machinery for justice" demonstrated an uncanny ability to just "collapse"
in the face of southern opposition.[11]

Nowhere was this opposition more consistent, more insistent, and more in
direct violation of not only the Constitution but also the civil rights statutes
and the Supreme Court's *Yarbrough* and *Smith v. Allright* decisions than in
the denial to African Americans of the right to vote. Beginning in the 1890s,
the South had erected a series of barriers that essentially blocked all but a relative handful of African Americans from voting. The extrication of black
Americans from the voting process was designed to abrogate their citizenship and reassert legalized white supremacy.[12] It was more than effective.

A lethal combination of poll taxes, election-day terrorism, white primaries, literacy tests, and "understanding" clauses had done their damage. The
understanding clause, for example, permitted an often uneducated election

11. Washington, "Civil Rights Section," 335–38; Clark quoted in Dray, *Hands of Persons
Unknown,* 452; Eleanor Bontecou, Oral History, Truman Library; Washington, "Civil Rights
Section," 342–43; Walter White to Mrs. (Marian Wynn) Perry, memo, October 4, 1946, Box
B112, File Perry, Marion, Wynn, 1945–49, Legal, NAACP Papers; Walter White to Truman,
telegram, June 15, 1946, Box 543, Official File 93 May–December 1946 [1 of 2], Truman
Papers. I thank professor of law and former attorney in the Civil Rights Division of the Department of Justice Michael Middleton for his help with and insight on the statutes.
12. Washington, "Civil Rights Section," 337; Kari Frederickson, *The Dixiecrat Revolt and
the End of the Solid South: 1923–1968* (Chapel Hill: University of North Carolina Press, 2001),
54; Lewis, "Negro Voter in Mississippi," 330–33; Emmons, "'Somebody Has Got to Do That
Work,'" 235; Lichtman, "Federal Assault," 346; J. Mills Thornton, III, *Dividing Lines: Municipal Politics and the Struggle for Civil Rights in Montgomery, Birmingham, and Selma* (Tusca-
loosa: University of Alabama Press, 2002), 1–2; C. Vann Woodward, *The Strange Career of Jim
Crow,* 3d ed. (New York: Oxford University Press, 1974), 74–93.

official to reject potential African American voters because they could not interpret the state constitution to the registrar's satisfaction or answer a question such as "How many bubbles are there in a bar of soap?" Then there was
the poll tax. States such as Mississippi and South Carolina had applied this
financial screw so effectively that voter turnout rates there were nearly 50
percent *below* the national average in both the 1944 and 1948 presidential
elections.[13]

The use of sheer terror was, of course, not out of the question either. The
"South's white supremacists," historian Glenn Feldman noted, "were not
about to surrender the region without a fierce struggle." Alabama, for example, had already passed the Boswell Amendment, a master compendium of
understanding clauses and disfranchisement tools, but for white Alabamians
it was still not enough. "Postwar Alabama was . . . tense," Feldman wrote.
"Klan violence was part and parcel of a situation in which black assertiveness
[and] voting registration efforts . . . clashed with determined white reaction."
One elderly southern man thus "greeted news of the [resurgence of the] Klan
by saying 'This will teach the niggers to stay put in their place. If they don't
we'll stack 'em up like cordwood.' "[14] That was no idle threat.

Georgia's gubernatorial candidate, Eugene Talmadge, for example, "campaigned largely on the issue of 'keep the niggers where they belong.' " He insisted that "if the good white people will explain it to the negroes around the
state just right I don't think they will want to vote." Talmadge's clarion call, as
intended, was deadly and resulted in at least five black corpses within a
month.[15]

The most vociferous advocate of violence was, without a doubt, however,
Mississippi senator Theodore Bilbo. He railed about "niggers . . . having
meetings all over the State." And he was apoplectic when he learned that
Jackson police had broken into one of those gatherings and found "Northern
niggers teaching them [black Mississippians] how to register and how to
vote." Outraged, the U.S. senator stood before his "Anglo-Saxon" throng and
invoked the god of white supremacy in a call to arms: "I call on every red-
blooded white man to use *any* means to keep the niggers away from the polls.

---

13. Lewis, "Negro Voter in Mississippi," 338; *To Secure These Rights*, 38; Anderson, *Eyes Off
the Prize*, 80.

14. Glenn Feldman, "Soft Opposition: Elite Acquiescence and Klan-Sponsored Terrorism
in Alabama, 1946–1950," *Historical Journal* 47:3 (September 1997): 756, 757.

15. Talmadge quoted in Anderson, *Eyes Off the Prize*, 63; "Resolution on Terrorism in the
South: Adopted by Pacific States Council of Furniture Workers," August 10–11, 1946, Box
548, Official File 93a, Truman Papers.

If you don't understand what that means you're just plain dumb. . . . I'm calling on every red-blooded American who believes in the superiority and integrity of the white race to get out and see that no nigger votes. . . . *And the
best time to do it is the night before.*"[16] Bilbo then menacingly directed, "If any
nigger tries to vote, use the tar and feathers and don't forget the matches."
Not surprisingly, the "reign of terror" soon began, punctuated with beatings,
floggings, economic extortion, and intimidation.[17]

As a result of this cocktail of barely legal and extralegal disfranchisement,
in 1944 there were no blacks registered as Democrats in the entire state of
Florida. In Bilbo's Mississippi of 1946, where nearly half the population was
black, the percentage of voting-age African Americans who actually went to
the polls was barely .001. Mississippi was so bad and the problem had been
allowed to fester for so long that the state "permitted fewer blacks to vote for
Lyndon Baines Johnson in 1964 than had been eligible to vote for William
McKinley in 1896." Given the unrelenting violence and "perils of democracy" faced by blacks determined to vote, one civil rights worker could only
describe America's Mississippi as "the land of the tree and home of the
grave."[18]

When confronted with this vicious denial of constitutional rights and a
stakehold in American citizenship, "the Negro could look only to Washington, where," unfortunately, "he found little help before 1965." In the late
1940s and early 1950s, the Civil Rights Section continually ran for cover behind the rationale that the Department of Justice had little or no statutory
authority to intervene. Department officials insisted, "Under present laws, . . .
the Justice Department cannot prosecute until a voter has been denied the

16. Bilbo quoted in F. Ross Peterson, "Glen H. Taylor and the Bilbo Case," *Phylon (1960–)*
31:4 (Fourth Quarter 1970): 346, and Lewis, "Negro Voter in Mississippi," 332 (emphasis in
original).

17. Jason Parkhurst Guzman, ed., *Negro Yearbook: A Review of Events Affecting Negro Life,
1941–1946* (Tuskegee, Ala.: Department of Records and Research, Tuskegee Institute, 1947),
2. Bilbo quoted in Jerry A. Hendrix, "Theodore G. Bilbo: Evangelist of Racial Purity," in *The
Oratory of Southern Demagogues*, ed. Cal M. Logue and Howard Dorgan (Baton Rouge:
Louisiana State University Press, 1981), 167; Martha Coble, "Bilbo Demands: 'Keep Negro
from Polls,'" *Akron Beacon Journal*, n.d. [ca. June 26, 1946], found in Box 543, Official File 93
May–December 1946 [1 of 2], Truman Papers; and "Death of a Demagogue," *American
Heritage*, July/August 1997, 99–100. Sidney Hillman to Truman, telegram, June 24, 1946, Box
543, Official File 93 May–December 1946 [1 of 2], Truman Papers; Frederickson, *Dixiecrat
Revolt*, 48.

18. Emmons, "'Somebody Has Got to Do That Work,'" 235; Lewis, "Negro Voter in Mississippi," 333; Neil R. McMillen, "Black Enfranchisement in Mississippi: Federal Enforcement and Black Protest in the 1960s," *Journal of Southern History* 43:3 (August 1977): 352,
354.

right to vote on Election Day. It cannot take civil action in advance against individual acts or conspiracies to deprive citizens of their voting rights." Thus, Bilbo's plan to keep blacks away from the polls the night *before* found more than sufficient legal cover in the Justice Department's interpretation of the law. This formula for inaction was tailor-made for ignoring reprisals— *after* the election—as well. Therefore, when a black man who had just voted had to flee the state of Florida and go into hiding after whites firebombed his home, the Justice Department held firm that "an investigation of this complaint has failed to disclose . . . any connection between this explosion and the attempted intimidation of the Negroes who voted" and, as a consequence, "no further action would be taken."[19]

As one scholar noted, African Americans' "only hope" to assert their franchise rights "lay in federal intervention, and for over eighty years the federal government had failed to act." This was despite the fact that President Truman had identified the protection of the vote against "organized terrorism" and "mob violence" as absolutely essential for a working democracy. This was also despite the fact that the President's Committee on Civil Rights (PCCR) asserted in its landmark report, *To Secure These Rights,* that "interference with the right of a qualified citizen to vote locally cannot today remain a local problem. . . . Can it be doubted that this is a right which the national government must make secure?" Yet, despite all this concern, which was buttressed by a recommendation from the PCCR that the Civil Rights Section be strengthened to meet its responsibilities, nothing of significance was done. As historian Richard Kluger noted, "Aside from pursuing an occasional voting-irregularity case or investigating a report of brutality at a federal prison, the civil-rights unit at the Justice Department was still pretty much the Tinker Toy it had been when Frank Murphy set it up in 1940." Thus, more than a decade after the section's founding, and several years after the PCCR's recommendations, law professor James Washington noticed that, despite the continuing disfranchisement of black Americans, "strangely missing from the reports on the activities of the Section are cases involving the use of the civil rights statutes to protect the Negro from interferences with his right to vote."[20]

19. McMillen, "Black Enfranchisement," 354; Justice officials quoted in Lewis, "Negro Voter in Mississippi," 349, and Emmons, "'Somebody Has Got to Do That Work,'" 240.

20. Lichtman, "Federal Assault," 346; Harry Truman to Walter White, June 6, 1946, Box 10, File N (Folder 1), Nash Files, Truman Papers; *To Secure These Rights,* 101; Kluger, *Simple Justice: The History of* Brown v. Board of Education *and Black America's Struggle for Equality* (New York: Vintage Books, 1977), 252; Washington, "Civil Rights Section," 342.

The Civil Rights Section's studied inaction certainly undercut Truman's call to make the federal government a "vigilant defender" of the Constitution. Yet, when it came to the critical issue of housing and home ownership, the federal government threw off its sackcloth of timidity and impotence and became a strong, vigilant defender—of racial segregation, discrimination, and the creation of black, impoverished, resource-deprived slums.

During the Great Depression, when the private mortgage industry was on the verge of collapse because of the banking crisis, the federal government, under the New Deal, stepped in and created an agency to throw Washington's power and financial resources behind a plan to increase home ownership for Americans. In 1937, this agency was supplanted by the Federal Housing Administration (FHA), whose "mortgage insurance eliminated the lending institution's risk in providing mortgage financing for properties meeting FHA standards." This allowed for lower downpayments, longer loan periods, and, thus, much more affordable monthly payments. "Within a year of its creation, FHA was insuring 40 percent of new home mortgages. Home building had doubled and mortgage costs were at an all-time low."[21]

There was a horrible downside to this success story, however. The FHA was "staffed by 'the very financial and real estate interests and institutions which led the campaign to spread racial covenants and residential segregation'" and their professional code of conduct was explicit in demanding the perpetuation of racially segregated neighborhoods: "A Realtor should never be instrumental in introducing into a neighborhood a character of property or occupancy, members of any race or nationality, or any individuals whose presence will clearly be detrimental to property values in that neighborhood." Thus, racial segregation and the undesirability of black people was the guiding principle of the FHA through, at least, the 1960s. In its 1939 *Underwriting Manual,* for example, the agency asserted that "if a neighborhood is to retain stability, it is necessary that properties shall continue to be occupied by the same social and racial classes." It was essential, the FHA continued, to not insert "inharmonious racial or nationality groups" into a community. Not surprisingly, then, "'Incompatible racial elements' was officially listed as a valid reason for rejecting a mortgage."[22]

21. Gary Orfield, "Federal Policy, Local Power, and Metropolitan Segregation," *Political Science Quarterly* 89:4 (Winter 1974–1975): 785.
22. William H. Brown Jr., "Access to Housing: The Role of the Real Estate Industry," *Economic Geography* 48:41 (January 1972): 68; Massey and Denton, *American Apartheid,* 54; Orfield, "Federal Policy," 786.

This racialized vision of home ownership dictated the FHA's adoption of a four-tiered, color-coded rating system for neighborhoods, which made it clear where and under what circumstances lending institutions could expect to have their loans underwritten by the federal government. For example, those neighborhoods that had a majority of African American residents were automatically coded "red" and strictly off-limits to FHA loans. Neighborhoods that abutted predominantly African American areas and appeared "in danger" of becoming black "virtually never received" federally underwritten loans. On the other hand, areas that were "new, homogenous"—that is, white—"and in demand in good times and bad" or areas that were stable and not threatened by black "invaders" consistently received federal support.[23]

Therefore, to maintain neighborhood stability and property values, the FHA, as part of its underwriting standard, demanded restrictive covenants. These covenants, which were enforced by the courts, required that white home owners could sell their homes only to other whites. That racial vise grip on the housing market was supposed to evaporate, however, under the heat of a searing Supreme Court decision in *Shelley v. Kraemer* (1948), in which the justices declared it unconstitutional to have the court system or other government authority enforce these racially restrictive covenants. Early on, the Truman administration weighed in on this decision as well, filing an amicus curiae brief in support of ending this discriminatory practice.[24]

Despite *Shelley*, restrictive covenants did not disappear. The FHA, the most important federal entity in shaping the residential housing market in the United States, deliberately ignored the ruling and "did not change" its open support of covenants until 1950. Even after that, the FHA still successfully adapted "an ongoing policy of racial separation" that allowed the agency to comply with the exact letter of the *Shelley* decision while defying the intent and spirit of the ruling. While "the FHA announced . . . that it would insure no more homes with new covenants, realtors soon learned that the agency had no objection to 'gentlemen's agreements.'" Therefore, those covenants, which were specifically designed to circumvent the *Shelley* ruling by making their enforcement the responsibility of neighbors or community boards instead of the government, were perfectly acceptable to and even encouraged by the FHA. Given the FHA's insistence on federally "subsidized

23. Massey and Denton, *American Apartheid*, 51; Philip H. Vaughan, "The City and the American Creed: A Liberal Awakening during the Early Truman Period, 1946–1948," *Phylon (1960–)* 34:1 (First Quarter 1973): 57.

24. Kluger, *Simple Justice*, 252–53; Dudziak, "Desegregation," 101, 105–6, 118.

discrimination," scholar Philip Vaughan could only remark that "the removal of restrictive covenants . . . certainly offered no cure-all."[25]

The FHA's actions redounded throughout America. Well into the 1960s, for example, "FHA procedures rendered whole cities ineligible for FHA-guaranteed loans simply because of a minority presence." In Missouri, between 1934 and 1960, St. Louis County, the suburban area legally separate from and hemming in the city of St. Louis, "received five times as many FHA mortgages as did the latter, and nearly six times as much loan money; [and] per capita mortgage spending was 6.3 times greater." Because of the financial and legal power of the federal government in the residential mortgage industry, "such blanket redlining sent strong signals to private lending institutions, which followed suit and avoided making loans within the affected areas." Without the capital to upgrade or maintain properties, without the ability to find buyers who could afford to purchase a home without tapping into the largest, low-interest-rate mortgage pool in the nation, housing values plummeted "and a pattern of disrepair, deterioration, vacancy, and abandonment" came to define America's cities. The deteriorating housing stock and quality of life were, however, attributed directly to the black inhabitants of the area and served only to reify the FHA's rationale for redlining and white suburban home owners' convictions that the mere presence of African Americans drove down property values.[26]

Not only did private lenders follow the FHA's lead in mortgage lending, but so, too, did the Veterans Administration (VA). As a consequence, although Truman insisted, "We must house the veteran—and I mean every veteran," in 1950 nonwhites received only 2 percent of the VA's guaranteed mortgages. Thus, while the federal government, through the VA and FHA, "financed more than $120 billion worth of new housing between 1934 and 1962," less than 1 percent of all those loans went to African Americans.[27]

Scholars and various commissions have clearly identified the federal government's role in the immediate postwar period as being instrumental in creating "the near-apartheid condition now existing in many metropolitan areas."

25. Brown, "Access to Housing," 66; Orfield, "Federal Policy," 788; Vaughan, "City and American Creed," 54, 57.
26. Massey and Denton, *American Apartheid,* 54–55; Sugrue, "Crabgrass-Roots Politics," 561.
27. Truman to Walter White, June 6, 1946, Box 10, File N (Folder 1), Nash Files, Truman Papers; Orfield, "Federal Policy," 785, 788–89; George Lipsitz, *The Possessive Investment in Whiteness: How White People Profit from Identity Politics* (Philadelphia: Temple University Press, 1998), 6; Dalton Conley, *Being Black, Living in the Red: Race, Wealth, and Social Policy in America* (Berkeley: University of California Press, 1999), 37.

The power of government "was invoked on behalf of segregation throughout the basic period of the development of the ghetto system and the construction of the early post–World War II suburbs." Historian Thomas Sugrue cogently argues that this use of the government to uphold segregation in housing and the creation and sustenance of whites-only suburbs was cloaked in the language of patriotism and citizenship. "Homeowners welcomed government assistance; in fact by World War II they began to view homeownership as a prerequisite of citizenship." Similarly, the FHA's "insistence that mortgages and loans be restricted to racially homogenous neighborhoods also resonated strongly with Detroit's white home owners. They came to expect a vigilant government to protect their segregated neighborhoods."[28]

African Americans, on the other hand, expected that the "vigilant defender" in Truman's clarion call for justice would break them out of the rat-infested ghettoes that the FHA and VA had helped erect. Truman, in fact, was committed to addressing the serious housing shortage that plagued the United States after the war. That commitment resonated throughout his presidency, from his first State of the Union Address. He even issued executive orders "to the FHA to deny financial assistance to new housing projects with racial or religious restrictions."[29] Yet, just as the Civil Rights Section and the FBI were ill equipped to deal with the president's pledge to ensure the right to vote in the United States, so, too, was the FHA unwilling to abide by Truman's directives for open housing.

Thus, a public housing and urban renewal bill that was supposed to alleviate the housing crisis, particularly in the inner city, looked more like a "Negro removal" bill with "devastating" consequences. "To get the projects moving, local officials often certified that replacement housing was available for poor blacks when there was none. Federal officials who knew they were lying accepted their assurances and provided funds." Faced with a growing throng of homeless, impoverished African Americans who had been uprooted and displaced by federal policy, the NAACP pushed Truman for a stronger and more effective executive order because the "problem was especially acute in several southern and border-state communities where Negroes, displaced by slum clearance programs, could not find replacement dwellings." The White House's response was to ask for patience. The NAACP had none and went to its supporters in Congress for relief. The Truman administration immediately

28. Sugrue, "Crabgrass-Roots Politics," 779, 784; Massey and Denton, *American Apartheid*, 55; Vaughan, "City and American Creed," 52, 54; Sugrue, *Origins of the Urban Crisis*, 62–63.
29. McCullough, *Truman*, 468, 470, 532, 586, 591, 628, 634, 642, 651, 666, 758, 915.

moved to block the NAACP's attempt to get fair housing legislation. "Charles Murphy, the President's special counsel and a key actor in congressional relations, . . . discouraged such remedies and assured the members of Congress that new rules from federal housing agencies were forthcoming." The FHA, of course, had no intention of issuing any regulation that would provide for integrated housing and was characteristically "unresponsive." The NAACP, therefore, kept pushing. To forestall an NAACP-sponsored congressional inquiry, Philleo Nash directed one of the association's chief congressional supporters to speak with "more responsive housing officials" in a smaller agency—not the FHA—who could assure the congressman that a new housing bill was not necessary.[30]

This scrambling to cover what needed to be exposed makes it clear that the Truman administration knew that the FHA was a problem—one that the administration had never truly dealt with. Nash wrote the president that "in 55 years [*sic*] of FHA operations, only 1.8 percent of FHA projects were available to Negroes, as compared to 35 percent of public housing projects." The results of FHA policy, Nash continued, were disastrous:

> Washington is typical. Its suburbs are ringed with "White Only" developments. Many of these are FHA financed. In the heart of D.C. is a handful of projects open to Negroes. Nearly all of them are FHA financed. This is commendable but it does not answer the problem.
>
> If this process is permitted to continue, our northern cities will grow into Negro "downtowns" surrounded by white suburbs.
>
> This is what lies at the heart of the D.C. school crisis. Only 35% of the District population is Negro, but over half its school population is Negro. This is a post-war change.[31]

One Truman biographer acknowledged that the president did not accomplish all he wanted to in the area of housing; but Truman had "set goals for the future." What that future portended, however, given the federally sponsored disinvestment in black communities and black Americans, was a ghettoized society struggling against bleak, violent despair.[32]

30. Orfield, "Federal Policy," 788; Joseph A. Pika, "Interest Groups under Roosevelt and Truman," *Political Science Quarterly* 102:4 (Winter 1987–1988): 665–66.

31. Pika, "Interest Groups," 665–66.

32. McCullough, *Truman*, 915; U.S. Riot Commission, *Report of the National Advisory Commission on Civil Disorders* (New York: Bantam Books, 1968); William Julius Wilson, *When Work Disappears: The World of the New Urban Poor* (New York: Alfred Knopf, 1997); Sugrue, *Origins of the Urban Crisis*; Andrew Hacker, *Two Nations: Black and White, Separate, Hostile, Unequal*, 2d ed. (New York: Ballantine Books, 1995).

No feature on the American scene, however, emphasized the bleakness, precariousness, and devaluation of black life more than the wave of lynching (legal and otherwise) that occurred after World War II. It was as if the usual suspects—Mississippi, Alabama, Georgia, South Carolina, Florida, Tennessee—rounded up their "usual suspects" and proceeded to try to push defiant, "uppity" African Americans back into their so-called proper, subordinate place in American society. One Alabaman noted, "If there is room for a National Association for the Advancement of Colored People . . . there is need for a League to Maintain White Supremacy." Similarly, a Georgian explained in clear, matter-of-fact terms that lynching has "got to be done to keep Mister Nigger in his place." Another man, who hated the radicalizing effect that World War II had had on African Americans, explained in no-frills language why he had to lynch a black veteran in Georgia. It was simple. Too many years in the army had ruined that "good nigger," who now thought that he was "as good as any white people."[33]

Thus, when Leon McTatie was accused of stealing a saddle, six white Mississippians, reliving the glory days of the Old South, grabbed the wrongly accused man and "whipped [him] to death."[34] The brutality, of course, did not end there:

> In Alabama, when an African-American veteran removed the Jim Crow sign on a trolley, an angry street car conductor took aim and unloaded his pistol into the ex-Marine. As the wounded veteran staggered off the tram and crawled away, the chief of police hunted him down and finished the job with a single bullet, execution style, to the head. In South Carolina, another veteran, who complained about the inanity of Jim Crow transportation, had his eyes gouged out with the butt of the sheriff's billy club. In Louisiana, a black veteran who defiantly refused to give a white man a war memento, was partially dismembered, castrated, and blow-torched until his "eyes 'popped' out of his head and his light complexion was seared dark." In Columbia, Tennessee, when African Americans refused to "take lying down" the planned lynching of a black veteran who had defended his mother from a beating, the sheriff's storm troopers, in an "attack . . . on a scale reminiscent of military operations in the last war," " 'drew up their machine guns and tommy guns, . . . fired a barrage of shots directly into the black area of town, and then moved in.' "[35]

33. Feldman, "Soft Opposition," 757; Frederickson, *Dixiecrat Revolt*, 54; Hyde Post, Andy Miller, and Peter Scott, "Murder at Moore's Ford," *Atlanta Journal-Constitution*, May 31, 1992, A/01.

34. "Lynching Record for 1946: Chronological Listing," n.d., Box 408, File Lynching: Lynching Record, 1946–1952, NAACP Papers.

35. Anderson, *Eyes Off the Prize*, 58.

As the body count soared, the NAACP demanded that the White House do something. If nothing else, these were veterans—men who had fought the Germans and the Japanese in the name and cause of democracy. Certainly, that democracy could now turn around and fight for them. One black man just flat out informed Truman that there was a problem and, more to the point, that the president was part of it. "I am a veteran and I feel very much discouraged about the way we are being treated after coming home at the end of the war. I feel like you can do something to give us more and better protection against our common enemy." But, once again, the Department of Justice was stymied. In the Columbia, Tennessee, case, Attorney General Tom Clark declared that the "federal grand jury had 'exhausted every possibility of disclosing a federal offense' and that despite a full FBI investigation, 'No one is able to furnish the names of the perpetrators of the acts of vandalism. The grand jury had scores of witnesses before it to no avail.'" And while Isaac Woodward's blinding was a "terrible disgrace" that led one veteran of the Spanish American War to write to Truman, "I could hardly keep from shedding tears as I read this report," no federal department, not Justice, not War, not the Veterans Administration, could see that it had any jurisdiction in this case.[36]

Then came the unbelievable horror of Monroe, Georgia: four young African Americans—two couples—ambushed, defenseless, and facing a lynch mob armed with enough firepower for a small militia. The two black women became nothing more than collateral damage in a fatal lesson aimed at their husbands, whose behavior—one stabbed a white man for "messing" with his wife, while the other came back from the army thinking he was equal to any white man—spelled an unspeakable death. Historian Laura Wexler described the results after the mortician had done his best:

> At the far end of the row lay Roger Malcolm, his face pocked with the plaster of paris Dan Young [the mortician] had used to conceal the damage to his face. But nothing could hide the hole in Roger Malcolm's cheek. It was larger than a quarter, the result of a shotgun fired at close range.
> Dorothy's body lay next to Roger's, a bandage covering her face where the right side of her jaw had been blown away. It was evidently her tooth

36. Walter White et al. to Truman, telegram, August 6, 1946, and Sammye T. Lewis to the President, telegram, July 27, 1946, Box 548, Official File 93a Lynching of (4) Negroes at Monroe, GA, July 25, 1946, Truman Papers; Clark quoted in Dray, *Hands of Persons Unknown*, 369–70, 372–73; R. R. Wright Sr. to Harry S. Truman, July 18, 1946, Box 543, Official File 93 May–December 1946 [1 of 2], Truman Papers.

that the white student had found on the ground near Moore's Ford the morning before and given to his friend for her charm bracelet.

Next to Dorothy lay her brother George. His right eye was covered with a bandage—it had been shot out—and his right ear, which had been partially shot off, was attached by tape.

And last in the row was Mae Murray Dorsey, whose . . . face, unlike the others, wasn't a record of her death.

Roger Malcolm was also castrated, "the privates halfway cut off, something kind of hanging." Mae Dorsey, who had miraculously kept her face, had her spine severed and her hands crushed as sixty bullets ripped through her body.[37]

Black America was shaken and outraged. "This time it has gone too far," one enraged black man declared. African Americans understood the dogma of states' rights clearly enough; what was so difficult to understand, however, was the paralyzing limits that the federal government placed on itself even in its own domain. "Is not the South a part of the United States," a Baptist minister angrily asked. Because surely there were some laws that even the South had to abide by when it came to the rights of American citizens. As far as the minister was concerned, the president acted as if he was "afraid to tell" the South "that it is wrong to lynch human beings" and "helpless women." The Reverend Lyslee continued to seethe. "If we have a democracy what price do the Negroes have to pay for it." The real question, one organization contended, was simply at what point did states' rights trump the constitutional rights of American citizens? One woman also threw "Dachau and Buchenwald" in Truman's face, compared them to Monroe, Georgia, and then dared the Justice Department to haul the killers into federal court or "forever be condemned as a silent partner" and "accomplice" in mass murder.[38]

The department, however, was not up to the challenge. Two "assistant U.S. attorneys . . . visited Monroe on the day after the Moore's Ford lynching" to determine if sections 51 and/or 52 had been violated. When the sheriffs told them that they had no idea there was going to be a lynching, "the federal lawyers told a reporter 'they didn't think there had been a violation of any federal law. They didn't think the civil rights statutes would apply.'" As

37. Wexler, *Fire in a Canebrake,* 87–88; Anderson, *Eyes Off the Prize,* 59.

38. Sammye T. Lewis to Truman, telegram, July 27, 1946; Rev. Wm. Lyslee to Harry S. Truman, telegram, July 26, 1946; Max Yergan (President, National Negro Congress) to the President, telegram, July 26, 1946; Barbara Boucree to the President, telegram, July 27, 1946, Box 548, Official File 93a Lynching of (4) Negroes at Monroe, GA, July 25, 1946, Truman Papers.

Wexler wryly noted, the "reporter, in turn, penned a rhetorical question that underscored the federal government's powerlessness in lynching cases. He asked, 'I wonder if it would comfort what is left of those four young Negroes, lying naked on slabs in the basement of Dan Young's funeral parlor, to know that their civil rights had not been violated . . . ?' " Walter White warned Truman that "very dark days are ahead" because of the department's lackluster, abysmal performance. Getting away with murder, White explained, only emboldened those who preferred "the law of the jungle" to the rule of democracy.[39]

Truman was also outraged. This was not the democracy he knew and loved. He wanted the Justice Department to go back and investigate again. He ordered Attorney General Clark to " 'push with everything you have' to determine if there has been a 'violation of any Federal statutes.' It just seemed to Truman that 'when the mob gangs can take four people out and shoot them in the back, and everybody in the country is acquainted with who did the shooting and nothing is done about it, that country is in a pretty bad fix from a law enforcement standpoint.' " Clark, however, returned empty-handed. They "just won't talk . . . we just couldn't get any citizens there to give us information, although we know they have it."[40]

It was at this point, disgusted by the killings in Georgia and "literally blue with anger when he heard that this returning veteran [Isaac Woodward] had been blinded on the way home from a camp from which he was discharged," that Truman ordered the creation of the President's Committee on Civil Rights. His administration assembled a high-powered team and an excellent support staff, who compiled an invaluable, detailed report. But that was pretty much the end of it. The PCCR did not have any authority, and its recommendations, for far too long, ended up in a Pandora's box surrounded by plagues, pestilence, and only a scintilla of hope. Indeed, one former White House aide, Jonathan Daniels, remarked with brutal honesty that "this report of the President's Committee has no force and effect beyond its publicity value." But it was that "publicity value" that the United States needed and used repeatedly to counter Soviet criticism of the Jim Crow leader of the Free

39. Wexler, *Fire in a Canebrake,* 111; Walter White to Truman, telegram, July 26, 1946, Box 548, Official File 93a Lynching of (4) Negroes at Monroe, GA, July 25, 1946, Truman Papers; Walter White to Eleanor Roosevelt, telegram, September 18, 1946, Box 3338, File NAACP, 1945–47, Roosevelt Papers.
40. Anderson, *Eyes Off the Prize,* 61; "Tom Clark's Testimony to the President's Committee on Civil Rights," Record Group 220, Box 14, Papers of the President's Committee on Civil Rights, Truman Library.

World and, equally important, to take Truman "off the hot seat" when yet another brutal lynching exposed the reality of southern gallantry.[41]

Of course, few paid much attention when a black veteran in Mississippi "was tied to a tree by a mob . . . and castrated with a razor blade," but few could ignore the horrific lynching of Willie Earle in South Carolina. Earle, epileptic and accused of stabbing a cab driver, was pulled out of a jail by more than twenty men, tortured, mutilated, and killed. "When the undertakers had finished," one journalist wrote, "I too found it hard to believe that a South Carolina mob, and not a gang of Nazis, had done this atrocious thing. Where there must have once been a right eye, there was only a socket. . . . Where once there was skin and bones on the left side of the face, there was only the undertaker's plaster trying to form a face."[42]

Once again the hue and cry for justice resounded all the way up Pennsylvania Avenue. Perhaps learning something from its initial sluggish response in Monroe, Georgia, when it took the president nearly a week to even mention the killings, the PCCR "immediately moved in on" the Willie Earle slaying, issued a press release, made it clear to the public that it was "'deeply concerned' over the lynching," and provided a progress report detailing the role of federal agents in investigating the case. Within a week of the killing, the PCCR chair reported, "State and local officers ha[d] arrested some twenty persons and ha[d] obtained confessions from twelve of these people." Because it was clear that "state authorities [were] making vigorous efforts to arrest and prosecute the guilty parties," the chairman of the PCCR offered that the Department of Justice would "make no effort to seek a federal indictment." Thus, although it seemed as if section 52 could come into play because Earle was pulled out of a jail, it was, in the PCCR's assessment,

41. *Conference of Scholars on the Truman Administration and Civil Rights: April 5–6, 1968, at the Harry S. Truman Library*, ed. Donald R. McCoy, Richard T. Ruetten, and J. R. Fuchs (Independence: Harry S. Truman Library Institute for National and International Affairs, 1968), 20; *To Secure These Rights*, vii–xi; Jonathan Daniels to Charles S. Johnson, August 29, 1947, Folder 585, Papers of Jonathan Daniels, Southern Historical Collection, Wilson Library, University of North Carolina at Chapel Hill; Anderson, *Eyes Off the Prize*, 107, 109–10, 147; Dudziak, *Cold War Civil Rights*, 12, 15, 18, 27, 34, 37, 38–39; David K. Niles to Matt Connelly, memo, February 19, 1947, Box 26, Civil Rights/Negro Affairs 1945–June 1947, Niles Papers, Truman Library; David K. Niles to Mr. Connelly, February 19, 1947, Box 543, Official File 93 1947 [3 of 3], Truman Papers.

42. "Negro Veteran Mutilated by Mississippi Mob," March 6, 1947, Box 55, WH Files-Minorities-Negro-General-Lynching-Newsclipping—1946–1947; B. M. Phillips, "Mob Victim's Mother Sobs Out Tale of Woe," [Baltimore] *Afro-American*, March 1, 1947, found in Box 55, WH Files-Minorities-Negro-General-Lynching-Newsclipping—Willie Earle South Carolina, Feb–Mar 1947, Nash Papers, Truman Library.

also clear that the deputy was "an elderly man" who did not appear to be a "party to a conspiracy." After all, the sixty-two-year-old jailer remarked, he was totally innocent of any wrongdoing. "They had shotguns and I danced to their music." So too, apparently, did the jury, which despite the grisly death, the detailed confessions, and the physical evidence, found all the murderers "not guilty."[43]

The fact that the verdict, which was "what one might have expected from twelve idiots in a madhouse," came shortly after Truman asked Congress for $400 million to bring democracy to Greece and Turkey, was more ironic and tragic than most could bear. Walter Reuther, the president of the United Auto Workers, denounced the jury's verdict as a "legal farce," one that would certainly come back to haunt the United States. "So long as lynch mobs are permitted to murder American citizens and go unpunished, these peoples of other nations will look with skepticism on our claim that we are the most democratic nation in the world." Once again, though, despite the high stakes, there was nothing the Justice Department could do. Tom Clark had made a pretty "good speech" on the case, but, as one southerner noted, "Eloquence doesn't stop lynching." And he was appalled that Clark refused to take the necessary steps to put an end to this ongoing reign of terror. "Successful prosecution of lynchers and conniving sheriffs" who "surrender . . . a prisoner to a lynching mob" was the only thing that would "stop them." The southerner then could not help but comment on the obvious: "While proposing to make the world 'Democratic' by . . . the arming of fascist governments like Turkey and Greece at a cost of millions (soon to become billions), it might be helpful to attempt even handed justice in the United States."[44]

43. Wexler, *Fire in a Canebrake,* 113; David K. Niles to Matt [Connelly], memo, February 19, 1947, Box 26, Civil Rights/Negro Affairs 1945–June 1947, Niles Papers; "President Truman's Civil Rights Committee Watches S.C. Lynching: Closest Attention Being Given, Chairman States," [Atlanta] *Daily World,* February 23, 1947, found in Box 55, WH Files-Minorities-Negro-General-Lynching-Newsclipping—Willie   Earle   South   Carolina, Feb–Mar 1947, Nash Papers; Robert K. Carr to All Members of the President's Committee on Civil Rights, memo, February 21, 1947, Box 26, Civil Rights/Negro Affairs 1945–June 1947, Niles Papers; "South Carolina Negro First Lynch Victim of 1947," *P.M.,* February 18, 1947, found in Box 55, WH Files-Minorities-Negro-General Lynching-Newsclipping—Willie Earle South Carolina, Feb–Mar 1947, Nash Papers.

44. Ted Le Berthon, "White Man's Views: Wrong for Acquitted Lynchers to Believe They are Christians," *Pittsburgh Courier,* June 21, 1947, found in Box 55, File WH Files-Minorities-Negro-General Lynching-Newsclipping—Willie Earle South Carolina, Feb–Mar 1947, Nash Papers; Walter Reuther to the President, telegram, May 27, 1947, Box 548, Official File 93a, Truman Papers; Albert E. Barnett to Tom Clark, May 24, 1947, Box 1099, Folder 7, Papers of the American Civil Liberties Union, Seeley Mudd Manuscript Library, Princeton University, Princeton, N.J.

What so many, like this man, understood as they watched the federal government's consistent inability to secure the vote, end housing discrimination, and protect American citizens, including veterans, from lynching, was that in contrast to the "caution and restraint" the Truman administration showed in dealing with the destructive forces engulfing the black community, its actions on the international stage were bold, innovative, and decisive. It was not as though the international problems were less intractable, the opponents less formidable, or the goals more attainable. In fact, they were not. At that time, the international system was in absolute chaos. The old multipolar system, with Britain as power broker, was in rubble, and the wartime alliance with the Soviet Union had rapidly disintegrated. Faced with these seemingly insurmountable odds, the Truman administration did not wallow in the politics of helplessness. Nor was the administration shackled by traditions that had outgrown their usefulness. Instead, Truman and his team devised strategies to cope with this new international situation. They decisively amassed the political will and savvy to break away from the Founding Fathers' sacred commandments against entangling alliances, standing armies, budget deficits, and "the man on horseback."[45] In fact, the administration not only did everything in its power to craft innovative programs, such as the Marshall Plan and the North Atlantic Treaty Organization (NATO), but it also removed ineffective or recalcitrant top administrators, such as Secretary of State James Byrnes and Gen. Douglas MacArthur, and replaced them with those who shared the president's vision and determination to get things done and done right.

Except, of course, in the area of civil rights. There, helplessness, hopelessness,

45. James F. Byrnes, *Speaking Frankly* (New York: Harper and Brothers, 1947); Daniel Yergin, *Shattered Peace: The Origins of the Cold War and the National Security State* (Boston: Houghton Mifflin Co., 1977); John L. Gaddis, *The United States and the Origins of the Cold War, 1941–47* (New York: Columbia University Press, 1972); Bruce R. Kuniholm, *The Origins of the Cold War in the Near East: Great Power Conflict and Diplomacy in Iran, Turkey, and Greece* (Princeton: Princeton University Press, 1980); Lloyd C. Gardner, *Architects of Illusion: Men and Ideas in American Foreign Policy, 1941–1949* (Chicago: Quadrangle Books, 1970); Melvyn P. Leffler, *A Preponderance of Power: National Security, the Truman Administration, and the Cold War* (Stanford: Stanford University Press, 1992); Michael J. Hogan, *A Cross of Iron: Harry S. Truman and the Origins of the National Security State, 1945–1954* (New York: Cambridge University Press, 1998); Mark R. Grandstaff, "Making the Military American: Advertising, Reform, and the Demise of an Antistanding Military Tradition, 1945–1955," *Journal of Military History* 60:2 (April 1996): 299–323; Robert M. Collins, *More: The Politics of Economic Growth in Postwar America* (Oxford: Oxford University Press, 2000), 1–36; Paul G. Pierpaoli, *Truman and Korea: The Political Culture of the Early Cold War* (Columbia: University of Missouri Press, 1999).

and mediocrity reigned. Not only were Truman's attorneys general—Tom Clark and J. Howard McGrath—lackluster, but they also shared many of the same traits, including a tendency to not "strain" themselves "in behalf of advancing Negro rights." Moreover, Truman's chief aide for minority affairs, David Niles, was also problematic. While he clearly saw his role as being the president's "ambassador" to liberal and Jewish organizations in New York, he was strikingly unconcerned about the condition of black Americans. The memos and letters that survived Niles's annual New Year's Day purge reveal a man who was contemptuous of African American leaders and the concerns they tried to bring to Truman's attention. In addition, Niles, from all accounts, had a "mania for anonymity" and "spent much of his time outside Washington." And when he was in the capital, he "slunk rather furtively around the corridors of the White House" and "alone among the senior Presidential assistants never attended HST's daily morning staff meeting." As a result, it was painfully "clear that the Minorities Office . . . was a rather isolated operation and, in that respect, rather different from the rest of the White House staff," which, Niles's key aide had to admit, "had its obvious disadvantages." Niles's administrative antics led one colleague to characterize Truman's chief point man on minority affairs as simply a "liability that HST inherited from FDR."[46] Yet, because the Cold War and black demands for citizenship had forced civil rights to the fore, the issue could not be totally ignored. Thus, "Negro affairs" became the province of Philleo Nash, who, unfortunately, did not have authority or access to make a significant impact. He, therefore, focused his efforts on working hard to develop among the black component of the New Deal coalition an "appreciation for the administration's 'good faith' efforts"—as opposed to actual accomplishments, which during the president's second term were virtually nil.[47]

46. Kluger, *Simple Justice*, 277; Pika, "Interest Groups," 651, 652; Francis H. Heller, ed., *The Truman White House: The Administration of the Presidency, 1945–1953* (Lawrence: Regents Press of Kansas, 1980), 52–56; David K. Niles to Matthew J. Connelly, January 6, 1947 [*sic*], Box 543, Official File 93 1948 [1 of 3], Truman Papers; Stephen J. Spingarn to Donald R. McCoy, memo, April 4, 1969, Box 42, File Civil Rights File-Civil Rights Correspondence Regarding—under Truman Administration, Spingarn Papers, Truman Library.

47. Heller, ed., *White House,* 54; Pika, "Interest Groups," 665; McCoy and Ruetten, *Quest and Response,* 148–49, 171–200; Berman, *Politics of Civil Rights,* 137–81; G. L. Bishop to Truman, July 8, 1949, Box 548, Official File 93B July–December 1949 [2 of 2], Truman Papers; "The 40th Annual NAACP Conference," by Edward Strong and William Taylor, Box 167–1, Folder 18, and Roy Wilkins to Officers of Branches/State Conference/Youth Councils and College Chapters, memo, October 21, 1949, found in Box 167–6, Folder 5, Edward Strong Papers, Moorland-Spingarn Research Center, Howard University, Washington, D.C.; Walter White, press release, April 3, 1952, Box 1235, Official File 413 (1950–53), Truman Papers.

Thus, as the president bade the country farewell, he could only direct the nation's attention to the fact that his administration had at least put the issue of civil rights on the nation's agenda and had established the groundwork for change. "We have made progress in spreading the blessings of American life to all of our people," Truman asserted. "There has been a tremendous awakening of the American conscience on the great issues of civil rights—equal economic opportunities, equal rights of citizenship, and equal educational opportunities for all our people, whatever their race or religion or status of birth." Yet, in truth, while there may have been some level of consciousness-raising, the actual attainment of civil rights, given the persistence of disfranchisement, lynching, and housing discrimination, left those facing the onslaught of Jim Crow wondering when this vaunted "progress" would finally catch up to them.[48]

In 1968, a group of scholars came together to discuss the Truman legacy on civil rights and met, by sheer happenstance, the day after Martin Luther King Jr. was assassinated and America's urban landscape became a smoldering inferno. Against this hellish backdrop the scholars discussed what Truman had accomplished and the various reasons he could not have done more. These included the power of the southern Democrats and the fact that, above all else, he was a "party man" and realized that to push too hard for civil rights would destroy the Democratic Party. But one scholar, acknowledging the external pressures on Truman, kept asking why the president did not do more in those areas where he had greater control. Why were there no appointments in the Department of Justice where the need was obviously so great? Why, Professor Flint Kellogg kept asking, did Truman seemingly find "it easier to move to integration in the armed forces than he did within the administration itself? What was the block here? Usually you'd think that would cause less uproar if he moved within administrative agencies than within the armed forces."[49]

In 1948, the labor secretary of the NAACP, Clarence Mitchell, had asked virtually the same question. But because Truman had at least done what no other modern president had, the association leadership decided that the man from Missouri, "though far from perfect," was still the best that black people could get under the circumstances.[50] That tendency to accept less and to

48. Martin Luther King Jr., *Where Do We Go From Here: Chaos or Community* (New York: Harper and Row, 1967), 8.

49. *Conference of Scholars*, ed. McCoy, Ruetten, and Fuchs, 10, 18, 22, 25, 28, 32–34.

50. Clarence Mitchell to Walter White, May 20, 1948, Box 633, File Harry S. Truman, 1946–49, and Alfred Baker Lewis to Walter White, December 19, 1947, Box 665, File

clutch at civil rights straws as if they are the silk threads of democracy has created an anomaly in American society in the area of civil rights (and only in the area of civil rights), where the mere act of trying—and not necessarily succeeding—becomes more than enough. At some point, as a democracy, we must realize it is not.

Wallace, Henry A.—General, 1945–48, NAACP Papers; Claude Barnett to Channing Tobias, April 10, 1948, and Channing Tobias to Philleo Nash, March 29, 1948, Box 14, File T (Folder 1), Nash Files, Truman Papers; William H. Hastie, Oral History, Truman Library.

MEMORANDUM TO Mr. Gael Sullivan   April 20, 1948

Subject: The Negro Vote   cc: Mr. Clark Clifford

        Jack Ewing last night gave us a shocking report on the Negro vote in New
York City. I had seen polls to the effect that from 20% to 30% of the Negro
voters were going to vote for Wallace, but he reported interviews with what
he said were the two best ward leaders in Harlem and in Brooklyn, both of whom
said about 75% of their voters were going to vote for Wallace.

        It seems to me that the Negro vote is one that it is within our power to
salvage. Here are some steps which have been suggested to me in discussions
with Philleo Nash and young Negro leaders of the caliber of George Weaver.

        (1) Congressman Dawson or whomever else you have in mind to head up the
Negro group for the campaign might be told that he was going to lead it. If
that were understood now, the feeling is that he could begin to get his group
lined up and preliminary steps could be taken.

        (2) The first preliminary step, they feel, would be the taking on of some-
one to handle the Negro press. They mean by that not just seeing that Committee
releases get to the large Negro papers, but that feature stories be dug up,
written up, and planted showing the things the Administration is doing for the
Negroes and making other points of interest to the Negro community. There is
a tremendous story in the work that is being done by the Housing Agency in
Negro housing, and it has never gotten adequate play.

        (3) Of course, the two things on top of their agenda are the Executive
Order promised by the President in his Report on Civil Rights for an FEPC for
the Executive branch of the Government, and the ending of discrimination in
the Armed Services. I gather that there is a great deal of feeling that the
issuance of the Executive Order would create another Southern revolt, and that
is why it is being held up. I do not know whether or not anyone has sounded
out the Southern leaders to see if this objection is valid. As regards the
second point, the heat may be taken off this somewhat by the meeting of Negro
leaders which Secretary Forrestal is calling in the near future to discuss the
problem of Negroes in the Armed Services. The military objection to it is that
with such an order they fear an immediate falling off of volunteers from the
Southern States, which are the best source of recruits for the Army.

        The judicious use of appointments, like that of Bill Hastie, is of course
tremendously effective. Are there any appointments coming up that you know of,
particularly in the large metropolitan areas where the depredations of the
Wallaceites are particularly severe? I understand there is a bill in to create
another Federal judgeship in eastern Pennsylvania, but that runs up against the
difficulty of Senate confirmation, which Philleo Nash believes would provoke

still another Southern revolt.

It might be well worthwhile to sit down with the Senator and Jack
Redding and review what we can do in this sector in the immediate future.

William L. Batt, Jr.

WLB:vw

August 18, 1948

Dear Ernie:

I appreciated very much your letter of last Saturday night from Hotel Temple Square in the Mormon Capital.

I am going to send you a copy of the report of my Commission on Civil Rights and then if you still have that antibellum proslavery outlook, I'll be thoroughly disappointed in you.

The main difficulty with the South is that they are living eighty years behind the times and the sooner they come out of it the better it will be for the country and themselves. I am not asking for social equality, because no such thing exists, but I am asking for equality of opportunity for all human beings and, as long as I stay here, I am going to continue that fight. When the mob gangs can take four people out and shoot them in the back, and everybody in the country is acquainted with who did the shooting and nothing is done about it, that country is in pretty bad fix from a law enforcement standpoint.

When a Mayor and a City Marshal can take a negro Sergeant off a bus in South Carolina, beat him up and put out one of his eyes, and nothing is done about it by the State authorities, something is radically wrong with the system.

On the Louisiana and Arkansas Railway when coal burning locomotives were used the negro firemen were the thing because it was a backbreaking job and a dirty one. As soon as they turned to oil as a fuel it became customary for people to take shots at the negro firemen and a number were murdered because it was thought that this was now a white-collar job and should go to a white man. I can't approve of such goings on and I shall never approve it, as long as I am here, as I told you before. I am going to try to remedy it and if that ends up in my failure to be reelected, that failure will be in a good cause.

I know you haven't thought this thing through and that you do not know the facts. I am happy, however, that you wrote me because it gives me a chance to tell you what the facts are.

Sincerely yours,

HARRY S. TRUMAN

Mr. E. W. Roberts
c/o Faultless Starch Company
Kansas City, Missouri

Note in longhand --

This is a personal & confidential communication and I hope you'll regard it that way - at least until I've made a public statement on the subject - as I expect to do in the South.

HST

(Envelope marked - Personal and Confidential)

Report enclosed - "To Secure These Rights" --
"The Report Of The President's Committee On Civil Rights"

President Harry S. Truman's Farewell Address and the Atomic Bomb

The High Price of Secrecy

Richard B. Frank

As the contents of the Farewell Address reflect, retrospective assessments of the presidency of Harry S. Truman customarily rank foreign affairs ahead of domestic matters. In the realm of statecraft, no event transcends the dropping of the atomic bombs. In the concise phrases contained in his Farewell Address in 1953, President Truman explained that atomic weapons became available in the summer of 1945. He affirmed that it was his decision to use the bomb. He maintained that the primary motivation for his decision was the belief that it would save hundreds of thousands of lives—both American and Japanese. Yet, only five years later, Truman refused to employ nuclear weapons in Korea. He defended that decision both as one grounded in a deeply ingrained American sense of morality and as one aimed to avoid World War III, a war that "might dig the grave not only of our communist opponents but also of our own society, our world as well as theirs."

The use of atomic weapons in 1945 spawned a vast and vastly contentious literature. President Truman's dual propositions in his Farewell Address that he decided to use the bombs and that his primary motive was to save lives—as well as the number of those lives saved—are all subjects that rise as peaks in this disputed terrain. It is impossible in this short discussion to range over the full universe of this controversy, much less all the events in 1945. What can be addressed here are just the most fundamental points. First, both the distance in time and the heat of the controversies generally have divorced much of the debate from the realities of 1945. Yet, without a firm grasp of those realities, especially the military and political strategies pursued by the United States and Japan, the use of atomic weapons cannot be judged. Second, the declassification of radio intelligence material between the late 1970s and the present has transformed our understanding of U.S. decision making. Finally, I will address the propositions Truman set forth in his Farewell Address concerning the use of atomic weapons in 1945 and, more important, what he was not able to divulge then that might well have prevented this whole controversy or certainly materially altered its shape.

I. The Realities of 1945

With few exceptions, Americans in 1945 believed fervently that the use of atomic weapons at Hiroshima and Nagasaki ended the Pacific War and saved countless lives. That conviction dominated national discourse for approximately two decades. Since that time, various scholars and writers have mounted multiple challenges to what one critic labeled the "patriotic orthodoxy." These challenges share three basic premises: first, that Japan's strategic position in the summer of 1945 was catastrophic; second, that her leaders recognized that their nation's situation was hopeless and thus were seeking to end the war; finally, that American leaders understood, thanks primarily to decoded Japanese diplomatic communications, that the Japanese knew they were defeated and were seeking to end the war. Thus, an array of critics argue that American leaders comprehended that neither atomic weapons nor an invasion of the Japanese home islands was necessary to end the war. Accordingly, they charge that American leaders deliberately used atomic weapons in pursuit of some other goal: to justify the enormous expenditure of funds; to satisfy (perverse) intellectual curiosity; to perpetuate the Manhattan Project as a bureaucratic empire; or to intimidate the Soviets.[1]

But the very first premise of this structure is wrong. The harsh reality is

1. For "patriotic orthodoxy," see Michael S. Sheery, "Patriotic Orthodoxy and American Decline," in *History Wars,* ed. David T. Linenthal and Tom Engelhardt (New York: Metropolitan Books, 1996). The summary of themes from the postwar critical literature is drawn from J. Samuel Walker, "The Decision to Use the Bomb: A Historiography Update," *Diplomatic History* 14 (Winter 1990), and Barton Bernstein, "The Struggle over History," in *Judgment at the Smithsonian,* ed. Philip Nobile (New York: Marlowe and Co., 1995).

that the key Japanese leaders in the summer of 1945 did not regard their situation as hopeless. On the contrary, driving them was a coherent and well-conceived military and political strategy called *Ketsu-Go* (Decisive Operation). Understanding both the particulars of Ketsu-Go and the investment of Japanese leaders in this strategy is the key to grasping not only why the war continued but also how and when it ended. Perhaps ironically, the starting point for examination of Ketsu-Go is the U.S. strategic planning in 1945 that Ketsu-Go anticipated.

Grand Strategy: American

President Franklin Roosevelt publicly articulated the national political goal at the Casablanca Conference in January 1943 as the unconditional surrender of the Axis powers. As it evolved over the next two years, unconditional surrender was not simply a slogan about victory but a policy about peace. It provided the legal authority for the extensive plans to renovate the internal structure of the Axis nations.[2]

The American military strategy forged to secure that national political goal by the Joint Chiefs of Staff (JCS) in the spring of 1945 was an unstable compromise of two conflicting visions. The U.S. Navy, led by Fleet Admiral Ernest King, had studied war with Japan since 1906. From these decades of analysis, naval officers distilled a number of principles about defeating Japan. None of these principles was more deeply embedded than the conviction that an invasion of the Japanese home islands would result in a bloodbath and thus represented absolute folly. Accordingly, naval leaders advocated ending the war in a campaign of blockade and bombardment, including intense aerial bombardment by sea- and land-based aircraft. The U.S. Army, led by General of the Armies George C. Marshall, never invested the same intellectual capital into examination of a conflict with Japan. The army had, however, explored the prospect of war with Japan in the 1930s and concluded

2. Michael D. Pearlman, *Unconditional Surrender, Demobilization, and the Atomic Bomb* (Fort Leavenworth, Kans.: Combat Studies Institute, U.S. Army Command and General Staff College, 1996), 1–8; Herbert P. Bix, *Hirohito and the Making of Modern Japan* (New York: HarperCollins, 2000), 496–98, and "Japan's Delayed Surrender: A Reinterpretation," *Diplomatic History* 19:2 (Spring 1995): 204. John Dower stresses that U.S. officials treated Japan's surrender as unconditional and initially kept the status of the emperor and the Imperial Institution vague to pressure Japanese elites into accepting the first occupation reforms (*Embracing Defeat: Japan in the Wake of World War II* [New York: W. W. Norton/New Press, 1999], 81–84).

that invasion might be necessary.[3] Thus, when the army turned attention to the problem of ending hostilities with Japan in 1944, it adopted a strategy of invasion of the home islands.

The JCS merged these two conflicting views into a strategic plan in May 1945. The Chiefs authorized the continuation and intensification of the strategy of blockade and bombardment until November 1. At that point, the United States would launch a two-phase invasion of the Japanese homeland under the overall code name of Operation Downfall. The first step, Operation Olympic, involved the seizure of approximately the southern third of Kyushu, the southernmost main Japanese home island, by the Sixth Army starting on November 1, 1945. Olympic would obtain air and naval bases to support a second phase, Operation Coronet, tentatively set for March 1, 1946, involving two armies to secure the Tokyo-Yokohama region.

As the JCS pointed out in the policy paper it adopted to support this strategy, the overall Allied war aim remained unconditional surrender. This would provide the legal authority to effect the far-ranging political changes in Japan designed to assure that she never again posed a threat to peace. As the JCS acknowledged, however, there was no historical precedent of surrender to a foreign power by the Japanese government for some two thousand years. Moreover, throughout the entire course of the Pacific War no Japanese unit had ever surrendered. Thus, the JCS cautioned that there was no guarantee that the surrender of the Japanese government could be obtained or that, even if a Japanese government would capitulate, the Japanese armed forces would comply with that surrender. Therefore, an invasion was vital because it was most likely to compel a surrender of the Japanese government. Moreover, an invasion would best position the United States to deal with the situation if there was no surrender or if the Japanese armed forces refused to comply with surrender by a Japanese government.[4]

The importance of this framework of U.S. strategic thinking cannot be overemphasized. The JCS appreciation shows that the ultimate American nightmare was not Operation Downfall, the two-phase initial invasion, but the absence of an organized capitulation of Japan's armed forces. In the latter case, the United States would face the prospect of defeating four to five million Japanese men under arms in the home islands, on the Asian continent,

---

3. Edward S. Miller, *War Plan Orange* (Annapolis: Naval Institute Press, 1991), 4, 29, 150, 164–65; Henry G. Cole, *The Road to Rainbow* (Annapolis: Naval Institute Press, 2003).

4. JCS 924/15, April 25, 1945, CCS 381 Pacific Ocean Operations (6–10–43), Sec. 11, Record Group [hereafter RG] 218, National Archives and Records Administration, Washington, D.C. [hereafter NARA].

and across the Pacific Ocean. This made even the potential casualties in Downfall only a down payment on the ultimate cost of the complete defeat of Japan. President Harry S. Truman reviewed the invasion strategy in June 1945. He authorized Olympic, the invasion of Kyushu, but he withheld sanction for Coronet.[5]

Grand Strategy: Japanese

New Year's Day 1945 found Japanese military and naval leaders sober but resolute. Their entrenched attitudes toward their American adversaries had remained constant since the summer of 1941; only their goals had altered. None of these men ever believed Japan could physically conquer the United States, and no Japanese leader questioned the ability of the United States to produce vast quantities of war materiel. But they calculated that America would be compelled to divert much of that materiel to Europe to counter Germany and Italy. The bedrock conviction shared by almost all Imperial Army officers and many Imperial Navy officers, however, was that Americans, lacking racial purity and the spiritual stamina of the Japanese populace, possessed only brittle morale. A lengthy, increasingly costly war would sap American will to see the war through and force American political leaders to negotiate an end to the conflict on terms favorable to Japan. Initially those terms would include Japanese control of resource areas in Southeast Asia. By 1945, Japanese militarists viewed the attainable terms as at least the preservation of the homeland with a political order in which their position remained dominant.[6]

Commonly skewing retrospective assessments of Japan's situation are the "War in the Pacific" maps that depict a line representing Japan's greatest advance in 1942 bulging halfway across the ocean and then a line nearly rubbing Japan's shores representing her situation in the summer of 1945. Senior leaders at Imperial General Headquarters in Tokyo understood that Japan had lost her navy and with it control of the Western Pacific right up to her shores. But the Imperial realm still included huge territories with vast resources and hundreds of millions of vassals on the continent and to the south—

5. "Minutes of Meeting Held at White House on Monday, June 18, 1945, at 1530," Xerox 1567, George C. Marshall Library, Lexington, Va.

6. Edward Drea, *In Service of the Emperor: Essays on the Imperial Japanese Army* (Lincoln: University of Nebraska Press, 1998), 11–13, 26–34, 45–46, 63, 89–90; Gerhard L. Weinberg, *World at Arms: A Global History of World War II* (Cambridge: Cambridge University Press, 1994), 245–59.

areas on those "War in the Pacific" maps American eyes often ignore. These territories also represented potential bargaining chips—some for Japan to retain as the profit from her gamble on war and others to trade away to secure those gains or, in the final accounting, at least the old order in the homeland.

Officers at Imperial Headquarters accepted that Japan's airpower was much diminished, but there remained thousands of planes and a bountiful supply of young men prepared to crash them into enemy ships. Above all, there was still a formidable army, backed by a stalwart civilian population, and the priceless asset of Japan's home soil, which negated all the advantages of an attacker dependent on machines rather than men. And senior leaders coupled a reassuring assessment of the current strategic picture with an acute appreciation of future U.S. intentions. Americans lacked the patience for a protracted strategy of blockade and bombardment; they therefore surely would seek to end the war quickly by an invasion of the Japanese homeland. If the initial assault could be repulsed, or even if its cost just could be made prohibitive, Japan could yet extricate herself from the war with honor. Thus, with this goal in mind the emperor sanctioned a new strategic directive published on January 20 that candidly declared the homeland itself would be the arena for the "final decisive battle" of the war.[7]

The Imperial Army's homeland defense scheme created two theaters of command. The First General Army (roughly equivalent to an American army group) with headquarters in Tokyo oversaw most of central and northern Honshu. The Second General Army with headquarters at Hiroshima exercised jurisdiction over forces on western Honshu, Shikoku, and Kyushu. Several Area Armies (effectively the equivalent of an American army) answered to each General Army. Imperial Headquarters separately entrusted the defense of Hokkaido, the northernmost home island, to the Fifth Area Army.

There were only twelve field divisions in all of Japan on New Year's Day 1945. With so few field units available, Imperial Headquarters embarked on a huge program of homeland reinforcement. From Manchuria came four di-

---

7. For the assessment at Imperial General Headquarters, see generally Boeicho Boei Kenshujo Senshi Shitsu (War History Office, Defense Agency) Senshi Shosho (War History Series) No. 57, *Hondo Kessen Junbi (2) Kyushu No Boei* (Preparations for the Decisive Battle on the Homeland [2] Defense of the Kyushu Area) (Tokyo), 159–64; *Reports of General MacArthur, Japanese Operations in the Southwest Pacific Area, Volume II, Part II* (Washington, D.C.: U.S. Government Printing Office, 1966), 577; Statement of Baron Suzuki, December 26, 1945, Interrogation No. 531, p. 308, Center for Military History, Washington, D.C.; and Edward Drea, *MacArthur's Ultra: Code Breaking in the War against Japan* (Lawrence: University Press of Kansas, 1992), 202.

visions, but by far and away the major increase in strength sprang from a February 26 order for a gigantic, three-phase mobilization program to create new legions. At the end of the mobilization, the forces available to defend the homeland would number sixty divisions (thirty-six field and counterattack, twenty-two coastal combat, and two armored divisions) and thirty-four brigades (twenty-seven infantry and seven tank). Counting the necessary logistic and administrative infrastructure, the mobilization would add 1.5 million men to the home defense commands. The aggregate strength of the homeland armies would total 2,903,000 men, 292,000 horses, and 27,500 motor vehicles.[8]

On April 8, staff officers in Tokyo completed the sprawling master defense plan known as Ketsu-Go for the impending struggle for the homeland and contiguous areas. This plan envisioned that American invaders would be confronted and crushed in one of seven key areas, with emphasis on Ketsu Number Three (the Kanto-Tokyo Area) and Ketsu Number Six (Kyushu).[9]

Three features marked the Ketsu-Go plan. First, the operations did not aim at destroying the enemy either at the water's edge (the tactics prior to mid-1944) or far inland (the tactics from mid-1944 to Ketsu-Go). The Japanese realized the folly of immediate beach defense in the face of massive American pre-landing bombardments, but they also grasped that their adversary could never be dislodged if permitted to consolidate his positions after a landing. Therefore, Ketsu-Go strived to destroy the beachhead, the perimeter established by the invader a few days after the landing, anchored on the coast but stretching only a few miles inland. The second distinctive feature of Ketsu-Go was the comprehensive devotion to *tokko* ("special attack" or suicide) tactics, not only the now routine air and sea efforts, but also ashore. The incorporation of the civilian population into the defense scheme represented the third highly singular feature of Ketsu-Go. Under the National Resistance Program, commanders would summon all able-bodied civilians, regardless of gender, to combat.[10]

8. *Hondo Kessen Junbi (2) Kyushu No Boei*, 177–82, 211–16, 278–92; Japanese Monograph No. 17, Appendix VII; *Reports of General MacArthur, Volume II, Part II*, 591–92, 605–7.

9. April 8 Imperial Headquarters Directive No. 2438: "Outline of Preparations for the Ketsu Go Operation," *Hondo Kessen Junbi (2) Kyushu No Boei*, 164–66, 264; *Reports of General MacArthur, Volume II, Part II*, 601. For a complete translation of this order, see *War in Asia and the Pacific, Volume 12: Defense of the Homeland and End of the War* (New York: Garland Publishing, 1980), 201–31.

10. *Reports of General MacArthur, Volume II, Part II*, 612.

Ketsu-Go on Kyushu

The Japanese did not rely on espionage or code breaking to reach their prescient assessment that the Americans would target Kyushu, and specifically southern Kyushu, for their initial invasion. Rather, the Japanese simply deduced their antagonist's intentions from the elementary clues of American operational techniques and obvious goals. American superiority in combat power during the Pacific War rested upon overwhelming air and sea power, not ground forces. It followed that U.S. invasion plans must encompass the ability to bolster their ground units with masses of planes and ships. While carrier-based aviation permitted an almost unlimited number of potential invasion sites, it represented just a fraction of available American airpower. If the United States employed ground-based air units, the invasion beaches must fall within fighter-plane range of the nearest bases.

In January 1945 the Japanese perceived shrewdly that by midyear the U.S advance would reach Okinawa. Thus, an arc representing American fighter-plane range from Okinawa foretold the likely American landing areas. Within that arc fell the southern ranges of Kyushu around Miyazaki, Shibushi Bay, and the Satsuma Peninsula. These comprised the most obvious targets with plentiful airfield sites and naval bases forming easy stepping-stones for an invasion of the Kanto (Tokyo) plain. In sum, the Japanese deduced three of the four designated invasion beaches exactly and were not that far off on the fourth.[11]

Although only one field division garrisoned Kyushu in January 1945, over the next five months the Imperial Army flooded the island with reinforcements that brought the defenders on Kyushu to fourteen field divisions, three tank brigades, and eight independent mixed (infantry) brigades. The aggravate forces numbered some 900,000 men. In the words of Maj. Gen. Sanada Joichiro, the deputy chief of staff of the Second General Army, Field Marshal Shunroku Hata, the commander of the Second General Army, and his staff believed that the struggle for Kyushu would be "the last chance to change the war situation in our favor."[12]

11. *Hondo Kessen Junbi (2) Kyushu No Boei*, 273–76, 294–95; Maj. Gen. Yasumasa Yoshitake, "Statement Concerning the Estimate of U.S. Army Plan of Invasion against Southern Kyushu during the Period from April 1945 to August 1945 and Changes in the Operational Plans and Preparations of the 57th Army," p. 5, Center for Military History.

12. *Hondo Kessen Junbi (2) Kyushu No Boei*, 294–96, 298–300, 458–59; Maj. Gen. Joichiro Sanada, "Statement on the Operational Preparations for the Defense of Kyushu," Doc. No. 58513, Center for Military History.

Feeble naval but formidable air forces backed this ground battle array. The Imperial Navy's surface naval forces amounted to a handful of cruisers, destroyers, and submarines. Many of these actually served to porter small, short-range suicide weapons close to their launching points. But Imperial Headquarters decided to devote all of Japan's airpower to Ketsu-Go. That meant converting thousands of training aircraft into suicide planes. By a drastic policy of declining combat and dispersing and hiding planes, the Japanese swelled their combat aircraft inventory in 1945. By midsummer, the Japanese fielded more than ten thousand aircraft to confront the invasion, about half already earmarked for kamikaze attacks. The great bulk of these planes defended Kyushu.[13]

Overall, the Imperial Army faced severe logistic shortfalls for the Ketsu Operation, notably in ammunition and weapon supplies. These acute shortages placed a premium on selecting priorities in distributing available equipment and ammunition. From the outset, Imperial Headquarters effectively staked its fortunes on Kyushu. Moreover, Imperial Headquarters prudently aimed to pack Kyushu with ample supplies and arms well before a landing and discounted the prospect of substantial replenishment after an invasion. As a result of these priorities, the general equipment situation on Kyushu was adequate based on a match of the authorized to the actual equipment levels—it was sumptuous compared to other regions save perhaps Tokyo.[14]

Preparations for Internal Defense and Resistance

Following their experience on Saipan, American planners incorporated the prospect of facing a "fanatically hostile population" into their situation estimates for an invasion of Japan. Two subsequent events fortified this expectation. The Philippines (excluding Leyte) contained 381,550 Japanese. Within this total were about 38,280 Japanese civilians, including government officials, businessmen, and farmers (and their families), as well as civilian employees of the Japanese armed forces. As the U.S. Army official history on the campaign would note: "except for the extremely aged and the very young, almost all of these Japanese civilians came to serve the armed forces in

13. Richard B. Frank, *Downfall: The End of the Imperial Japanese Empire* (New York: Random House, 1999), 204–11.

14. Statement of Lt. Col. Ohta Kyoshi (Staff Officer in Charge of Transportation and Line of Communications of the Sixteenth Area Army), pp. 1–3; Statement of Lt. Col. Iwakoshi Shinroku, Doc. No. 62800, Center for Military History. For a further discussion of postwar evidence on Japanese logistics see Frank, *Downfall*, 176–77.

one way or another." Almost exactly two-thirds of the 381,550 Japanese in the Philippines (not counting Leyte) died, but there is no explicit breakdown of losses among these civilians. Then much worse came on Okinawa, where at least 35,000 and perhaps as many as 100,000 to 150,000 civilians may have perished.[15]

In March 1945, Imperial Headquarters moved to make this American nightmare a reality and to establish a seamless fusion of the military, the government, and the people. On March 24, Imperial Headquarters directed the formation the following month of Area Special Policing units to be placed under the area commanders. These organizations would represent the practical merger of the governmental and civilian spheres. Every village or town would form its own platoon or company composed of local inhabitants, and it would become a part of an Area Special Policing unit of about three hundred. These formations afforded a pool of auxiliary combat or combat support units, as illustrated by their direct attachment to operational units, usually in coastal areas. The members were scheduled for call-up in May, June, and July for periods of three to four days each for rudimentary but morale-boosting instruction.[16]

On March 27, Public Law Number 30 mobilized all citizens in the coastal areas to contribute to the decisive battle strategy by lending their hands to fortification, transportation, construction, or other tasks. This followed the decision by the cabinet on March 18 to enact the Decisive Battle Educational Measures Guidelines, which suspended all school classes, except grades one to six, from April 1, 1945, to March 31, 1946. All of these students—and their teachers—would be mobilized for the production of food and military supplies, air raid work, and other activities to facilitate the decisive battle.

On March 23, the cabinet ordered the formation of the Patriotic Citizens Fighting Corps across the whole nation. This corps constituted a mechanism for inducting the whole body of citizens and permitting military authorities to call them up upon invasion. The entire public, in effect, became subject to mobilization under the "Volunteer Enlistment Law." This applied to all men from fifteen to sixty years of age and all women seventeen to forty. They were organized into Volunteer Fighting units and subject to military discipline

15. Robert Ross Smith, *Triumph in the Philippines* (Washington, D.C.: U.S. Government Printing Office), 694, app. H-2; Thomas M. Huber, *Japan's Battle of Okinawa April–June 1945* (Leavenworth: Combat Studies Institute, U.S. Army Command and General Staff College, 1990), 13; George Feifer, *Tennozan: The Battle of Okinawa and the Atomic Bomb* (New York: Ticknor and Fields, 1992), 532–33; Frank, *Downfall*, 71–72.

16. *Hondo Kessen Junbi (2) Kyushu No Boei*, 406–9, 414–15.

and control through the local area commands. The scale of these organizations was formidable: a tabular representation of these units in Kumamoto prefecture in southern Kyushu, for example, gives a breakdown by subjurisdiction and then notes that the figures represented all the citizens in the age groups, a total of more than one million persons.[17]

What this sea of civilians lacked besides training was arms and even uniforms. One mobilized high school girl, Yukiko Kasai, found herself issued an awl and instructed: "Even killing just one American soldier will do. You must prepare to use the awls for self-defense. You must aim at the enemy's abdomen." Many civilians found themselves drilling with sharpened staves or spears. Japan lacked the cloth to put those civilians now transformed as combatants into uniforms—one senior general spoke of his hope to provide them with patches on their civilian clothes. This lack of distinguishing identification would undoubtedly have made it impossible at normal combat range for a soldier or marine to identify which civilians represented the Japanese armed forces and which did not, a sure prescription for vast numbers of deaths. At least one U.S. Fifth Air Force intelligence officer took the Japanese at their publicly broadcast word of total mobilization and declared in a July 21 report: "the entire population of Japan is a proper Military Target . . . THERE ARE NO CIVILIANS IN JAPAN."[18]

The significance of these designs cannot be exaggerated. Japanese authorities intended this mobilization to create a gigantic pool of untrained men and women who would be married to tactical units where they would perform direct combat support and ultimately combat jobs. This would literally add tens of millions to the strength of the ground combat units, albeit of little formal combat power due to their lack of training and equipment. It would also guarantee huge civilian casualties and make the disturbing American nightmare of a "fanatically hostile population" a reality. By mustering millions of erstwhile civilians into the area swept by bombs, artillery, and small arms fire, Japan's military masters willfully consigned hundreds of thousands of their countrymen to death. Moreover, by deliberately tramping down any distinctions between combatants and noncombatants, they would compel

---

17. Ibid., 410–13.

18. Thomas R. Havens, *Valley of Darkness* (Lanham, Md.: University Press of America, 1986), 188–90; Statement of Lt. Gen. Yoshizumi Masao, former chief Military Affairs Bureau, Army Section, Imperial General Headquarters, December 22, 1949, Doc. No. 61388, p. 3, Center for Military History; W. F. Craven and J. L. Cate, eds., *The Army Air Forces in World War II*, vol. 5, *The Pacific: Matterhorn to Nagasaki June 1944 to August 1945* (Washington, D.C.: Office of the Chief of Air Force History, 1953), 696.

American soldiers and marines to treat virtually all Japanese as combatants, or fail to do so at their peril.

Ketsu-Go versus Olympic

American officers subjected the proposed massive amphibious assault on Kyushu to several postwar assessments. A comprehensive study by the staff of the V Amphibious Corps, while allowing that the struggle would have been "costly," overall tended to deprecate Japanese prospects. The compilers of this report, however, acknowledged that they had secured copies of very few enemy plans and orders, that demobilization had disorganized and dispersed Japanese units, and that they confronted many conflicts in the testimony of Japanese officers. This analysis likewise was skewed by the fact that the Japanese units facing the V Amphibious Corps were the weakest Imperial Army detachments on Kyushu.[19]

Even with the far better perspective offered by the much more comprehensive Japanese material, the assessment of the V Amphibious Corps study that Ketsu-Go could not defeat Olympic still appears sound. In essence, American firepower and materiel were simply too overpowering to permit the defeat of Olympic. While the exact costs of the struggle on Kyushu can never be known with certainty, a reasonable approximation can be ventured. The Japanese would probably have committed at least a half million combatants and sustained at least 200,000 to 250,000 killed. Probably another 380,000 Japanese fatalities would have occurred among the erstwhile civilian population, overwhelmingly among those press-ganged into militias. A fair speculation on American losses, based on a troop list of about 681,000, the lower planning ratio for losses proposed by the JCS planners in April 1945, and the campaign lasting no more than ninety days, would yield projected casualties of 132,385, including 25,741 killed and missing. To these would be added naval casualties ranging from 7,228 to 12,942 killed, and 16,809 to

19. V Amphibious Corps, Operations Report, Occupation of Japan, Appendix 3 to Annex Charlie, The Japanese Plan for the Defense of Kyushu, pp. 1, 39, Marine Corps History Center, Washington, D.C. Other important assessments include: (1) British Combined Observers (Pacific), "Report of Operation OLYMPIC and Japanese Countermeasures," April 4, 1946, CAB 106, No. 97, Public Record Office Kew, England; (2) Report of Reconnaissance Southern Kyushu, IX Corps Zone of Operation, December 3–5, 1945, RG 407, Entry 427, WWII Operations Reports, IX Corps 209–2.0, NARA; and (3) File: Intelligence Specialist School and Information, Edmund J. Winslett Papers, U.S. Army Military History Institute, Carlisle, Pa.

30,098 wounded. This brings combined U.S. land and sea losses to the range of 149,194 to 162,483, of whom between 32,969 and 38,683 would be killed.[20] All of these numbers are based on very conservative assumptions.

But the real significance of Ketsu-Go versus Olympic does not rest in conjectures about outcomes or human costs. The Japanese comprehended astutely that they need not repulse Olympic to attain their overarching political objective, which was to find the American pain threshold in casualties that would induce American policy makers to parley for terms to the taste of Japanese militarists. Moreover, they correctly perceived that this threshold comprised not just the raw number of losses in Olympic but also the implications those casualties carried. The Japanese did not have to reach the ultimate American pain threshold in the battle against Olympic. They only needed to convince U.S. policy makers and the public that the bloodletting on Kyushu foretold an unbearable cost to root out all the Japanese defenders in the home islands—and perhaps those spread across Asia and the Pacific.

The American tolerance for casualties to secure unconditional surrender was never tested in reality, so it cannot be certified, but there are several benchmarks from which it may be judged. First, with total battle deaths for the war at 290,907, each additional 29,900 dead increased the war's cost by 10 percent. Moreover, and perhaps more telling, the highest death total for any one month of the war, 20,325 in March 1945, could easily have been exceeded in the first thirty days of Olympic. Because battle casualties fell in great disproportion on combat as opposed to support troops, battle casualties ashore of only 92,500—a number well within Japanese capabilities—would have doubled the losses for the entire war among the assault divisions.[21] This carried dire implications for combat effectiveness and morale. Any soldier or marine infantryman slated for Olympic who believed the atomic bomb saved him from death or injury had solid grounds for this belief. The other men earmarked for Olympic, whatever their job, would have become unwilling

20. Frank, *Downfall*, 190–95.

21. Ibid., 134. American battle casualties were not spread evenly across all branches but were overwhelmingly concentrated in the infantry. For the war as a whole, the infantry accounted for 80 percent of U.S. Army fatalities in ground units. *Army Battle Casualties and Nonbattle Deaths in World War II, Final Report, 7 December 1941–31 December 1946*, Statistical and Accounting Branch, Office of the Adjutant General, p. 5, gives totals from which the percentage of infantry casualties is extracted. The same data show artillery sustained 5.2 percent and engineers 4.2 percent of all battle deaths for the war among ground branches. The assumption that 92,500 overall casualties results in a doubling of losses in the assault divisions is derived by multiplying this number by 80 percent to approximate the 74,239 casualties Olympic divisions had already sustained. Frank, *Downfall*, 122.

participants in a gigantic and deadly game of kamikaze roulette where random chance determined who lived and who died.

There is at least one contemporary suggestion of what a key policy maker deemed unacceptable: General Marshall recoiled sharply at estimates from Gen. Douglas MacArthur's headquarters in the Pacific of casualties exceeding 100,000 for Olympic. Indeed, Marshall's message inviting MacArthur to disavow such projections explicitly cited President Truman's sensitivity to casualties, plainly a matter with heavy political freight.[22] By these measures, if Ketsu-Go against an unaltered Olympic produced casualties in the 140,000 to 160,000 range, the implications for the ultimate cost of obtaining unconditional surrender may possibly have been enough to secure Japanese political objectives—or at least Japanese leaders possessed a sound basis to believe this. The more probable alternative, however, is that losses in that range in Olympic might have driven American strategy back to a blockade and bombardment aimed at starving out Japan at a cost of millions of deaths, mostly civilian.

In Tokyo, it was not the military but the political implications for Ketsu-Go that stood preeminent. According to a postwar statement from Maj. Gen. Amano Masakazu, chief of the Operations Section, Imperial General Headquarters, assessed the outlook for Ketsu-Go as follows: "We were absolutely sure of victory. It was the first and the only battle in which the main strength of the air, land and sea forces were to be joined. The geographical advantages of the homeland were to be utilized to the highest degree, the enemy was to be crushed, and we were confident that the battle would prove to be the turning point in political maneuvering."[23]

The most critical attitude of all was that of War Minister Anami Korechika, and the evidence on his views is overwhelming. He was convinced that Ketsu-Go would succeed. The chief of staff of the Imperial Army, Gen. Umezu Yoshijiro, argued even after Soviet intervention that it did not compel surrender because it made no difference in the prospects for Ketsu-Go.[24] A realistic assessment of Ketsu-Go as the Japanese saw it shows that the belief

22. Marshall to MacArthur, June 19, 1945, and MacArthur to Marshall, June 19, 1945, RG 4, USAFPAC Correspondence WD, folder 4, MacArthur Memorial Archive, Norfolk, Va.

23. Statement of Maj. Gen. Amano Masakazu, June 10, 1950, Doc. No. 59617; see also statement December 29, 1949, Doc. No. 54480, Center for Military History.

24. Statements of Lt. Gen. Yoshizumi, Masao, Former Chief Military Affairs Bureau, Army Section, Imperial General Headquarters, December 22, 1949, Doc. No. 54484, p. 4; Doc. No. 54485, pp. 2, 3; Doc. No. 61338, p. 3; Statement of Col. Hayashi Saburo, Doc. No. 54482, p. 3. A mass of statements attest to Anami's confidence in the prospects for Ketsu-Go. Hayashi related in another interview, "I think War Minister Anami's ideas of continuing the war was

that Japan could salvage something from her war other than unconditional surrender was grounded in solid fact.

Validation

Quite apart from the illumination of retrospective assessments, powerful contemporary validation for Ketsu-Go emerges from the reaction of U.S. leaders once radio intelligence compromised Japanese plans. American intelligence originally calculated that on November 1, 1945, the scheduled date for Olympic, the Japanese would protect Kyushu with only six field divisions, and just three of these would defend the southern Kyushu target area. The Japanese were expected to deploy ultimately eight to ten field divisions with an aggregate of 350,000 troops against Olympic. The Imperial Army and Imperial Navy would have available only 2,500 to 3,000 planes to support these troops.[25]

From July 9 and continuing well into August, radio intelligence (code-named Ultra or Magic) unmasked the massive buildup of Japanese forces in the homeland in general and the even more disturbing evidence of a huge

---

that he wanted to make peace after dealing a heavy blow to the enemy" (Doc. No. 61436, p. 5). Col. Matsutani Sei reported, "It seems to me that General Anami had hopes of concluding peace in early August on fairly advantageous terms after at least inflicting a blow in Japan proper upon the enemy" (statement, January 13, 1950, Doc. No. 54227, p. 2). Maj. Gen. Nagai Yatsuji, chief of the Military Affairs Section, War Ministry, commented that Anami believed strongly in the idea that the tide of war could be turned by a decisive battle on the homeland. Apparently he thought that by taking advantage of this opportunity, an "Honorable peace could be concluded" (statement of December 27, 1949, Doc. No. 54228, p. 2). In the mildest of these, Col. Arao Okikatsu, also an important staff officer at the War Ministry, stated, "War Minister Anami was confident of victory to some extent (at least lessen the conditions in the Potsdam Proclamation)" (statement of December 27, 1949, Doc. No. 54226, p. 2). As for Umezu's critical comment in August, see Memorandum of Vice Admiral Hoshina Zenshiro, Doc. No. 53437; Statement of Ikeda Sumihisa, December 27, 1949, Doc. No. 54483. These two documents are the "minutes" of the Imperial Conference in the early hours of August 10, 1945. All documents are at the Center for Military History.

25. The estimate that the initial Japanese capability was to garrison Kyushu with six divisions with only three in the southern part of the island is mentioned repeatedly in planning documents from at least mid-1944 and reiterated in Downfall, Strategic Plans for Operations in the Japanese Archipelago, author's copy. (A copy of the Downfall plan may be found in OPD 350.05, Sec. 1, RG 165, NARA.) MacArthur's projection of ultimate Japanese capabilities is from the same Downfall plan. General Marshall's estimate before Truman of ultimate Japanese strength of eight to ten divisions and 350,000 men is found in "Minutes of Meeting Held at White House on Monday, 18 June 1945." These minutes make no mention of reference to Japanese air capabilities.

bolstering of Kyushu centered on the proposed landing areas. By war's end, intelligence had identified thirteen of the fourteen field divisions (nine in the southern half of the island) and five of the eleven brigades on Kyushu. The final revised estimate of August 20 credited the Japanese with all fourteen field divisions and an aggregate of 625,000 troops on Kyushu.[26]

An equally dark picture emerged with regard to Japanese airpower, although differences existed between various intelligence centers. By the surrender date the newly created Joint Army-Navy Committee on the Japanese Air Forces estimated Japanese air strength in the homeland at 5,911. The intelligence center for the Commander in Chief Pacific Fleet (CINCPAC) calculated by August 13 that the Japanese had 10,290 aircraft available for homeland defense. The actual total was about 10,700.[27]

As this collage of alarming intelligence accumulated, it was passed to civilian and uniformed leaders. By July 29, Maj. Gen. Charles A. Willoughby, General MacArthur's intelligence chief, declared that further unchecked increase of Japanese strength on Kyushu threatened "to grow to [the] point where we attack on a ratio of one (1) to one (1) which is not the recipe for victory."[28]

Senior staff officers of the Joint Chiefs of Staff in Washington shared doubts about Olympic with Willoughby and Nimitz. "There is every indication that the Japanese have been giving the highest priority to the defense of Kyushu and particularly to southern Kyushu," noted the Joint Intelligence Committee (JIC) in an early August report. It rated southern Kyushu, followed by Shikoku, northern Kyushu, and the Kanto plain, as the focus of Japanese attention.[29]

The day the first atomic bomb was dropped on Hiroshima, August 6, in Washington the Joint War Plans Committee of the Joint Chiefs of Staff forwarded a report entitled "Alternatives to 'Olympic'" to the Joint Staff Plan-

26. Joint Intelligence Committee, "Japanese Reaction to an Assault on the Sendai Plain," J.I.C. 218/10, August 10, 1945 (final revision August 20, 1945); the total for Kyushu includes the Tsushima Fortress that was under the Fifty-sixth Army; Geographic File 1942–45, CCS 381 Honshu (7–19–44) Section 4, RG 218, Box 90, NARA.

27. SRS-486, July 19, 1945; SRS-507, August 9, 1945, and SRMD-008, p. 266, July 16, p. 2; August 13, p. 297, RG 457, NARA; United States Strategic Bombing Survey, Report No. 62, Military Analysis Division, *Japanese Air Power* (Washington, D.C.: U.S. Government Printing Office, 1946), 24–25, 70. For a discussion of the various numbers offered concerning Japanese air strength in the homeland, see Frank, *Downfall*, 182–83 and notes.

28. General Headquarters, United States Army Forces Pacific, Military Intelligence Section, General Staff, "Amendment No. 1 to G-2 Estimate of the Enemy Situation with Respect to Kyushu," July 29, 1945, p. 1, Gen. John J. Tolson Papers, U.S. Army Military History Institute (a copy is also in Record Group 4, Box 22, MacArthur Memorial Archive).

29. Joint War Plans Committee, J.W.P.C. 397, August 4, 1945 (with attached copy of "Defensive Preparations in Japan"), Joint Intelligence Committee, RG 218, NARA.

ners, a body just below the Joint Chiefs themselves. Noting the alarming fresh intelligence estimates of Japanese preparations on Kyushu, the committee observed: "The possible effect upon Olympic operations of this build-up and concentration is such that it is considered commanders in the field should review their estimates of the situation, reexamine objectives in Japan as possible alternatives to Olympic, and prepare plans for operations against such alternate objectives." An attached draft message to MacArthur and Nimitz commented that while the dramatic increase in Japanese strength did not yet require a change of the directive, it did compel focus on the prospects for Olympic and mandate that commanders formulate "alternate plans and submit timely recommendations." It advised, "Operations against extreme northern Honshu, against the Sendai area, and directly against the Kanto Plain are now under intensive study [in Washington]."[30]

The Joint Staff Planners formally reviewed these reports on August 8, two days after Hiroshima and one day before Nagasaki. Probably because of this timing, the minutes of their meeting show the planners temporized. They "took note of . . . the fact that the Joint War Plans Committee is preparing studies on alternate objectives with a view to presentation to the Joint Chiefs of Staff."[31]

But General Marshall had already acted. On August 7, Washington time, he sent the following dispatch to MacArthur:

Intelligence reports on Jap dispositions which have been presented to me and which I understand have been sent to your Staff are that the Japanese have undertaken a large buildup both of divisions and of air forces in Kyushu and Southern Honshu. The air buildup is reported as including a large component of suicide planes which the intelligence estimate here considers are readily available for employment only in the vicinity of their present bases. Concurrently with the reported reinforcement of Kyushu, the Japanese are reported to have reduced forces north of the Tokyo plain to a point where the defensive capabilities in Northern Honshu and Hokkaido appear to be extraordinarily weak viewed from the standpoint of the Japanese General Staff. The question has arisen in my mind as to whether the Japanese may not be including some deception in the sources from which our intelligence is being drawn.

In order to assist in discussions likely to arise here on the meaning of reported dispositions in Japan proper and possible alternate objectives to

30. Ibid.
31. Joint Staff Planners, Minutes of 213th Meeting, August 8, 1945, Xerox 1540, part 9, George C. Marshall Papers, Marshall Library.

Olympic, such as Tokyo, Sendai [northern Honshu], Ominato [extreme northern Honshu], I would appreciate your personal estimate of the Japanese intentions and capabilities as related to your current directive and available resources.

Marshall provided a copy of this message to Admiral William Leahy, Truman's chief of staff.[32]

"I am certain," intoned MacArthur in the expeditious "personal estimate" of August 9, "that the Japanese air potential reported to you as accumulating to counter our Olympic operation is greatly exaggerated." While he allowed the possibility of some increases on Kyushu, he deprecated "the heavy strengths reported to you in southern Kyushu." MacArthur insisted that Allied tactical airpower, in addition to the B-29 force, would "quickly seek out and destroy" Japanese air potential and "practically immobilize" and "greatly weaken" Japanese ground forces in southern Kyushu.

"In my opinion," declared MacArthur, "there should not be the slightest thought of changing the Olympic operation." The purpose of Olympic, he stressed, was to obtain air bases to cover a strike into "the industrial heart of Japan." Olympic was "sound and will be successful." After critiquing the proposed alternatives, MacArthur ended with a peroration that selectively recalled history and played up to Marshall's own admitted doubts that perhaps the Japanese had cleverly managed to hoodwink Ultra: "Throughout the Southwest Pacific Area campaigns, as we have neared an operation intelligence has invariably pointed to greatly increased enemy forces. Without exception, this buildup has been found to be erroneous. In this particular case, the destruction that is going on in Japan would seem to indicate that it is very probable that the enemy is resorting to deception."

MacArthur's conclusion contained an extraordinarily brazen lie about past history in his theater, where his intelligence officers consistently underestimated, not overestimated, Japanese strength. But behind this lie was something else. Marshall had observed to Secretary of War Henry Stimson in December 1944 that MacArthur was "so prone to exaggerate and so influenced by his own desires that it is difficult to trust his judgment."[33] It defies

32. OPD (WAR) [Marshall] to MACARTHUR WAR 45369; CINCAFPAC [MacArthur] to WARCOS [Marshall] C 31897, CINCPAC Command Summary, book 7, pp. 3508–10. The exchange is also found in OPD Top Secret Incoming Msg July 28–August 17, 1945, RG 165, Box 39, NARA.
33. Drea, *MacArthur's Ultra*, 180–85, 229–30; Diary of Henry S. Stimson, December 27, 1944, Yale University Library, New Haven, Conn.

logic to doubt that MacArthur's resort to falsehood now was motivated in large measure by his personal interest in commanding the greatest amphibious assault in history.

After receipt of MacArthur's self-serving estimate late on August 9 (Washington time), Admiral King moved to intervene decisively in the controversy over Olympic. He gathered both Marshall's original query and MacArthur's reply into a package and sent both "Eyes Only" to Nimitz asking CINCPAC for "your comments." But while King passed the order for a response "Eyes Only" to Nimitz, he required that Nimitz send a copy of his "comments" to MacArthur. King did not, however, set a deadline for Nimitz's response.

King clearly aimed to bring on an explosive interservice confrontation over Olympic, and probably the whole invasion strategy. On April 30, he had informed his colleagues on the Joint Chiefs of Staff that he agreed to permit orders to be issued for an invasion only so that the necessary preparations could be put in train to maintain that option. But he also had warned that the Joint Chiefs would be revisiting this issue in August or September. Now, precisely as he predicted, this had come to pass.[34]

Nimitz had advised King "Eyes Only" on May 25 that he no longer supported an invasion of Japan, and thus no army officer was aware of this fact. King now forced Nimitz either to avow support for Olympic (an action that can be safely ruled out given the intelligence developments since May 25) or to break the interservice consensus behind Olympic in particular and the invasion strategy in general. It was obvious that if Nimitz withdrew his endorsement of Olympic, he would create a major confrontation with the army institutionally, as well as personally between MacArthur and himself. By the time Nimitz received King's order, however, a second atomic bomb had been dropped and the Soviet Union had entered the war. Moreover, very shortly thereafter evidence appeared for the first time that Japan might be seriously contemplating peace. Indeed, the next major message from King to Nimitz, only some thirteen hours after the order for Nimitz to declare his position on Olympic, began, "This is a peace warning." Nimitz understandably hesitated to see if events would deliver him from the onerous duty of igniting what was certain to be a firestorm over American strategy to end the war.[35]

34. Memorandum for the Joint Chiefs of Staff, Subject: Campaign Against Japan, April 30, 1945, 381 POA (6–10–43), Sec. 12, RG 218, Box 169, NARA.
35. CINCPAC to COMINCH [commander in chief, U.S. Navy] 051725, May 1945, CINCPAC Command Summary, book 6, January 1945 to July 1945, Naval History Center, Washington, D.C. "Eyes Only" means a private communication between commanders that would not be available to anyone else, save perhaps the discrete communicator who performed

While Nimitz temporized, on August 12 Marshall received a situation estimate from Maj. Gen. Clayton Bissell, his chief intelligence officer. Bissell projected that "large, well disciplined, well armed, undefeated Japanese ground forces have a capacity to offer stubborn fanatic resistance to Allied ground operations in the homeland and may inflict heavy Allied casualties." Bissell further calculated, "Atomic bombs will not have a decisive effect in the next 30 days."[36] The following day, August 13, Maj. Gen. John E. Hull, the assistant chief of staff for operations at the War Department, telephoned Col. L. E. Seeman of the Manhattan Project at the express direction of General Marshall. Hull explained that the chief of staff believed the two atomic bombs "have had a tremendous effect on the Japanese as far as capitulation is concerned," but Marshall doubted that further atomic bombing would influence any Japanese decision to end the war. Therefore, Marshall commissioned Hull to examine an alternative strategy to reserve all additional atomic weapons produced and then deploy them in direct (that is, tactical) support of the invasion "rather than [on] industry, morale, psychology, etc." The upshot of this conference was an estimate that seven bombs probably would be ready for use by October 31.[37]

Thus, in the last weeks of the war American leaders faced the prospect that Ketsu-Go had made Olympic not unnecessary but unthinkable. They were embroiled in the opening moves of a massive confrontation between the army and navy over the whole invasion strategy.

Diplomatic Intercepts

As noted above, a major issue in the controversy over how the Pacific War ended surrounds American comprehension of Japanese diplomacy through

the coding and decoding. COMINCH AND CNO TO CINCPAC ADV HQ 092205, August 1945 (headed "KING TO NIMITZ EYES ONLY"), and attached copies of CIN-CAFPAC to WARCOS C 31897 and OPD (WAR) to MACARTHUR WAR 45369, CINCPAC Command Summary, book 7, pp. 3508–10, Naval History Center. This section of the Command Summary contains closely held or "Eyes Only" traffic. The daily narrative in the Command Summary is silent on this exchange. The conclusion that Nimitz never replied to King is based on an exhaustive search of voluminous message files, including those dealing with secret flag officer communications, with the invaluable assistance of the staff of the Naval History Center.

36. Maj. Gen. Clayton Bissell, Memorandum for the Chief of Staff, Subject: Estimate of the Japanese Situation for the Next 30 Days, August 12, 1945, RG 165, Entry 422, Box 12, Executive No. 2, Item No. 11, NARA.

37. Telephone conversation General Hull and Colonel "Seaman," 1325, August 13, 1945, Verifax 2691, George C. Marshall Papers, Marshall Library.

message intercepts. The significance of these messages, however, must be viewed in light of their full disclosures as to the authority and substance of Japanese peace maneuvers. They also must be judged against the backdrop of the military intercepts.

The body of evidence customarily cited by critics as evidence of Japan's efforts to end the war comprises an assortment of messages from Japanese diplomats as well as certain military or naval attachés in Europe. These individuals sent dispatches from Stockholm, Switzerland, and the Vatican. Some of them also contacted American diplomats or officers of the Office of Strategic Services (OSS). But the intercepts revealed that these individuals must be styled as "peace entrepreneurs" because none of them—with the sole exception of the Japanese ambassador in Moscow—represented the policy of the Japanese government. The official stand of the Japanese government was the Fundamental Policy adopted in June 1945 and expressly sanctioned by the emperor. This declared that Japan would fight to the finish. None of these diplomats in Europe possessed any official authority to deviate from that policy—a fact made clear to American policy makers by code breaking.[38]

The exception to this picture arose in extreme secrecy within an inner cabinet formally titled the Supreme Council for the Direction of the War. Known in shorthand as the Big Six, this body consisted of Prime Minister Suzuki Kantaro, Foreign Minister Togo Shigenori, Army Minister Anami Korechika, Navy Minister Yonai Mitsumasa, Chief of the Imperial Army General Staff Umezu Yoshijiro, and Chief of the Imperial Navy General Staff Toyoda Soemu. The Big Six contrived an initiative in May 1945 to secure the services of the Soviet Union as a mediator to negotiate an end to the war. The emperor intervened in June 1945 to buttress this effort by authorizing a special envoy acting in his name to pursue the démarche. What essentially prevented this initiative from success, and indeed what severed it from reality, was the requirement that the Big Six could act only with unanimous agreement. In fact, the Big Six could never agree upon what Japan would offer the Soviet Union for its services as a mediator. The Big Six never even reached a substantive discussion of what terms Japan would find acceptable

---

38. Frank, *Downfall*, 86–102, 114–15. A recent and comprehensive restatement of the thesis that the Magic Diplomatic Summary and Office of Strategic Service reports demonstrated that Japan was actively seeking peace may be found in Gar Alperovitz, *The Decision to Use the Atomic Bomb and the Architecture of an American Myth* (New York: Alfred A. Knopf, 1995), 23–28, 292–93, 295–97. Interestingly, even Alperovitz concedes, "None of these approaches, of course, carried formal official authorization, and, accordingly, were treated with considerable caution."

for terminating hostilities because War Minister Anami insisted that Japan had not lost the war.[39]

Thanks to the diligent work of U.S. and British code breakers, Japan's secret diplomatic traffic was routinely available to policy makers. The intercepts appeared in a daily publication known as the Magic Diplomatic Summary. This summary was distributed to a select band of officials, with the White House at the top of the list. But in order to maintain security, the daily summaries were available for perusal only for that day. After the policy maker examined his copy, it was retrieved and all but a record copy destroyed. Hence, the editors of the summary drafted it like a small daily newspaper. Topics appeared under headlines. The editors provided continuity and context for the messages because the recipients did not have a library of back copies. The editors employed both summary and verbatim quotation of key passages from the messages.[40]

Besides the Magic Diplomatic Summary the intervention by the emperor in June 1945 with regard to the Soviet initiative also generated a separate analysis. This was forwarded on June 13 to General Marshall, who was at the Potsdam conference. This analysis termed the prospect that the initiative represented a genuine effort of the emperor to intervene in favor of peace despite opposition from the military as "remote." It assessed as the probable motivating force behind this move a well-coordinated effort by the Japanese government to stave off defeat in the belief that Soviet intervention could be purchased at a proper price and that an attractive peace offer would appeal to war weariness in the United States. The message to General Marshall noted that Assistant Secretary of State Joseph Grew, the leading Japanese expert within the U.S. government, agreed with these conclusions.[41]

A reading of all of Magic Diplomatic Summaries does not disclose a Japan teetering near capitulation. First, as noted above, the summaries clearly reveal that only the effort through the Japanese ambassador to Moscow carried any official sanction. Second, an examination of the exchanges between the Japanese ambassador to Moscow and the foreign minister discloses a chasm between Japanese aspirations and any real prospect for peace. The Japanese ambassador in Moscow was Sato Naotake, a former foreign minister. He was not one to mince words at this time of crisis. Sato challenged the very bona fides of the effort. He demanded to know on July 15 whether the effort car-

39. Alperovitz, *Decision to Use the Bomb,* 101–2, 227–28.

40. Ibid., 104–5.

41. Memorandum for the Deputy Chief of Staff from Deputy Assistant Chief of Staff, G-2, July 13, 1945, reel 109, item 2581, Marshall Library.

ried any official sanction from the government and military in light of the Fundamental Policy adopted in early June to continue the war to the end.[42]

Sato's wires also raised a constant refrain: there was no prospect of enlisting Soviet help unless Japan could articulate concrete terms for ending the war. On July 13, Sato flatly told Tokyo that the best Japan could hope for was "virtually [the] equivalent of unconditional surrender." On July 17, Foreign Minister Togo responded with a message pointing out: "Please bear particularly in mind, however, that we are not seeking the Russians' mediation for anything like unconditional surrender." This provoked a rejoinder from Ambassador Sato in Moscow that he wished to clarify his position—that when he stated that the best Japan would hope for was virtually unconditional surrender, he meant that this must include the maintenance of the imperial institution. The Magic Diplomatic Summary of July 22, 1945, correctly informed its readers that Sato's message had "advocated unconditional surrender provided the Imperial House was preserved." Thus, the Magic Diplomatic Summary demonstrates that the concept of a modified unconditional surrender assuring the continuation of the imperial institution was placed squarely before the key decision makers in Japan in mid-July 1945. This is precisely the diplomatic move that critics argued could have procured Japan's surrender without recourse to atomic bombs. What then was the foreign minister's reply? Togo responded flatly that Japan was unable to consent to unconditional surrender "under any circumstances whatever."[43] Thus, the Magic Diplomatic Summary shows that U.S. policy makers could see by July 22, 1945, that merely advancing some guarantee of the imperial institution was not sufficient to obtain a Japanese capitulation.

But still more telling than the contents of these diplomatic intercepts is their context. The relative trickle of diplomatic intercepts stood in contrast to a torrent of military intercepts. Those military intercepts demonstrated without exception that Japan was preparing for a final battle at the very sites of the proposed invasion. No American decision maker in 1945 doubted that it was the militarists, not Japan's Foreign Service, that dominated policy making in Japan. Nor could any American policy maker forget that Japanese diplomats were conducting sham negotiations in Washington at the time of Pearl Harbor. Thus, there was not one stream of intercepts but two. And the one that carried the most weight demonstrated not only that there was no

42. Magic Diplomatic Summary No. 1208, July 16, 1945, RG 457, NARA.
43. Ibid., No. 1206, July 14; No. 1207, July 15; No. 1212, July 18; No. 1214, July 20; No. 1215, July 21; No. 1216, July 22, 1945.

prospect for negotiation to end the war but also that American presumptions as late as June 1945 as to the prospects for an invasion were grossly wrong.

II. The Farewell Address

The Decision

What might have struck Harry Truman as one of the oddest twists in the controversy over the atomic bombs is the dispute over whether he, in fact, "decided" to use them. On the one hand, historian Gar Alperovitz agrees with President Truman in a backhanded fashion. In *The Decision to Use the Atomic Bomb and the Architecture of an American Myth,* Alperovitz argues that American leaders consciously chose to use the atomic bombs, even though they realized the bombs no longer were needed to secure Japan's surrender. Ulterior purposes motivated that choice, specifically the intimidation of the Soviet Union. The late Stanley Goldberg advanced a mutation of this position. He allowed that the bombs might well have been used to save lives and to intimidate the Soviets. But Goldberg argued that two other factors weighed in the decision to use the bomb: the desire of the civilian and military leaders who directed the Manhattan Project to protect their reputations, and the manipulations fueled by the personal ambitions of the project's director, Maj. Gen. Leslie Groves.[44]

The rival school ironically argues that Truman did not make a decision in the robust sense that the president himself carefully examined and weighed alternatives or settled a division among his advisers. This school presents the events as the virtually inevitable implementation of a long-standing assumption. That assumption, born at the same moment as the decision to create the bomb, was that if it would work, it would be used.[45] As *Downfall* records, the presumption that the bomb would be used represented

> a key element in Roosevelt's potent legacy to Truman. Thus, any notion that these policy makers agonized over the question of use or that Truman

44. Alperovitz, *Decision to Use the Bomb,* 466–70, 496, 516–21, 569–70, 627–28, 747, 758–59; Stanley Goldberg, "Racing to the Finish," in *Hiroshima's Shadow: Writings on the Denial of History and the Smithsonian Controversy,* ed. Kai Bird and Lawrence Lifschultz (Stony Creek, Conn.: Pamphleteer's Press, 1998).

45. The earliest articulation of this thesis was by Barton Bernstein in "Roosevelt, Truman, and the Atomic Bomb, 1941–45: A Reinterpretation," *Political Science Quarterly* 90 (Spring 1975): 23–69. It is instructive that David McCullough in his Pulitzer Prize–winning biography of Truman incorporates this theme; see *Truman* (New York: Simon and Schuster, 1992), 424–25, 435–44.

made a personal and lonely decision to use the bomb misconstrues the decision process. Later, Groves stated that Truman's decision was one of non-interference—basically, a "decision not to upset the existing plans." But Truman's noninterference transpired in the context of a policy that arrived before him carrying the unanimous sanction of his principal advisers on the issue, all of whom save Byrnes had similarly served Roosevelt. None of these advisers had been moved to reexamine the issue of use, and thus there was no catalyst for Truman to do so.[46]

With the benefit of further reflection on these matters and particularly on Truman himself, I would amend my analysis. It still remains, in my view, best to regard these events objectively as a process involving the implementation of an assumption. Further, Ultra and Magic disclosures on the Japanese build-up to resist the invasion and Japanese diplomacy certainly buttressed any assumption about using the bombs. These disclosures would almost certainly have trumped any substantive challenge to unleashing nuclear weapons. But the implementation of an assumption framework ignores or understates another aspect of the process. As Truman had not been party to the secret of the atomic bomb, as were his advisers, it cannot be fairly argued that he was operating from the same long-standing assumption. Moreover, even if you see the order as inevitable in the context of the objective circumstances of July 1945, Truman knew what anyone with command responsibility knows: you bear the ultimate responsibility for acts or omissions on your watch. Thus, when Harry Truman emphasized it was his decision, he was affirming his enormous subjective sense of ultimate responsibility.

Casualties

In the Farewell Address, Truman justified the use of the atomic bombs against Japan on essentially utilitarian grounds. He maintained that the reason he authorized their use was to save lives, both American and Japanese. The number of lives saved he figured to be in the hundreds of thousands. Among the many strands within the controversy over the atomic bombs, this is the area labeled as "the casualty issue." It bids to be the most passionately debated part of the controversy.

The main lines of the debate are as follows. Critics allege that there was no contemporary justification for the huge figures for potential American losses to invade Japan offered after the war by Truman and members of his

46. Frank, *Downfall*, 257.

government, particularly Secretary of War Stimson. They hold that the contemporary documents, particularly those prepared for a key meeting on June 18, 1945, provide far lower figures. They vehemently insist that there is no contemporary support for the assertion by Stimson in an influential article in 1947 that U.S. losses could have reached the one million range. They also point out that Truman after 1945 was inconsistent in his statements about potential U.S. casualties and at various times offered numbers from the hundreds of thousands to a half-million deaths. In sum, they essentially charge that U.S. leaders in 1945 did not fear huge U.S. casualties and therefore retrospective citation of such numbers is not only without justification and thus false, but also constitutes evidence that there must have been some other "real reason" the United States used atomic bombs.[47]

Truman's defenders have countered with various arguments. Many of them, particularly veterans who were earmarked to participate in the invasion of Japan, insist just as vehemently that one million casualties is realistic. To some of them, the one million figure has assumed talismanic significance.[48] I believe that Truman's defenders are far closer to the truth than his critics, but the reasons for this are more complex than most of his defenders have articulated. Here, however, there is only space for a synopsis.

Let me start with a brief tutorial for those unversed in the military lexicon. The word *casualty* is not a synonym for *death*. "Casualties" include service members who are killed, wounded, and missing. "Missing" is a category for those unaccounted for after battle. They may be prisoners of war, or they may have been killed, but their remains have not been recovered. The ratio of those killed to those wounded was roughly four to one, with the missing constituting an additional few percentage points of the total ground casualties. Against the Japanese, missing usually translated into dead, but with the remains not recovered. In sea and air combat, the ratios of killed to wounded generally ran closer to one to one. More individuals went missing, but again most of them perished.[49]

47. Alperovitz, *Decision to Use the Bomb*, 466–70, 496, 516–21, 569–70, 627–28, 747, 758–59; Goldberg, "Racing to the Finish"; Barton Bernstein, "A Postwar Myth: 500,000 Lives Saved," *Bulletin of Atomic Scientists* 42 (June–July 1986): 38–40; Rufus Miles, "Hiroshima: The Strange Myth of a Half Million Lives Saved," *International Security* 10 (Fall 1985): 121–40. The key postwar article on the use of the bombs by Henry L. Stimson was "The Decision to Use the Atomic Bomb," *Harper's*, February 1947.

48. Robert P. Newman, *Truman and the Hiroshima Cult* (East Lansing: Michigan State University Press, 1995); D. M. Giangreco, "Casualty Projections for the U.S. Invasions of Japan, 1945–46: Planning and Policy Implications," *Journal of Military History* 61 (July 1997): 521–81; Paul Fussel, *Thank God for the Atomic Bomb and Other Essays* (New York: Summit Books, 1998).

49. *Army Battle Casualties*, 5, 10; Navy Department, Division of Medical Statistics, Bureau of Medicine and Surgery, *The History of the Medical Department of the United States Navy in*

While casualties certainly figured in the strategic deliberations of the JCS, it was almost invariably only on a broad subjective basis. The key reason for this was that there were too many variables, some of which were always unknown beforehand, to predict casualties precisely. In fact, there was no agreed method for making such predictions either at the level of the JCS or even between the two Pacific Theater commanders.[50] Efforts at quantitative estimates of potential casualties rested in the warrants of those charged with providing personnel replacements and medical treatment.

What is unusual about the invasion of Japan is that for once the JCS did find the issue of such significance that it was addressed quantitatively. In the final paper adopted by the JCS as its policy statement on the invasion, there is a section on casualties. This section, however, does not give absolute totals. Rather it offers analogies to protracted operations in Europe and a sample of Pacific campaigns. These analogies are drawn only as a formula for casualties per thousands of men committed to the campaign per day. Obtaining an overall figure requires taking the formula in that paper and multiplying it out, using the number of men committed and an estimated length for the campaign in days. When you do this you get eye-popping numbers ranging from approximately 349,000 to 1.2 million for Downfall.[51]

Throughout 1945, Secretary of War Stimson was plagued by profound doubts as to whether he had made a grave error in setting the size of the army ground forces. He feared the army was too small to finish the war with both Germany and particularly Japan. In this running controversy, he commissioned an outside study by two academics to determine whether the selective service system and the army were properly geared to draft and to train sufficient men to meet the demands of finishing the war with Japan. This study affirmed the plans in effect. Those plans provided for 1.2 million men to enter

---

World War II, The Statistics of Disease and Injuries, Navmed P-1318, vol. 3 (Washington, D.C.: U.S. Government Printing Office, 1950), 3, 170.

50. Giangreco, "Casualty Projections," 528–31. Compare the casualty projections by Nimitz of 49,000 for the first thirty days alone with projections of 22,576 by MacArthur's staff for the same period. Even subtracting the 5,000 navy casualties that Nimitz includes and MacArthur's staff did not incorporate, the difference is still almost 100 percent. Commander in Chief Pacific and Pacific Ocean Area, Joint Staff Study OLYMPIC Naval and Amphibious Operation, Preliminary Draft, May 13, 1945, RG 165, Box 1842, NARA; MacArthur to Marshall, June 16, 1945, RG 4, USAFPAC Correspondence, WD Folder 4, MacArthur Memorial Archive. As for the JCS, see the paper cited in the next note in which two different formulas were set out that produced widely different projections.

51. Joint Chiefs of Staff, JCS 924/15, April 25, 1945, CCS 381 Pacific Ocean Operations (6–10–43), Sec. 12, RG 218, NARA; Frank, *Downfall,* 136–37. What this formula did in effect was ignore all the unknowable variables in favor of the only two numbers that U.S. officers could obtain with certainty: U.S. losses and the number of days of the campaign.

the services on an annual basis from June 1945. Of these, the army alone planned to turn out about 764,000 infantry replacements. In other words, in 1945 America was prepared to replace more than one million men in its armed forces each annum.[52]

Truman called a meeting in June 1945 to address the invasion of Japan. The memorandum summoning the JCS to this conference explicitly stated that casualties were his chief concern. In preparation for this meeting, the army massaged the estimates downward to produce projections of 193,500 casualties for Olympic and Coronet, of which 43,500 would be deaths. But the army did not even present these numbers to Truman. Rather, it simply presented some analogies of loss ratios in various Pacific battles.[53]

Then, as noted above, the radio intelligence revelations demonstrated that Japanese strength on Kyushu and before Tokyo vastly exceeded prior estimates, thus implying drastically greater casualties. As far as we know, however, no one bothered to attempt a recalculation of likely casualties. Instead, the validity of the whole operation was placed in doubt. When Truman met with his key advisers to examine the initial Japanese peace proposal on August 10, Secretary of War Stimson warned that if an organized capitulation of Japanese armed forces could not be obtained, the United States might face "a score of bloody Iwo Jimas and Okinawas all over China and the New Netherlands (Indonesia)." A score of Iwo Jimas translates into 634,100 casualties (including 171,720 killed and missing), while a score of Okinawas equals 982,660 casualties (including 250,400 killed and missing).[54] And Stimson's remarks *do not* include casualties in an invasion of Japan.

So what does all this tell us about the great controversy as to potential American losses in an invasion of Japan? First, the root problem was that no American policy maker knew with assurance whether it would be possible to obtain an organized surrender by Japan's government and armed forces. If Japan's armed forces did not surrender, the United States faced an unpre-

52. Robert R. Palmer, Bell I. Wiley, and William R. Keast, *The Procurement and Training of Ground Combat Troops* (Washington, D.C.: Office of the Chief of Military History, Department of the Army 1948), "The Provision of Enlisted Replacements"; *Selective Service and Victory: The Fourth Report of the Director of Selective Service* (Washington, D.C.: U.S. Government Printing Office 1948), table 140, p. 595.

53. Memorandum to JCS, June 17, 1945, Xerox 1567, George C. Marshall Papers, Marshall Library; JWPC 369/1, "Details of the Campaign Against Japan," June 15, 1945, ABC 385, RG 319, NARA; JCS 1388, June 16, 1945, "Details of the Campaign against Japan," Report by the Joint Staff Planners, Geographic File 1942–45, 381 Japan (6-14-45), RG 218, Box 118, NARA; "Minutes of Meeting Held at White House on Monday, June 18, 1945."

54. Diary of Henry S. Stimson, August 10, 1945, Yale University Library.

dictable future with the prospect of defeating in detail four to five million Japanese combatants across the home islands, the Asian continent, and the Pacific. This was the scenario Secretary of War Stimson referred to in his 1947 article that used the million figure. Cast in this light, there is nothing exaggerated about such a number. Indeed, Stimson by analogy made the same point on August 10, 1945, long before any controversy arose, so the argument that the million number was invented after the fact has no validity. Second, there was no single officially sanctioned method for estimating potential casualties. Third, anyone of ordinary common sense could foresee that American casualties might fall anywhere along a wide spectrum ranging from the hundreds of thousands to a million. Indeed, if the campaign in Japan degenerated into guerrilla warfare stretching out for years as Admiral Leahy cautioned at the meeting on June 18, 1945, it was by no means clear that a million was the top end of the range.[55] The reality that there was a spectrum of realistic numbers also is consistent with the fact that various numbers were provided by Truman over the years.

More important, there is no doubt that Truman and others were profoundly concerned about casualties. The written record shows Truman stated this clearly in June 1945. Certainly, Secretary of War Stimson was concerned. The navy, in fact, believed that an actual invasion of Japan was folly precisely because of the likely huge casualties, but the navy did not bother to quantify that number; instead, King aimed for the jugular: kill any invasion plan in August or September 1945. Only the army, and only to sell the invasion in June, jiggled the estimates downward—probably because the army sincerely believed what proved to be faulty estimates of likely Japanese strength. Finally, as to American casualties, by early August 1945 it was startling clear from radio intelligence that any prior estimate of U.S. losses was woefully inadequate because it did not account for the huge increases in Japanese deployment to meet Olympic and Coronet.

There is yet another dimension to the casualty issue that, in my view, has not been sufficiently factored into this debate. Soviet intervention was not cost free in terms of civilian casualties. On the Asian continent, some 2.7 million Japanese nationals fell into Soviet hands in 1945. Only a third of these were military personnel. Of this total, between about 340,000 and 370,000 died or disappeared in Soviet hands. Most of these were civilians. As we now know, the Soviets were on the cusp of landing on Hokkaido, the main northerly home island, as the war ended. Had the Soviets seized

55. "Minutes of Meeting Held at White House on Monday, June 18, 1945."

Hokkaido and inflicted the same loss on civilians, another 400,000 Japanese would have perished. In China, some ten to possibly twenty-two million died during World War II, about 80 percent of them noncombatants.[56] That is a rate of approximately 100,000 to 200,000 per month. Thus, permitting the war to continue added to the Chinese death toll at that rate. Finally, as I discuss in detail in a chapter in *What If? 2*, had the war continued for even a few weeks, the switch of American strategic bombing to the Japanese rail system would have triggered a famine that would have killed millions of Japanese by November 1946.[57] Thus, alternatives to the nuclear weapons were not cost free, nor did the use of the bombs represent the most costly manner in which the war might end.

The Omissions

For good reason, allied radio intelligence success in World War II was called the Ultra Secret. For nearly thirty years only modest fragments of the story about American success against Japanese codes leaked out, primarily involving the intercepts prior to Pearl Harbor, the success before the Battle of Midway, and a few diplomatic intercepts in 1945. A veil remained over the massive penetration of Japanese systems, and a complete blackout masked the success against the German cryptographic systems.[58]

There are two fundamental reasons the secret was preserved. The first was the honor of those with knowledge of the success who observed their pledge of silence. It is amazing that literally thousands possessed at least some part of the secret, yet with only a handful of exceptions, nothing leaked out. A good example is the diary of Secretary of War Stimson. Although the diary

56. William F. Nimmo, *Behind a Curtain of Silence: Japanese in Soviet Custody, 1945–1956* (New York: Greenwood Press, 1998), chap. 7, esp. 115–17; John Dower, *War without Mercy: Race and Power in the Pacific War* (New York: Pantheon, 1986), 298–99, and *Embracing Defeat*, 50; Frank, *Downfall*, 356. Chinese fatalities in the ten million range are reported in Newman, *Truman and the Hiroshima Cult*, 134–39, and Dower, *War without Mercy*, 295–96. Weinberg's magisterial *World at Arms*, 894, gives fifteen million as a "reasonable approximation," and Dower, *Embracing Defeat*, sets the number as "perhaps 15 million." The twenty-two million figure is from James C. Hsiung and Steven I. Levine, eds., *China's Bitter Victory* (New York: M. E. Sharpe, 1992), 295 and note. Hsiung based his figures on work in Chinese archives in Nanking. The lowest-range numbers are two million, mentioned by Newman and Dower; however, these appear to be confined to military losses.

57. Richard B. Frank, "No Bomb: No End," in *What If? 2*, ed. Robert Cowley (New York: G. P. Putnam's Sons, 2001).

58. Frank, *Downfall*, 103–6.

contains many references to the atomic bomb, it contains no recognizable references to code breaking. But I suspect that another reason the secret was maintained was pragmatic. Because the recipients only had transitory opportunities to read intelligence reports based on Ultra or Magic, and were forbidden to maintain written records, it would have been nearly impossible for any policy maker to recall details of the intercepts. For example, just between April 12 and August 15, the daily Magic Diplomatic Summary provided to President Truman totaled 2,068 pages. Military intercepts would have at least equaled this number.[59]

Had Truman or the members of his government been at liberty to set out the evidence provided by radio intelligence, it is hard to envision the controversy arising, or certainly evolving as it did. What might President Truman have said? I would suggest the following amendments to the Farewell Address would have summarized his case.

> Meanwhile, the first atomic explosion took place out in the New Mexico desert.
>
> The war against Japan was still going on. We did not know whether the Japanese government would surrender. We did not know whether the millions of Japanese soldiers and sailors under arms would obey the decision of the government to surrender. We knew from decoded Japanese messages that Japanese leaders in Tokyo would not accept a surrender that would deprive them of the power to rule Japan and prepare for another war. We also knew that they were preparing a gigantic battle against our planned invasion and that they had anticipated exactly where we intended to land. With this knowledge, I made the decision that the atomic bomb had to be used to end the war. I made the decision with the conviction it would save hundreds of thousands of lives—Japanese as well as American.

With these phrases President Truman could have set out the key facts about this momentous event and probably foreclosed or reshaped any subsequent controversy. But to do so would have been to damage his country with startling revelations about what came to be called Ultra Secret. Perhaps characteristically, even when his personal reputation was near a nadir, Harry Truman refused to place self above country.

---

59. Magic Diplomatic Summaries, April 12 to August 15, 1945, RG 457, NARA. The page count is my own. It includes the appendixes.

July 25 1945

We met at 11 A.M. today. That is Stalin, Churchill and the U.S. President. But I had a most important session with Lord Mountbatten & General Marshall before that. We have discovered the most terrible bomb in the history of the world. It may be the fire distruction prophesied in the Euphrates Valley Era, after Noah and his fabulous Ark.

Anyway we think we have found the way to cause a disintegration of the atom. An experiment in the New Mexican desert was startling — to put it mildly. Thirteen pounds of the explosive caused the complete disintegration of a steel tower 60 feet high, created a crater 6 feet deep and 1200 feet in diameter, knocked over a steel tower ½ mile away and knocked men down 10,000 yards away. The explosion was visible for more than 200 miles and audible for 40 miles and more.

This weapon is to be used against Japan between now and August 10th. I have told the Sec. of War, Mr Stimson to use it so that military objectives and soldiers and sailors are the target and not women and children. Even if the Japs are savages, ruthless, merciless and fanatic, we as the leader of the world for the common welfare cannot drop this terrible bomb on the old Capitol or the new.

He & I are in accord. The target will be a purely military one and we will issue a warning state-ment asking the Japs to surrender and save lives. I'm sure they will not do that, but we will have given them the chance. It is certainly a good thing for the world that Hitlers crowd or Stalins didnot discover this atomic bomb. It seems to be the most terrible thing ever discovered, but it can be made the most useful

136

At 10:15 I had Gen. Marshall come in and discuss with me the tactical and political situation. He is a level headed man — so is Montgomery.

At the Conference Poland and the Bolshviki land grab came up. Russia helped herself to a slice of Poland and gave Poland a nice slice of Germany taking also a good slice of East Prussia for herself. Poland has moved in up to the Oder and the west Niesse, taking Stettin and Silesia as a fait accomplished. My position is that according to commitment made at Yalta by my predecessor Germany was to be divided into four occupation zones, one each for Britain, Russia and France and the U.S. If Russia chooses to allow Poland to occupy a part of her zone I am agreeable but title to territory cannot and will not be settled here. For the fourth time I restated my position and explained that territorial cessions had to be made by treaty and ratified by the Senate.

We discussed reparations and movement of populations from East Germany, Czekoslavakia, Austria Italy and elsewhere. Churchill said Maisky had so defined war booty as to include the German fleet and merchant marine, It was a bomb shell and sort of paralyzed the Russkies, but it has a lot of merit.

AUG 7 9 05 PM 1945

WU8O LG GOVT

WINDER GA AUG 7 427P

THE PRESIDENT

(PERSONAL DELIVERY) THE WHITE HOUSE

PERMIT ME TO RESPECTFULLY SUGGEST THAT WE CEASE OUR EFFORTS TO
CAJOLE JAPAN INTO SURRENDERING IN ACCORDANCE WITH THE POTSDAM
DECLARATION. LET US CARRY THE WAR TO THEM UNTIL THEY BEG US TO
ACCEPT THE UNCONDITIONAL SURRENDER. THE FOUL ATTACK ON PEARL
HARBOR BROUGHT US INTO WAR AND I AM UNABLE TO SEE ANY VALID
REASON WHY WE SHOULD BE SO MUCH MORE CONSIDERATE AND LENIENT
IN DEALING WITH JAPAN THAN WITH GERMANY. I EARNESTLY INSIST
JAPAN SHOULD BE DEALT WITH AS HARSHLY AS GERMANY AND THAT SHE

SHOULD NOT BE THE BENEFICIARY OF A SOFT PEACE. THE VAST MAJORITY
OF THE AMERICAN PEOPLE, INCLUDING MANY SOUND THINKERS WHO HAVE
INTIMATE KNOWLEDGE OF THE ORIENT, DO NOT AGREE WITH MR. GREW IN
HIS ATTITUDE THAT THERE IS ANY THING SACROSANCT ABOUT HIROHITO.
HE SHOULD GO. WE HAVE NO OBLIGATION TO SHINTOLISM. THE COMPTEMT-
UOUS ANSWER OF THE JAPS TO THE POTSDAM ULTIMATUM JUSTIFIES A
REVISION OF THAT DOCUMENT AND STERNER PEACE TERMS.

IF WE DO NOT HAVE AVAILABLE A SUFFICIENT NUMBER OF ATOMIC
BOMBS WITH WHICH TO FINISH THE JOB IMMEDIATELY, LET US CARRYON
WITH TNT AND FIRE BOMBS UNTIL WE CAN PRODUCE THEM.

I ALSO HOPE THAT YOU WILL ISSUE ORDERS FORBIDDING THE
OFFICERS IN COMMAND OF OUR AIR FORCES FROM WARNING JAP CITIES

THAT THEY WILL BE ATTACKED. THESE GENERALS DO NOT FLY OVER JAPAN AND THIS SHOWMANSHIP CAN ONLY RESULT IN THE UNNECESSARY LOSS OF MANY FINE BOYS IN OUR AIR FORCE AS WELL AS OUR HELPLESS PRISONERS IN THE HANDS OF THE JAPANESE, INCLUDING THE SURVIVORS OF THE MARCH OF DEATH ON BATAAN WHO ARE CERTAIN TO BE BROUGHT INTO THE CITIES THAT HAVE BEEN WARNED.

THIS WAS A TOTAL WAR AS LONG AS OUR ENEMIES HELD ALL OF THE CARDS. WHY SHOULD WE CHANGE THE RULES NOW, AFTER THE BLOOD, TREASURE AND ENTERPRISE OF THE AMERICAN PEOPLE HAVE GIVEN US THE UPPER HAND. OUR PEOPLE HAVE NOT FORGOTTEN THAT THE JAPANESE STRUCK US THE FIRST BLOW IN THIS WAR WITHOUT THE SLIGHTEST WARNING. THEY BELIEVE THAT WE SHOULD CONTINUE TO STRIKE THE JAPANESE UNTIL THEY

ARE BROUGHT GROVELING TO THEIR KNEES. WE SHOULD CEASE OUR APPEALS TO JAPAN TO SUE FOR PEACE. THE NEXT PLEA FOR PEACE SHOULD COME FROM AN UTTERLY DESTROYED TOKYO. WELCOME BACK HOME. WITH ASSURAN-CES OF ESTEEM

RICHARD B RUSSELL US SENATOR.

August 9, 1945

Dear Dick:

I read your telegram of August seventh with a lot of interest.

I know that Japan is a terribly cruel and uncivilized nation in warfare but I can't bring myself to believe that, because they are beasts, we should ourselves act in the same manner.

For myself, I certainly regret the necessity of wiping out whole populations because of the "pigheadedness" of the leaders of a nation and, for your information, I am not going to do it unless it is absolutely necessary. It is my opinion that after the Russians enter into war the Japanese will very shortly fold up.

My object is to save as many American lives as possible but I also have a humane feeling for the women and children in Japan.

Sincerely yours,

HARRY S. TRUMAN

Honorable Richard B. Russell
Winder
Georgia

140

WB71 114 2 EXTRA

AUG 9 11 22 AM 1945

WUX NEWYORK NY AUG 9 1945 1046A

HONORABLE HARRY S TRUMAN

PRESIDENT OF THE UNITED STATES THE WHITE HOUSE

MANY CHRISTIANS DEEPLY DISTURBED OVER USE OF ATOMIC BOMBS
AGAINST JAPANESE CITIES BECAUSE OF THEIR NECESSARILY
INDISCRIMINATE DESTRUCTIVE EFFORTS AND BECAUSE THEIR USE SETS
EXTREMELY DANGEROUS PRECEDENT FOR FUTURE OF MANKIND. BISHOP
OXNAM PRESIDENT OF THE COUNCIL AND JOHN FOSTER DULES CHAIRMAN
OF ITS COMMISSION ON A JUST AND DURABLE PEACE ARE PREPARING
STATEMENT FOR PROBABLE RELEASE TOMORROW URGING THAT ATOMIC
BOMBS BE REGARDED AS TRUST FOR HUMANITY AND THAT JAPANESE

NATION BE GIVEN GENUINE OPPORTUNITY AND TIME TO VERIFY FACTS
ABOUT NEW BOMB AND TO ACCEPT SURRENDER TERMS. RESPECTFULLY
URGE THAT AMPLE OPPORTUNITY BE GIVEN JAPAN TO RECONSIDER
ULTIMATUM BEFORE ANY FURTHER DEVASTATION BY ATOMIC BOMB IS
VISITED UPON HER PEOPLE

FEDERAL COUNCIL OF THE CHURCHES OF CHRIST IN AMERICA

SAMUEL MCCREA CAVERT   GENERAL SECRETARY.

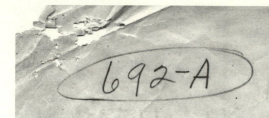

August 11, 1945

My dear Mr. Cavert:

I appreciated very much your telegram of
August ninth.

Nobody is more disturbed over the use of
Atomic bombs than I am but I was greatly   × PP7 1
disturbed over the unwarranted attack by   × 197-
the Japanese on Pearl Harbor and their
murder of our prisoners of war. The only   × 400 N.
language they seem to understand is the
one we have been using to bombard them.   ×190-8

When you have to deal with a beast you have   ×197
to treat him as a beast. It is most re-
grettable but nevertheless true.

                    Sincerely yours,

                        HARRY S. TRUMAN

Mr. Samuel McCrea Cavert   × PP7 33
General Secretary
Federal Council of   × 213
     The Churches of Christ in America
New York City, New York

×692-A-Misc.

142

Harry S. Truman, History, and Internationalism

The 1953 Farewell Address and U.S. Foreign Relations

Mary Ann Heiss

Fewer than a dozen paragraphs of Harry S. Truman's Farewell Address to the American People deal with what might be termed general foreign policy or international relations. Yet these relatively brief passages highlight some of the most important and far-reaching international initiatives in U.S. history: the founding of the United Nations in 1945; the expulsion of Soviet troops from Iran in 1946; the Truman Doctrine in the spring of 1947; the Marshall Plan that June; the Berlin airlift of 1948–1949; the postwar U.S. military assistance program; and the postwar U.S.-initiated security pacts. Truman's motivation in enumerating his foreign policy successes, as Richard Kirkendall makes clear, was to rebut contemporary critics who viewed his presidency as a failure, particularly in the area of foreign relations. Given Truman's keen sense of history, he was writing for future readers as well. For in the end, Truman believed that historians, not his contemporaries, would set his reputation and rank him in relation to his thirty-two predecessors—and, as of this writing, now ten successors. As he himself proclaimed, "It's our duty to tell our viewpoint, and then let future generations decide what's right and wrong."[1] Although Truman was not speaking directly about the Farewell

---

1. Truman's sentiments on the role of historians in judging his presidential record are expressed in Ralph E. Weber, ed., *Talking with Harry: Candid Conversations with President Harry*

Address here, his remarks surely sum up his sentiments about one of its purposes.

During his time in the White House, Harry Truman's approval ratings were, quite simply, abysmal. Poll after poll taken throughout his presidency revealed substantial voter criticism, rising dissatisfaction with his job performance, and general concern about his fitness for office. At its lowest point (late 1951), his approval rating was only 23 percent, lower even than Richard Nixon's at the peak of the Watergate scandal. To be sure, Truman's poor standing was not solely related to his foreign policy. Critics of that policy were vocal enough, however, to create the popular perception that Truman's foreign policy record left much to be desired.[2]

As Truman no doubt expected, historians have been much kinder, and polls and surveys of scholars have consistently judged him a successful president. Some polls count him among the nation's all-time ten "best" chief executives. Others rank him as "near great," just a notch below the agreed-upon "big four": Abraham Lincoln, Franklin D. Roosevelt, George Washington, and Thomas Jefferson. Truman's Farewell Address, while not the source of the thirty-third president's rising status among historians, certainly makes a case for high standing by laying out his accomplishments, both generally and in the specific case of foreign relations. With regard to the latter, many of those traits on which Truman has been judged most highly, such as toughness and decisiveness, are directly evident in his administration's various international initiatives.[3]

S. Truman (Wilmington, Del.: SR Books, 2001), 96. On the president's desire to defend his record in the Farewell Address, see, in addition to Kirkendall's Introduction, above, Halford R. Ryan, *Harry S. Truman: Presidential Rhetoric* (Westport, Conn.: Greenwood Press, 1993), 127–32. Truman's love of history is noted throughout his two-volume memoirs: *Memoirs*, vol. 1, *Year of Decisions,* and vol. 2, *Years of Trial and Hope* (Garden City: Doubleday, 1955–1956). See also Francis H. Heller, ed., *The Truman White House: The Administration of the Presidency, 1945–1953* (Lawrence: Regents Press of Kansas, 1980), 46.

2. See William E. Pemberton, *Harry S. Truman: Fair Dealer and Cold Warrior* (Boston: Twayne, 1989), ii, and Bruce Kuklick, *The Good Ruler: From Herbert Hoover to Richard Nixon* (New Brunswick: Rutgers University Press, 1988), esp. chap. 5, "A Problem of Authority."

3. For Truman's position in historians' polls, see Martin D. Tullai, "A Presidential Dozen," *World and I* 18 (February 2003): 272; "When Historians Rate America's Presidents," *U.S. News and World Report* 95 (November 21, 1983): 54; Robert K. Murray and Tim H. Blessing, "The Presidential Performance Study: A Progress Report," *Journal of American History* 70 (December 1983): 535–55; Douglas A. Lonnstrom and Thomas O. Kelly II, "Rating the Presidents: A Tracking Study," *Presidential Studies Quarterly* 27 (Summer 1997): 591; Gary M. Maranell, "The Evaluation of Presidents: An Extension of the Schlesinger Polls," *Journal of American History* 57 (June 1970): 104–13; and Tom Kynerd, "An Analysis of Presidential Greatness and 'President Rating,'" *Southern Quarterly* 9 (April 1971): 309–29. Foreign policy

At its most basic level, Harry Truman's Farewell Address opens a window into what Truman himself considered to be the primary accomplishments of his administration. It also provides an opportunity to assess the president's claims. How have historians judged the various foreign policy "triumphs" detailed in Truman's address? Was Truman's use of history both in shaping his foreign policy in practice and in evaluating it in the address accurate and appropriate? (In other words, did Truman truly "learn" from history?) Did the Truman administration's foreign policy really mark the triumph of internationalism, as the address maintains? And how did the Farewell Address seek, albeit indirectly, to present Truman's conception of the U.S. national identity during the early Cold War period? These and related questions provide the basis for what follows.

Before examining the specific foreign policy accomplishments detailed in the Farewell Address, some general observations are appropriate. One is to note the overwhelming focus on the Cold War among the policies included in the address, a focus that makes perfect sense given Truman's belief, expressed in the address, that that conflict had overshadowed American life during his administration and was "the overriding issue of our time." Upon consideration, in fact, it becomes clear that the foreign policy Truman outlines forms a coherent whole organized around containing Soviet expansion as a prelude to eventually destroying the Communist system worldwide. As the subsequent discussion will reveal, the initiatives outlined in the address also focus in great measure on efforts in Europe and the Mediterranean. The address omits almost entirely the world's developing nations, or what some label the Third World. This First World focus, when coupled with the emphasis on the Cold War, results in an address that slights large portions of the globe— portions that would become crucial for the foreign policies of Truman's successors. Finally, the foreign relations successes that Truman outlines all demonstrate strength and decisiveness, or what might simply be termed grit, traits that have helped Truman attain and retain his present high place among rankings of presidential success. With these basic observations in

---

is addressed in Jack E. Holmes and Robert E. Elder Jr., "Our Best and Worst Presidents: Some Possible Reasons for Perceived Performance," *Presidential Studies Quarterly* 19 (Summer 1989): 529–57, and Robert Underhill, *FDR and Harry: Unparalleled Lives* (Westport, Conn.: Praeger, 1996), 147–66, which speculates that Truman's popularity stemmed from his foreign policy. For a negative assessment of Truman that emphasizes foreign policy, see Arnold A. Offner, *Another Such Victory: President Truman and the Cold War, 1945–1953* (Stanford: Stanford University Press, 2002).

mind, a look at the specific foreign policy initiatives Truman outlines is now in order.

The first initiative to be addressed in Truman's roughly chronological survey is the San Francisco Conference to create the United Nations. As Truman notes, the conference was planned long before he assumed the presidency, and it was his "first decision" as president to hold it as scheduled, less than two weeks after the death of Franklin D. Roosevelt. Truman goes on in the address to herald the United Nations, which embodied the principles articulated in the 1941 Atlantic Charter, as one of the great foreign policy successes of his administration. Perhaps more important for a president ever cognizant of the role of history in shaping his policies, both foreign and domestic, Truman notes in his address that by taking a leading role in helping "to found and to sustain the United Nations," the United States was somehow atoning for its post–World War I failure to join the League of Nations. Clearly, Truman saw U.S. membership in the United Nations as a positive development—and one, in his eyes, that helped to prevent a third world war. Indeed, proof of his faith in the United Nations comes in the fact that furthering its goals played a prominent role in the justifications that he and other members of his administration would make for other important foreign policy initiatives outlined in the Farewell Address—namely, the Truman Doctrine and the Marshall Plan.[4]

Historians have joined Truman in seeing the formation of the United Nations as a positive development, though they have tempered their praise with

4. The Atlantic Charter may be found in Michael D. Gambone, ed., *Documents of American Diplomacy: From the American Revolution to the Present* (Westport, Conn.: Greenwood Press, 2002), 256–57. The idea that post–World War II involvement in the world would right the nation's previous failure to join the League of Nations was a long-standing one for Truman. See Alonzo Hamby, "Harry S. Truman and the Origins of the Truman Doctrine," in *The Truman Doctrine of Aid to Greece: A Fifty-Year Retrospective*, ed. Eugene T. Rossides (Washington, D.C.: American Hellenic Institute Foundation, 1997), 16–18; and Evan Luard, *A History of the United Nations*, vol. 1, *The Years of Western Domination, 1945–1955* (New York: St. Martin's Press, 1982), 3–16. Truman, in fact, supported the concept of the United Nations even before its creation. For one account, see J. Phillipp Rosenberg, "The Belief System of Harry S Truman and Its Effect on Foreign Policy Decision-making during His Administration," *Presidential Studies Quarterly* 12 (Spring 1982): 230. And he used support for UN principles as a justification for two key foreign policy initiatives outlined in Harry S. Truman, "Special Message on Greece and Turkey: The Truman Doctrine," March 12, 1947, *Public Papers of the Presidents: Harry S. Truman, 1945–1953*, 8 vols. (Washington, D.C.: U.S. Government Printing Office, 1961–1966), 3 (1947): 176–80; and "The Marshall Plan (Economic Cooperation Act of 1948)," in Thomas G. Paterson and Dennis Merrill, eds., *Major Problems in American Foreign Relations: Documents and Essays*, vol. 2, *Since 1914*, 4th ed. (Lexington, Mass.: D. C. Heath, 1995), 261.

realistic assessments of the organization's shortcomings. In 1945, there were high hopes that the United Nations would ultimately maintain world peace and prevent conflict. Supporters believed it would accomplish what the League of Nations had not: true collective security and prosperity the world over. And since then, it has accomplished quite a lot.[5] But given the grossly over-inflated expectations that surrounded its creation, it was perhaps inevitable that the United Nations would disappoint. It often became mired in the Cold War tensions that gripped so many other facets of life in the postwar period. At times, too, it became a tool of the large powers and did not always give smaller states a chance to exert their influence, although this was more true of the Security Council than of the General Assembly. It did not always fulfill the promise of its much-ballyhooed charter. It did not prevent war. And it embodied an unwise and perhaps even utopian idealism of world cooperation that failed to take account of human foibles and fallibility.[6] Nevertheless, the world is better for the existence of the United Nations, and Truman is justified in highlighting the role he played in bringing it into existence.

The second foreign policy action that Truman mentions in his address—and the first that can be entirely attributed to him—is the successful 1946

5. An excellent account of the origins of the United Nations that notes many of the problems that would later emerge is Robert C. Hilderbrand, *Dumbarton Oaks: The Origins of the United Nations and the Search for Postwar Security* (Chapel Hill: University of North Carolina Press, 1990). For contemporary support for the United Nations among the U.S. public, see Robert D. Accinelli, "Pro-U.N. Internationalists and the Early Cold War: The American Association for the United Nations and U.S. Foreign Policy, 1947–52," *Diplomatic History* 9 (Fall 1985): 347–62; William Abbott Scott and Stephen B. Withey, *The United States and the United Nations: The Public View, 1945–1955* (New York: Manhattan Publishing Co., 1958); and Kenneth W. Thompson, *Political Realism and the Crisis of World Politics* (Princeton: Princeton University Press, 1960). One recounting of the success of the United Nations since 1945 is John Allphin Moore and Jerry Pubantz, *To Create a New World? American Presidents and the United Nations* (New York: Peter Lang, 1999), 11–12.

6. On the Truman administration's experiences with the United Nations, see Gary B. Ostrower, *The United Nations and the United States* (New York: Twayne, 1998), 39–65, and, for a very different perspective, James Barros, *Trygve Lie and the Cold War: The UN Secretary-General Pursues Peace, 1946–1953* (DeKalb: Northern Illinois University Press, 1989). Various shortcomings are discussed in Luard, *History of the United Nations;* George T. Mazuzan, *Warren R. Austin at the U.N., 1946–1953* (Kent, Ohio: Kent State University Press, 1977); Thomas Franck, *Nation against Nation: What Happened to the U.N. Dream and What the U.S. Can Do about It* (New York: Oxford University Press, 1985); Carol Anderson, *Eyes Off the Prize: The United Nations and the African American Struggle for Human Rights, 1944–1955* (New York: Cambridge University Press, 2003); Max Harrelson, *Fires All around the Horizon: The U.N.'s Uphill Battle to Preserve the Peace* (Westport, Conn.: Praeger, 1989); Geoff Simons, *The United Nations: A Chronology of Conflict* (New York: St. Martin's Press, 1994); and Walter A. McDougall, *Promised Land, Crusader State: The American Encounter with the World since 1776* (Boston: Houghton Mifflin, 1997).

effort to end the Soviet military presence in Iran. The Soviet troops were a lingering result of the Allied wartime desire to protect Iran's oil resources from German encroachment and to ensure the flow of Lend-Lease aid to the Soviet Union. To this end, American, British, and Soviet troops had all been deployed to Iran. But while the American and British troops had been withdrawn within six months of the war's conclusion, Soviet troops remained, confirming the fears of many in Washington that the nation's former ally was determined to secure a stake in Iran's rich oil resources for itself. Specifically, the Soviets seemed determined to encourage a nascent separatist movement in the northern Iranian province of Azerbaijan. The prevailing Western wisdom was that pulling the province away from Iran would ultimately lead to a Soviet takeover in Tehran, cancellation of the Anglo-Iranian Oil Company's concession, and Soviet control of Iranian oil. It would also confirm suspicions that Soviet designs on Iran were similar to earlier Soviet moves on Manchuria. Again, American officials looked to history to guide their policy making. Determined to prevent the "loss" of Iran, the Truman administration, as the president relates, forced the Soviets to withdraw through diplomatic pressure, most notably at the new United Nations, which heard the Iran case during its inaugural session in January 1946. (Witness again Truman's reliance on the United Nations as an instrument of U.S. foreign policy.) By standing firm against the Soviets in Iran, the administration was also writing its own historical "lesson," as it would conclude that toughness with Moscow got results.[7]

The scholarly assessment of the 1946 Iran crisis shares some features of Truman's but departs from it in others. Historians generally credit the administration with firmness and give it high marks for making clear its determination to prevent Soviet encroachment into oil-rich Iran. They also laud Truman and his advisers for securing their goals diplomatically rather than militarily—despite Secretary of State James F. Byrnes's bellicose declaration that the crisis would finally give Washington the chance to "give it to [Moscow] with both barrels!" Less positively, while historians have noted the firm U.S. posture on the Iran question, they also point out that the United Nations

---

7. The general contours of the Iranian crisis may be followed in Bruce R. Kuniholm, *The Origins of the Cold War in the Near East: Great Power Conflict and Diplomacy in Iran, Turkey, and Greece* (Princeton: Princeton University Press, 1980), 304–50. A briefer account is Richard Pfau, "Containment in Iran, 1946: The Shift to an Active Policy," *Diplomatic History* 1 (Fall 1977): 359–72. The role of the United Nations in resolving the crisis is highlighted in Wm. Roger Louis, *The British Empire in the Middle East, 1945–1951: Arab Nationalism, the United States, and Postwar Imperialism* (Oxford: Oxford University Press, 1984), 62–73.

was unable to prevent the crisis or, in the end, really to resolve it. (Resolution, of course, came only when the Iranian government traded an oil concession in northern Iran for removal of the Soviet troops. The troops were withdrawn, but the Iranian Majlis refused to ratify the concession.) Thus, an episode that supposedly demonstrates the Truman administration's resolve also makes plain the weakness of the United Nations as a truly effective keeper of the peace. It is also possible to question the administration's assumptions about Soviet motives in the Iran crisis. Definitive evidence about Moscow's aims in Iran is not yet available, so scholars cannot be sure that Truman and his advisers were correct in ascribing to the Soviets the basest and most aggressive of designs. Preliminary evidence from Soviet archives, in fact, suggests that there was no grand Soviet plan to take over the government of Iran and that Stalin's stance was a response to what he perceived as threatening Anglo-American oil interests near the Soviet border.[8] The scholarly assessment of the 1946 Iran crisis must thus be described as a mixture of positive and negative. The administration did achieve its goal of removing Soviet troops from a strategically important area, but at the cost of circumventing the United Nations and without apparent consideration for its own role in influencing Soviet policy.

The strength that Truman lauds in his administration's handling of the Soviet threat in Iran is also evident in his description of the U.S. response to a perceived Soviet threat to Greece and Turkey. The Greek and Turkish crises, like the troubles in Iran, had their origins in World War II. In Greece, wartime had brought domestic conflict between pro-monarchist, non-Communist elements that collaborated with the Nazi occupation and left-leaning forces, including some Communists. After Germany's defeat, the British sought to restore and support the monarchy and found themselves confronted with significant left-leaning opposition elements that received aid from Bulgaria, Yugoslavia, and Albania (but not, to any appreciable degree, the Soviet Union). In time, the conflict became an all-out civil war. The crisis in Turkey stemmed from long-standing Soviet desires for a warm-water Black Sea port

---

8. Byrnes quoted in Mark H. Lytle, "Containment and American Foreign Policy, 1945–1963," in *Modern American Diplomacy*, rev. ed., ed. John M. Carroll and George C. Herring (Wilmington, Del.: Scholarly Resources, 1996), 141. A positive assessment is Kuniholm, *Origins of the Cold War*, 378–82. Barros, *Trygve Lie and the Cold War*, 68–80, makes clear the weakness of the United Nations. For the debate on Soviet policy, see Natalia I. Yegorova, "The 'Iran Crisis' of 1945–46: A View from the Russian Archives," Working Paper #15, Cold War International History Project (CWIHP), Washington, D.C., 1996. This and other materials published by the CWIHP may be found at the project's web site, www.wilsoncenter.org/cwihp.

that would serve as a gateway to the Mediterranean and the whole of the Middle East. By early 1947, the Soviets had amassed troops on their border with Turkey, presumably in preparation for an armed effort to take the Turkish Straits. Viewed through the lens of the Soviet designs on Iran, the situations in Greece and Turkey seemed to presage an all-out drive by Moscow to control what was commonly referred to as the "Northern Tier."[9]

In February 1947, the British announced that financial constraints were forcing their withdrawal from Greece (and from neighboring Turkey), an announcement that necessitated—and received—a careful and considered response from Washington. Committed by that time to the containment doctrine articulated in George F. Kennan's Long Telegram of the previous year, the Truman administration knew instinctively that it would step in and take up the burden of defending Greece and Turkey from Communist advances. As Truman notes in the Farewell Address, "Something had to be done at once, or the Eastern Mediterranean would be taken over by the communists." Accordingly, the administration sponsored a four-hundred-million-dollar economic and military aid bill for Greece and Turkey, a bill that the president decided to endorse personally before a joint session of Congress. But Truman's March 12, 1947, speech did much more than simply stump for approval of the aid package. In often apocalyptic language, the president described the bipolarization of the world without ever actually mentioning the Soviet Union and made his case for a more activist U.S. foreign policy. "No other nation in the world," Truman maintained, was "willing" or "able" to provide the aid necessary to save Greece and Turkey. "The free peoples of the world," he averred, looked to the United States "for help in maintaining their freedoms." Failing to act would call into question the nation's world role and squander the "$341,000,000,000" the United States had spent winning World War II. Lest the American people draw the conclusion that aiding Greece and Turkey in their struggle against Communism was purely an act of altruism, the president went on to claim that the aid package was "no more than a frank recognition that totalitarian regimes imposed on free peoples, by direct or indirect aggression, undermine the foundations of international peace and

9. For the outlines of this story, see Randall B. Woods and Howard Jones, *Dawning of the Cold War: The United States' Quest for Order* (Athens: University of Georgia Press, 1991), chap. 5; and Kuniholm, *Origins of the Cold War*, 399–433. Correctives to the overwhelming Greek focus in the literature are Melvyn P. Leffler, "Strategy, Diplomacy, and the Cold War: The United States, Turkey, and NATO, 1945–1952," *Journal of American History* 71 (March 1985): 807–25; and Eduard Mark, "The War Scare of 1946 and Its Consequences," *Diplomatic History* 21 (Summer 1997): 383–415.

hence the security of the United States." Couched in these terms, aid to Greece and Turkey became a crucial matter for U.S. survival.[10]

Scholarly assessments of the Truman Doctrine have been mixed. On the positive side, the administration has been credited with protecting the strategically important Mediterranean region, countering what seemed to be aggressive Soviet designs on Greece and Turkey, and setting the course for a more active U.S. foreign policy in general. Defenders of the Truman Doctrine also hail its importance as a symbol to potential U.S. allies elsewhere, as it demonstrated Washington's determination to do what was necessary to halt the spread of Communism.[11] On a more negative note, however, a number of criticisms have been launched at both the Greek-Turkish aid package in particular and the larger Truman Doctrine that it spawned. Many observers, at the time and since, have rightly been troubled by the lengths to which the administration went to back nondemocratic elements in Greece. For these critics, the Truman Doctrine subverted traditional American values such as free government and democracy by tying the nation to a repressive regime that did not reflect the will of the majority—an apparent and somewhat ironic violation of the very principles the United States was supposedly defending in the Truman Doctrine. It also established a pattern of intervention that would be repeated in other parts of the world, such as Korea and Indochina. Another problem for some scholars has been the Truman Doctrine's grandiose rhetoric and expansive nature. In making the case for U.S. aid to Greece and Turkey in the way that he did, Truman implied that the nation's worldwide interests knew no bounds. Such an implication, some scholars believe, was improper, inaccurate, and unduly threatening to the Soviet Union. It may also have helped to generate hope of U.S. aid in other places and disappointment when that aid was not forthcoming. (To cite just

10. Truman, "The Truman Doctrine," 177, 178. The Long Telegram may be found in Gambone, ed., *American Foreign Policy*, 298–305. Kennan expounded on the Long Telegram's main themes in "The Sources of Soviet Conduct," *Foreign Affairs* 25 (July 1947): 566–82. For thoughtful and provocative analysis of Kennan's thinking and its implications, see Michael J. Hogan, *A Cross of Iron: Harry S. Truman and the Origins of the National Security State, 1945–1954* (New York: Cambridge University Press, 1998), 10, 12–17. See also John Lewis Gaddis, "Was the Truman Doctrine a Real Turning Point?" *Foreign Affairs* 52 (January 1974): 386–402.

11. See Bruce R. Kuniholm, *The Near East Connection: Greece and Turkey in the Reconstruction and Security of Europe, 1946–1952* (Brookline, Mass.: Hellenic College Press, 1984), for the strategic importance of those two countries in administration thinking. Generally laudatory accounts of the Truman Doctrine include Howard Jones, *"A New Kind of War": America's Global Strategy and the Truman Doctrine in Greece* (New York: Oxford University Press, 1989), and Kuniholm, *Origins of the Cold War*.

one example, Iranian officials were deeply chagrined that their nation was not included in the aid package.) Some scholars have also criticized the administration for sidestepping the United Nations and formulating a unilateral U.S. response to the Greek and Turkish crises, at least a tacit admission of the international organization's weakness. Others have also noted the connection between the seemingly global campaign against Communism and McCarthyism, which gripped the United States during the final years of the Truman administration and effectively destroyed the administration's domestic credibility on international issues after 1950. Scholars have even questioned the basis on which the Truman Doctrine was formulated, noting the imprecision with which Truman described especially the situation in Greece and suggesting a multitude of reasons for the administration's failure to present the situation as it truly existed. All in all, scholars have criticized a number of features and implications of the Truman Doctrine and do not unanimously join Truman in considering it a resounding success.[12]

The fourth foreign policy initiative Truman outlines in the Farewell Address is the Marshall Plan, which, he proudly proclaims, "saved Europe." Formally known as the European Recovery Program and unveiled just twelve weeks after the Truman Doctrine, the Marshall Plan was first announced by Secretary of State George C. Marshall in a commencement speech at Harvard

12. Generally critical accounts of the Truman Doctrine include Lawrence S. Wittner, *American Intervention in Greece, 1943–1949* (New York: Columbia University Press, 1982); Jon V. Kofas, *Intervention and Underdevelopment: Greece during the Cold War* (University Park, Pa.: Pennsylvania State University Press, 1989); Zachary Karabell, *Architects of Intervention: The United States, the Third World, and the Cold War, 1946–1962* (Baton Rouge: Louisiana State University Press, 1999), chap. 1; and David F. Schmitz, *Thank God They're on Our Side: The United States and Right-Wing Dictatorships, 1921–1965* (Chapel Hill: University of North Carolina Press, 1999). Thought-provoking explorations of the rhetoric of Truman's speech may be found in Robert L. Ivie, "Fire, Flood, and Red Fever: Motivating Metaphors of Global Emergency in the Truman Doctrine Speech," *Presidential Studies Quarterly* 29 (September 1999): 570–91, and Robert J. McMahon, "'By Helping Others We Help Ourselves': The Cold War Rhetoric of American Foreign Policy," in *Critical Reflections on the Cold War: Linking Rhetoric and Memory*, ed. Martin J. Medhurst and H. W. Brands (College Station: Texas A & M University Press, 2000), 233–46. For links between the Truman Doctrine and domestic developments see Richard M. Freeland, *The Truman Doctrine and the Origins of McCarthyism: Foreign Policy, Domestic Politics, and Internal Security, 1946–1948* (New York: Knopf, 1971), and Athan Theoharis, *Seeds of Repression: Harry S. Truman and the Origins of McCarthyism* (Chicago: Quadrangle, 1971). For imprecision see Deborah Welch Larson, *Origins of Containment: A Psychological Explanation* (Princeton: Princeton University Press, 1985). The true nature of Soviet involvement, based on newly released Soviet sources, is discussed in Artiom A. Ulanian, "The Soviet Union and 'the Greek Question,' 1946–53: Problems and Appraisals," in *The Soviet Union and Europe in the Cold War, 1943–53*, ed. Francesca Gori and Silvio Pons (New York: St. Martin's Press, 1996), 144–60.

delivered on June 5, 1947. Alarmed by the slow progress of European recovery from the devastation of war—and worried about the implications of that slow recovery—Marshall proposed a concerted U.S. program of financial assistance. By the time the Marshall Plan was fully subsumed under the Mutual Security Agency in 1952, almost thirteen billion dollars had flowed under its auspices to the war-torn nations of Western Europe. For Truman, the Marshall Plan was another example of his administration not repeating the errors of the first postwar period. Instead of retreating into an isolationist shell as he believed the nation had done in 1919, the United States after World War II went "ahead with other free countries to help build their economies and link us all together in a healthy world trade."[13]

Unlike the Truman Doctrine, the Marshall Plan has received effusive and almost universal praise from scholars; according to one, it justifiably "has attained virtual policy canonization." The reasons for such adulation are obvious. The Marshall Plan restored hope to a demoralized and vulnerable continent and thereby staved off the spread of Communism. It furthered the cause of European integration and laid important seeds for such subsequent institutions as the Common Market and the European Union. It assuaged French fears of German revitalization and made Germany's entry into NATO possible. It marked a triumph for internationalist thinking in U.S. policy making circles. It paved the way for a bipartisan foreign policy, no mean feat given the bitter disagreements that had theretofore characterized the making of U.S. foreign policy. And this list just scratches the surface. In the words of historian Michael J. Hogan, it was simply "one of the most successful peacetime foreign policies launched by the United States in this century."[14] Such criticisms as have been launched at the Marshall Plan are concentrated in two main areas. Some scholars claim that the plan was unnecessary, that Europe by 1947 had taken control of its own recovery and did not really need

13. The Marshall Plan was announced in "Press Release Issued by the Department of State, June 4, 1947," remarks by Secretary of State George C. Marshall at Harvard University June 5, 1947, U.S. Department of State, *Foreign Relations of the United States, 1947* (Washington, D.C.: U.S. Government Printing Office, 1972), 3:237–39. For an interesting exploration of the speech see Ferald J. Bryan, "George C. Marshall at Harvard: A Study of the Origins and Construction of the 'Marshall Plan' Speech," *Presidential Studies Quarterly* 21 (Summer 1991): 489–502. The fullest and best account of the Marshall Plan is Michael J. Hogan, *The Marshall Plan: America, Britain, and the Reconstruction of Western Europe, 1947–1952* (New York: Cambridge University Press, 1987).

14. Charles S. Maier, "American Visions and British Interests: Hogan's Marshall Plan," *Reviews in American History* 18 (March 1990): 102; Hogan, *Marshall Plan,* 445. For another positive assessment of the Marshall Plan, see Robert A. Pollard, *Economic Security and the Origins of the Cold War, 1945–1950* (New York: Columbia University Press, 1985), chap. 5.

U.S. assistance. Others have denounced the plan as a threatening, anti-Soviet gesture that confirmed Joseph Stalin's suspicions about U.S. policy and solidified the division of Europe, a contention that preliminary evidence from Soviet archives seems to support.[15] Nevertheless, by all reasonable standards, the Marshall Plan must be judged one of the Truman administration's greatest foreign policy successes.

Truman moves from the Marshall Plan to another of what he considers his administration's international successes, "the heroic Berlin airlift." The stage for the airlift was set in June 1948 when road, rail, and canal routes into western Berlin, located deep within the Soviet zone of Germany, were closed, leaving residents without access to food, fuel, and medicine. As has been well documented, both by Truman and by historians, the president viewed the Berlin blockade as a test of strength. It generated significant debate within the administration, and more than one voice counseled withdrawal from a city that seemed indefensible. The president's oft-quoted response to such advice, however, was simple. "We're staying," he said. "Period." The subsequent airlift provided a relatively safe, nonconfrontational way to make U.S. determination to remain in Berlin clear, not only to the Soviets but also to Berliners and others to whom the United States had made promises—explicit or implicit. The nation's credibility was on the line in Berlin, the president believed. And he was determined that that credibility not be damaged on his watch.[16]

15. The argument that the Marshall Plan was unnecessary has been made most forcefully by Alan Milward, *The Reconstruction of Western Europe, 1945–1951* (London: Methuen, 1984). The argument that it was unduly threatening to the Soviets may be found in Vladislav Zubok and Constantine Pleshakov, *Inside the Kremlin's Cold War: From Stalin to Khrushchev* (Cambridge: Harvard University Press, 1996), 50–51, and Vojtech Mastny, "Stalin and the Militarization of the Cold War," *International Security* 9 (Winter 1984–85): 109–29. Supporting evidence for this idea comes in Scott D. Parrish and Mikhail M. Narinsky, "New Evidence on the Soviet Rejection of the Marshall Plan, 1947," Working Paper #9, CWIHP, Washington, D.C., 1994.

16. Truman quoted in Ernest R. May, "America's Berlin: Heart of the Cold War," *Foreign Affairs* 77 (July/August 1998): 150. The president's own sentiments may easily be followed in Truman, *Years of Trial and Hope,* 122–31. For general outlines of the blockade see Daniel F. Harrington, "The Berlin Blockade Revisited," *International History Review* 6 (February 1984): 88–112; Carolyn Woods Eisenberg, *Drawing the Line: The American Decision to Divide Germany, 1944–1949* (New York: Cambridge University Press, 1996), chap. 10; and Roger G. Miller, *To Save a City: The Berlin Airlift, 1948–1949* (College Station: Texas A & M University Press, 2000), which provides excellent coverage of the logistical side of the airlift. Truman's motives for standing firm in Berlin are well covered in Rosenberg, "Belief System of Truman," 235–57. For the concept of credibility in U.S. foreign policy generally, see Robert J. McMahon, "Credibility and World Power: Exploring the Psychological Dimension in Postwar American Diplomacy," *Diplomatic History* 15 (Fall 1991): 455–71.

As with many of Truman's other foreign policy initiatives, historical reviews of the Berlin airlift reveal both praise and criticism. To be sure, defenders of the airlift have been numerous. And they have highlighted such facts as the symbolic statement it sent to Moscow and the rest of the world and the lack of any meaningful Soviet opposition to it to support their claim that the airlift was indeed something to crow about. Other scholars, though, have seen the airlift in a less positive light. One source of criticism has been the way the administration conveniently downplayed or omitted altogether the role that Western (that is, U.S.) moves toward trizonal fusion in Germany and the creation of a common western German currency played in precipitating the blockade in the first place. For these scholars, the administration had pursued an aggressive, openly hostile, and anti-Soviet policy in Germany and only reaped the whirlwind when the Soviets blockaded Berlin. Critics have also come down on the administration for failing to fully pursue UN action on the blockade question, a development that appears to fly in the face of Truman's long-standing personal commitment to the United Nations and his belief in its power to maintain the peace.[17]

U.S. military assistance programs also find mention (and not much more) in Truman's survey of the international successes of his administration. Although the president does not provide specifics, he is obviously referring to the aid programs administered under the 1949 Mutual Defense Assistance Act and the 1951 Mutual Security Act. U.S. military aid fit neatly into the administration's activist foreign policy agenda and demonstrated its belief that military might, whether concentrated directly in the United States or wielded by its allies, would prevent Soviet aggression and intimidation around the globe. This was especially the case after the outbreak of war in Korea in June 1950. The military aid programs also conformed to the third of four broad "courses of action" that Truman had laid out in his January 1949 inaugural address. That course called for U.S. "military advice and equipment to free nations which will cooperate with us in the maintenance of peace and security." Of course, a large portion of the aid that flowed to Turkey and

---

17. Questions about the sinister nature of Soviet policy in Berlin are raised in Avi Shlaim, *The United States and the Berlin Blockade, 1948–49: A Study in Crisis Decision-Making* (Berkeley: University of California Press, 1983), and in Michail M. Narinskii, "The Soviet Union and the Berlin Crisis, 1948–49," in *Soviet Union and Europe in the Cold War,* ed. Gori and Pons, 57–75. Criticism of the administration's failure to work through the United Nations may be found in Daniel F. Harrington, "United States, United Nations, and the Berlin Blockade," *Historian* 52 (February 1990): 262–85, and Barros, *Trygve Lie and the Cold War,* 136–56.

especially Greece under the Truman Doctrine was military in nature. As Soviet-American tensions deepened after 1947, it seemed logical for the administration to rely on more overtly militaristic measures of containment.[18]

The Truman administration's decision to embark on a program of military assistance, like its other international initiatives, has received much scholarly attention, some positive, some negative. Those scholars who support the military assistance program usually do so with the argument that such assistance was a necessary—and ultimately effective—strategy for dealing with a hostile and militaristic Soviet Union. They also maintain that military aid demonstrated the commitment of the United States to its allies, that it literally put the nation's money where its mouth was. Scholarly critics of the military assistance program have been many. Some decry how that program militarized the Cold War struggle, some how it probably encouraged Soviet hostility and aggression. Another common criticism is that military assistance was often provided to nations that were less than stellar examples of democracy and freedom, often with untoward results. Greece under the Truman Doctrine was an early example of this criticism. Iran was another, though by no means was it alone. The military assistance program has also been taken to task for its potentially destabilizing regional effects—for introducing military hardware into regions such as the Middle East that could be used to disrupt relations between states—and for how arms aid can affect domestic politics in recipient nations.[19] Clearly, scholars have not judged the administration's military assistance programs as an overwhelmingly positive development.

The final foreign relations success Truman delineates in the Farewell Address is the U.S. role in helping to engineer a number of important international agreements, namely "the North Atlantic Pact, the Rio Pact binding the Western Hemisphere together, and the defense pacts with the countries of the Far Pacific." These pacts or alliances grew out of the ever present and all-

18. Harry S. Truman, "Inaugural Address," January 20, 1949, *Public Papers: Truman, 1949,* 114. The bases for military assistance may be found in Appendix D, "Mutual Defense Assistance Act of 1949," and Appendix F, "Mutual Security Act of 1951," in Lawrence S. Kaplan, *A Community of Interests: NATO and the Military Assistance Program, 1948–1951* (Washington, D.C.: Office of the Secretary of Defense, Historical Office, 1980), 214–22, 224–39. The program in general is addressed in Chester A. Pach Jr., *Arming the Free World: The Origins of the United States Military Assistance Program, 1945–1950* (Chapel Hill: University of North Carolina Press, 1991).

19. Criticisms of military assistance may be found in Schmitz, *Thank God They're on Our Side;* Mark J. Gasiorowski, *U.S. Foreign Policy and the Shah: Building a Client State in Iran* (Ithaca: Cornell University Press, 1991); and Michael T. Klare, *American Arms Supermarket* (Austin: University of Texas Press, 1984).

consuming Cold War and were designed to project U.S. power into regions considered important for national security and thereby deter possible Soviet aggression. The Rio Pact, officially named the Inter-American Treaty of Reciprocal Assistance, was negotiated in late 1947 and went into force a year later. It bound the signatories, which included most of the nations of the Western Hemisphere, in "solidarity and cooperation" and "mutual assistance and common defense." The North Atlantic Treaty, negotiated in April 1949 and entered into force in August, joined the United States with Canada and ten European nations in "self-help and mutual aid . . . to develop their individual and collective capacity to resist armed attack . . . against the territorial integrity, political independence or security of any of the Parties." The pacts with the "Far Pacific" nations to which Truman refers are undoubtedly the security pacts with Australia and New Zealand, the Philippines, and Japan, all signed in the late summer and early fall of 1951. They, too, bound the United States to strategically important allies in alliances of mutual defense and cooperation. Unlike the Rio Pact or NATO, though, these agreements were not negotiated until after the outbreak of war in Korea and should be seen as part of the administration's ever widening policy of global containment. They show how dangerous the world had become, in the eyes of Truman administration officials, by 1951.[20]

These pacts were important components of the Truman administration's internationalist foreign policy and symbols of its realization that the Cold War necessitated departures from time-honored U.S. policies. In a clear and complete break with the nation's unilateralist (some would say isolationist) past, and in atonement for the failure after World War I to join the League of Nations, these pacts, and NATO in particular, resulted in entangling alliances that bound the United States to other nations—many of them located some distance from U.S. shores. Not since the 1778 treaties with France had the nation been involved in such an agreement. And in the space of a few years the Truman administration negotiated a number of them, each designed to respond to a possible Soviet threat in a nation or region deemed

20. "Inter-American Treaty of Reciprocal Assistance," September 12, 1947, TIAS no. 1838, and "North Atlantic Treaty," April 14, 1949, TIAS no. 1964, in *Treaties and Other International Agreements of the United States of America,* vol. 4 (Washington, D.C.: U.S. Government Printing Office, 1955); "Multilateral Security Treaty between Australia, New Zealand, and the United States of America," September 1, 1951, TIAS no. 2493; "Mutual Defense Treaty between the United States of America and the Republic of the Philippines," August 30, 1951, TIAS no. 2529; and "Security Treaty between the United States of America and Japan," September 8, 1951, TIAS no. 2491, in *United States Treaties and Other International Agreements*, vol. 3, pt. 3 (Washington, D.C.: U.S. Government Printing Office, 1954).

important to U.S. security. As such, these alliances were components of the revolution in foreign policy orientation that Truman outlines in the Farewell Address. No longer would the United States "fail to act in concert with other peoples against aggression." No longer would "slavery and darkness" threaten the world because the United States and other "free men were paralyzed for lack of strength and unity and will." Instead, as Truman notes, the United States had accepted the responsibilities of "world leadership" and demonstrated "speed and courage and decisiveness . . . against the Communist threat."[21]

Due to their long-term impact and continuing importance, the Truman administration's mutual defense pacts—most notably NATO—have received much scholarly attention, and, like the other initiatives discussed in Truman's address, have netted both praise and criticism. Scholars have hailed NATO in particular, and the other mutual security pacts to a lesser degree, as a milestone in the development of U.S. postwar internationalism, as a meaningful institution that has stood the test of time. In assessing NATO, historian Norman A. Graebner has also pointed out the organization's "symbolic demonstration of the cultural and political unity of Western civilization in the twentieth century."[22] As with Truman's other foreign policy initiatives, criticisms have been raised. One, vocally expressed at the time and echoed in scholarly literature since, bemoaned the abandonment of tradition inherent in the mutual defense pacts. Although Truman sees the abandonment of the particular tradition of unilateralism, of not acting effectively on the world stage, as a positive development, some critics have not. To them, the administration erred grievously in eschewing the advice contained in the nation's first presidential farewell address, the one George Washington presented in print in 1796. Washington's address is much more advisory than Truman's. In fact, it is almost entirely so, with much of that advice pertaining to the conduct of the nation's foreign affairs. In his address, Washington counseled his fellow Americans to cultivate "just and amicable feelings towards all" nations. "Antipathy in one nation against another," he warned, "disposes each more readily to offer insult and injury, to lay hold of slight causes of umbrage, and

21. On Truman's earlier articulation of these ideas, see Hamby, "Truman and the Origins of the Truman Doctrine," 16–18.

22. Graebner, "Reflections on a Turning Point," in *NATO: The Founding of the Atlantic Alliance and the Integration of Europe*, ed. Francis H. Heller and John R. Gillingham (New York: St. Martin's Press, 1992), 432. Positive assessments of the postwar security pacts may be found in Lawrence S. Kaplan, *The United States and NATO: The Formative Years* (Lexington: University Press of Kentucky, 1984); Don Cook, *Forging the Alliance: NATO, 1945–1950* (New York: Arbor House, 1989); and Peter Duignan, *NATO: Its Past, Present, and Future* (Stanford: Hoover Institution Press, 2000).

to be haughty and intractable when accidental or trifling occasions of dispute occur." To his mind, it should be the "true policy [of the United States] to steer clear of permanent alliances with any portion of the foreign world," while "temporary alliances [should be contemplated only] for extraordinary emergencies." For those who subscribed to this Washingtonian belief system, alliances such as NATO were frightening stuff indeed. The postwar security pacts have also been criticized as unduly threatening to the Soviet Union, which was unlikely to launch a conventional attack in any of the areas to which the United States was making commitments.[23] As these and other criticisms illustrate, like the administration's other foreign policy initiatives, the post–World War II mutual defense pacts have received a mixed review from scholars.

What general conclusions may be drawn about the specific foreign policy decisions that Truman covers in his Farewell Address? Several thoughts come to mind. One relates to the president's use of history and historical analogy. As the address makes clear, the president lamented deeply the failure of the United States after World War I to take a forceful stand in defense of freedom. "We withdrew from world affairs," he notes. "We failed to act in concert with other peoples against aggression." "We helped to kill the League of Nations." In Truman's mind, these policies of "weakness and indecision," as well as appeasement of Germany and Japan during the 1930s, led directly to the horrors of World War II. Like many in his time, Truman was much influenced by the supposed lessons of the World War eras, which included the importance of standing firm against aggression, cooperating with like-minded peoples and nations in formulating policies for global good, and accepting one's responsibility to the community of nations.[24]

But more than simply revealing Truman's grasp of the nation's past mistakes, the Farewell Address also attempts to demonstrate his success in avoiding those mistakes when formulating policy in the post–World War II

23. U.S. Senate, *Washington's Farewell Address to the People of the United States*, 106th Cong., 2d sess., 2000, S. Doc. 106–21, 23, 27, 29. For the potentially provocative effects of the postwar alliances see Phillip A. Karber and Jerald A. Combs, "The United States, NATO, and the Soviet Threat to Western Europe: Military Estimates and Policy Options, 1945–1963," *Diplomatic History* 22 (Summer 1998): 399–429.

24. Collectively, these ideas have been referred to as the "Munich analogy." See Joseph M. Siracusa, "The Munich Analogy," in *Encyclopedia of American Foreign Policy*, ed. Alexander DeConde, Richard Dean Burns, and Fredrik Logevall (New York: Scribner, 2002), 2:443–54, and Göran Rystad, *Prisoners of the Past? The Munich Syndrome and Makers of American Foreign Policy in the Cold War Era* (Lund, Sweden: DWK Gleerup, 1982).

period. Instead of the indecision and vacillation of the past, "speed and courage and decisiveness" in moving "against the Communist threat" prevailed.
The United States under Truman's direction formulated and implemented "a
new set of policies to attain peace—positive policies, policies of world leadership, policies that express faith in other free people." The determined stance
in Iran, the Berlin airlift, and the various military initiatives of the administration were all evidence that the United States would not passively allow
Communist aggression to challenge world peace. The United Nations marked
the U.S. determination to join with other nations in the cause of peace and
prosperity. And the Truman Doctrine, the Marshall Plan, and the postwar alliances and pacts all bespoke the nation's acceptance of a position of world
leadership.

Truman certainly "used" history in formulating foreign policy and in defending that policy in his Farewell Address, but did he demonstrate that he
had truly learned from it?[25] This question, and the broader issue of the use of
history by policy makers generally, has received a fair amount of scholarly attention. The prevailing consensus seems to be that while history can be a
valuable tool for policy makers, most use it improperly. The literature on the
subject of using history in policy making is replete with examples of poorly
made analogies, simplistic and superficial comparisons, and incorrect conclusions.[26] In the case of Truman's use of history, the verdict is mixed. To take
the president's less successful use of history first, it was probably not accurate
to equate Soviet policy following World War II with German and Japanese
aggression before and during the war. Soviet policy did not manifest a con-

25. This essay will not deal with Truman's use of history and historical analogy with regard
to the war in Korea. On that subject generally, see Yuen Foong Khong, *Analogies at War: Korea,
Munich, Dien Bien Phu, and the Vietnam Decisions of 1965* (Princeton: Princeton University
Press, 1992).

26. On the uses of history by policy makers, see Bruce Kuklick, "Tradition and Diplomatic
Talent: The Case of the Cold Warriors," in *Recycling the Past: Popular Uses of American History,*
ed. Leila Zenderland (Philadelphia: University of Pennsylvania Press, 1978), 116–31; George
E. Mowry, "The Uses of History by Recent Presidents," *Journal of American History* 53 (June
1966): 5–18; Francis L. Loewenheim, *The Historian and the Diplomat: The Role of History and
Historians in American Foreign Policy* (New York: Harper and Row, 1967); Ernest R. May,
"Lessons" of the Past: The Use and Misuse of History in American History (New York: Oxford
University Press, 1973); Richard E. Neustadt and Ernest R. May, *Thinking in Time: The Uses
of History for Decision-Makers* (New York: Free Press, 1986); George C. Herring, "Vietnam,
American Foreign Policy, and the Uses of History," *Virginia Quarterly Review* 66 (Winter
1990): 1–16; and Edwin M. Yoder, *The Historical Present: Uses and Abuses of the Past* (Jackson:
University Press of Mississippi, 1997). An excellent collection of writings on this subject is
Stephen Vaughn, *The Vital Past: Writings on the Use of History* (Athens: University of Georgia
Press, 1985).

certed drive for territorial acquisition, and even had such territorial designs existed, they certainly were never implemented. Thus, the inferences drawn in the Farewell Address that the Soviet Union was another version of Nazi Germany and Imperial Japan cannot be sustained. With regard to the lessons Truman and his generation took from the interwar experience, however, the judgment is more positive. While it cannot be said definitively that U.S. membership in the League of Nations would have prevented World War II, it is fair to say, as Truman does, that the U.S. retreat into itself after 1919 did not help the cause of world peace or prosperity. U.S. unilateralism, what some would call isolationism, was not a far-sighted policy and certainly not one that served international purposes. (Whether that policy was wise or justified is not the issue here.) Simply put, Truman was probably right in taking from the U.S. interwar experience the lesson that standing aloof from international events served neither the nation nor the world. It was therefore logical for him to chart a different course in foreign relations than the failed course of the past. In a further nod to the past, but with an acknowledgment that nowhere in the Farewell Address does Truman use the term, it is noteworthy that the foreign policy Truman implemented was firmly rooted in the Wilsonian tradition, founded as it was on "internationalism, interventionism, and collective security." It was a policy consciously meant to vindicate the views of Woodrow Wilson and other internationalists of an earlier generation, but despite its clear and obvious links to the past, it was one that was designed to last well into the future.[27]

The description of Truman's foreign policy as Wilsonian suggests a second point of consideration: did the foreign policies outlined in the Farewell Address constitute a real change from the nation's purported isolationist past and the triumph of a form of internationalism? To that question, the answer must be an unequivocal yes. This is not the place to debate the administration's reasons for embarking on an internationalist foreign policy in the years after World War II. Historians of U.S. foreign relations have been addressing questions of motivation for years—and they are likely to continue to do so for many years to come. The point here is that, for whatever reasons, the United States did indeed embark on a dramatically different foreign policy in the post–World War II period. This new policy included extensive financial

27. Kuklick, "Tradition and Diplomatic Talent," 118, notes the foundations of Truman's foreign policy. For Wilsonianism in general, see Tony Smith, "Wilsonianism," in *Encyclopedia of American Foreign Policy*, ed. DeConde, Burns, and Logevall, 3:617–26. The Wilson-Truman connection is explored in Anne R. Pierce, *Woodrow Wilson and Harry Truman: Mission and Power in American Foreign Policy* (Westport, Conn.: Praeger, 2003).

and military aid programs to nations outside the Western Hemisphere, the first U.S. entangling military alliances since the late eighteenth century, and a crusading, missionary spirit that propelled the nation toward ever more expansive involvement with the outside world. Spurred by their fear of Communist expansion, guided by the containment doctrine, and determined that the United States remain a major international player, Truman and his advisers fashioned a multipronged strategy that involved new U.S. commitments throughout the world. They utilized diplomatic maneuvers, economic and military assistance, and bilateral and multilateral alliances to defend what they saw as the nation's global interests. In so doing, they spurred a revolution in U.S. foreign relations, the consequences of which remain in play today.[28]

The long-term importance of the internationalist features of the Truman administration's foreign policy is manifestly visible in the policies of Truman's successors. The five decades since Truman delivered his Farewell Address have not witnessed a return to isolationism or unilateralism in U.S. foreign relations. On the contrary. The nation remains deeply involved in the United Nations and NATO, even if those organizations have not always pursued policies or made decisions that suited U.S. purposes. It continues to maintain military relationships with other nations, to provide them with economic and military assistance, and to play a leading role in international affairs. Even the end of the Cold War, the conflict that provided the initial rationale for the revolution in foreign relations that characterized the Truman years, did not bring an end to the U.S. commitment to the larger world. So despite minor quibbles with or criticisms of the individual foreign policy initiatives of the Truman administration, it is clear that those initiatives added up to a real revolution in U.S. foreign policy that has endured the test of time.

A related conclusion about the administration's foreign policies as a whole is to note the multiplicity of strategies they revealed for attaining the same

28. Comprehensive and illuminating discussions of the terms *isolationism* and *internationalism* in a U.S. sense may be found in Manfred Jonas, "Isolationism," and Warren F. Kuehl and Gary B. Ostrower, "Internationalism," in *Encyclopedia of American Foreign Policy*, ed. DeConde, Burns, and Logevall, 2:337–51, 241–58. A still valuable discussion of early steps toward internationalism, and especially educating the American people on that idea, may be found in Warren F. Kuehl, "Webs of Common Interests Revisited: Nationalism, Internationalism, and Historians of American Foreign Relations," *Diplomatic History* 10 (Spring 1986): 102–20. On the ideological transformation of the move toward internationalism, see Wallace J. Thies, "Learning in U.S. Policy toward Europe," in *Learning in U.S. and Soviet Foreign Policy*, ed. George W. Breslauer and Philip E. Tetlock (Boulder: Westview Press, 1991), 158–207, and Joseph M. Siracusa, *Into the Dark House: American Diplomacy and the Ideological Origins of the Cold War* (Claremont, Calif.: Regina Books, 1998).

result—preventing the spread of Communism. U.S. membership in the United Nations, an international organization designed to prevent conflict and ensure peace and prosperity the world over, demonstrated U.S. resolve after World War II to play a role in world affairs and fulfilled Truman's goal of getting the United States to work "in concert with other peoples against aggression." In his mind at least, it helped to prevent yet another world war. International contacts, albeit of a more military nature, also characterized NATO, the various multilateral and bilateral defense treaties to which the United States became a signatory during the Truman presidency, and the U.S. military assistance program. The aid rendered Greece and Turkey under the Truman Doctrine was also mostly military. To be sure, the administration did employ nonmilitary tactics, such as the Marshall Plan, to combat the spread of Communism through economic means. (It also employed tactics not mentioned in Truman's Farewell Address, such as the Bretton Woods institutions.) But ultimately even the European Recovery Program lost its economic focus as it was subsumed under the Mutual Security Program in the early 1950s, a development due largely to the Korean War.[29] Clearly, the outbreak of war in Korea, which marked the first "hot" conflict of the Cold War, also marked the militarization of the U.S. policy of containment.

Finally, it is also possible to view the foreign policy initiatives outlined in the Farewell Address in terms of how Truman conceptualized the nation and its place in the world. To be sure, Truman did not frame his international discussion in the Farewell Address in quite this way. But it is evident that he had a well-defined sense of what the United States was all about and that he desired to use his administration's foreign policy to project his vision of the nation the world over. One indication that the president thought in terms of "identity" comes in his response to the suggestion that atomic weapons be used to end the war in Korea. In rejecting such a proposal, the president says simply, "we are not made that way." Other indications come in his repeated references to the nation's "free society," to the "ideals" and "principles" for which it stands, and to his "deep and abiding faith in the destiny of free men." Truman's positive assessment of the potential of "free men," in fact, echoed throughout the public statements and addresses of his presidency, from his very first address to a joint session of Congress on April 16, 1945, through

29. For other economic strategies in U.S. foreign relations, see Diane B. Kunz, *Butter and Guns: America's Cold War Economic Diplomacy* (New York: Free Press, 1997). The growing militarization of U.S. foreign aid policy is explored in Robert A. Pollard, "Economic Security and the Origins of the Cold War: Bretton Woods, the Marshall Plan, and American Rearmament, 1944–50," *Diplomatic History* 9 (Summer 1985): 271–89.

the Farewell Address in January 1953.[30] It reflected Truman's belief in an American mission, and it colored the way he approached foreign-policy making during his administration.

If containing the spread of Communism was the "official," stated goal of Truman's foreign policy, the Farewell Address also hints at an unstated but nonetheless real goal—implementation of Truman's "dream" of refashioning the world in the U.S. image. The president's conception of what the nation stood for was a positive one, grounded in an optimistic version of its history and exemplified in his administration's activist, internationalist foreign policy. The Marshall Plan sparked economic prosperity and fostered free trade, long-standing U.S. goals. The Truman Doctrine kept Greece "free and independent." The other foreign policy initiatives also contributed to the furthering of Truman's vision by helping to make the free world "stronger, more united, more attractive to men on both sides of the Iron Curtain." Motivated by the Cold War these policies surely were. But they also reflected Truman's deep and abiding confidence in the power and inherent goodness of the United States. Critics of the administration's foreign policy would clearly question such assumptions, with some justification. Yet their criticisms do not negate the fact that Truman's Farewell Address (especially those portions dealing with international affairs) reflects a positive image of the nation and demonstrates the clear pride that Truman felt not only about the nation but also about the role he had played in crafting its post–World War II foreign policy. It was a policy based on history. It was a policy grounded in internationalism. And it was a policy tailored to American ideals and designed for the long haul.

Locksley Hall   Tennyson 1842

For I dipt into the future, as far
    as human eye could see,
Saw the Vision of the world, and all
    the wonder that would be;

Saw the heavens fill with commerce,
    argosies of magic sails,
Pilots of the purple twilight dropping
    down with costly bales;

Heard the Heavens fill with shouting,
    and there rained a ghastly dew,
From the nations' airy navies grappling
    in the central blue;

Far along the world-wide whisper
    of the south-wind rushing warm
With the standards of the peoples plung-
    ing through the thunder-storm;

Till the war-drum throbb'd no longer,
    and the battle flags were furl'd
In the Parliament of man, the Federation
    of the world.

CONFIDENTIAL: The following address of the President, to be delivered
at the signing of the Atlantic Pact in the Departmental Auditorium,
Washington, D. C., MUST BE HELD IN STRICT CONFIDENCE until released.

NOTE: Release is automatic at 4:30 P.M., E.S.T., today, Monday, April 4,
1949. The same release applies to all newspapers and radio stations.

          PLEASE GUARD AGAINST PREMATURE PUBLICATION OR RADIO ANNOUNCE-
MENT.

                         CHARLES G. ROSS
                         Secretary to the President.

- -

          On this historic occasion, I am happy to welcome the
Foreign Ministers of the countries which, together with the United
States, form the North Atlantic community of nations.

          The purpose of this meeting is to take the first step toward
putting into effect an international agreement to safeguard the peace
and prosperity of this community of nations.

          It is altogether appropriate that nations so deeply conscious
of their common interests should join in expressing their determination
to preserve their present peaceful situation and to protect it in the
future.

          That we are about to do here is a neighborly act. We are
like a group of householders, living in the same locality, who decide
to express their community of interests by entering into a formal
association for their mutual self-protection.

          This treaty is a simple document. The nations which sign
it agree to abide by the peaceful principles of the United Nations,
to maintain friendly relations and economic cooperation with one
another, to consult together whenever the territory or independence
of any one of them is threatened, and to come to the aid of any one
of them which may be attacked.

          It is a simple document, but if it had existed in 1914 and
in 1939, supported by the nations which are represented here today,
I believe it would have prevented the acts of aggression which led
to two World Wars.

          The nations represented here have known the tragedy of those
two wars. As a result, many of us took part in the founding of the
United Nations. Each member of the United Nations is under a solemn
obligation to maintain international peace and security. Each is bound
to settle international disputes by peaceful means, to refrain from
the threat or use of force against the territory or independence of any
country, and to support the United Nations in any action it takes to
preserve the peace.

          That solemn pledge -- that abiding obligation -- we re-affirm
here today.

          We rededicate ourselves to that obligation, and propose this
North Atlantic Treaty as one of the means to carry it out.

          Through this treaty we undertake to conduct our inter-
national affairs in accordance with the provisions of the United
Nations Charter. We undertake to exercise our right of collective
or individual self-defense against armed attack, in accordance with
Article 51 of the Charter, and subject to such measures as the
Security Council may take to maintain and restore international
peace and security.

Within the United Nations, this country and other countries have hoped to establish an international force for the use of the United Nations in preserving peace throughout the world. Our efforts to establish this force, however, have been blocked by one of the major powers.

This lack of unanimous agreement in the Security Council does not mean that we must abandon our attempts to make peace secure.

Even without that agreement, which we still hope for, we shall do as much as we can. And every bit that we do will add to the strength of the fabric of peace throughout the world.

In this treaty, we seek to establish freedom from aggression and from the use of force in the North Atlantic community. This is the area which has been at the heart of the last two world conflicts. To protect this area against war will be a long step toward permanent peace in the whole world.

There are those who claim that this treaty is an aggressive act on the part of the nations which ring the North Atlantic.

This is absolutely untrue.

The pact will be a positive, not a negative, influence for peace, and its influence will be felt not only in the area it specifically covers but throughout the world. Its conclusion does not mean a narrowing of the interests of its members. Under my authority and instructions, the Secretary of State has recently made it abundantly clear that the adherence of the United States to this pact does not signify a lessening of American concern for the security and welfare of other areas, such as the Near East. The step we are taking today should serve to reassure peace-loving peoples everywhere and pave the way for the world-wide stability and peaceful development which we all seek.

Twice in recent years, nations have felt the sickening blow of unprovoked aggression. Our peoples, to whom our governments are responsible, demand that these things shall not happen again.

We are determined that they shall not happen again.

In taking steps to prevent aggression against our own peoples, we have no purpose of aggression against others. To suggest the contrary is to slander our institutions and defame our ideals and our aspirations.

The nations represented here are bound together by ties of long standing. We are joined by a common heritage of democracy, individual liberty, and the rule of law. These are the ties of a peaceful way of life. In this pact we merely give them formal recognition.

With our common traditions we face common problems. We are, to a large degree, industrial nations, and we face the problem of mastering the forces of modern technology in the public interest.

To meet this problem successfully, we must have a world in which we can exchange the products of our labor not only among ourselves, but with other nations. We have come together in a great cooperative economic effort to establish this kind of world.

We are determined to work together to provide better lives for our people without sacrificing our common ideals of justice and human worth.

But we cannot succeed if our people are haunted by the constant fear of aggression, and burdened by the cost of preparing their nations individually against attack.

In this pact, we hope to create a shield against aggression and the fear of aggression -- a bulwark which will permit us to get on with the real business of government and society, the business of achieving a fuller and happier life for our citizens.

We shall, no doubt, go about this business in different ways. There are different kinds of governmental and economic systems, just as there are different languages and different cultures. But these differences present no real obstacle to the voluntary association of free nations devoted to the common cause of peace.

We believe that it is possible for nations to achieve unity on the great principles of human freedom and justice, and at the same time to permit, in other respects, the greatest diversity of which the human mind is capable.

Our faith in this kind of unity is borne out by our experience here in the United States in creating one nation out of the variety of our continental resources and the peoples of many lands.

This method of organizing diverse peoples and cultures is in direct contrast to the method of the police state, which attempts to achieve unity by imposing the same beliefs and the same rule of force on everyone.

We believe that our method of achieving international unity through the voluntary association of different countries dedicated to a common cause is an effective step toward bringing order to our troubled world.

For us, war is not inevitable. We do not believe that there are blind tides of history which sweep men one way or the other. In our own time we have seen brave men overcome obstacles that seemed insurmountable and forces that seemed overwhelming. Men with courage and vision can still determine their own destiny. They can choose slavery or freedom -- war or peace.

I have no doubt which they will choose. The treaty we are signing here today is evidence of the path they will follow.

If there is anything certain today, if there is anything inevitable in the future, it is the will of the people of the world for freedom and peace.

- - - - - - - - - -

OCTOBER 22, 1949

CONFIDENTIAL: The following address of the President, to be delivered
at the laying of the cornerstone of the Secretariat Building of the
permanent United Nations Headquarters in New York on Monday, October
24, 1949, MUST BE HELD IN STRICT CONFIDENCE UNTIL RELEASED and no
portion, synopsis or intimation may be given out, broadcast or published
in advance of the hour of release.

NOTE: Release is automatic at 12:30 o'clock, P.M., Eastern Standard
Time, Monday, October 24, 1949. The same release applies to all radio
announcers and news broadcasters, both in the United States and abroad.

PLEASE GUARD AGAINST PREMATURE PUBLICATION OR RADIO ANNOUNCEMENT.

CHARLES G. ROSS
Secretary to the President

- -

President Romulo, Mr. Lie, Distinguished Representatives and
Fellow Guests:

We have come together today to lay the cornerstone of the
permanent headquarters of the United Nations. These are the most
important buildings in the world, for they are the center of man's
hope for peace and a better life. This is the place where the nations
of the world will work together to make that hope a reality.

This occasion is a source of special pride to the people of
the United States. We are deeply conscious of the honor of having the
permanent headquarters of the United Nations in this country. At the
same time, we know how important it is that the people of other nations
should come to know at first hand the work of this world organization.
We consider it appropriate, therefore, that the United Nations should
hold meetings from time to time in other countries when that can be done.
For the United Nations must draw its inspiration from the people of
every land; it must be truly representative of and responsive to the
peoples of the world whom it was created to serve.

This ceremony marks a new stage in the growth of the United
Nations. It is fitting that it should take place on United Nations Day,
the fourth anniversary of the day the Charter entered into effect.
During the four years of its existence, this organization has become a
powerful force for promoting peace and friendship among the peoples of
the world. The construction of this new headquarters is tangible proof
of the steadfast faith of the members in the vitality and strength of the
organization, and of our determination that it shall become more and more
effective in the years ahead.

The Charter embodies the hopes and ideals of men everywhere.
Hopes and ideals are not static. They are dynamic, and they give life
and vigor to the United Nations. We look forward to a continuing growth
and evolution of the organization to meet the changing needs of the
world's peoples. We hope that eventually every nation on earth will be
a fully qualified and loyal member.

We who are close to the United Nations sometimes forget that
it is more than the procedures, the councils and the debates, through
which it operates. We tend to overlook the fact that the organization
is the living embodiment of the principles of the Charter — the re-
nunciation of aggression and the joint determination to build a better
life.

But if we overlook this fact, we will fail to realize the
strength and power of the United Nations. We will fail to understand
the true nature of this new force that has been created in the affairs
of our time.

The United Nations is essentially an expression of the moral
nature of man's aspirations. The Charter clearly shows our determination
that international problems must be settled on a basis acceptable to the
conscience of mankind.

169

Because the United Nations is the dynamic expression of what all the peoples of the world desire, because it sets up a standard of right and justice for all nations, it is greater than any of its members. The compact that underlies the United Nations cannot be ignored -- and it cannot be infringed or dissolved.

We in the United States, in the course of our own history, have learned what it means to set up an organization to give expression to the common desire for peace and unity. Our Constitution expressed the will of the people that there should be a United States. And through toil and struggle the people made their will prevail.

In the same way, I think, the Charter and the organization served by these buildings express the will of the people of the world that there shall be a United Nations.

This does not mean that all the member countries are of one mind on all issues. The controversies which divide us go very deep. We should understand that these buildings are not a monument to the unanimous agreement of nations on all things. But they signify one new and important fact. They signify that the peoples of the world are of one mind in their determination to solve their common problems by working together.

Our success in the United Nations will be measured not only in terms of our ability to meet and master political controversies. We have learned that political controversies grow out of social and economic problems. If the people of the world are to live together in peace, we must work together to establish the conditions that will provide a firm foundation for peace.

For this reason, our success will also be measured by the extent to which the rights of individual human beings are realized. And it will be measured by the extent of our economic and social progress.

These fundamental facts are recognized both in the language of the Charter and in the activities in which the United Nations has been engaged during the past four years. The Charter plainly makes respect for human rights by nations a matter of international concern. The member nations have learned from bitter experience that regard for human rights is indispensable to political, economic and social progress. They have learned that disregard of human rights is the beginning of tyranny and, too often, the beginning of war.

For these reasons, the United Nations has devoted much of its time to fostering respect for human rights. The General Assembly has adopted the Universal Declaration of Human Rights and the Convention on Genocide. Other important measures in this field are under study.

I am confident that this great work will go steadily forward. The preparation of a Covenant on Human Rights by the Human Rights Commission is a task with which the United States is deeply concerned. We believe strongly that the attainment of basic civil and political rights for men and women everywhere -- without regard to race, language or religion -- is essential to the peace we are seeking. We hope that the Covenant on Human Rights will contain effective provisions regarding freedom of information. The minds of men must be free from artificial and arbitrary restraints, in order that they may seek the truth and apply their intelligence to the making of a better world.

Another field in which the United Nations is undertaking to build the foundations of a peaceful world is that of economic development. Today, at least half of mankind lives in dire poverty. Hundreds of millions of men, women and children lack adequate food, clothing and shelter. We cannot achieve permanent peace and prosperity in the world until the standard of living in under-developed areas is raised.

It is for this reason that I have urged the launching of a vigorous and concerted effort to apply modern technology and capital investment to improve the lot of these peoples. These areas need a large expansion of investment and trade. In order for this to take place, they also need the application of scientific knowledge and technical skills to their basic problems -- producing more food, improving health and sanitation, making use of their natural resources, and educating their people.

To meet these needs, the United Nations and its agencies are preparing a detailed program for technical assistance to under-developed areas.

The Economic and Social Council last summer defined the basic principles which should underlie this program. The General Assembly is now completing and perfecting the initial plans. The fact that the Economic Committee of the Assembly voted unanimously for the resolution on technical assistance shows that this is a common cause which commands united support. Although differences may arise over details of the program, I fervently hope that the Members of the United Nations will remain unanimous in their determination to raise the standards of living of the less fortunate members of the human family.

The United States intends to play its full part in this great enterprise. We are already carrying on a number of activities in this field. I shall urge the Congress, when it reconvenes in January, to give high priority to proposals which will make possible additional technical assistance and capital investment.

I should like to speak of one other problem which is of major concern to the United Nations. That is the control of atomic energy.

Ever since the first atomic weapon was developed, a major objective of United States policy has been a system of international control of atomic energy that would assure effective prohibition of atomic weapons, and at the same time would promote the peaceful use of atomic energy by all nations.

In November, 1945, Prime Minister Attlee of the United Kingdom, Prime Minister King of Canada and I agreed that the problem of international control of atomic energy should be referred to the United Nations. The establishment of the United Nations Atomic Energy Commission was one of the first acts of the first session of the General Assembly.

That Commission worked for three years on the problem. It developed a plan of control which reflected valuable contributions by almost every country represented on the Commission. This plan of control was overwhelmingly approved by the General Assembly on November 4, 1948.

This is a good plan. It is a plan that can work and, more important, it is a plan that can be effective in accomplishing its purpose. It is the only plan so far developed that would meet the technical requirements of control, that would make prohibition of atomic weapons effective, and at the same time promote the peaceful development of atomic energy on a cooperative basis.

We support this plan and will continue to support it unless and until a better and more effective plan is put forward. To assure that atomic energy will be devoted to man's welfare and not to his destruction is a continuing challenge to all nations and all peoples. The United States is now, and will remain, ready to do its full share in meeting this challenge.

Respect for human rights, promotion of economic development, and a system for control of weapons are requisites to the kind of world we seek. We cannot solve these problems overnight, but we must keep everlastingly working at them in order to reach our goal.

No single nation can always have its own way, for these are human problems, and the solution of human problems is to be found in negotiation and mutual adjustment.

The challenge of the twentieth century is the challenge of human relations, and not of impersonal natural forces. The real dangers confronting us today have their origins in outmoded habits of thought, in the inertia of human nature, and in preoccupation with supposed national interests to the detriment of the common good.

As members of the United Nations, we are convinced that patience, the spirit of reasonableness, and hard work will solve the most stubborn political problems. We are convinced that individual rights and social and economic progress can be advanced through international cooperation.

Our faith is in the betterment of human relations. Our vision is of a better world in which men and nations can live together, respecting one another's rights and cooperating in building a better life for all. Our efforts are made in the belief that men and nations can cooperate, that there are no international problems which men of good will cannot solve or adjust.

Mr. President, Mr. Lie, the laying of this cornerstone is an act of faith -- our unshakable faith that the United Nations will succeed in accomplishing the great tasks for which it was created.

But "faith without works is dead." We must make our devotion to the ideals of the Charter as strong as the steel in this building. We must **pursue** the objectives of the Charter with resolution as firm as the rock on which this building rests. We must conduct our affairs foursquare with the Charter, in terms as true as this cornerstone.

If we do these things, the United Nations will endure and will bring the blessings of peace and well-being to mankind.

- - - - - - - - -

Truman and Korea

An Assessment of Presidential Performance

William Stueck

Growing up in a small, conservative Connecticut town in the 1950s and early 1960s, I did not hear much of Harry Truman's side of the Korean War. In my home, Truman was called "hair-breath Harry," the meaning of which I never understood, except that it was not a compliment; his firing of Gen. Douglas MacArthur was described as "when the humming-bird called home the hawk." During my teens, when an old naval commander moved in next door, I did learn of Truman's claim that the most important thing he did while president was to win the Korean War. "I got news for him," the old sea dog would grumble; "We didn't win the Korean War! Those sons-a-bitches in Washington wouldn't let ole MacArthur finish the job." It was not until the late 1960s and graduate school that I was exposed to Truman's case, first in British writer David Rees's classic *Korea: The Limited War* and then in political scientist John Spanier's more polemical *The Truman-MacArthur Controversy and the Korean War*.[1] Now, after thirty-five years of research, reflection, and writing on the Korean War, I have before me the task of commenting on Truman's self-assessment regarding the event as manifested in his Farewell

1. Rees, *Korea: The Limited War* (New York: St. Martin's Press, 1964), and Spanier, *The Truman-MacArthur Controversy and the Korean War* (Cambridge: Harvard University Press, 1959). For an appreciative assessment of the former book, see William Stueck, "The Korean War as History: David Rees' *Korea: The Limited War* in Retrospect," http://www.archives.gov/research_room/research_topics/cold_war_history_conference/stueck_paper.html.

Address of January 1953. My old neighbor will probably roll over in his grave at the result; my dad will be more tolerant, but quietly skeptical.

As Richard Kirkendall points out, most of Truman's address dealt with foreign policy. Predictably, the outgoing president focused on the Cold War, which he characterized as "this conflict between those who love freedom and those who would lead the world back into slavery and darkness." History would "remember my term in office as the years when the 'cold war' began to overshadow our lives," he acknowledged, but also would "say that in those eight years we have set the course that can win it." "We have succeeded in carving out a new set of policies to attain peace," Truman declared. "We have averted World War III up to now, and we may already have succeeded in establishing conditions which can keep that war from happening as far ahead as man can see." He went on to contrast this record with the U.S. course during the interwar period, when "we withdrew from world affairs—we failed to act in concert with other peoples against aggression—we helped to kill the League of Nations—and we built up tariff barriers that strangled world trade."

It was in the second and third of these four areas that U.S. action in Korea, beginning in late June 1950, provided a stark contrast. "Most important of all," Truman asserted at the end of a recital of measures taken since 1946 to contain the Soviet Union, "we acted in Korea." The Soviet-supported North Korean regime had launched military "aggression" across the thirty-eighth parallel in a "probing" or "testing" action. Had "we let the Republic of Korea go under, some other country would be next, and then another." Such developments would have drained "the courage and confidence of the free world," just as had occurred in the 1930s, and the United Nations would have gone "the way of the League of Nations."

Given the self-serving and partisan context within which these comments appeared, they have aged remarkably well. Truman and his successors did avert World War III, and Truman and his advisers set the United States on a course in which, over time, the Cold War was won. On Korea, Truman ignored the nationalistic and civil dimensions of the outbreak of war, but most likely he did not err in characterizing it as a probing action from Moscow's perspective.[2] Soviet leader Joseph Stalin gave his North Korean counterpart

2. For the nationalistic and civil dimensions of the war, see Bruce Cumings, *The Origins of the Korean War*, 2 vols. (Princeton: Princeton University Press, 1981, 1990). For an effort to balance the civil and nationalistic dimensions with the international ones, see William Stueck, *Rethinking the Korean War: A New Diplomatic and Strategic History* (Princeton: Princeton University Press, 2002), 60–83.

Kim Il-sung the green light and the wherewithal to attack South Korea at a time when he possessed no master plan for military aggression—or even a clear intention to move Soviet or Soviet-sponsored forces aggressively in another area. Yet as Kathryn Weathersby points out, fundamental to Stalin's decisions was the belief that the United States would not intervene to save South Korea, and in part this calculation derived from the U.S. refusal to effectively resist the Communist victory in China. Had the Korean venture succeeded, therefore, Stalin may well have seen the opportunity to move against other nations not explicitly protected by Washington from attack.[3] As for the United Nations, we must recall that the North Korean move came while the Soviets were boycotting the Security Council and were promoting an international "peace" campaign that included Communist bloc governments and leftist parties in the West and Third World. Some believed that this movement sought to provide the foundation for a new organization that would compete with the largely U.S.-dominated United Nations.[4] When the United States succeeded in pushing two resolutions through the Security Council supporting its position on Korea, it became apparent to Stalin that participation in that body was in Soviet interests. Had U.S.-UN resistance in Korea proved ineffectual, Stalin might have continued to boycott the Security Council as a prelude to total Soviet withdrawal from the international organization. The Korean War did not strengthen the United Nations, but the success of the North Korean attack might well have led to its destruction as a broadly based international body.[5]

Why couldn't the United States have written off South Korea in June 1950 while using the North Korean attack as a call to arms in the United States, Europe, and Japan for a political and military effort that would have deterred Stalin and his allies from acting aggressively elsewhere? South Korea,

---

3. Weathersby, "The Soviet Role in the Korean War: An Assessment of the State of Knowledge," in *The Korean War: Interpretive Essays,* ed. William Stueck (Lexington: University Press of Kentucky, 2004). Weathersby draws this conclusion from a summary of Stalin's comments to Kim Il-sung in April 1950, which included the following statement: "Americans left China and did not dare to challenge the new Chinese authorities militarily." See Evgeniy P. Bajanov and Natalia Bajanova, "The Korean Conflict, 1950–1953: The Most Mysterious War of the 20th Century—Based on Secret Soviet Archives," 41; this is an English translation of an unpublished manuscript by two Russian scholars with access to the Presidential Archives in Moscow (copy in author's possession).

4. Marshall Shulman, *Stalin's Foreign Policy Reappraised* (Cambridge: Harvard University Press, 1963).

5. This point is developed further in William Stueck, *The Korean War: An International History* (Princeton: Princeton University Press, 1995), 369–70.

after all, was *not* of vital strategic significance, nor was it a good place to tie down large numbers of American troops. The answer is that, after having created an independent South Korea—and having done so through the United Nations—to have abandoned it in the face of overt military assault risked seriously undermining allied confidence in U.S. leadership and domestic confidence in the Truman administration.[6] These developments would have greatly magnified the difficulty for Truman, both abroad and at home, in mobilizing the support necessary to build up the military strength essential to contain the Soviet bloc. We cannot with any assurance say that the reinforced U.S.-led coalition emerging from the Korean War could have been replicated without the effective U.S.-UN resistance to North Korea that actually occurred.

But was the strengthening militarily of the Western coalition really essential? Was there a need for the massive military buildup that occurred in the United States and western Europe in the years following June 1950, or did Truman and his advisers and allies perceive a Soviet threat that did not exist? While it is possible to quibble on details, the record of Soviet behavior through the North Korean attack and what we now know about the Soviet side indicate that Truman pursued the wise course. Stalin surely had no master plan for aggression or world conquest, but he did take a series of military or quasi-military actions that revealed an expansionist thrust and a determination to probe U.S. intentions. In his Farewell Address, Truman mentioned actions involving Iran, Greece, Turkey, and Berlin. He might have added Manchuria, where Stalin ignored agreements with the Americans and Chinese Nationalists by giving assistance to the Communists and then withdrew troops in the spring of 1946 only under U.S. pressure.[7] By mid-1950 developments related to the military balance of power were in progress that, left to continue over several more years, would have produced a most dangerous situation indeed. After an initial period of demobilization following World War II, the Soviets began a military buildup in 1949.[8] The successful test of an atomic device and the Communist victory in China during 1949 added significantly to the military potential of the Soviet camp. Stalin's green light to Kim Il-sung was at least in part a result of Mao Zedong's advance in China,

6. American diplomat Charles E. Bohlen later recalled that, when told of the U.S. decision to provide military assistance to South Korea, French Foreign Minister Robert Schuman declared, in an obvious reference to the 1930s, "Thank God, this will not be a repetition of the past." See Bohlen, *Witness to History: 1929–1969* (New York: Norton, 1973), 291–92. For a contemporary report of relief in western Europe at the strong U.S. response to the North Korean attack, see *New York Times,* July 2, 1950, 4:1.

7. Odd Arne Westad, *Cold War and Revolution: Soviet-American Rivalry and the Origins of the Chinese Civil War* (New York: Columbia University Press, 1993), 163.

8. David Holloway, *Stalin and the Bomb* (New Haven: Yale University Press, 1994), 240–41.

Mao's desire for a close alliance with the Soviet Union, and the growing weakness of the United States in East Asia.[9] Without the increase in military strength sparked by the Korean War, by the mid-1950s the United States and its NATO allies would have faced a Soviet bloc with a continuing advantage in conventional forces in Europe and a capacity to launch a nuclear attack on the American homeland. The implications of such a development, given past Soviet behavior, are not comforting to imagine.

If Truman's statements of January 1953 about his reaction to the North Korean attack nearly three years earlier appear sound—and even put him in a rather heroic light—his omissions cast his overall performance regarding Korea in a different perspective. Those omissions may be grouped in three broad categories: (1) the U.S. failure to prevent the North Korean attack altogether; (2) the U.S. failure to end the war quickly and at minimal cost once it had started or, worse still, the failure to end it at all; and (3) the U.S. failure to win a decisive victory in the war. The second and third categories represent, to some degree, conflicting strains of thought, which will be addressed below. The immediate task is to assess Truman's role in and responsibility for the American failure to deter the North Koreans from attacking.

The logic for holding Truman at least partly responsible here is clear-cut. He was a man proud of his ability to make decisions as chief executive. "The buck stops here" was a fundamental principle of governance in Truman's Oval Office, and one of its obvious implications was that the president must not only render final judgments on important and difficult issues but also take responsibility for those judgments and their consequences. Truman had signed off on the decisions to intervene in Korea at the end of World War II, to take the Korean issue to the United Nations in 1947, and to press there for the creation of an independent government below the thirty-eighth parallel. Those decisions provided the foundation for the beliefs that the North Korean attack of June 1950 constituted aggression and that the United States must act to resist it. That being the case, Truman should have been more diligent in advance in conveying to the other side a sense of U.S. commitment to South Korea.

The point becomes all the stronger given the available evidence about deliberations among Communist leaders preceding the North Korean move. Kim Il-sung first approached Stalin regarding an attack on the South in March 1949, when he visited Moscow. The Soviet leader told his guest to be patient, that his forces currently lacked "overwhelming superiority over the troops of the South," that U.S. soldiers remained in the Republic of Korea

9. See Bajanov and Bajanova, "Korean Conflict," 40–41.

and would probably "interfere in case of hostilities." He also noted that an agreement existed between Washington and Moscow on the thirty-eighth parallel, providing an additional reason for the United States to intervene if the North attacked. Should South Korea attack first, however, then Kim could launch a counterattack and be assured of widespread support.[10]

Kim approached the Soviets again in August. The last American occupation troops had withdrawn in June, thus eliminating the risk of immediate U.S. involvement. The prospect of American intervention was further reduced, Kim argued, by the fact that the agreement on the thirty-eighth parallel was merely to divide the zones of occupation between Soviet and U.S. forces in the aftermath of Japan's surrender. With the occupation forces of both sides gone and independent regimes in place in North and South Korea, the 1945 agreement was no longer pertinent. Furthermore, Kim asserted, recent clashes of his forces with those of the Republic of Korea in the South indicated that his were clearly superior. Again Stalin demurred, emphasizing that the North should take the offensive only in response to an attack from the South.[11]

It was not until late January 1950 that Stalin showed a willingness to reconsider Kim's request, and he gave a conditional go-ahead to the North Korean leader only the following April. A summary of Stalin's conversations with Kim in Moscow during that month indicates that the Communist victory on mainland China, the American withdrawal from there without a fight, and the recent conclusion of a military alliance between Moscow and Beijing had altered the situation in Korea in the Soviet leader's mind. In addition, "according to information coming from the United States . . . the prevailing mood is not to interfere," a mood reinforced by the successful Soviet test of an atomic bomb the previous August. Even so, Stalin emphasized the need for the North to prepare carefully in order to win a quick military victory so "the Southerners and the Americans . . . won't have time to put up a strong resistance and to mobilize international support." Stalin also insisted that Kim gain Mao Zedong's advance approval for the attack. If Kim did run into difficulty with the Americans, it would be up to China, not the Soviet Union, to give him direct assistance. Kim received Mao's approval in mid-May on a trip to Beijing.[12]

10. Ibid., 18.
11. Ibid., 17–19, 29–33; *Bulletin* of the Cold War International History Project 5 (Spring 1995): 6–8.
12. Bajanov and Bajanova, "Korean Conflict," 41–43, 48–53; Chen Jian, *China's Road to the Korean War: The Making of the Sino-American Confrontation* (New York: Columbia University Press, 1994), 111–13.

These deliberations suggest that, had the United States conveyed to the Soviets a determination to defend South Korea, Stalin would not have approved an attack and given Kim the means to carry it out. The Soviet leader was concerned about the American response to a North Korean attack throughout the period from March 1949 to June 1950, but in early 1950 he reversed an earlier conclusion and decided that strong U.S. intervention was unlikely on the peninsula. Certainly the U.S. withdrawal of occupation forces from Korea in June 1949 and the refusal of Washington to intervene in China to halt the Communist advance influenced his thinking, but so too did evidence emanating from within the United States. Kathryn Weathersby argues that Stalin may have received information on NSC-48, a top-secret U.S. planning document regarding East Asia of late December 1948, through the British spy Kim Philby. Weathersby and others, myself included, have speculated that Secretary of State Dean Acheson's speech at the National Press Club in Washington, in which Korea was omitted from the American defense perimeter in the Pacific, encouraged Stalin to go along with Kim's desires. So did defeat by the U.S. House of Representatives a week later of a bill for aid to Korea.[13] If these were not enough, Truman's annual budget proposal to Congress in January included less than fourteen billion dollars overall for defense, a figure well below that anticipated a year earlier.[14] Subsequent statements by Acheson and Sen. Tom Connally, a Democrat and chairman of the Senate Foreign Relations Committee, if anything strengthened Stalin's belief that a rapid North Korean military campaign against the South, reinforced by massive uprisings there against the conservative regime of Syngman Rhee, would face no effective resistance from American forces.[15] The best evidence indicates that Stalin could have been deterred from supporting Kim and that Kim, at least for the present given his dependence on Soviet support, would not have moved without Stalin's green light.

13. Weathersby, "Soviet Role in the Korean War"; Stueck, *Korean War,* 32–36. For dissenting views of Acheson's speech and its affect, see Cumings, *Origins of the Korean War,* 2:408–38, and James I. Matray, "Dean Acheson's Press Club Speech Reexamined," *Journal of Conflict Studies* 22 (Spring 2002): 28–55.

14. Michael J. Hogan, *A Cross of Iron: Harry S. Truman and the Origins of the National Security State, 1945–1954* (New York: Cambridge University Press, 1998), 285.

15. For Acheson's statement before the Senate Foreign Relations Committee on March 7, 1950, see U.S. Department of State *Bulletin,* March 20, 1950, 454. This journal, of course, was a public document easily accessible to Soviet officials. For Senator Connally's statement, see *U.S. News World Report,* May 5, 1950. For Acheson's reply to this statement that South Korea was likely to fall to the Communists, see U.S. Department of State, *Foreign Relations of the United States, 1950, Korea* (Washington, D.C.: U.S. Government Printing Office, 1976), 7:67n1.

Why did American deterrence fail in Korea? An answer to this question does not exonerate Truman from responsibility, but it does suggest that he deserves a measure of sympathy given the complexity of American politics, both partisan and bureaucratic, and the scope of the challenges he faced in the years immediately following World War II.

The first point to be made is that, during his term, Truman initiated foreign policies that engaged the United States abroad on a level unprecedented in peacetime in the nation's history. In doing so, he had to contend with a Congress sometimes controlled by the opposition Republican Party. Even when in his own party's hands, the legislative branch included influential individuals, some Democrats, who were dubious of a high level of activism outside the Western Hemisphere and the spending levels necessary at home to sustain it.[16] He also had to grapple with an American public anxious to move on to a better life following a decade and a half of depression and war. World War II had brought about a drastic reconfiguration of power on the Eurasian land mass, a change with huge implications regarding the need for the United States to exercise its power abroad; but Truman's predecessor had done little to prepare Americans for the new burdens that accompanied this change. As a result, once Germany surrendered in May 1945 the clamor for rapid demobilization of the armed forces picked up steam, and when Japan followed suit four months later the pressure became overwhelming. By the time of Truman's call in March 1947 for a campaign to assist "free peoples who are resisting attempted subjugation by armed minorities or by outside pressures," U.S. armed forces were a mere shell of their former selves and the bulk of Congress and the public rested comfortably in the assumption that America's atomic monopoly represented a cost-effective method of protecting the country from any foreseeable military threat.[17]

This was the context within which Korea policy was shaped prior to June 25, 1950. For example, as the Republican-dominated Congress accepted Truman's proposals regarding aid to Greece and Turkey and prepared to consider an even larger program for economic assistance to Europe, it reduced by two hundred million dollars administration budget requests for the War Department for fiscal year 1948. These cuts included reductions in army civilian employees by 58,371 and officers by 12,500. Both of these categories were

16. See, for example, Susan Hartmann, *Truman and the 80th Congress* (Columbia: University of Missouri Press, 1971), 65, 161–62, 169–73.

17. For a discussion of congressional attitudes toward defense spending, see Edward A. Kolodziej, *The Uncommon Defense and Congress, 1945–1953* (Columbus: Ohio State University Press, 1966), 33–123.

heavily represented in occupation duties abroad. Simultaneously, congressional leaders discouraged the administration from submitting a major economic aid bill for Korea. The U.S. occupation of Korea already faced serious difficulties, and these developments reflected the need of the Truman administration to make hard choices regarding its priorities abroad. With the Joint Chiefs of Staff concluding in September 1947 that the United States had "little strategic interest" in maintaining troops in Korea, that any advantage gained by the Soviet Union from control of the entire peninsula could be neutralized by American airpower in Japan and Okinawa, Washington moved decisively toward ending the occupation. Essentially, the Pentagon preferred to write off Korea as an investment gone bad, but the State Department insisted that the United States had an important commitment to at least the southern half of the country. With the Soviet Union refusing to accept American plans for a unified, independent Korea, the United States worked through the United Nations in forming an independent government, the Republic of Korea (ROK), below the thirty-eighth parallel. The State Department managed to get through Congress a program of limited economic and military assistance to the fledgling ROK and to delay the final withdrawal of U.S. troops. Yet in 1948 the legislative branch passed a large tax cut over Truman's veto.[18] With the onset of recession in early 1949, the reduction of federal revenues led to a substantial deficit, thus reinforcing the predisposition in the executive branch and Congress to focus defense policy on airpower and atomic weapons. In June 1949, despite lingering concerns in the State Department, the last American combat units left Korea, leaving only five hundred military advisers to assist in training the ROK army.[19]

In the year prior to the North Korean attack, Truman faced the tasks in foreign policy of pushing through Congress a major arms aid package for Europe and the renewal of funding for the Marshall Plan. He also had to resist pressure for an undesirable increase in U.S. involvement in the civil war in China. The State Department remained concerned about Korea, yet that country possessed no important constituency in the United States, and any effort to single it out for attention would run into indifference in the Pentagon and/or added pressure from pro–Chiang Kai-shek forces in Congress and the press for new assistance to Nationalist China. Besides, American intelligence assessments indicated that North Korea was unlikely to launch an

---

18. William Whitney Stueck Jr., *The Road to Confrontation: American Policy toward China and Korea, 1947–1950* (Chapel Hill: University of North Carolina Press, 1981), 81–82, 84–88, 98–102; Hartmann, *Truman and the 80th Congress*, 132–37.

19. Stueck, *Road to Confrontation*, 98–109, 153–59.

all-out attack in the near future because it continued to have a chance to overthrow the ROK through assistance to antigovernment guerrillas below the thirty-eighth parallel. The ROK's internal weakness and the oft-expressed desire of its president, Syngman Rhee, to take military action against the North to unite the peninsula made Washington reluctant to provide large-scale arms assistance. Given Korea's marginal strategic significance to the United States and the uncertainty, both locally and otherwise, regarding the circumstances under which a conflagration might occur on the peninsula, Washington could not afford to make an advance commitment to military action there.[20]

The problem with the above analysis is that it omits Truman's contribution to the events described. If we are to give the president credit for his leadership from 1947 to 1949 in warning the country of the Soviet threat and pushing through Congress a series of measures to contain it, we must also acknowledge the limits of his leadership regarding the military dimension of the threat. It was not as if he was lacking in advice from his underlings in the Pentagon, who wanted to use the Czech crisis of March 1948 as an instrument for a major buildup of U.S. military forces. Truman accepted only modest increases in military manpower levels, however, and when the leading administration hawk, Secretary of Defense James Forrestal, left office in early 1949 he was replaced by Louis Johnson, who was only too willing to implement his boss's desire to keep a tight rein on defense spending. Truman, historian Paul Pierpaoli remarks, was "a legendary fiscal conservative," a proponent of the view that budget deficits would undermine national economic strength, America's primary asset in its struggle with the Soviet Union. His determination to implement domestic welfare programs that would add hundreds of millions of dollars to federal expenditures strengthened his resolve to limit military expenditures. Finally, he possessed deeply ingrained suspicions and fears of a national security state, believing that empowerment of the military brass and/or national security managers would undermine American democracy and that the military services could get along with what they had if only they would rid themselves of redundancies in weapons and personnel rooted in their inability to agree on missions.[21] The president continued to resist a substantial increase in overall military spending even after the successful Soviet test of an atomic bomb and the Communist victory in mainland China. Although he did not explicitly reject NSC-68, a planning document

---

20. Ibid., 153–71.
21. Paul G. Pierpaoli Jr., *Truman and Korea: The Political Culture of the Early Cold War* (Columbia: University of Missouri Press, 1999), 18.

that appeared on his desk in April 1950 asserting the need for a massive increase in the military budget, he made no move to implement it. In early May he actually stated publicly that the next year's budget would be smaller than the current one.[22]

Clearly Truman's attitude toward defense spending contributed to a disjunction between America's growing commitments abroad and the means available to fulfill them. Even if we concede that an explicit commitment to South Korea's defense was unwarranted prior to June 25, 1950, we must acknowledge that the continuing desire of the Pentagon to withdraw American troops from the peninsula and its lack of enthusiasm for bolstering State Department efforts at deterrence there were in part a result of the president's determination to hold down the defense budget.

It is unrealistic to expect Truman and his advisers, in the immediate aftermath of World War II, to have constructed and implemented a fully coherent national strategy. The Soviet threat was not widely accepted until early 1946, and its precise nature remained contested for some time after that.[23] Yet, in addition to the existence of numerous advocates of higher defense spending, there was no shortage of expert analysts who believed that the American economy could thrive with higher defense budgets, even if this meant substantial budget deficits over the short term. Most prominent of these was Leon Keyserling, who became chairman of the Council of Economic Advisers in late 1949 following the resignation of the more conservative Edwin Nourse. Keyserling was Truman's appointee, but prior to June 1950 the commander in chief showed no inclination to use Keyserling's thinking as justification for increased military expenditures.[24]

Whatever Truman's failures prior to the North Korean attack, there can be no doubt that his response to this event was swift and vigorous. Within a week, he committed American troops to the defense of the ROK, and over

22. *Public Papers of the Presidents of the United States: Harry S. Truman, 1945–1953,* 8 vols. (Washington, D.C.: U.S. Government Printing Office, 1961–1966), 6 (1950): 286. For a powerful indictment of Truman's position on defense spending prior to the Korean War, see Robert A. Pollard, "The National Security State Reconsidered: Truman and Economic Containment, 1945–1950," in *The Truman Presidency,* ed. Michael J. Lacey (New York: Woodrow Wilson Center for Scholars and Cambridge University Press, 1989), 205–34.

23. I am using John Lewis Gaddis's definition of *strategy* here: "the process by which ends are related to means, intentions to capabilities, objectives to resources." See his *Strategies of Containment: A Critical Appraisal of Postwar American National Security Policy* (New York: Oxford University Press, 1982), viii.

24. For Nourse's struggle with Keyserling and the latter's ascendance, see Hogan, *Cross of Iron,* 276–91. For Truman's response to NSC-68, see 301–4.

the next two months he asked Congress for new funding for foreign arms assistance, the Atomic Energy Commission, and the Pentagon's budget that virtually doubled heretofore projected expenditures for fiscal 1951. These were merely the first steps in what became the implementation of NSC-68 and the creation of a national security state.[25]

Some scholars who defend Truman for intervening in Korea criticize him for an excessive military buildup at home and for an overconcentration of power in the executive branch. I have argued above for the prudence of a military buildup, while conceding that its size is open to debate. It deserves mention, however, that Truman was by no means on the extreme side of contemporary disputes over the size of the military buildup. Moreover, due to restraining forces in both the executive and legislative branches, the buildup was not nearly as large as some believed was necessary.[26] On executive power, broader agreement exists that Truman erred in refusing to go to Congress for at least a resolution approving his action in Korea and that this refusal represented an important step in the development of the "imperial presidency" that peaked in the Johnson and Nixon years.[27]

Criticism is also widespread of Truman's conduct of the war in the fall of 1950, when he altered the original mission of the intervention from restoring

25. See ibid., 304–65.

26. For a nuanced treatment of Truman's position on military spending, see Hogan, *Cross of Iron*. For a sharp critique, see Arnold A. Offner, *Another Such Victory: President Truman and the Cold War, 1945–1953* (Stanford: Stanford University Press, 2002), 458–60, 468–70. For an account that emphasizes the role of American political culture in averting excessive militarization and concentration of power in the executive, see Aaron L. Friedberg, *In the Shadow of the Garrison State: America's Anti-Statism and Its Cold War Strategy* (Princeton: Princeton University Press, 2000).

27. See, for example, Offner, *Another Such Victory*, 376–78. For a more balanced assessment of the extent and limits of presidential power, see Stueck, *Rethinking the Korean War*, 238. Alonzo L. Hamby notes that "probably it was a mistake not to [go to Congress for approval] but hardly the enormous error often discerned from retrospective critics" (*Man of the People: A Life of Harry S. Truman* [New York: Oxford University Press, 1995], 539). Whatever the domestic political and constitutional arguments for congressional action, it is not clear that a declaration of war against North Korea would have served as a source of restraint either on presidential power at home or U.S. action abroad. By stoking passions at home for a militant campaign against Communism, such a declaration might have made it more difficult for Truman to limit the war, especially after the Chinese entered the conflict. By the logic of Truman's critics here, after all, China's intervention in the fall of 1950 would have dictated a congressional declaration of war against the new mainland regime as well, with serious implications regarding expansion of the war beyond Korea and the implementation of the Sino-Soviet alliance. Truman might have avoided these problems, however, had he asked Congress in July for a resolution of support for action to implement the recent U.N. Security Council resolutions on Korea.

the boundary of the thirty-eighth parallel to destroying North Korean forces and constructing a pro-American government throughout the peninsula. Rather than leading to an end to the fighting well before the end of the year, as a halting of UN ground forces at or near the old boundary line probably would have done, the headlong march to the Yalu River brought the Chinese Communists into the fray and extended the war's duration indefinitely against a secondary enemy and in a location far removed from Europe, the key battlefield of the Cold War. The march beyond the narrow neck of Korea located just north of the cities of Pyongyang and Wonsan was especially ill advised, as it overextended UN ground units in a manner that left them vulnerable to strong Chinese counterattacks, undermined allied confidence in Washington's judgment, and greatly weakened Truman at home.

However faulty Truman's leadership may have been during the fall of 1950, the point needs to be made up front that halting UN forces at the thirty-eighth parallel in late September and early October would have had serious international and domestic drawbacks; even with a half-century of hindsight it is not clear that this approach would have been the wisest to follow. Most important here is that the thirty-eighth parallel was an indefensible line. As such, its reestablishment was unlikely "to restore international peace and security in the area," the phrase used in the U.S.-drafted UN Security Council resolution of the previous June 27, which called for action "to repel the armed attack" by North Korea.[28] In international relations as in life, of course, "security" is a relative rather than an absolute concept, but surely the United States had ample justification after June 25 to seek a boundary in Korea that possessed good natural barriers to being breached. A second problem with a halt at the thirty-eighth parallel was that it would have created a split between the United States and the ROK, whose leader, Syngman Rhee, was a fierce proponent of unification by any means necessary. The United States had helped to divide the country in 1945 and to perpetuate that division in 1948, while at the same time identifying unification as a continuing objective. To have denied ROK forces an opportunity to achieve that objective following North Korea's breach of the peace in June would have produced serious and potentially long-term difficulties for the United States in Korea. A third problem was that Truman and his Democratic Party were engaged in an intense battle at home for continued control of the federal government, and calling a halt to UN forces in Korea at the thirty-eighth parallel, especially following the sharp reversal of military conditions on the peninsula

---

28. U.N. document S/1511.

brought about by the Inchon landing, would have produced intensified attacks from the Republicans regarding the alleged timidity of American policy toward East Asia as a congressional election campaign reached its peak.[29]

In all three areas, a case can be made that most of the major elements of the policy Truman set in place in late September were the best suited to produce a positive result. The new orders sent to Gen. Douglas MacArthur, the commander of UN forces in Korea, on September 27 read in part: "Under no circumstances . . . will your forces cross the Manchurian or U.S.S.R. borders of Korea, and, as a matter of policy, no non-Korean ground forces will be used in the northeast provinces bordering the Soviet Union or in the area along the Manchurian border." Although "as a matter of policy" was a less absolute prohibition than "under no circumstances," and had possibly tragic future consequences, the idea behind this directive was that all UN ground forces would march as far north as the narrow neck of the peninsula just north of Pyongyang and Wonsan, and then ROK troops would move on to the northern border on their own, with the assistance of UN (mostly U.S.) air and naval power.[30]

This approach presented the possibility of (1) establishing a defensible line (either at the northern boundary of Korea if all went well, or at the narrow neck if otherwise), (2) a unified peninsula, and (3) a U.S. victory in East Asia that would have undermined perceptions at home of Democratic weakness in combating Communism in the region. If the Chinese Communists intervened, as they threatened to do at the end of September and early October, American ground forces at least would have been at a line they might have been able to defend, their sensitivity to the Chinese in halting well south of the Manchurian border would have made Beijing's position less attractive before international opinion, and criticism on the home front could have been contained by pointing to the improved position of friendly forces in Korea compared to the period before June 25 and the likely cost, in lives and treasure, of pursuing a more ambitious course.

Admittedly, any non-Korean ground effort across the thirty-eighth parallel increased the prospect of Chinese intervention, and that includes even a

29. A majority of American editorial writers as well as a majority of Americans questioned in a national poll favored a military effort to unite Korea. See U.S. Department of State, Office of Public Opinion Studies, "Fortnightly Survey of American Opinion on International Affairs," September, October 1950, Record Group 59, National Archives II, College Park, Md.

30. U.S. Department of State, *Foreign Relations of the United States, 1950,* 7:781; Dean Acheson, *Present at the Creation: My Years in the State Department* (New York: W. W. Norton, 1969), 452–55.

very limited move in search of a defensible line. Arguably, the safest approach from all perspectives except domestic politics was to establish such a line while announcing to the North Koreans and the Chinese that any effort to counter it would produce an all-out campaign to unite the peninsula. On the domestic front, Truman undermined his own flexibility in August by permitting his underlings to make public comments that encouraged expectations of a UN campaign to unite Korea. On the thirty-first, the president himself stated in a radio broadcast that "the Koreans have a right to be free, independent, and united" and that the United States, "under the guidance of the United Nations," would "do [its] part to help them enjoy that right."[31] Had the administration launched a summer campaign to encourage caution rather than boldness in Korea, the domestic climate in the fall might have been easier to manage, although there can be little doubt that the Republicans would have attempted to use any restraint by the United States to their partisan advantage.[32]

Truman boxed himself in still further on Korea in early October, when at American behest the UN General Assembly passed a resolution reiterating the international body's objective of "a unified, independent and democratic Government of Korea," first stated in November 1947, and then called for "all appropriate steps . . . to ensure conditions of stability throughout Korea."[33] In essence, the resolution defined victory on the peninsula *not* as the originally stated aim of reestablishing the thirty-eighth parallel, or even restoring "peace and security in the area," but as a united anti-Communist Korea.[34] By the time Chinese intervention became apparent in late October, therefore, any settlement short of Korea's unification under a friendly regime could not be considered anything but a defeat. Ironically, the president who before June 25 had failed to place protection of half of Korea high enough on his list of priorities now elevated its unification to a level that soon would have dire consequences for his presidency and his country.

31. U.S. Department of State *Bulletin* 23 (September 11, 1950): 407; Stueck, *Road to Confrontation,* 207–8.

32. The Truman administration did follow a policy of restraint regarding Taiwan during the summer while, despite a public row with General MacArthur, maintaining extensive public support. The Korean case was more difficult, however, as American soldiers were fighting and dying there in response to perceived Communist aggression. See Stueck, *Korean War,* 75.

33. Ibid., 904–5.

34. Richard E. Neustadt, *Presidential Power: The Politics of Leadership* (New York: John Wiley and Sons, 1960), 123. Concerned about broad international support for a ground campaign in North Korea, the United States could have proposed a resolution authorizing such action as necessary "to restore international peace and security in the area," an inherently ambiguous aim. There is no indication that the Truman administration considered this course.

Truman's ill-advised management of the Korean issue reached its apogee from mid-October to late November. During this period he permitted Mac-Arthur to move non-Korean ground units beyond the narrow neck in Korea and then to continue offensive operations in the face of irrefutable evidence of Chinese intervention. The result was a devastating Chinese counteroffensive in late November. Dean Acheson later referred to this development as "one of the most terrific disasters that has occurred to American foreign policy" and "the greatest disaster which occurred to the Truman administration."[35]

In his memoirs, Acheson wrote, "I have an unhappy conviction that none of us [advising the president], myself prominently included, served him as he was entitled to be served." Truman told political scientist Richard Neustadt many years after the event that MacArthur "was commander in the field. You pick your man, you've got to back him up. That's the only way a military organization can work. I got the best advice I could and the man on the spot said this was the thing to do. . . . So I agreed. That was my decision."[36] It was, indeed; yet Truman had not followed MacArthur's earlier advice regarding Taiwan, nor did he follow the field commander's subsequent advice on Korea, eventually firing him from all his commands. It was apparent by November 1950 that MacArthur placed an importance on East Asia in general that ran contrary to administration thinking, which was committed to a Europe-first strategy. Truman faced a very difficult set of circumstances in the fall of 1950, both domestic and international, and he did not receive sage advice from any of his top advisers. Still, he made the final choices, and on Korea he chose badly. The overall success of his presidency in the area of foreign policy derived in large part from his ability and willingness to choose people as his subordinates who were better informed and often more sophisticated than himself—and to follow their advice. There are times, nonetheless, when greatness in leadership requires an ability to rise above the wisdom and courage of subordinates, and in this instance Truman failed the test.

If his administration never fully recovered from that failure, Truman did manage in Korea to both contain Communism and contain the war. The president refused to panic in the face of China's counteroffensive, rejecting either withdrawal from Korea unless absolutely necessary or expansion of the war beyond the peninsula, as MacArthur wanted. In early April 1951, with UN forces back in the area of the thirty-eighth parallel and Chinese forces

35. "Princeton Seminars," February 13, 1954. This is the transcript, available in photocopied form at the Truman Library, of a series of retrospective discussions by high foreign policy officials in the Truman administration shortly after they left office.
36. Acheson, *Present at the Creation*, 466; Neustadt, *Presidential Power*, 128.

preparing to mount a new offensive, Truman cobbled together a consensus among his advisers that the wayward general must go, mustered the courage to do the deed, and then rode out the storm. When the Chinese spring offensives failed, he approved an attempt to negotiate an end to the fighting. Armistice talks began in July.

Yet when he left office a year and a half later, the shooting still had not stopped. The continuing war in Korea was a key in the defeat of the Democratic Party in the election of 1952 and in Truman's low ratings in public opinion polls.[37] So the issue remains: should Truman have done something differently between the Chinese intervention in late 1950 and his departure from office?

The first step in addressing this question is to evaluate MacArthur's proposed course of a naval blockade of and air attacks on China. At the time, this course was rejected on several grounds. First, it might have led to direct Soviet intervention in the war with airpower, ground forces, or both. Given the Soviets' proximity to Korea and their ability to strike Japan from the air, such intervention might well have forced a UN retreat from the peninsula and caused severe damage to U.S. airpower in Japan. Second, even if the Soviets did not intervene directly in Korea or attack Japan, their airpower in the Far East was sufficient to have inflicted serious losses on U.S. air forces operating over Manchuria. The combination of loss of planes and expenditure of bombs, including perhaps atomic bombs, over China would have depleted the capacity of the United States to launch its war plan against the Soviet Union.[38] As it was, American planners were uncertain that an atomic offensive against the Soviet homeland would destroy Moscow's war-making capacity. Given its conventional superiority in Europe, the Soviet army might well have marched to the English channel and bombed U.S. air bases in the British Isles, thus weakening the most important launching pads for the strategic offensive against the Soviet Union. Third, whether in an expanded war in northeast Asia or an all-out war in Europe that grew out of it, allied support was uncertain. NATO allies were uniformly opposed to expanding the war beyond Korea, and a U.S. flaunting of their views might have torn the young alliance asunder at a time when unity was most needed.[39] To Truman and his top advisers, the prospect of victory in Korea and/or a quick

37. Robert A. Divine, *Foreign Policy and U.S. Presidential Elections* (New York: New Viewpoints, 1974), 2:50–70; Hamby, *Man of the People*, 615.

38. Marc Trachtenberg, "'A Wasting Asset'? American Strategy and the Shifting Nuclear Balance, 1949–1954," *International Security* 13 (Winter 1988–1989): 20–36.

39. Stueck, *Korean War*, 132–38, 148–57, 178–82.

end to the war was never sufficiently alluring to warrant the risks that accompanied the effort.

A half-century later, with our access to huge bodies of formerly secret documents from both sides in the war, Truman's decision to limit the war to Korea appears sound. Although it is clear now as then that Stalin preferred to avoid a direct clash with the United States either in northeast Asia or in Europe, it is also apparent that he was willing to take considerable risk in aiding the Chinese and even to encourage them to pursue total victory in Korea. He, too, was impressed with divisions generated in the Western camp by U.S. conduct in Korea. Despite the Soviet Union's lack of full preparedness for war, he was well aware that the future might produce an enemy—with West Germany and Japan rearmed and the United States fully mobilized—far more potent than at present.[40] During the fall of 1950, he had resisted pressure from Pyongyang and Beijing to become directly involved in the fighting, but later, with China fully engaged against the Americans and the Western alliance approaching the breaking point, U.S. escalation of the war beyond the peninsula might well have led Stalin to take the plunge. Had he done so, the United States *might* have emerged victorious from the ensuing conflagration, but at a huge cost to life and treasure and, in all likelihood, to the trust and allegiance of its European allies. To his credit, Truman chose patience and internationalism over impulsiveness and unilateralism.

But what of more aggressive action within Korea to place greater diplomatic pressure on the enemy? Here the goal would not have been Communist acquiescence in total defeat on the peninsula, as MacArthur wanted, but rather enemy acceptance of an early end to the fighting on terms as or more attractive to the United States than the ones ultimately secured by the Eisenhower administration in mid-1953.

There is no doubt that during the last seven months of 1951 Chinese and North Korean forces were at a military disadvantage in Korea and that, after this, their integration of Soviet artillery and completion of deep, well-manned lines of defense made any significant UN gain on the ground extremely difficult and costly.[41] It is also true that in November 1951, after recent

40. See Stalin's letter to Kim Il-sung of October 8, 1950, translated by Alexandre Mansourov in *Bulletin* of the Cold War International History Project 6–7 (Winter 1995–1996): 116. Also Stueck, *Rethinking the Korean War*, 134–36.

41. Shu Guang Zhang, *Mao's Military Romanticism: China and the Korean War, 1950–1953* (Lawrence: University Press of Kansas, 1995), chaps. 7, 9; U.S. Army, *United States Army in the Korean War: Truce Tent and Fighting Front*, by Walter G. Hermes (Washington, D.C.: U.S. Government Printing Office, 1966), chap. 5.

UN ground gains of several miles at various points along the battlefront, Washington imposed concessions regarding an armistice line on its negotiators at Panmunjom against the passionate advice of the UN commander, Gen. Matthew B. Ridgway. The concessions included a provision that the final line would not be altered from the existing point of contact between the contestants so long as other issues for an armistice were resolved within thirty days. This provision, in turn, led the Eighth Army commander in Korea, Gen. James Van Fleet, to order an end to all offensive ground operations.[42] These facts would have been relatively insignificant had Truman not, in February 1952, decided to take a firm stand in favor of the principle of no forced repatriation of prisoners of war. Had he been willing to give ground on that issue, an armistice would have been achieved two months later. As it was, the Communists resisted the American position on POWs until June 1953, thus delaying an end to the fighting for more than a year.

The capacity of UN ground forces, without reinforcements, to advance substantially farther than they did any time between June and December 1951 remains debatable, although there is general agreement that any advance would not have been beyond the narrow neck. It is debatable as well whether or not an advance would have softened the Communist negotiating position at an earlier date. The Chinese, after all, could (and did) augment their forces in Korea, both in manpower and in Soviet firepower, and they were extraordinarily sensitive about making concessions under military pressure. The farther north UN forces advanced, the more difficult it would have been for Mao's "new China" to claim victory in the war—or even avoid a perception of defeat. In addition, any UN advance would have increased U.S. and allied casualties, increased the already considerable pressure on the home front to end the fighting, and undermined European support for American conduct of the war. On the other hand, the key Chinese concession on POWs in 1953 came after the United States had stepped up the air war over North Korea and threatened, in the face of allied pressure to the contrary, to escalate still further.[43]

The strongest case to be made against Truman is that, in late 1951, he permitted an end to military pressure on the ground in Korea while major issues remained to be resolved in the armistice talks. He did this without comprehending the potential significance of an unconventional stand on the POW

---

42. Stueck, *Korean War,* 236–43.

43. Ibid., 236–43, 313–30. It should be noted, though, that Stalin died in March 1953, which was probably the most important factor in the Communist move toward ending the war.

issue or even having made up his mind that that stand would be adopted. He adopted that position as firm only after the Communists had used the respite on the battlefield to improve their relative military position.[44]

Another criticism often directed at Truman is that his stand on POWs itself was unjustified. It was of dubious legality under the Geneva Convention of 1949, to which the United States was a signatory, and conditions in the POW camps in South Korea were such as to make it difficult for prisoners to express their true feelings toward repatriation. Many American military officials were against Truman's position because it gave priority to enemy rather than allied prisoners. The stance, it was feared, would at best keep American prisoners in Communist hands for longer than necessary and at worst lead to additional Americans dying or not being returned. Delay of an armistice, of course, also would lead to continuing battlefield casualties on the UN side.[45]

The case for no forced repatriation was not without merit, however. In practice, the Communists had flaunted the Geneva Convention from the beginning, treating UN POWs miserably. The Communists' list of POWs held in their custody numbered a mere 11,559, whereas the UN Command classified some 100,000 of its troops as missing in action. During the early months of the war alone, Communist news releases and radio broadcasts claimed the capture of more than 65,000 enemy soldiers. The UN Command list numbered 132,000 prisoners, with 37,000 more being classified as civilian internees because they had begun the war as residents of the South and, in some cases, had even been in the ROK army. The Communists reported 188,000 of their soldiers as missing. Whether or not we include the civilian internees, the UN list was far closer, proportionately or in absolute numbers, to the enemy's own estimates than was the case on the other side. Why should the bad behavior of the Communists be rewarded, some asked, with the return to the Communists of more than ten times the number of men returned to the United Nations, men who could then be reintegrated into Communist armies to fight another day? Rather, why not uphold the principle of no forced repatriation in this case so as to encourage soldiers in Communist armies in the future to defect rather than fight? Fearing such an outcome, Communist leaders might think twice about launching military aggression. At least the enforcement of no forced repatriation in Korea would represent a great propaganda victory in the war of ideas between the democratic United States

44. Ibid., 241–48, 258–65.
45. Ibid., 258–65. For a sharply critical analysis of Truman's policy on POWs, see Offner, *Another Such Victory,* 408–17, 469–70.

and the authoritarian Soviet Union. Pragmatic considerations aside, with memories still fresh of the brutal mistreatment of POWs forcibly returned to the Soviet Union following World War II, the humanitarian impulse was not without weight.[46]

Whatever the wisdom of Truman's decision, it was very much his own, as the State Department was divided on the issue and the Pentagon and UN Command essentially favored an all-for-all exchange.[47] The president's motives remain uncertain. His moral revulsion growing out of his experience with the return of prisoners to the Soviet Union during 1945 and 1946 probably played a role, as did his accumulated frustration and anger over dealing with Communist powers that he believed, as he wrote in his private journal, possessed "no sense of honor and no moral code."[48] He also worried that an end to the war might compromise the rearmament program at home.[49] It is doubtful that he preferred to continue the war, but his concern here may have led him to pursue its end with a bit less determination.

As things turned out, the rearmament program did continue through 1952, as did the war. If Truman must take a share of the blame for the unpreparedness that helped bring on the war in 1950, and if the prudence of his stand on POWs remains very much in doubt, there is no question that he used the conflict in Korea to put the United States in a much stronger military position vis-à-vis the Soviet Union.

Political leadership is an enterprise fraught with imprecision. Leaders are forever called upon to make decisions under the pressure of time and with incomplete information. Once decisions are made, they often take on lives of their own, closing off options and setting the course of events in directions that few anticipated or desired. Leadership in the United States is inherently untidy, with presidents constantly being restrained by a system and a populace that prioritizes restrictions on power. With these realities in mind, and with the records of dozens of other presidents available for comparison,

46. Stueck, *Korean War,* 244–45, 259–60, 264.

47. Ibid., 244–45, 250–51, 258–65.

48. Diary entry for January 27, 1952, Box 333, President's Secretary's Files, Truman Papers, Truman Library. On the experience with return of prisoners to the Soviet Union after World War II, see Mark R. Elliott, *Pawns of Yalta: Soviet Refugees and America's Role in Their Repatriation* (Urbana: University of Illinois Press, 1982).

49. U.S. Department of State, *Foreign Relations of the United States, 1951* (Washington, D.C.: U.S. Government Printing Office, 1983), 7:1244n, 1290–96. For evidence that Truman's fear was justified, see Pierpaoli, *Truman and Korea,* 119–59, and Friedberg, *In the Shadow of the Garrison State,* 122–23.

Truman's performance on Korea as chief executive merits a mixed grade, but one weighted toward the higher end.

Although Truman's actions and oversights contributed to the outbreak of war in June 1950, his early response was largely sound, including his action to bolster American military power. While he erred badly in the fall of 1950 with his overly aggressive campaign to unite Korea, he did not compound his mistake by expanding the war beyond the peninsula. Rather, he successfully escalated the military buildup and continued multilateral diplomacy to strengthen the Western alliance. In other words, Truman learned from his mistakes rather than compounding them and left the United States in a strong position to compete effectively with the primary enemy, the Soviet Union.

True, his legacy included questionable positions in Korea on POWs and elsewhere in East Asia on aid to the French in Indochina and to the Nationalist government on Taiwan. Yet the first of these was soon resolved advantageously by his successor, who experienced the good fortune of Stalin's death shortly after assuming office. The course in Indochina, however flawed, was a substantial distance in scope and time from the tragic intervention there under President Lyndon B. Johnson.[50] As for Taiwan, the consequences of Truman's move to protect the Nationalists in the aftermath of the North Korean attack of June 1950 remain with us to this day. We must recognize, though, that in addition to interjecting what turned out to be a dangerous, long-term dimension to the U.S. relationship with the People's Republic of China, Truman also made possible the eventual emergence of Taiwan as both an economic powerhouse and a working democracy, a success story for American policy in the underdeveloped world.

A comparison of this record with those of two highly rated wartime presidents of the twentieth century, Woodrow Wilson and Franklin D. Roosevelt, does not necessarily diminish Truman. Wilson led the United States into war only after failing to mediate an end to a massive European conflict and at least in part because he did not arm his country to a degree that forced the belligerents to take him seriously. To be sure, Wilson governed at a time when Americans were even less accustomed than during Truman's era to the

---

50. A debate has long existed as to whether the policies of Truman and Eisenhower during the 1950s weighted the scales overwhelmingly toward the escalation that Johnson chose in 1965. For two recent accounts that emphasize Johnson's personality, rather than structural factors rooted in past policies, see Fredrik Logevall, *Choosing War: The Lost Chance for Peace and the Escalation of War in Vietnam* (Los Angeles: University of California Press, 1999), 398–99, and Robert Dallek, *An Unfinished Life: John F. Kennedy, 1917–1963* (Boston: Little, Brown and Co., 2003), chap. 15.

thought of military preparedness, yet the country was hardly devoid of prominent advocates of that approach. Wilson deserves high marks for his performance once the nation was at war, but he overreached himself in its aftermath, thus contributing mightily to the withdrawal of the United States from a position of international leadership and responsibility. If his ideas eventually provided much of the framework for a successful U.S. global strategy in the Cold War, his clumsiness at home during 1919 and 1920 left the country ill-equipped to face the challenges of the next generation. Clearly this cannot be said of Truman.

As for Roosevelt, although he inherited a weak hand in foreign policy given prevailing conditions and attitudes at home, he did not provide path-breaking leadership in handling the emerging crises in either East Asia or Europe. The best that can be said for him—and this is well worth saying—is that when he finally maneuvered the country into war, he did so in a manner that produced widespread unity. What he did not do was to prepare the American people particularly well for the challenges of the postwar era. Given the nature of American political culture, it is perhaps too much to expect him to have managed the war adeptly while giving the population a realistic sense of the responsibilities they were likely to face in its aftermath. And he did make significant moves in that direction with the Bretton Woods and Dumbarton Oaks conferences of 1944. To have attempted more might well have left the nation in the same position that Wilson did when he retired in 1921.

Even so, the last point helps us to appreciate the extraordinary challenges that Truman faced upon assuming office and, indeed, throughout his presidency. Undeniably, the road he followed was laced with bumps and potholes, and his negotiation of them was far from flawless. If our standard is perfection or the immediate judgment of his contemporaries, his performance falls well short; if it is historical comparison and the perspective provided by the passage of time, the claims of his Farewell Address are not without merit.

156

DEPARTMENT OF STATE

~~TOP SECRET~~ *Memorandum of Conversation*

LIMITED DISTRIBUTION

DATE: June 25, 1950

SUBJECT: Korean Situation

PARTICIPANTS: The President

Secretary Acheson   Secretary Pace
Secretary Johnson   Secretary Finletter
Secretary Matthews   General Bradley
                             Admiral Sherman
~~COPIES XXX~~   Mr. Webb   )   General Vandenberg
             Mr. Rusk   )   General Collins
             Mr. Hickerson) State
             Mr. Jessup   ) Dept.

The persons listed above met with the President for dinner at Blair House at 7:45 PM. Before dinner General Bradley read a memorandum prepared by General MacArthur in which he emphasized his views about the importance of denying Formosa to the Communists.

After dinner the discussion began around the table. The President called on the Secretary of State to open the discussion.

MR. ACHESON summarized the various problems which he thought the President should consider. The first point was the question of authorizing General MacArthur to supply Korea with arms and other equipment over and above the supplies of ammunition presently authorized under the MDAP program. He recommended that this be done. He suggested that our air cover should be used to aid in the evacuation of the women and children from Seoul and that our air force should be authorized to knock out northern Korean tanks or airforce interfering with the evacuation. He then mentioned the resolution adopted by the Security Council and suggested that consideration should be given to what

further

~~TOP SECRET~~

further assistance we might render to Korea in pursuance
of this or a supplementary Security Council resolution.
He next suggested that the President should order the Seventh
Fleet to proceed to Formosa and prevent an attack on Formosa
from the mainland. At the same time operations from Formosa
against the mainland should be prevented. He said that he
did not recommend that General MacArthur should go to
Formosa until further steps had been decided upon. He said
that the United States should not tie up with the Generalissimo.
He thought that the future status of Formosa might be determined
by the UN.

THE PRESIDENT interposed "or by the Japanese Peace Treaty".

MR. ACHESON finally suggested that our aid to Indochina
should be stepped up.

GENERAL BRADLEY said that we must draw the line
somewhere.

THE PRESIDENT stated he agreed on that.

GENERAL BRADLEY said that Russia is not yet ready for
war. The Korean situation offered as good an occasion for
action in drawing the line as anywhere else and he agreed
with the actions suggested by Mr. Acheson. He said that
jets flying over her would have a great morale effect on
the South Koreans even if they were unable to spot the
North Korean tanks. He said that naval action could help
on the East Coast. He questioned the value of sending
materiel which the Koreans were not trained to use. He
mentioned the F-51's in this connection. He said that we
should act under the guise of aid to the United Nations.
He proposed that we should move fleet units now in Subic Bay.
He thought it would probable not be necessary for them to
shoot but that they might frighten off the North Korean
amphibious forces. He questioned the advisability of putting
in ground units particularly if large numbers were involved.

GENERAL COLLINS reported on a telecon with Tokyo.
General MacArthur is shipping the mortars, artillery, and
so on with ammunition. These supplies will reach the Koreans
within the ten-day period for which they already have
supplies. The F-51's are available in Japan for Korean
pilots to fly back. The Korean pilots will be flown from
Kimpo. General Collins urged that authority be given
MacArthur to send a survey group to Korea.

ADMIRAL SHERMAN

ADMIRAL SHERMAN said that the Russians do not want war now but if they do they will have it. The present situation in Korea offers a valuable opportunity for us to act. Korea is a strategic threat to Japan; this was the conclusion which he reached in his studies during the war when we were planning our attacks on Japan. He favored sending a survey group from Tokyo and increasing the strength of KMAG. He thought we should stop the use of the sea as a means of attack on South Korea. This was the logical correlary of the views stated by the Secretary of State. On Formosa he thought we must adjust our position to our general occupation position in Japan. He thought that MacArthur fitted into that situation as SCAP. He agreed, as had General Bradley, that in the Formosa operation we must apply our guarantees against military action both ways, that is to prevent attacks from Formosa as well as on Formosa. We could not otherwise justify our action. He said it would take two days to bring the fleet up from the Philippines. It need not be used if we decided against such action but the movement should be ordered now. He wished also to move some ships from the mainland as far as Pearl Harbor, for example, at least one carrier.

THE PRESIDENT asked about Russian fleet strength in the Far East and Admiral Sherman gave him the details.

GENERAL VANDENBERG agreed that we must stop the North Koreans but he would not base our action on the assumption that the Russians would not fight. He said that we could knock out the North Korean tanks with our air if only the North Korean air force is involved. However, Russian jets might come into action and they would be operating from much closer bases. In regard to Formosa he pointed out that all places were interrelated. Formosa was therefore important only in relation to other places.

THE PRESIDENT asked about Russian air strength in the Far East.

GENERAL VANDENBERG gave him the information including the fact that a considerable number of Russian jets are based on Shanghai.

THE PRESIDENT asked whether we could knock out their bases in the Far East.

GENERAL

~~TOP SECRET~~

GENERAL VANDENBERG replied that this might take some time. He said it could be done if we used A-Bombs.

MR. PACE expressed doubts about the advisability of putting ground forces into Korea. He stressed the need for speed and for encouraging General MacArthur to take action.

MR. MATTHEWS also stressed the need for prompt action and said that we would get popular approval.

MR. FINLETTER said we should go as far as necessary in protecting our evacuation. He expressed some doubt on the additional items which had been suggested by the Secretary of State. He said our forces in the Far East were sufficient if the Russians do not come in. He advised that only the necessary decisions be made that night. He thought that General MacArthur should be authorized to go beyond mere evacuation. He stressed the analogy to the situation between the two world wars. He thought we should take calculated risks hoping that our action will keep the peace.

MR. JOHNSON agreed with Mr. Acheson's first recommendation concerning instructions to General MacArthur but thought the instructions should be detailed so as not to give him too much discretion. He thought there should not be a real delegation of Presidential authority to General MacArthur. He mentioned the three islands south of Okinawa in the Ryukyus which could be made ready in a few days as air bases. He pointed to the fact that they are already under our jurisdiction and said that the Formosan situation could be handled from them. He agreed with the views that had been expressed by Mr. Finletter. He was opposed to committing ground troops in Korea.

MR. WEBB, MR. JESSUP, MR. RUSK and MR. HICKERSON made brief comments in amplification of Mr. Acheson's statements.

THE PRESIDENT confirmed his decision that the following orders should be sent:

    1. General MacArthur was to send the suggested supplies to the Koreans.

    2. General MacArthur was to send a survey group to Korea.

    3. The

TOP SECRET

3. The indicated elements of the fleet were to be sent to Japan.

4. The Air Force should prepare plans to wipe out all Soviet air bases in the Far East. This was not an order for action but an order to make the plans.

5. Careful calculation should be made of the next probable place in which Soviet action might take place. A complete survey should be made by State and Defense Departments.

.He stressed that we are working entirely for the United Nations. We would wait for further action until the UN order is flouted.

He wished the State Department to prepare a statement for a message for him to deliver in person to Congress on Tuesday indicating exactly what steps had been taken. He wished the Department to put its best brains on it and said that there were plenty of them there.

He said he was not yet ready to put MacArthur in as Commander-in-Chief in Korea.

He said our action at this moment would be confined to the United Nations and to Korea.

He said that our air was to continue to give cover for evacuation destroying tanks if necessary.

He asked whether more bazookas and possibly recoiless rifles could be sent.

GENERAL BRADLEY said that on the recoiless rifles we had few available and that there was also a shortage of ammunition.

THE PRESIDENT again emphasized the importance of making the survey of possible next moves by the Soviet Union. He also emphasized that no statement whatever was to be made by any one to the press until he speaks on Tuesday. It was absolutely vital that there should be no leak in regard to this matter and he wished everyone to be careful. They should not even make any background comment to the press.

MR. ACHESON

TOP SECRET

MR. ACHESON pointed out that he and Secretary Johnson were scheduled to appear before the Congressional Appropriations Committee tomorrow and wondered whether any statements should be made on the Korean situation. The President said that he thought no comment on this question should be made by either of the Secretaries at that time.

ADMIRAL SHERMAN inquired whether he had been authorized to move fleet units from California to Pearl Harbor.

THE PRESIDENT said that he was.

In response to further questions THE PRESIDENT said that our air cover should take action against North Korean tanks if this were necessary.

S/A PJessup:mtb   TOP SECRET

THE WHITE HOUSE
WASHINGTON

Nov 25' 50

Wake Island.

We arrived at dawn. Gen.
MacArthur was at the airport
with his shirt unbuttoned,
wearing a greasy ham and eggs
cap that evidently had been
in use for twenty years.

He greeted the President
cordially and after the photo-
graphers had finished their
usual picture orgy the President
and the General boarded an
old two door sedan and drove

203

to the quarters of the Air-
line manager on the Island.

For more than an hour
they discussed the Japanese and
Korean situation.

The General assured the
President that the victory
was won in Korea, that
Japan was ready for a peace
treaty and that the Chinese
Communists would not
attack.

THE WHITE HOUSE
WASHINGTON

A general discussion was
carried on about Formosa.
The General brought up his
statement to the Veterans of
Foreign Wars, which had been
ordered withdrawn by the
President. The General said
that he was sorry for any
embarassment he'd caused,
that he was not in politics
at the time and that the
politicians had made a "chump"
(his word) of him in 1948 and

that it would not happen again. He assured the President that he had no political ambitions.

He again said the Chinese Commies would not attack, that we had won the war and that we could send a Division to Europe, from Korea in January 1951.

The Truman Prophecy

Randall B. Woods

In his Farewell Address, Harry Truman dared to look into the future. He lamented the fact that he "had hardly a day in office that has not been dominated by this all-embracing struggle—this conflict between those who love freedom and those who would lead the world back into slavery and darkness. And always in the background there has been the atomic bomb." But history would judge, he predicted, that his administration had set the course for victory in the Cold War; the blueprint to which he referred, of course, was the strategy of containment. Although historians still debate the meaning and implications of containment, there was by 1952 little doubt in Truman's mind. He had tried rolling back the "bamboo curtain" in Korea and had rejected the strategy as too risky.[1] He had accepted George Kennan's original definition stated first in the Long Telegram of 1946 and then in the "Mr. X" article in *Foreign Affairs*. America and its free-world allies should through military strength and mutual aid contain the forces of international Communism within their current boundaries until, inevitably, Communism's various components should collapse of their own internal contradictions.[2] The people behind the Iron Curtain, oppressed, exploited—indeed, enslaved—would someday choose freedom over tyranny, justice over exploitation, God over

1. Bruce Cummings, *The Origins of the Korean War,* 2 vols. (Princeton: Princeton University Press, 1981), and William Stueck, *The Korean War: An International History* (Princeton: Princeton University Press, 1995).
2. Randall B. Woods and Howard Jones, *Dawning of the Cold War: The United States' Quest for Order* (Athens: University of Georgia Press, 1991).

atheism, and capitalism over Marxism. No system whose rulers lived in fear of their own people could survive. "Whether the communist rulers shift their policies of their own free will—or whether the change comes about in some other way," he declared, "I have not a doubt in the world that a change will occur." There would dawn then a new age of peace and prosperity, "an age when we can use the peaceful tools that science has forged for us to do away with poverty and human misery everywhere on earth." Francis Fukiyama could not have said it better.[3] There were two prophecies, then: that containment would achieve its objective—the demise of the international Communist conspiracy—and that the end of the Cold War would usher in a new era of international understanding and global prosperity. As a survey of American foreign policy since the Farewell Address demonstrates, Truman proved to be as wrong in his second prediction as he was right in the first.

When he was inaugurated president in 1953, Dwight Eisenhower was not fundamentally unhappy with the foreign policies America had followed since 1945. As NATO's first commander in chief, he had been a loyal advocate of Truman's containment policy. Like former Secretary of State Dean Acheson and Republican senators Robert Taft of Ohio and Joseph McCarthy of Wisconsin, he believed in the existence of a monolithic Communist threat directed from the Kremlin that, if the United States and its allies were not ever-vigilant, would spread Communism across the globe through a combination of intimidation, subversion, and, if circumstances were right, armed aggression. Eisenhower disagreed with both Taft and McCarthy in other areas, however. The principal threat was not Communist burrowing from within, and the United States could not entrust its security to chains of island bases in the Atlantic and Pacific. Rather, the principal menace was from abroad and was best countered by U.S.-led alliance systems and American-financed programs of overseas economic and military aid. Despite Republican rhetoric, continuity rather than change was the watchword during the Eisenhower administration in foreign as well as domestic policy. The task ahead, all agreed, was to contain Communism within its current boundaries until inevitably the Sino-Soviet empire rotted from within.[4]

During the Eisenhower era the United States refused to become involved in "brushfire" wars in part because it had learned the "lessons" of Korea and in part because the nation's conventional forces were allowed to deteriorate dramatically. The neglect was intentional, a byproduct of the administration's defense policy. Almost as soon as they took office Eisenhower, Secretary of

---

3. Fukiyama, *The End of History and the Last Man* (New York: Free Press, 1993).
4. Robert A. Divine, *Eisenhower and the Cold War* (New York: Oxford University Press, 1981).

State John Foster Dulles, Secretary of the Treasury George Humphrey, and Secretary of Defense Charles Wilson had to come to grips with the problem of how to reconcile a reduced budget (they were Republicans, after all) with a militantly anti-Communist posture. The chief lesson Ike and his associates drew from Korea was that limited wars fought with conventional weaponry on the periphery of the Communist world only drained the nation's resources and weakened its allies' resolve. Secretary Humphrey continually preached that big, expensive government, including bloated defense budgets, would corrupt the currency, drain capital away from the private sector, and do what the Soviet Union could never do—destroy the Republic from within. Yet the Communist threat was ever-present.[5]

The administration's synthesis of the seemingly antithetical objectives of military economy and global defense was the doctrine of strategic deterrence, which Dulles dubbed "massive retaliation." In order to get "more bang for the buck," the administration would concentrate its funds on the Air Force, specifically the Strategic Air Command (SAC), deliverer of the atomic bomb. Instead of becoming bogged down in a land war in Asia, Latin America, or the Middle East, the United States in any direct confrontation with the forces of international Communism would brandish its nuclear arsenal. When it or its allies were faced with aggression from the Soviet Union or its proxies, Dulles argued, the United States must be prepared to go to the brink of nuclear war. "The ability to get to the verge without getting into the war is the necessary art," he told a *Life* reporter in 1956.[6] Under the plan worked out by Humphrey and Wilson, total military expenditures would drop from about fifty billion dollars in 1954 to thirty-five billion by 1957. In 1955 President Eisenhower asserted America's willingness to use nuclear weapons if necessary. Massive retaliation was based on a kind of clear internal logic. If in fact all Communist roads led to Moscow and every Marxist revolution threatened to expand the area of Soviet influence, it was absurd to battle the manifestations of the disease. The most efficient response was to destroy the source of the cancer itself. This logic obtained, however, only so long as the United States maintained a clear superiority over the Soviet Union in both nuclear weaponry and means of delivery.[7]

Brinkmanship and alliance building proved to be ineffective strategies.

5. Richard H. Immerman and Robert Bowie, *Waging Peace: How Eisenhower Shaped an Enduring Cold War Strategy* (New York: Oxford University Press, 1998).

6. Randall B. Woods, *Quest for Identity: America since 1945* (New York and Fort Worth: Harcourt, Brace, 2001), 121.

7. Saki Dockrill, *Eisenhower's New Look National Security Policy, 1953–1961* (New York: St. Martin's Press, 1996).

The Soviets sought to project their power not through military aggression but rather through forging ideological links with anticolonial, revolutionary leaders in developing areas and providing non-Western governments with economic and military aid. During the first Eisenhower administration, Dulles refused to recognize the crucial role of economic assistance, stressing arms support almost exclusively. Covert operations such as that in Guatemala seemed somewhat more successful, but the victories won were short-term and in the end very costly. Washington seemed oblivious to the fact that indigenous nationalism and local rivalries were far more important in Third World crises than the East-West confrontation. In its obsession with the Cold War, the Eisenhower administration tended always to align the United States with entrenched, pro-Western oligarchies and to see revolutionary nationalism as part of the international Communist conspiracy. As a result, American policy frequently drove local nationalist movements into the arms of Communist China and the Soviet Union.[8]

Meanwhile, advances in Soviet rocketry seemed to render "massive retaliation" and "brinkmanship" irrelevant. On October 4, 1957, the Soviet Union shocked the West by sending the world's first earth satellite, Sputnik ("traveling companion" in Russian), into orbit. That accomplishment, realized before the United States had perfected its own missile system, upset the scientific and potentially the military balance between the two countries. On November 2 the Russians launched Sputnik II, with a payload six times heavier than that carried by the first Russian vehicle, again proving their apparent superiority in missile technology.[9] This demonstration of engineering acumen devastated most Americans. *Newsweek* devoted a sizable portion of its first issue after the launch to lamenting the deplorable state of American science and education. Democratic senator Stuart Symington of Missouri, a former secretary of the air force, warned that "unless our defense policies are promptly changed, the Soviets will move from superiority to supremacy. If that ever happens our position will become impossible."[10] The Soviet Union also possessed the most powerful army in the world and was developing a

---

8. John Lewis Gaddis, *Strategies of Containment: A Critical Appraisal of Postwar American National Security Policy* (New York: Oxford University Press, 1982), and Frank Ninkovich, *The Wilsonian Century: U.S. Foreign Policy since 1900* (Chicago: University of Chicago Press, 1999).

9. Craig Campbell, *Destroying the Village: Eisenhower and Nuclear War* (New York: Columbia University Press, 1998); Robert A. Divine, *The Sputnik Challenge* (New York: Oxford University Press, 1993); and Peter J. Roman, *Eisenhower and the Missile Gap* (Ithaca: Cornell University Press, 1995).

10. Woods, *Quest for Identity*, 138.

navy second only to that of the United States. Even Secretary Dulles admitted that Russia had overcome the "preponderance of power" that the United States had enjoyed since 1945.[11]

Although he recognized the importance of agriculture, the budget, labor-management problems, and social issues, John F. Kennedy's overriding interest was foreign affairs. The great bulk of his inaugural address was devoted to it, and he frequently justified policies designed to get the nation moving on the home front in terms of America's ongoing competition with the Soviet Union. Despite the attention he gave it, however, Kennedy's foreign policy suffered from a basic contradiction. He and his advisers insisted that they were out to make the world safe for diversity, that under their leadership the United States would abandon the status quo policies of the past and support change, especially in the developing world.

The Kennedy people did not object to the Eisenhower administration's intervention into the internal affairs of other nations but rather to the fact that it usually intervened ineptly and always to prop up the status quo. In a special address to Congress in May 1961, the president declared that "the great battleground for the defense and expansion of freedom today is . . . Asia, Latin America, Africa and the Middle East, the lands of the rising peoples."[12] According to Arthur Schlesinger Jr., Kennedy fully understood that in Latin America "the militantly anti-revolutionary line" of the past was the policy most likely to strengthen the Communists and lose the hemisphere. He and his advisers planned openings to the left to facilitate "democratic development." Specifically, the administration projected an ambitious foreign-aid program that would promote social justice and economic progress in the developing nations and in the process funnel nationalist energy into pro-democracy, anti-Communist channels. Modernization through American aid would ensure that evolution rather than revolution would characterize the political histories of the newly emerging nations.[13]

At the same time, the administration saw any significant change in the world balance of power as a threat to American security. Kennedy, McGeorge Bundy, Dean Rusk, and Robert McNamara took very seriously Nikita Khrushchev's January 1961 speech offering support for "wars of national liberation"; it was, they believed, evidence of a new Communist campaign to seize

11. Melvyn P. Leffler, *A Preponderance of Power: National Security, the Truman Administration, and the Cold War* (Stanford: Stanford University Press, 1992).

12. Woods, *Quest for Identity*, 182.

13. Jorge I. Dominguez, *To Make a World Safe for Revolution: Cuba's Foreign Policy* (Cambridge: Harvard University Press, 1989).

control of anticolonial and other revolutionary movements in economically underdeveloped regions. If the Third World was not to succumb to the siren song of Marxism-Leninism, with all the implications that would pose for the international balance of power, then the United States and other "developed" countries would have to demonstrate that economic progress could take place within a democratic framework. But the logic of this position, as John Gaddis has pointed out, was that the United States really would need a world resembling itself in order to be secure.[14] During the Kennedy years, the United States determined to support only those revolutionary movements that were democratic, favorable toward or at least tolerant of free enterprise, and staunchly anti-Communist. But the logic of the monolithic Communist threat and the domino theory coupled with the strength of domestic anti-Communism forced the administration to sacrifice freedom and democracy on the altar of anti-Communism. Thus did the United States decide to support various military regimes in Latin America, the Middle East, and Asia. Kennedy's reluctant support of Ngo Dinh Diem's ouster in Vietnam led to a succession of military governments in Saigon, virtually ensuring a confrontation with the forces of Vietnamese nationalism.[15]

Lyndon Johnson was in basic agreement with the foreign policies of the Kennedy administration; indeed, as vice president he had helped to shape them. Military preparedness and realistic diplomacy would contain Communism within its existing bounds. In order to keep up morale among America's allies and satisfy hard-line anti-Communists at home, the United States needed to continue to hold fast to Berlin, oppose the admission of Communist China to the United Nations, and confront and blockade Cuba. He was aware of the growing split between the Soviet Union and Communist China and the possibilities inherent in it for dividing the Communist world. He also took a flexible, even hopeful view of the Soviet Union and Khrushchev. It was just possible, he believed, that Russia was becoming a status quo power and as such would be a force for stability rather than chaos in the world. The United States must continue its "flexible response" of military aid, economic assistance, and technical/political advice in response to the threat of Communism in the developing world, but there was nothing wrong with negotiating with the Soviets at the same time in an effort to reduce tensions. To all appear-

14. Michael R. Beschloss, *The Crisis Years: Kennedy and Khrushchev, 1960–1963* (New York: Edward Burlingame Books, 1991), and Thomas G. Paterson, *Contesting Castro: The United States and the Triumph of the Cuban Revolution* (New York: Oxford University Press, 1994).
15. George M. Kahin, *Intervention: How America Became Involved in Vietnam* (New York: Knopf, 1986).

ances, then, Johnson was a cold warrior, but a flexible, pragmatic one. Nevertheless, the Texan was no more ready than his predecessor to unilaterally withdraw from South Vietnam or seek a negotiated settlement that would lead to neutralization of the area south of the seventeenth parallel.[16]

But America's agonizing entanglement in the Indochinese wars was not rooted simply in one man's personality and philosophy. The imposing political coalition supporting the war in Vietnam consisted of conservative anti-Communists who defined national security in terms of bases and alliances and who were basically xenophobic, along with liberal reformers who were determined to safeguard the national interest by exporting democracy and facilitating overseas social and economic progress. Spearheading the first group were former isolationists like Henry Luce who believed that if the United States could not hide from the world it must control it, rabid anti-Communists who saw any expansion of Marxism-Leninism as a mortal threat to the United States, and elements of the American military and corporate establishments with a vested interest in the Cold War. Joining these realpolitikers, true believers, and political opportunists were the leading lights of the liberal community—Arthur Schlesinger, Dean Acheson, Joseph Rauh (head of Americans for Democratic Action), and Hubert Humphrey. Products of World War II, these internationalists saw America's interests as being tied up with those of the other members of the global community. They opposed Communism because it constituted a totalitarian threat to the principles of cultural diversity, individual liberty, and self-determination that they hoped would prevail at home and abroad. Moreover, as others have pointed out, in the overheated atmosphere generated by the Cold War, anti-Communism was a political necessity for liberals whose views on domestic issues made them ideologically suspect. Conservatives and their liberal adversaries may have differed as to their notions of the ideal America but not over whether America was ideal or over whether it was duty bound to lead the international community into a new era of prosperity and stability.[17]

America's obsession with Cuba and Vietnam distorted its relationship with the rest of the world. Its opposition to revolutions in those countries destroyed its credibility with revolutionary nationalists everywhere and of every ideological persuasion. It stretched the nation's military and economic resources to the breaking point and polarized domestic politics and society.

16. Lloyd C. Gardner, *Pay Any Price: Lyndon Johnson and the Wars for Vietnam* (Chicago: I. R. Dee, 1995).

17. Randall B. Woods, *J. William Fulbright, Vietnam, and the Search for a Cold War Foreign Policy* (New York: Cambridge University Press, 1998).

The United States was not able to overthrow Castro, but it made allegiance to the anti-Castro crusade a litmus test for every government in the hemisphere. Nor was it able to defeat revolutionary nationalism in Vietnam. The ongoing war there strained the North Atlantic alliance, creating fears among America's allies that the United States had lost both the will and the ability to help defend Western Europe. In its determination to combat Communism on every front, it seemed, America had rendered itself incapable of defeating it on any. Many policy makers and sophisticated observers in the United States understood the imbalance and distortion Vietnam and Cuba had introduced into American foreign policy, but the strength of domestic anti-Communism barred them from pursuing a more pragmatic course.[18]

It is inconceivable that Richard Nixon could have been elected president without the Cold War. He made his career as a professional anti-Communist, and the ultimate proof of his commitment to the faith was the more than twenty-five thousand Americans who died in Vietnam during his watch. It is somewhat ironic, therefore, that the term *détente* is associated with his presidency. He and Henry Kissinger were determined to create a new world order in which, through military intimidation and economic incentives, the Soviet Union and Communist China could be transformed into traditional, interest-driven nation-states. Thus the famous Nixon trips to Beijing and Moscow. But neither the Communist superpowers nor Nixon's America was willing to give up the nuclear weapons, missiles, and alliance systems that were the stuff of the Cold War, and the president's paranoia at first distracted and then destroyed his administration.[19]

The principal themes of the Carter foreign policy were human rights and open diplomacy. During the 1976 presidential campaign the Democratic candidate had lashed Henry Kissinger for his secrecy and balance-of-power approach to foreign affairs. "Our Secretary of State simply does not trust the judgment of the American people," he told the Chicago Council on Foreign Relations. He pledged open covenants openly arrived at, echoing Woodrow Wilson's Fourteen Points. His promise to make American foreign policy conform to its lofty principles also echoed Wilsonian rhetoric. The president declared that he would make the Helsinki accords on human rights—free-

18. H. W. Brands, *The Wages of Globalism: Lyndon Johnson and the Limits of American Power* (New York: Oxford University Press, 1995).

19. Gregory D. Cleva, *Henry Kissinger and the American Approach to Foreign Policy* (Cranbury, N.J.: Associated University Presses, 1989); Seymour M. Hersh, *The Price of Power: Kissinger in the Nixon White House* (New York: Summit Books, 1983); and Jeffrey P. Kimball, *Nixon's Vietnam War* (Lawrence: University Press of Kansas, 1998).

dom of expression, freedom of migration, freedom from economic exploitation—the criteria for U.S. dealings with other countries. Carter and Secretary of State Cyrus Vance were mindful of the "lessons" of Vietnam; the secretary of state understood the limits that constrained American policy and perceived correctly that, for most of the developing world, issues of nationalism, decolonization, and socioeconomic justice were more important than the Cold War. Nevertheless, the president insisted, the United States did not have to aid countries oppressing and exploiting their populations, and it should be free to condemn violations of human rights at any and every opportunity. It should be noted, too, that Carter's political advisers believed that human rights was a "no-lose" issue that would attract not only liberals but cold warriors as well because of its implicit attack on the Soviet Union.[20]

The president's belief that he could make morality the basis of American foreign policy and simultaneously safeguard the nation's strategic and economic interests was flawed. It showed a basic ignorance of history and international politics. Woodrow Wilson's dealings with Mexico from 1913 through 1917 demonstrated that no matter how well intentioned U.S. intervention in the affairs of other countries was, it was inevitably interpreted as imperialism by both friend and foe and was utilized by authoritarian, repressive regimes to rally support that would not otherwise have been forthcoming.[21]

The invasion of Afghanistan, bordering the Soviet Union, China, and Pakistan, angered and frightened Carter and his advisers. It marked the first time Soviet troops had directly intervened in a nation outside Eastern Europe. Perhaps most alarming, the Kremlin invoked the Brezhnev Doctrine, last used to justify the Czech invasion of 1968, which held that the Soviet Union had the right to use force to correct any "deviation from socialism" in Marxist states. For the Carter administration, the invasion of Afghanistan raised the specter of a Soviet military takeover of the entire Middle East. Ironically, the Kremlin was acting in part to prevent the spread of Islamic fundamentalism into the Soviet republics of central Asia, the same fundamentalism that was responsible for the holding of the American hostages in Iran. Carter vehemently denounced the Afghan adventure, broadened and deepened ties with China, stopped grain sales to the Soviet Union, approved covert CIA aid to the Afghan rebels, and, in his most controversial move,

20. Kenneth Morriss, *Jimmy Carter: American Moralist* (New York: Oxford University Press, 1996), and Erwin C. Hargrove, *Jimmy Carter as President: Leadership and the Politics of the Public Good* (Baton Rouge: Louisiana State University Press, 1988).

21. Gaddis Smith, *Morality, Reason, and Power: American Diplomacy in the Carter Years* (New York: Hill and Wang, 1986).

called for a boycott of the Olympic games scheduled for Moscow the summer following the invasion. In his State of the Union Address in January 1980, the president announced what came to be known as the "Carter Doctrine": "an attempt by any outside force to gain control of the Persian Gulf region will be regarded as an assault on the vital interests of the United States of America, and as such an assault will be repelled by use of any means necessary, including military force."[22] Carter's hard-line response to the Soviet invasion of Afghanistan merely angered friend and foe alike without affecting the fundamental situation.

Ronald Reagan's view of Soviet Communism seemed frozen in the mid-1950s. The Kremlin, Reagan was convinced, was at the head of a worldwide conspiracy to export totalitarianism to all parts of the globe. At his first press conference, the president declared that the Soviets were "prepared to commit any crime, to lie, to cheat" in order to facilitate the spread of Marxism. For Reagan as for members of the "moral majority," Soviet Communism represented all the negative forces abroad in the world: atheism, state socialism, immorality. Likewise, anti-Communism was a crucial component of the struggle to resurrect the hallowed principles of liberty, free enterprise, patriotism, and family values. For Reagan, the Soviet Union was truly "the Evil Empire."[23] The president's principal foreign policy advisers—Secretary of State Alexander Haig and his successor, George Shultz, Secretary of Defense Caspar Weinberger, National Security Adviser Richard Allen, and Ambassador to the United Nations Jeane Kirkpatrick—all shared their chief's fear of an overweening Soviet state, although some were far more ideological than others, and they differed dramatically about how to deal with the red menace.

Defenders of the Reagan administration would later claim that its huge defense budgets were deliberate attempts to spend the Soviet Union into bankruptcy. It is unclear whether this was the case, whether Reagan and Weinberger really believed their own propaganda about Soviet arms superiority, or whether the administration was simply serving its military industrial constituency. What is certain is that the administration embarked on a massive arms buildup and rejected meaningful arms control negotiations with the Soviets.[24]

In the spring of 1983 Reagan unveiled an ambitious new defense plan that threatened the concept of mutual assured destruction (MAD) and virtually

22. Woods, *Quest for Identity*, 314.
23. David E. Kyvig, *Reagan and the World* (New York: Greenwood Press, 1990).
24. William W. Kaufmann, *Glasnost, Perestroika, and U.S. Defense Spending* (Washington, D.C.: Brookings Institution, 1990).

assured an escalation of the arms race. In order to deal with the Soviet Union's "margin of superiority," the United States would launch the Strategic Defense Initiative (SDI). Labeled "Star Wars" by its critics, the new defense system would consist of lasers and particle beams projected from ground stations and satellites in space. These "death rays" would allegedly destroy incoming enemy missiles before they entered the earth's atmosphere. Those few that slipped through would easily be taken care of by the anti-ballistic missile (ABM) system, according to the administration. Domestic critics of the plan claimed that SDI was both impractical and outrageously expensive. Soviet leader Yuri Andropov denounced SDI as a deliberate attempt by the United States to undermine the concept of mutually assured destruction, the basis for global peace since the late 1950s. It would, he declared, "open the floodgates of a runaway race of all types of strategic arms, both offensive and defensive."[25]

Many Americans who voted for Ronald Reagan in 1984 did so in spite of his confrontational posture toward the Soviet Union. They were particularly worried about the arms buildup and the Reagan administration's apparent unwillingness to negotiate. Statements from various government officials alluding to the survivability of a nuclear war sent a shiver up the nation's collective spine. A Pentagon representative declared that all an American family had to do to get through a thermonuclear blast would be to "dig a hole, cover it with a couple of doors, and then throw three feet of dirt on top." When another member of the Reagan team assured a congressional committee that the mail would go through in the wake of a nuclear exchange, one member observed that it would be difficult to deliver where there were "no addresses, no streets, no blocks, no houses." A group of antinuclear doctors and scientists refuted the notion that the world could survive and thrive in the wake of a missile attack. The physicians predicted that nuclear war would bring on "the last epidemic." Scientists presented data to prove that the dust and smoke from a nuclear exchange would produce a prodigious global cloud that would obscure the sun for a year, bring on a "nuclear winter," and undermine the very basis of life on earth.[26]

The only bright spot in this exceedingly depressing picture was a dramatic and promising change in the leadership of the Soviet Union. Andropov had died in early 1984 following a long illness and was succeeded by Konstantin Chernenko, another aging autocrat who repressed his countrymen and pursued

25. Donald C. Baucom, *The Origins of SDI, 1944–1983* (New York: Oxford University Press, 1992).
26. Woods, *Quest for Identity,* 376, 385.

a hard line abroad. Upon Chernenko's death in March 1985, Mikhail Gorbachev became general secretary of the Communist Party of the Soviet Union (CPSU). Gorbachev represented a new generation of Soviet leaders—educated, nonideological technocrats who had shed the paranoia of Stalin's generation. In his midfifties, charismatic, and cosmopolitan, Gorbachev was, like Peter the Great, fascinated by rather than fearful of Western technology and culture. Steeped in philosophy, law, and agricultural economics, he was married to a woman who held a doctorate in philosophy. Gorbachev was determined to save socialism, the CPSU, and the Soviet Union by modernizing them. He understood that his country had fallen behind the United States, Japan, West Germany, and even some developing countries in technological innovation and economic output. The only way to reverse his country's dramatic and inevitable decline, Gorbachev reasoned, was through policies of perestroika (social and economic reform) and glasnost (democracy and openness to the international community). Specifically, economic progress would require the substitution of some free market mechanisms for collectivization in the Soviet economy. Rewards would have to be tied to productivity, certain industries decentralized, and the principle of private ownership applied to certain sectors, especially agriculture. And the Soviet Union would have to cooperate with the capitalist countries. That cooperation, Gorbachev perceived, would pay dividends in two ways. It would give the Soviet Union access to Western technology and markets and allow the Kremlin to divert resources from its monstrous military machine to the civilian sector. The Soviet Union would remain a single-party state, but Russians could choose from Communist candidates at certain levels, and their representatives would have authentic input into national decisions.[27]

To create an opening to the West, Gorbachev took a number of unilateral steps. He stopped his country's nuclear testing program, halted the deployment of intermediate-range missiles in Eastern Europe, and called for on-site inspection to enforce future arms control treaties. He concluded agreements with Japan and West Germany for the exchange of nonnuclear technology, and he replaced his hard-line foreign minister, Andrei Gromyko, with the pragmatic, sophisticated Edward Shevardnadze. During the summer of 1985 the new Soviet leader departed for a whirlwind tour of Europe, Latin America, and the United States. His sincerity and charm particularly

27. Anders Aslund, *Gorbachev's Struggle for Economic Reform: The Soviet Reform Process, 1985–1988* (Ithaca: Cornell University Press, 1989), and Seweryn Bialer and Michael Mandelbaum, *Gorbachev's Russia and American Foreign Policy* (Boulder: Westview Press, 1988).

impressed the hard-nosed British prime minister, Margaret Thatcher, who upon Gorbachev's departure declared him a man with whom the West could do business.

Throughout his first five years in office Ronald Reagan had steadfastly refused to meet face-to-face with a Soviet chief of state. Perhaps because he sensed in Gorbachev the dawning of a new era or perhaps because his wife's astrologer advised that the time was right, the president agreed to a summit in Geneva in November 1985. The meeting was only partially successful. While Nancy Reagan and Reisa Gorbachev competed for the attention of the cameras, the two heads of state disagreed over the second proposed Strategic Arms Limitation Treaty (SALT II) and SDI. Although he chided Gorbachev for continuing human rights violations in the Soviet Union, Reagan was his usual cordial self, and Gorbachev retained his composure, determined to keep the channels open for future negotiation. The summit ended on a high note. At dinner the Reagans discovered that the Gorbachevs were movie buffs and regaled them with fascinating anecdotes of their life in Hollywood.[28]

A year later with very little prior publicity, Reagan and Gorbachev met in Reykjavik, Iceland. During the previous year the Soviet leader had taken a very aggressive stance on arms control issues. His overall goal, he stated, was the total elimination of nuclear weapons by the turn of the century. As the meeting opened, Gorbachev took the initiative, proposing 50 percent cuts in ICBMs as a prelude to their eventual elimination. Not to be outdone, Reagan, to the consternation of his advisers, suggested scrapping all American— and possibly British and French—nuclear weapons within ten years in return for Russian acquiescence in the construction and deployment of the Strategic Defense Initiative. The Soviets were as puzzled as Reagan's top aides. Why would SDI be necessary with a full-scale nuclear build-down under way? Gorbachev, suspecting that the Americans were trying to establish clear nuclear superiority, rejected Reagan's proposal, and the Reykjavik meeting broke up. Nevertheless, the two leaders departed on a friendly note. The path to disarmament was still open. As the Gorbachev-Reagan relationship ripened, individuals on both sides of the Iron Curtain began tentatively to anticipate an end to the Cold War.

Perestroika and glasnost, coupled with high military budgets in the United States and President George Herbert Bush's policy of watchfulness, led to a series of events that saw Gorbachev's replacement with the ultrapragmatic

---

28. Michael Schaller, *Reckoning with Reagan: America and Its President in the 1980's* (New York: Oxford University Press, 1992).

Boris Yeltsin, the end of one-party rule in what became the former Soviet Union, and, with the breaching of the Berlin Wall in 1989, the collapse of the Soviet satellite system in Eastern Europe. That same year, twenty-five thousand U.S. troops invaded Panama; for the first time in forty years, American intervention was justified on grounds other than the need to combat the forces of international Communism; the Cold War was over.

Harry Truman's prophecy concerning the end of the Cold War proved more or less true, but it did not mean, as he implied and Francis Fukiyama claimed, an end to history. As repressive and exploitative as it was, Soviet Communism had suppressed or controlled ancient tribal, sectarian, and religious animosities. In its anti-Communist obsession the United States had made deals with many devils. But the Long Peace, to use John Lewis Gaddis's term, had imposed a certain order on the world.[29] The end of the Cold War brought the end of a global confrontation that had threatened mankind with nuclear annihilation, but it also marked the end of a world system that contained blood-and-soil nationalism. "The Tigris and Euphrates Valley can be made to bloom as it did in the times of Babylon and Nineveh," Harry Truman had said in his Farewell Address. "Israel can be made the country of milk and honey as it was in the time of Joshua." But the end of the Cold War did not pave the way to Utopia. The lion did not lie down with the lamb. The second part of the Truman prophecy was as misguided as the first was insightful.

The fact that in the wake of the Cold War warfare, bloodshed, and refugees became primarily intranational rather than international have not made them less devastating or dangerous. Tribal hatreds have led to genocide in Rwanda, Burundi, and other parts of Africa. Freed from the threat of coercion by Soviet power and state Communism, the Balkans once again succumbed to ethnic and religious hatreds. The polyglot Soviet empire began to unravel as Chechnians and other long-oppressed minorities sought independence from Mother Russia. In the Middle East, Arab and Jew, Sunni and Shiia, Kurd and Turk continued to fight and bleed. The disintegration of the Communist bloc together with the intensification of ethnic and religious rivalries has led to the proliferation of nuclear technology. Arguably, during the 1990s the world stood closer to a nuclear incident than it had at any time during the Cold War, including the Cuban Missile Crisis.[30]

29. Gaddis, *The Long Peace: Inquiries into the History of the Cold War* (New York: Oxford University Press, 1987).

30. James Chace, *The Consequences of the Peace: The New Internationalism and American Foreign Policy* (New York: Oxford University Press, 1992); John Lewis Gaddis, *We Now Know:*

Bill Clinton assumed the presidency at a time unique in the history of American foreign relations. The end of the Cold War left the United States in a position of unquestioned preponderance. Its economy was 40 percent larger than that of its nearest competitor, and its defense spending equaled that of the six next highest combined, many of which were Washington's close allies. The United States led the world in higher education, scientific research, and advanced technology. As it faced the last decade of the twentieth century, America possessed great power and freedom of action but no overriding enemy and no clear idea of its objectives. *Globalization* would be the byword of the 1990s, but as Sandy Berger observed, "It can expand access to technology that enriches life—and technology that destroys it. It can equalize economic opportunity—and accentuate economic disparity. It can make dictatorships more vulnerable to the spread of liberating ideas—and democracies more vulnerable to the spread of terrorism, disease, and financial turmoil."[31]

As the world was to learn, the Clinton administration would advance five major foreign policy goals: (1) to shrink the military-industrial complex and use the "peace dividend" to advance social and economic security in the United States; (2) to reduce the risk of major war in Europe, East Asia, and the Middle East, largely by remaining militarily involved there; (3) to reduce the threat posed by weapons of mass destruction; (4) to foster a more open and productive world economy; and (5) to attempt to build a world order compatible with basic American values by encouraging the growth of democracy and by acting forcefully to curb major human rights abuses. These goals were hardly controversial; indeed, they were virtually indistinguishable from those of both Bushes.

As far as creating and distributing a peace dividend, Clinton proved as good as his word. The Clinton budget marked the first decline in defense spending since the Cold War began. In regard to his second objective, Clinton had to limit America's direct military role and encourage key allies to bear a heavier burden because domestic support for overseas military operations was fragile. But he deserves credit for holding NATO together at a time when its principal reason for being—the Cold War—was waning. Under American leadership, NATO assumed the broader role of guaranteeing peace and security

---

Rethinking Cold War History (New York: Oxford University Press, 1997); and Stanley Hoffmann, *World Disorders* (New York: Rowman and Littlefield, 1999).

31. Berger, "A Foreign Policy for the Global Age," *Foreign Affairs* 79 (November/December 2000): 23–24.

throughout Europe. In Asia the reaffirmation of the Japanese-American security treaty in April 1995 defused Japanese concerns about a continued U.S. military presence and constituted a powerful symbol of America's continued engagement in the region. As far as international economics was concerned, Bill Clinton was as committed to free trade and American participation in a global economy as had been his Republican predecessors. With a great deal of effort he pushed through Congress the North American Free Trade Agreement (NAFTA), which provided for the gradual elimination of tariffs and other trade barriers between the United States on the one hand and Canada and Mexico on the other.

As President Clinton came into office, the pressure on him to intervene militarily to relieve the Serbian siege of Sarajevo and to stop the bloodshed throughout Bosnia became intense. He insisted, however, that the Bosnian nightmare was a matter for NATO and the UN and that the members of those organizations in closest physical proximity to the strife-torn region, namely France and Germany, should take the lead. Privately, the Clinton administration had decided that it would intervene in Bosnia only when and if the parties involved showed a willingness for peace. Despite its professed sympathy for human rights, the Clinton administration was afraid of becoming bogged down in another Vietnam-type conflict. In 1995, after years of bloody fighting and ethnic cleansing, and a crushing economic embargo imposed on Yugoslavia by the United Nations, the Serbs, Croats, and Muslims agreed to a cease-fire and to Bosnia-wide elections for a parliament and a three-person presidency. The Dayton Accords (named for the Ohio city where the negotiations took place) were to be backed by a sixty-thousand-person NATO force, including twenty thousand American troops.

The best the Clinton administration was able to do—indeed, perhaps the best any administration could have done facing the immediate post–Cold War world—was to manage the supernational and subnational threats to U.S. security in ways that minimized their damage to the nation's vital interests. The supernational threat took the form of a growing globalization of grievance networks, including the transnational network of terror groups active from South and Central Asia to southern Russia to the Middle East and Africa. All shared a messianic hatred of open, tolerant societies. The subnational threat was the challenge to the nation-state from the potential disintegration of ethnically diverse societies. The Clinton administration, like its predecessor and successor, had no real answer to the question of how to balance legitimate demands for self-determination against the danger of unleashing new grievances. How do the forces of order and peaceful change confront and defeat the unscrupulous who simultaneously manipulate religious fundamentalism and seek to mobilize the disinherited of the earth in their own quest for power?[32]

Although Harry Truman's record as a crystal-ball gazer is mixed, the architects of America's post–Cold War policy have much to learn from him and his foreign policies. Certainly, until the mid-twentieth century, and even beyond, the strongest impulse in America's approach to the rest of the world was isolationism. Throughout its history the republic had considered itself a people apart. Its role in world affairs was perceived primarily as that of a shining example to the less fortunate peoples of the earth. North America first and then the entire Western Hemisphere were, of course, excepted. Even as it became an integral part of the world economy, the United States avoided entanglement in the affairs of the Great Powers. The United States intervened abroad militarily only when it was convinced that its direct economic and strategic interests were threatened, and then only temporarily; the approach was to defeat the enemy and retreat within fortress America. The notion that the United States would have to embrace military alliances, foreign aid, and the constant risk of bloodshed in a foreign land came only with the Cold War. It was during Truman's watch that the United States first became acquainted with the benefits and burdens of internationalism. It was then that the republic was forced to learn to live with ambiguity, to equate victory with the maintenance of the status quo. As the triumphalism of the early 1990s quickly faded, the Clinton and Bush administrations came to realize that, though the enemies and problems they faced were different from those confronted by Harry Truman, his realism, pragmatism, and patience would serve the nation just as well in 2000 as they had in 1950.

32. William G. Hyland, *Clinton's World: Remaking American Foreign Policy* (Westport, Conn.: Praeger, 1999).

WHO WON THE COLD WAR?

"Ideology is the curse of public affairs because it converts politics into a branch of theology and sacrifices human beings on the altar of dogma."[3] In its name, tens of millions of people died during this bloodiest of all centuries, in the furnaces of the Third Reich and in the Gulag, in Cambodia and Mao's China. We are living at the end of a century which saw the rise and fall of two of the most pernicious ideologies in history, fascism and communism. They each portrayed themselves as the antithesis of the other, but in fact they had a great deal in common. I lived much of my life watching one, then the other, grow in power. From the twenties through the seventies—half a century, more than half a lifetime—one or both of these alien philosophies threatened not only our freedom, but the very concept of freedom. That the century ends with the apparent triumph of the idea of freedom is a tribute, above all, to the human spirit.

Today, in the wake of the collapse of communism in Eastern Europe, its near (and I hope imminent) collapse in the Soviet Union, and its return to a police state in China, we can begin to look back on the policies that were put into place by the U.S. after World War II as a completed period of world history. Now that it has come to an end in the region in which it began—Eastern Europe—it is timely to address the question of who won the Cold War.

The events with which the eighties ended and the nineties began were, above all, a result of the failure of communism as both an economic theory and a political system. Neither the theory nor the system worked, and all that was left was a collection of police states which had lost the ability to use limitless force and repression to retain control. Mikhail Gorbachev recognized this and let Eastern Europe go, although that could not have been his original intention. Thus, credit for the liberation of Eastern Europe—the second end to the Second World War, so to speak—should go first and foremost to their own skillful and courageous leaders, and to Mikhail Gorbachev's decision not to intervene.

American policy, though, made an important contribution to these events. Many will step forward to seek credit for the triumph of freedom in Eastern Europe. The Reagan conservatives will claim that the bloated defense budgets of the eighties and President Reagan's muscular rhetoric turned the tide in Eastern Europe. Others will credit President Carter's human rights policies or his support of the resistance in Afghanistan, and some may even search the debris of Vietnam for evidence that our stand there, however costly, bought time for freedom to take root in other corners of the world.

Perhaps, in some minor incremental manner, all these events contributed to the flow toward freedom. But the policy that truly succeeded was born during the great era of American foreign policy, when, in less than three years, President Truman unveiled the Truman Doctrine, the Marshall Plan, NATO, and Point Four. Over the next forty years, the essential core of President Truman's policies survived fierce domestic debate, domestic politics, even the four great challenges of the last forty years—the Korean War, McCarthyism, Vietnam, and Watergate—and was accepted as the framework of our foreign policy by every President from Eisenhower to Bush.

President Truman knew we were embarking on a long and difficult struggle with an uncertain outcome, but he and most of his advisers nevertheless believed that if we held the line against further Soviet expansion, eventually communism would start its own painful transformation into something less dangerous and more open. He could not imagine then that his policy would require a commitment of more than forty years, that it would at times threaten to tear our own nation apart, that we would veer from overinvolvement to neo-isolation, and that it would be misapplied and overextended in Vietnam. With characteristic directness, President Truman did not agonize over the details. He simply announced the policy because he felt it was right. In my years in Washington, this was the most enduring event with which I was associated. Its consequences and its legacy would keep the fires of freedom burning until communism reached the point of collapse from within.

As I watched the collapse of communism, I thought back to the report George Elsey and I had produced for President Truman in 1946, and to George Kennan's prophetic writings of the same era. We had both argued for resistance to Soviet expansion, and offered the hope that if we could "restrain," or "contain," the Soviets, the country would eventually be transformed by internal pressures. In America, both the Left, with its readiness to accept communism as inevitable, and the Right, which searched for the enemy within and advocated a swollen and wasteful American military establishment, had been wrong. In the forty-fifth year after our report, I believed that communism was not only morally and intellectually bankrupt and discredited—as it had been for a long time—but it was also dying as a framework for government. It will survive for a while longer in certain areas, perhaps including North Korea, Vietnam, Cuba, and China, neither as an economic system nor as a viable ideology, but only as a justification for a police state. Its death, however, seemed to me virtually certain. In the eloquent words of the Yugoslav dissident and former communist Milovan Djilas:

> Communism is contrary to human nature. . . . Human nature is pluralistic in its being. Human nature is sinful. If human nature were perfect, communism might be possible, but that would be a "dead" society. Human nature is evil and at the same time gentle and good. The constant struggle of different tendencies in us is essential for the existence of humanity. . . . Capitalism functions better than communism because it is closer to human nature. Communism has failed and will fail because human nature cannot live without freedom, without choices, without facing alternatives. . . . Man can be restricted for a while, but not for generations.[4]

"A Very Dangerous Course"
Harry S. Truman and the Red Scare

Ellen Schrecker

One of the things Harry Truman did not mention in his Farewell Address was McCarthyism. In January 1953, the Red Scare was hardly something that Truman and his staff could overlook. Its omission from the Farewell Address was a conscious decision; the original draft of the speech by Richard Neustadt contained several paragraphs on the subject. Neustadt's formulation was what one might have expected. It pointed to the dangers facing the United States "in the world" and then echoed Franklin Roosevelt's inaugural address in its warning against "the spread of fear among us here at home." Reiterating a conceptualization that had become standard among civil libertarians during the 1950s, Neustadt explained that "if we once yield to fear, it may destroy the very liberties that we are striving to defend." There was an explicit reference to the menace of Communism, and then came the heart of the message: "But I really think there is still greater menace in some of the shouting and witch hunting that is going on today. And I tell you, we won't have much left, if we ever let our Bill of Rights, our basic guarantee of freedom, get trampled under in the rush to save ourselves from communists." The draft's language then turns folksy:

> You know, it has been said I must be a very "radical" fellow, even "soft" on communists, because I have expressed my opposition to bad laws and bad practices which masquerade today under the label of anti-communism.

Well, I am neither "radical," nor "soft." I am just an old-fashioned fellow
who wants to turn the clock back—way back, back to the Founding fathers,
back to the basic faith that first created our Republic.

A quotation from Jefferson, Madison, or Washington was to complete this
section, along with a final peroration about the need for "faith in the creative
human spirit, faith in the dignity and worth of every human soul" and "the
freedoms that have made our Republic a good place for men."[1]

It is hard to tell why this passage or one like it never made it into later
drafts of the speech. Certainly, at a moment when the Red Scare seemed at
its peak—with three major congressional investigating committees working
the field—there was no question about the relevance of the excised passage.
Maybe the president and his speechwriters did not want to rain on their own
parade.

There is considerable irony here, for it is possible to argue that Truman's
record on civil liberties—a contradictory one, as we shall see—nonetheless
contained moments that in retrospect reflect well on the president. Neustadt
knew his leader; the language of the excised passage was familiar in the White
House. It expresses, in words that the beleaguered chief executive might very
well have used, Truman's opposition to the Red Scare that so severely blighted
his presidency.

That opposition was more than rhetorical. Truman was, in some very basic
ways, a gut civil libertarian. Strangely enough, for a national leader whose administration saw so much political repression, Harry Truman seems to have
been far more concerned with protecting individual rights than any other
modern president—with the possible exception of Jimmy Carter. His attachment to the Bill of Rights, though far from sophisticated, was deep and long-
lasting. No doubt it owed much to his midwestern populism, to his passion
for history and reverence for the Founding Fathers, and to an innate sense of
fairness that would not let ordinary people be pushed around.[2] It was also intensified by his personal friendship with Max Lowenthal, an uncompromis-
ing liberal in the Brandeisian mold who tried to stiffen the president's spine
on matters of civil liberties. Time and again, in his private correspondence, as
well as his comments to members of his staff, Truman cited the need to protect individuals from unjust persecution. Typically, he tended to indulge in

1. Neustadt draft of Harry S. Truman Farewell Address, January 10, 1953, Charles S.
Murphy papers, courtesy of Dennis Bilger, Truman Library.
2. Alonzo L. Hamby, *Man of the People: A Life of Harry S. Truman* (New York: Oxford University Press, 1995), 428–29.

barnyard epithets when referring to those, including members of his own administration such as J. Edgar Hoover, who abused people's rights or indulged in "police state tactics."[3] Joe McCarthy, of course, got the choicest language—a "blatherskite," "a liar and a crook," and "a ballyhoo artist."[4] But whatever the vocabulary, there is no mistaking the depth and sincerity of Truman's concern.

So why was his administration's record so awful? During the high point of the Cold War revisionism of the 1960s and 1970s, Harry Truman got as much flak for developing what later came to be known as McCarthyism as any other individual—including Senator McCarthy. Historians have noted that the administration's loyalty-security program of 1947, with its list of proscribed organizations and concept of "guilt by association," triggered much of the repression. They have also pointed out that Truman's Justice Department handled the key political trials of the era—the Hollywood Ten, Alger Hiss, the Rosenbergs, and the top leaders of the American Communist Party. Naturally, none of these revisionists blame Truman for *everything*. Still, most agree that Truman was, if not directly responsible for starting the conflagration, at least pretty careless with matches. His desire to gain domestic support for the heavy military and financial commitment he felt the Cold War required tempted him to exaggerate the dangers of Communism. Unfortunately, once he began to disseminate an overly hyped and ideological portrayal of the Communist threat in the international arena, he was unable to offer a more realistic assessment of its relative insignificance at home. As his biographer Robert J. Donovan put it, "to obtain authority for what he considered necessary measures against Soviet expansionism, he appealed to anti-Communist feelings at home. To be in a position to take a tough stance against the dangers of communism abroad, he took a tough stance against domestic communism."[5]

3. Stephen J. Spingarn, memo for the file, July 22, 1950, Box 31, Internal Security File, National Defense and Individual Rights, Vol. I [2 of 2], Spingarn Papers, Truman Library.

4. Truman to T. H. Van Sant, February 12, 1952, Personal "V," and Truman to Clif Langsdale, November 29, 1950, Box 881, Missouri Folder 1, President's Secretary's Files, Truman Papers, Truman Library; Robert J. Donovan, *Tumultuous Years: The Presidency of Harry S Truman, 1949–1953* (1982; rpt. Columbia: University of Missouri Press, 1996), 166.

5. Athan Theoharis, *Seeds of Repression: Harry S. Truman and the Origin of McCarthyism* (Chicago: Quadrangle, 1971); Richard M. Freeland, *The Truman Doctrine and the Origins of McCarthyism: Foreign Policy, Domestic Politics, and Internal Security, 1946–1948* (New York: Knopf, 1971); Robert Griffith and Athan Theoharis, eds., *The Specter: Original Essays on the Cold War and the Origins of McCarthyism* (New York: New Viewpoints, 1974); Donovan, *Tumultuous Years*, 27.

It is easy, with a historian's twenty-twenty hindsight, to see how Truman's anti-Communism subverted his civil libertarianism. Most mainstream liberals of the early Cold War subscribed to a similar set of beliefs. They viewed Communism as so antithetical to the American system that its adherents did not deserve the protection of the Bill of Rights. Thus, they were willing to stand up for the rights of innocent liberals but would not lift a finger if the alleged subversive really was a Communist. They opposed what they considered "McCarthyism" because it violated individual rights, but also because they believed that its attacks on Cold War liberals and policy makers actually aided the Communist cause. It was not until much later that some of them recognized how damaging their selective approach to civil liberties had been. Truman, of course, was in a different position. Not only did he avoid defending Communists (whom he tended to view as an alien species), but he was, at least nominally, responsible for persecuting them. Still, while the president may not have acknowledged his own complicity in what happened, he was definitely disturbed by the excesses of the congressional committees and the internal security apparatus. He did, as some of his actions indicated, sincerely want to do the right thing. That he could not—even by his own lights—was the result of several factors over which he had no control. One, which has long been recognized, was the opposition he faced from a hostile Congress, dominated by a conservative coalition of Republicans and southern Democrats. The other was his inability to rein in the repressive activities of members of his own administration—most notably, those of J. Edgar Hoover and the FBI. Had Truman been able to control the situation, Communists would certainly have been unwelcome in positions of influence, but the broader inquisition might not have taken place.

When Truman took over the White House, he found himself facing an anti-New Deal coalition of conservative Republicans and southern Democrats. Long hostile to FDR's liberal reforms and his alleged partiality to organized labor, some of these right-wingers claimed to see Moscow's hand in the New Deal policies and agencies they disliked. Roosevelt's death did not make these charges disappear, and the Communists-in-government issue Truman inherited was to plague him throughout his administration. When it first arose, however, the issue, though annoying, did only peripheral damage. The House Un-American Activities Committee (HUAC), for example, took up the matter at its very first hearings in 1938 when it began to probe for reds within the WPA and other New Deal agencies. For the next few years, HUAC's chairman, Texas congressman Martin Dies, continued to fling McCarthyesque allegations that the administration was riddled with reds, accompanying his charges with lists of suspect employees. Congress paid attention to HUAC, even if Roosevelt did not, and in June 1941 appropriated $100,000 to the FBI to investigate the federal workforce and report back. Although Hoover assumed that the potential subversives his agents uncovered would be fired, the administration essentially shoved the FBI's findings under the rug.[6] The issue gained further currency during the 1944 presidential election, when Republican candidate Thomas Dewey attacked Roosevelt for dallying with the American Communist Party in order to curry favor with his Russian ally.[7] Nonetheless, neither Dies nor Dewey drew blood; the Communists-in-government issue had little resonance at a time when the United States and the Soviet Union were on the same side against Hitler. Still, Communism had never been popular, and the New Deal did, in fact, harbor people who were in or near the Communist Party. Thus, when the Cold War made the issue salient, conservatives in Congress and elsewhere were ready to wield it against the incumbent administration.[8]

Truman's postwar honeymoon was brief. By the middle of 1946, as conflict with the Soviet Union abroad and labor unrest at home were darkening the political scene, Congress began to look at the loyalty of federal employees. Revelations about a Canadian spy ring raised questions about American security; HUAC, which had just become a permanent committee, made noises about subversives in the government; and Nevada's powerful senator Pat McCarran slipped a rider into the State Department's appropriation bill giving the secretary summary power to dismiss security risks. The most immediate danger, however, emanated from the House Post Office and Civil Service Committee, which had authorized a three-man subcommittee to investigate the loyalty of federal employees. The subcommittee's report, transmitted to Truman late in July, criticized the government's security procedures and recommended that he appoint a commission to "make a thorough study of existing laws and the adequacy of existing legislation; . . . and present to the Congress at the earliest time practicable . . . a complete and unified program that will give adequate protection to our government against individuals whose primary loyalty is to governments other than our own."[9] The

6. D. Milton Ladd to J. Edgar Hoover, Harry Dexter White FBI file, no #; Ellen Schrecker, *Many Are the Crimes: McCarthyism in America* (Boston: Little, Brown, 1998), 108–15.

7. Robert J. Donovan, *Conflict and Crisis: The Presidency of Harry S Truman, 1945–1948* (1977; rpt. Columbia: University of Missouri Press, 1996), 233.

8. For a more extended discussion of anti-Communism and the Roosevelt administration, see Schrecker, *Many Are the Crimes*, chap. 3.

9. Jennings Randolph to Truman, July 25, 1946, Box 871, Official File, President's Temporary Commission on Employee Loyalty, Truman Papers.

Cabinet discussed the matter, but Truman was in no hurry to accede to the House committee's request. His administration was already easing suspected Communists out of their jobs, and no one in the White House felt that Communist subversion was a major threat. Truman, in a February 1947 letter to former Pennsylvania governor George H. Earle, discounted the "Communist 'bugaboo,' " reiterating his essentially populist conviction that "the country is perfectly safe so far as Communism is concerned—we have too many sane people." Attorney General Tom C. Clark also downplayed the situation, at one point telling another Cabinet member that some of the FBI's early accusations were "a lot of bull." Clark Clifford recalled a similar mindset among Truman's White House aides. "My own feeling was that there was not a serious loyalty problem. I felt the whole thing was being manufactured. We never had a serious discussion about a real loyalty problem. . . . It was a political problem."[10]

But it was a political problem that threatened to explode after the Republicans won the congressional elections of 1946. Within a few weeks of the GOP's victory at the polls, Truman appointed the Temporary Commission on Employee Loyalty. Its ostensible mission was to overhaul the government's procedures for assessing the loyalty of federal workers; its real mission, Truman later confessed to the FCC's Clifford Durr, was "to take the ball away from Parnell Thomas," the incoming chair of HUAC.[11]

It is unclear what kind of procedures the president may have had in mind. But if Truman's conception of a viable loyalty program was fuzzy, such was not the case with some of his subordinates within the executive branch. J. Edgar Hoover of the FBI knew exactly what he wanted such a program to contain: provisions that would give his agency control over its implementation. World War II had seen a vast expansion of the bureau's jurisdiction, budget, and personnel; and its director was determined to retain and, if possible, augment them. A brilliant bureaucratic politician whose dedication to building up the FBI's power and influence was matched only by the intensity of his antipathy to radicalism, Hoover recognized that he could carry out both missions if he could monopolize the government's internal security operations. Thus, from the start, he worked to ensure that his men would be in

10. Arthur S. Flemming, memo to Attorney General, July 22, 1946, Box 871, Official File, President's Temporary Commission on Employee Loyalty, and Truman to Geo. H. Earle, February 28, 1947, Box 880, Official File 263, Truman Papers; D. M. Ladd to Hoover, January 24, 1952, H. D. White file, #24; Carl Bernstein, *Loyalties: A Son's Memoir* (New York: Simon and Schuster, 1989), 197–98.

11. Donovan, *Conflict and Crisis*, 293.

charge of investigating and vetting the loyalty of every federal worker and would do so in accordance with his own essentially authoritarian worldview. As we shall see, Hoover's preemption of the loyalty-security program was only one of several instances in which the FBI director undermined Truman's more humane approach to the issue of domestic Communism.[12]

Less than a week after the House Civil Service Committee recommended that the president establish a commission to study employee loyalty, Hoover whisked a memo to the attorney general about the type of individual the Justice Department should appoint as its representative on the proposed commission. He even named a name. Sure enough, when the commission finally came into being, there was Hoover's candidate, A. Devitt Vanech, not only representing the Justice Department but chairing the body as well. "I want you to know how much I appreciate the confidence you have evidenced in me," Vanech wrote the director on the day his appointment was announced, "and assure you that I will do everything within my power to make a success of this assignment."[13] And he did. Since the commission had only two months to produce a report, it could not study the issue in depth and had to rely on the expertise of the preexisting internal security bureaucracy. In practice this meant that the FBI's view of the threat of Communism and the way to combat it came to dominate the commission's recommendations. Although some members of the body had doubts about the seriousness of the threat, the FBI brushed them off. According to Stephen J. Spingarn, a Treasury Department representative, soon to become the White House's point man on internal security matters, when the bureau's assistant director, D. Milton Ladd, was asked to specify the nature of the threat, "he stated that Communists in the Government present a substantial problem. However, he presented almost no factual information to support this statement."[14] Nor did Vanech press him to.

When the commission finally rendered its report, the FBI's fingerprints

12. The most useful studies of J. Edgar Hoover are Richard Gid Powers, *Secrecy and Power: The Life of J. Edgar Hoover* (New York: Free Press, 1987), and Athan Theoharis and John Stuart Cox, *The Boss: J. Edgar Hoover and the Great American Inquisition* (Philadelphia: Temple University Press, 1988).

13. Hoover, memo to Tom C. Clark, July 25, 1946, and A. Devitt Vanech to Hoover, November 25, 1946, Box 1, Vanech Papers, Truman Library. See also Alan D. Harper, *The Politics of Loyalty: The White House and the Communist Issue, 1946–1952* (Westport, Conn.: Greenwood Publishing Co., 1969), and Eleanor Bontecou, *The Federal Loyalty-Security Program* (Ithaca: Cornell University Press, 1953).

14. Memo for the File, January 14, 1947, Box 7, Treasury Department/President's Temporary Commission 1946, Spingarn Papers.

were all over the document. Embodied in Truman's Executive Order 9835 of March 21, 1947, the program required name checks for every federal employee against the files of the FBI as well as against those of the Civil Service Commission, HUAC, military intelligence, and similar agencies. If that initial search turned up "derogatory information," a full field investigation by the FBI would follow. The bureau then would submit its report to the individual departments, which could take action if they found "reasonable grounds for belief in disloyalty." On the surface, the process seemed fair enough. In order to prevent arbitrary dismissals, the employees had to be given formal charges and granted a hearing. They could also appeal their cases through several layers of agency boards as well as a central Loyalty Review Board. There were, however, some serious problems with these procedures, most of them the result of the FBI's reluctance to allow interference with its established investigative techniques.[15]

Communists, it was clear, were the primary target. But the Communist Party was a secret organization whose members concealed their affiliation. As a result, investigators had to rely on indirect evidence in order to identify someone as a party member. The method they employed relied on a kind of political profiling, based on a pattern of behaviors and associations that were assumed to be prevalent among people in the Communist movement. The main indicator was membership in what were then known as "front organizations," groups that usually operated within the penumbra of the American party. Adopting this method of identification with its assumptions that there were few differences between Communists and people who supported their causes opened the process up to abuse, especially since EO 9835 made "membership in, affiliation with or sympathetic association with" such organizations grounds for dismissal. *Sympathetic association* was a slippery term that, in the hands of narrow-minded bureaucrats, could even include socializing with one's parents. Almost as slippery were the criteria for selecting the proscribed organizations. The attorney general was to list them; but until the federal judiciary stepped in, he could do so on any grounds he wanted—and without a hearing.[16]

15. Bontecou's fifty-year-old study, *The Federal Loyalty-Security Program,* remains the best overview of the program.

16. Executive Order 9835, Prescribing Procedures for the Administration of an Employees' Loyalty Program in the Executive Branch of the Government, 12 *Fed. Reg.* 1935. Reprinted in Bontecou, *The Federal Loyalty-Security Program,* 275–81. For a good sampling of the charges brought against federal employees, see Adam Yarmolinsky, ed., *Case Studies in Personnel Security* (Washington, D.C.: Bureau of National Affairs, 1955).

Charging people with guilt by association was bad enough, even if they could have been able to rebut the charges against them. But in most cases, that turned out to be impossible. Again, the FBI was the culprit. It refused to give the accused workers and the agencies that employed them access to its files or information about the sources of its information. Doing so, Hoover explained, in a memo to the attorney general, would not only have revealed the names of secret informants who "have been painstakingly developed over a period of years," but would also have revealed the bureau's bugs and wiretaps. As a result, "much of the valuable material which we have received in the past and which would otherwise not be available to the Government could no longer be obtained."[17] The director was paranoid about retaining the secrecy of his bureau's files. Not only was national security at stake, but so too, Hoover and his allies were wont to claim, were the privacy and reputation of the individuals under investigation. To avoid smearing innocent men and women, the files could not be released. There was considerable hypocrisy in the director's insistence that he was protecting people's rights. What he really cared about was preserving the FBI's reputation and ensuring that his agents' unauthorized activities never became public.[18] Unfortunately, maintaining the secrecy of the bureau's files by refusing to let federal employees know who had accused them of disloyalty often made it impossible for those employees to mount a viable defense.

From the start, the loyalty-security program came under attack. Civil libertarians homed in on the injustices that "guilt by association" and unknown informants could create. Max Lowenthal, who acted as the president's liberal conscience, was outspoken in his opposition to the program.[19] Truman was unhappy as well. He was aware of Hoover's agenda and tried to limit the FBI's jurisdiction by encouraging the Civil Service Commission to carry out most of the investigations the program called for. The "Pres feels very strongly anti FBI," White House aide George Elsey noted, "and sides positively with [Civil Service Commissioners Harry B.] Mitchell and [Frances] Perkins. Wants to be sure and hold F.B.I. down, afraid of 'Gestapo.'" But Truman had neither the clout nor the desire to take on the director, especially since even his own advisers recognized that the FBI's previous experience in the field of

17. Hoover, memo to Attorney General, January 29, 1947, Box 1, File ADV: Loyalty Commission, Vanech Papers.

18. Athan G. Theoharis, "In-House Cover-up: Researching FBI Files," and Anthony Marro, "FBI Break-in Policy," both in *Beyond the Hiss Case: The FBI, Congress, and the Cold War*, ed. Theoharis (Philadelphia: Temple University Press, 1982), 20–128.

19. Elsey, Memo for Mr. Clifford, September 19, 1949, Box 69, Internal Security, Federal Employees Loyalty Program, EO 9835, Elsey Papers, Truman Library.

internal security gave it an advantage over other agencies. Moreover, as Truman well knew, Hoover had powerful allies on the Hill. "J. Edgar will in all probability get this backward looking Congress to give him what he wants," Truman complained. And in fact it did, reversing the administration's priorities and giving the FBI more than twice as much money for the loyalty program investigations as for the Civil Service Commission.[20]

Truman had little more control over other aspects of the program. Since it was designed to serve as a political buffer against a Republican-dominated Congress that was seeking to profit from the Communists-in-government issue, he felt compelled to appoint conservatives to the Loyalty Review Board. Its chair, Seth Richardson, was an old-line Republican who had served as assistant attorney general under Herbert Hoover, and the rest of its members had solid business, legal, and academic credentials. Officials who administered the program at lower levels were similarly conservative, if not more so, since their careers depended on ensuring that potential subversives did not escape their purview. As Eleanor Bontecou noted, "There appears to have been a rather general acceptance by the appointing authorities of the theory voiced by a spokesman for one agency that liberal intellectuals should not be chosen." Over time, Truman and his subordinates responded to their right-wing critics by tightening up the program—relaxing the standard for proof from "reasonable grounds" to "reasonable doubt" and reviewing the cases of people who had already been cleared. Even so, despite the administration's precautions, the loyalty program did not serve its intended purpose. It could not contain the Communists-in-government issue.[21]

Hoover had been skeptical from the start. Ever since the Roosevelt administration retained many employees the FBI had targeted as potential subversives, the director had been upset about what he felt was a lackadaisical attitude toward security. Early in 1945, the discovery of classified documents in the offices of *Amerasia*, a left-wing publication dealing with East Asian affairs, intensified Hoover's frustration. The FBI's investigation revealed that a few State Department and military employees had been leaking materials to the magazine. Although he was anxious to prosecute, his superiors for a number of reasons, including the FBI's own missteps, were not. After arresting six people in June, the Justice Department dropped the prosecution, apparently because of a deal with the defendants. Hoover was furious, but

20. Donovan, *Conflict and Crisis*, 296–97; Elsey memo, May 2, 1947 for CMC, Clifford Memo for the President, May 23, 1947, Box 69, Internal Security, Federal Employees Loyalty Program, EO 9835, Elsey Papers.

21. Bontecou, *The Federal Loyalty-Security Program*, 47, 280–82.

unable to prevail. The case, however, festered for years, ultimately resurfacing in Joe McCarthy's charges against the Truman administration.[22]

Hoover's distress increased in the fall of 1945 when Vassar graduate Elizabeth Bentley walked into the bureau's New York office and began to spill a story about her activities as the courier for a ring of Communist espionage agents within the federal government. Bentley named more than eighty people, including State Department employee Alger Hiss and an assistant secretary of the Treasury, Harry Dexter White. Their names were not new to the FBI. Some of these people had been on Dies's lists or else had been fingered by other defectors like *Time* magazine editor Whittaker Chambers. While the bureau tried—unsuccessfully—to reinsert Bentley into the KGB apparatus, it interviewed the people she identified, tapped their phones, and put them under surveillance. Although it did find circumstantial evidence to support Bentley's story, it did not collect enough material to support a conviction.[23] No one confessed, and the corroborating KGB telegrams that were deciphered by the VENONA code-breaking project a few years later were considered too secret to be produced in court. (They were, in fact, considered too secret to be revealed to the president and attorney general!)[24]

Even as the FBI and Justice Department tried to assess the prospects for a prosecution, they were also considering what to do about those of Bentley's agents still on the federal payroll. Hoover had, of course, immediately notified the White House about the case. But he and his superiors in the Justice Department were sending mixed signals about whether the alleged spies should be fired or kept under surveillance in order to obtain evidence that could be used in court. Such evidence never appeared and, as FBI Assistant Director D. Milton Ladd later explained, "We were reluctant to see this case prosecuted as it was our view that the facts would not sustain a prosecution." Nonetheless, despite the bureau's strong reservations, the department took the case to a New York City grand jury at the beginning of 1947. Knowing that the government could not indict the alleged spies, the FBI director tried to get them fired.[25] A few were. Many simply left the government, recogniz-

22. Theoharis and Cox, *The Boss,* 241–46; Harvey Klehr and Ronald Radosh, *The Amerasia Spy Case: Prelude to McCarthyism* (Chapel Hill: University of North Carolina Press, 1996).

23. Memo, Ladd to Hoover, November 26, 1945, Bentley-Silvermaster file #108x12. The most useful source on Elizabeth Bentley is Kathryn S. Olmsted, *Red Spy Queen: A Biography of Elizabeth Bentley* (Chapel Hill: University of North Carolina Press, 2002).

24. Daniel Patrick Moynihan, *Secrecy: The American Experience* (New Haven: Yale University Press, 1998), 69–72.

25. Ladd to Hoover, November 12, 1953, H. D. White file, #59; Hoover, memo to Attorney General, January 27, 1947 in Summary Brief on H. D. White, in L. V. Boardman to Hoover,

ing that the Cold War federal bureaucracy was no place for people with their political backgrounds. Hoover, meanwhile, showered the executive branch with memos about these people's subversive activities. But the memos were vague, and many officials were unwilling to act on the basis of what they felt was incomplete information. The Treasury Department, for example, where several of Bentley's people were employed, tried for more than a year to get the attorney general to send more information, but to no avail.[26] Meanwhile, Hoover, who had little patience for such punctiliousness, was becoming increasingly annoyed with the administration's failure to purge itself.[27] EO 9835 offered no assistance, since, contrary to the director's advice, the Loyalty Review Board lacked the power to fire anyone.

By the summer of 1948, it was clear that the New York grand jury was not going to indict Bentley's suspects for espionage. Rather than fold their tents and slink back to D.C., the federal attorneys running the operation decided to prosecute the Communist Party's top leaders under the 1940 Smith Act for conspiring to "teach and advocate" the "violent overthrow" of the American government. This was a prosecution that Hoover and his lieutenants had been hoping to mount ever since the end of World War II. A trial that branded the Communist Party as a criminal conspiracy would not only bolster the FBI's "educational campaign" to alert the American people to the danger of Communism, but it would also legitimate many aspects of the government's internal security program. On his own initiative, Hoover had ordered his men to compile a thick prosecutorial brief against the American Communist Party; and he was more than happy to send it on to the Justice Department.[28] Although the Smith Act indictments looked like an election-

---

August 26, 1954, H. D. White file, #1245; Ladd to Hoover, November 12, 1953, H. D. White file, #59.

26. A. L. M. Wiggins (acting secretary of the treasury) to Attorney General, October 13, 1947; Spingarn memo, October 14, 1947; Spingarn memo to Wiggins, October 16, 1947, all in Box 7, File Treasury Department Loyalty cases, 1947–48, Spingarn Papers.

27. Allen Weinstein, *Perjury: The Hiss-Chambers Case* (New York: Knopf, 1978), 357–66; Hoover, memo to Clyde Tolson, February 24, 1947, and E. A. Tamm, memo to Hoover, December 8, 1947, both in Belmont to Ladd, November 11, 1953, H. D. White file, #75; Ladd to Hoover, memo, January 21, 1947, Carl Marzani file, #70; Powers, *Secrecy and Power,* 280–91.

28. U.S. Congress, Senate, Select Committee to Study Governmental Operations with Respect to Intelligence Activities, *Final Report,* book 3, "Supplementary Detailed Staff Reports on Intelligence Activities and the Rights of Americans," 94th Cong., 2d sess., April 23, 1976, 429–39 (hereafter SDSRIARA); SAC [special agent in charge], Portland, to Hoover, October 8, 1945, Smith Act Trials file, #13; John F. X. McGohey, handwritten memorandum on preparations for the Smith Act prosecution, Box 1, John F. X. McGohey Papers, Truman Library.

year ploy on the part of the Truman administration to preempt the Communist issue, in reality neither the president nor the attorney general knew about the prosecution in advance. "I have been accused of filing cases against communists in order to bolster the president's image," Tom Clark told a later interviewer, "but there is no truth to this. The president never talked to me about it at all."[29] Clark was, in fact, surprised and annoyed to find that his underlings were taking the case to court; and Truman, it seems, may not have been informed about it at all. However, once the prosecution got under way and proved to be a success, the administration began to cite it as evidence of its diligence in fighting Communism.[30] By then, however, Truman had pretty much lost the public relations battle, for his congressional enemies had at last struck pay dirt with the Communists-in-government issue.

The turning point came in 1948. All but two of Bentley's people were gone from the federal payroll, and the loyalty-security program was proving so efficacious in screening out potential subversives that the KGB's Washington bureau was reduced to obtaining information from the daily press.[31] But it was an election year, and the Communists-in-government issue was too juicy for Republican politicians to overlook, especially when the FBI director was sending them useful information. Since Hoover was paranoid about covering his bureau's tracks, we do not have (or at least this author does not have) a complete picture of the FBI's collaboration with the congressional investigating committees. What we do have indicates that the director's impatience with what he considered the administration's laxity in firing suspected Communists finally impelled him to leak material, often through intermediaries, to favored congressmen. While it is possible that HUAC and the other committees might have embarrassed the Truman administration on the issue even without the FBI's assistance, it is clear that the collaboration proved politically lethal. In March, the HUAC chair, Parnell Thomas, who had been relatively restrained on the Communists-in-government issue during the loyalty-security program's initial year, launched an attack on the

29. Donovan, *Tumultuous Years*, 27.

30. Spingarn Memo for file, July 12, 1950, Box 31, Internal Security File, National Defense and Individual Rights, Vol. I [2 of 2], Spingarn Papers; Murphy and Spingarn, Memo for the President, August 14, 1950, Box 1, Chron File 1947–56 July 1950, Richard E. Neustadt Papers, Truman Library; Peyton Ford to Pat McCarran, January 4, 1950, Box 7, File Assistant to the President/White House Desk Manual, Constitutionality of S2311, Spingarn Papers.

31. Spingarn Memo for Attorney General, September 9, 1948, Box 30, White House Assignment, memorandums, letters, Spingarn Papers; Allen Weinstein and Alexander Vassiliev, *The Haunted Wood: Soviet Espionage in America—The Stalin Era* (New York: Random House, 1999), 286–89.

atomic scientist Edward U. Condon, then serving as head of the Commerce Department's Bureau of Standards. Claiming that Condon was the "weakest link" in the nation's security, Thomas pressed the administration for Condon's loyalty files.[32] Truman refused, announcing in an official directive on March 13 that keeping those files within the executive branch "is necessary in the interest of our national security and welfare, to preserve the confidential character and sources of information furnished, and to protect Government personnel against the dissemination of unfounded or disproved allegations. It is necessary also in order to insure the fair and just disposition of loyalty cases."[33] Thomas was something of a loose cannon and his charges, though clearly a nuisance, did not do much damage to the White House.

Such was not the case with the investigation of Elizabeth Bentley's allegations that Sen. Homer Ferguson of Michigan took up a few months later. He brought Bentley to the stand at the end of July and asked Truman for the files of some of the federal employees she had fingered. HUAC got into the act as well. Its political agenda was obvious; the presidential campaign was getting under way and, as Parnell Thomas explained, the chairman of the Republican National Committee "was urging me . . . to set up the spy hearings. At the time he was urging me to stay in Washington to keep the heat on Harry Truman."[34] Not only did the committee subpoena Bentley and some of the people she had accused, but it also called up Whittaker Chambers to corroborate her testimony. Chambers, who had defected from the Soviet underground in the late 1930s, had been trying to alert official Washington to the presence of his former associates ever since 1939. He identified several of the same people Bentley had, most notably Harry Dexter White and Alger Hiss. White, who had a serious heart condition, denied all the charges against him and then died three days later of a massive heart attack. Hiss denied the charges as well, insisting that he had never met Chambers.[35]

Recognizing the partisan agenda behind the hearings, Truman tried to brush them off, claiming that the committees had uncovered nothing the FBI did not already know and that, as the grand jury discovered, there was not enough evidence for a criminal prosecution. He refused to hand over any

32. Harper, *Politics of Loyalty,* 62.

33. Donovan, *Conflict and Crisis,* 414; Truman directive, March 13, 1948, Box 68, Internal Security—Congressional Loyalty Investigations (1), Elsey Papers.

34. Memo for Clifford, August 2, 1948, Box 68, Internal Security—Congressional Loyalty Investigations (2), Elsey Papers; Donovan, *Crisis and Conflict,* 414.

35. The most useful studies of the Hiss case are Weinstein, *Perjury,* and Sam Tanenhaus, *Whittaker Chambers: A Biography* (New York: Random House, 1997).

loyalty files and attacked the "public hearings now under way [which] are serving no useful purpose. On the contrary, they are doing irreparable harm to certain persons, seriously impairing the morale of Federal employees, and undermining public confidence in the Government." At the end of his statement, the president was asked by a reporter whether he thought the hearings were a "red herring" to distract the voters from Congress's failure to enact the administration's legislative program. Little realizing that he was about to inflict massive damage on his administration, Truman repeated his interlocutor's words. "They are simply a 'red herring' to keep from doing what they ought to do."[36]

Unbeknownst to Truman and Hiss, J. Edgar Hoover was feeding information to the committees, especially to HUAC's most effective member, first-term California congressman Richard M. Nixon, who used it to dramatize the allegation that the administration was soft on Communism. By the end of August, it was clear that the Bentley and Hiss revelations were having an impact. Truman remained relatively unconcerned about the charges, but some of his aides, who worried about the forthcoming election, did not. "It is a major Republican issue," George Elsey mused on August 26. "It is getting worse, not better. . . . It is the Administration's weakest link. There is paydirt here, and the Republicans had no intention of being diverted by appeals from anguished liberals who see the Bill of Rights transgressed." Elsey's bleak assessment turned out to be wrong—at least for the moment. Thomas E. Dewey, the Republican contender, did not take advantage of the Communists-in-government issue. During the primaries, he had openly refused to support outlawing the Communist Party and, having found red-baiting unrewarding in 1944, had no desire to revisit that terrain. According to the chair of the Republican Party, "He thought it degrading to suspect Truman personally of being soft on Communism."[37] The Republicans would not make that mistake again.

While Dewey went on his genteel way to defeat, the Hiss case unfurled. Chambers had not initially claimed that any of his associates in the Communist Party's Washington underground were involved with espionage. He added that charge after Hiss sued him for slander, when he sought to bolster his defense by providing a sheaf of government documents that he said the

36. Statement by the President, August 5, 1948, Box 35, Internal Security File/Loyalty Program [2 of 4], Spingarn Papers; Hamby, *Man of the People*, 453.
37. Elsey, "Random thoughts 26 August," Box 68, Internal Security—Congressional Loyalty Investigations (2), Elsey Papers; Richard Norton Smith, *Thomas E. Dewey and His Times* (New York: Simon and Schuster, 1982), 493–94, 507–8.

former State Department official had delivered to him. By that point, it was clear that the administration had to do something. Under pressure from Nixon, who staged a dramatic raid on Chambers's pumpkin patch to force the Justice Department to act, the government indicted Hiss for perjury—the statute of limitations for espionage having run out. Although it took two trials before the prosecution got a conviction, the Hiss case gave real heft to the Communists-in-government issue. Truman's "red herring" turned out not only to be a red, but to be a spy as well. Moreover, the administration had been repeatedly warned about Hiss and had repeatedly ignored that warning.[38] For conspiracy-minded Republicans, frustrated by their defeat in 1948, this was "paydirt" indeed.

The Communist victory in China brought an additional Republican onslaught against the administration. China had never been bipartisan territory; Republican politicians, though reluctant to make a commitment in Europe, had long pressed for greater involvement in East Asia. While Truman and his foreign-policy advisers recognized that the United States could not intervene in any effective way to preserve Chiang Kai-shek's Nationalist regime, Chiang's supporters in Congress and elsewhere, the so-called China lobby, disagreed and were demanding ever more assistance. When Chiang was finally forced from the mainland in the middle of 1949, these people blamed the administration for letting him down. It was then not much of a leap to connect the Nationalists' defeat with the Communists-in-government issue and exploit the whole business for partisan ends. With the Hiss case still in the headlines, Republicans began to circulate charges that Communist subversion within the State Department had somehow brought about the "loss of China." South Dakota senator Karl Mundt made it explicit: Hiss with his "effective Harvard accent" had influenced the policy "which has helped bring about the entire subjugation of China by Communist forces directed from Moscow."[39] This was, of course, the scenario that Sen. Joseph McCarthy was to embellish early in 1950 as he began to brandish his alleged lists of Communists within the government.

It is important to realize that McCarthy, at least at this point in his career, was echoing charges that many other politicians had been making. If we discount his personal flamboyance, the main thing that distinguished him from

38. Hoover to Attorney General, January 17, 1949, enclosure in Nichols to Tolson, November 14, 1953, H. D. White file, #825.
39. Lewis McCarroll Purifoy, *Harry Truman's China Policy: McCarthyism and the Diplomacy of Hysteria, 1947–1951* (New York: New Viewpoints, 1976); Donovan, *Tumultuous Years*, 135.

his Republican colleagues was his willingness to give names and numbers, thus transforming the vague "loss of China" into real accusations against real people—even if the charges themselves had little basis in reality. Although Truman could not completely ignore McCarthy's allegations, he did not take them very seriously. On March 3, he told one of his aides, then under attack from McCarthy, that the senator "is just a ballyhoo artist who has to cover up his shortcomings by wild charges. I don't think you need pay any particular attention to him." Ignore him, in other words, and he will go away. But McCarthy did not go away. The Republican leadership encouraged him to keep on attacking. And the Democrats, who at first did not realize how feckless the Wisconsin senator was, feared that he had a second Hiss case in his pocket. As George Elsey recalled, "No one had any experience in dealing with the likes of McCarthy. He could out-yell everyone and evade being pinned down to the facts. The State Department was worried because they had picked up a lot of employees during the postwar reorganization, and they were not sure exactly what they had."[40] As a result, the administration and its congressional allies decided to respond to the senator's charges by investigating them, presumably to show how little merit they contained. But the investigation, by a subcommittee of the Senate Foreign Relations Committee under the direction of Maryland senator Millard Tydings, backfired. Instead of squelching McCarthy, it amplified him. The advent of the Korean War gave further salience to his charges: now State Department subversives had brought the United States into a war.[41]

To make matters worse, J. Edgar Hoover was by then completely disenchanted with the administration. The denouement occurred in June 1949 in a Washington courtroom where a former Justice Department employee named Judith Coplon was on trial for transmitting unauthorized materials to a Soviet engineer who worked for the United Nations. The VENONA project had alerted the FBI to Coplon's activities the previous year, and the bureau put her under surveillance. On March 4, 1949, the G-men who had been trailing her and her Russian contact all over New York City finally made the arrest near Union Square. In her purse was a batch of official documents, including twenty-six FBI reports that had been copied from the Justice

40. Donovan, *Tumultuous Years*, 166, 172–73.
41. The most useful studies of Joseph McCarthy's political career are Robert Griffith, *The Politics of Fear: Joseph R. McCarthy and the Senate*, 2d ed. (Amherst: University of Massachusetts Press, 1987); David Oshinsky, *A Conspiracy So Immense: The World of Joe McCarthy* (New York: Free Press, 1983); and Thomas Reeves, *The Life and Times of Joe McCarthy* (New York: Stein and Day, 1982).

Department's files. Since Coplon had been caught in the act, her conviction was a sure thing.[42] The only problem, at least from the FBI director's point of view, was that the trial judge wanted the documents produced in court in order to prove that Coplon had been endangering national security. Allowing FBI reports to reach the public eye would, Hoover insisted, violate executive privilege and infringe on the privacy of individuals; worse yet, the director explained to the attorney general, it would destroy the bureau's "effectiveness to discharge its responsibilities in the more important field of internal security." In reality, of course, Hoover was worried that the materials in Coplon's handbag would embarrass the bureau, and he urged the Justice Department to abandon the prosecution rather than hand over the files. The director lost that battle, since other members of the Truman administration wanted to show that they could be tough on spies. When the documents became public, they revealed that the FBI had been spying on private citizens, among them the actor Frederick March. Hoover never forgave his superiors.[43] And, when McCarthy came on the scene, the FBI director rushed to assist him.

By the summer of 1950, Truman had lost control of the situation. He could restrain neither the FBI nor the conservatives in Congress. Moreover, he was also becoming upset about the accumulating evidence that his own subordinates within the federal bureaucracy were abusing people's rights while administering the loyalty-security program. The Coplon case's revelations of FBI misconduct made him sympathetic to calls for a high-level investigation of the bureau, but he realized that he lacked the political clout to implement it. Nor did he have the staff to supervise what the rest of the executive branch was doing in the field of internal security.[44] At the same time, he was still struggling to keep Congress from obtaining access to the administration's personnel records. There had been considerable jockeying throughout the spring and early summer over the Tydings subcommittee's request for the loyalty files of the men and women McCarthy had fingered. At first Truman stood firm, insisting that his earlier refusals to let Congress review such ma-

---

42. Ironically, because the FBI had wiretapped her conversations with her defense attorney and failed to get the appropriate warrant for her arrest, Coplon was able to overturn her convictions (she had two trials) on appeal. For information about the Coplon case, see Marcia and Thomas Mitchell, *The Spy Who Seduced America: Lies and Betrayal in the Heat of the Cold War, the Judith Coplon Story* (Montpelier, Vt.: Invisible Cities Press, 2002).

43. Hoover, memo to Tolson, Ladd, Nichols, Belmont, November 9, 1953, H. D. White file, #43; Hoover to Morris Ernst, November 23, 1953, File 100, Morris L. Ernst papers, Harry Ransom Humanities Research Center, University of Texas at Austin; Theoharis and Cox, *The Boss,* 256–61; Theoharis, "In-House Cover-up," 26–28.

44. Theoharis and Cox, *The Boss,* 262–63; Hamby, *Man of the People,* 428.

terials still held. But eventually he gave in and allowed the subcommittee's staff to look them over.[45]

The Korean War turned a mess into a disaster. Not only did it reinvigorate McCarthy's charges, but it also pushed Congress into passing the deeply flawed Internal Security Act of 1950, otherwise known as the McCarran Act. The original impetus for that legislation had come from none other than Richard Nixon, who in the spring of 1948 joined his HUAC colleague Karl Mundt in proposing a measure to cripple the Communist Party by forcing it and its front groups to register with the federal government. The problems with this legislation were legion. Not only was it so vaguely worded that it could conceivably threaten all manner of perfectly harmless organizations, but the registration provisions for individual members of those groups clearly violated the Fifth Amendment's prohibitions against self-incrimination. Although the bill had sailed easily through the House of Representatives, it got bogged down in the Senate Judiciary Committee, where some heavy hitters, including former Chief Justice Charles Evans Hughes, raised questions about its constitutionality. It was reintroduced the following year, and, when the Korean War broke out, the Republicans put the measure on their "Must List," while few of the Democrats who opposed the bill were willing to do so publicly. Truman was against the measure from the start and, in his usual blunt manner, expressed his disappointment with the behavior of "a lot of people on the Hill [who] should know better but had been stampeded into running with their tails between their legs."[46]

Also working its way through Congress that summer was some fairly repressive legislation that the Justice Department had requested. Some of it was designed to plug holes in the existing internal security laws, like extending the statute of limitations for espionage, but other measures were more questionable, especially those that allowed for the indefinite detention of deportable aliens who could not return to their countries of origin. Truman did not support this legislation, but no doubt because he lacked the staff to keep on top of everything that was going on, he did not realize that the Justice Department was still pushing the measure. As one of his aides noted, the

45. J. Howard McGrath to Truman, memo, March 17, 1950, Box 880, Official File 419K, Truman Papers; Donovan, *Tumultuous Years,* 174.

46. Spingarn, memo, July 21, 1950, Box 31, Internal Security File, National Defense and Individual Rights, Vol. I [1 of 2], and memo for the file, July 22, 1950, Box 31, Internal Security File, National Defense and Individual Rights, Vol. I [2 of 2], Spingarn Papers; William R. Tanner and Robert Griffith, "Legislative Politics and 'McCarthyism': The Internal Security Act of 1950," in *The Specter,* ed. Griffith and Theoharis, 174–89; Tanner, "The Passage of the Internal Security Act of 1950" (Ph.D. diss., University of Kansas, 1970).

president had become increasingly concerned about his own administration's policy and its "tendency to be formulated in a security vacuum without regard to other important considerations, notably whether encroachment on individual rights." He felt, the aide continued, "that I.S. [internal security] legislative policy has tendency to be formulated in security branches of Government (FBI, Immigration, Intelligence services) and course upward to top where it is approved without adequate considerations from other angles."[47] In short, even his own subordinates did not always share Truman's veneration for the Bill of Rights.

Nor, of course, did the Republicans and southern Democrats who pushed the McCarran Act through Congress over the president's veto. The legislative history of that measure is replete with misunderstandings and mixed signals as both the Truman administration and its congressional allies struggled to prevent its passage. Probably no strategy would have succeeded, given the poisonous concatenation of the Korean War, an approaching election, and the frantic desire of liberal politicians not to appear soft on Communism. Truman had been meeting with congressional leaders off and on over the course of the summer in an attempt to come up with something that would defuse the rush for enactment of what was essentially the revived Mundt-Nixon bill. Still, many liberals within Congress and elsewhere felt that the Truman administration was not giving them much help. An ACLU lobbyist on the Hill noted "a tremendous amount of resentment among the top Democratic Senators at the bungling ineptitude with which the White House has handled this whole subject. They feel it will very likely cost some of them their election."[48] Truman sent Congress a message on August 8 explaining what his administration had done and was doing to deal with the threat of subversion and warning the lawmakers not to "enact laws which would seriously damage the right of free speech," but the bill the administration offered a few days later merely tweaked existing laws. The congressional liberals doubted that it would prevent the passage of the Mundt-Nixon measure. In its place, they decided to propose legislation authorizing the FBI to round up potential subversives in an emergency.[49]

47. Spingarn notes for 5/19/50 talk with Attorney General, 5/18/50, Box 28, Assistant to President, White House, Desk Manual, Internal Security, Spingarn papers.
48. Mary Ann Baldinger, quoted in William W. Keller, *The Liberals and J. Edgar Hoover: Rise and Fall of a Domestic Intelligence State* (Princeton: Princeton University Press, 1989), 40. I have relied heavily on Keller's thoughtful treatment of the FBI, the liberals, and the passage of the Internal Security Act of 1950.
49. Tanner and Griffith, "Legislative Politics and 'McCarthyism.'"

J. Edgar Hoover had been seeking such authority for years; it would legitimize the bureau's ongoing practice of keeping Communists and other potential subversives under surveillance.[50] While there is no evidence that the director actually worked with Paul Douglas, Hubert Humphrey, and the other Senate liberals to construct the measure, it is clear that they were hoping to establish their anti-Communist credentials by invoking the FBI. Such had been Hoover's success in creating the bureau's image as a professional, apolitical outfit that liberals, who should have known better, and even Harry Truman, who certainly did, tended to cite the FBI when they were fighting the witch-hunters. The HUAC, McCarthy, and their allies were sloppy and reactionary—far better to leave the task of dealing with spies and saboteurs to what Attorney General Clark called "the continuous but quiet watchfulness of the Federal Bureau of Investigation."[51] While Truman may have been sending mixed signals about whether he would support the liberals' ploy, it made little difference. When the so-called concentration camp measure reached the Senate floor, it was simply folded into the Mundt-Nixon registration bill along with the administration's requested changes in the existing legislation. Only seven senators voted against it. (The House had just passed a similar measure, sans detention provisions, by a lopsided 354–20 vote.)

No one inside the White House had ever doubted that Truman would veto the McCarran Act. What comes through most clearly in the internal memos that circulated within his staff is the depth and intensity of his opposition to the measure's infringement on civil liberties. According to one of his staff members, Truman had told a newspaper editor

> of the importance he attached to the Bill of Rights and had stated flatly that he would veto any legislation that reached him which did not fully square with that document.
>
> The President repeated that statement to us, saying that he would veto any legislation such as the Mundt-Nixon bill which adopted police-state tactics and unduly encroached on individual rights, and he would do so regardless of how politically unpopular it was—election year or no election year.[52]

While the arguments that the White House constructed to persuade Congress, first, not to pass the bill and, then, to uphold Truman's veto stressed

---

50. SDSRIARA, 461.

51. Keller, *Liberals and J. Edgar Hoover,* 36–71.

52. Spingarn, memo for the file, July 22, 1950, Box 31, Internal Security File, National Defense and Individual Rights, Vol. I [2 of 2], Spingarn Papers.

that the measure would be counterproductive in the struggle against Communism, those formulations were standard Cold War rhetoric, clearly designed to convince wavering Democrats that they could safely uphold the president's veto without appearing soft on Communism. Invariably, Truman and his supporters pointed out the effectiveness of the administration's current activities—the Smith Act prosecution, the loyalty-security program, and the deportations carried out by the Immigration and Naturalization Service. They often reiterated J. Edgar Hoover's argument that outlawing the Communist Party or making it register would force the party underground where it would be much more difficult to watch. They also noted that the affected organizations were sure to litigate, a process that could take years and seriously delay the measure's implementation. Finally, as the president warned Congress on August 8, "if such legislation were held unconstitutional, as it well might be, it would make martyrs out of our worst enemies and create public sympathy for them."[53]

Truman's real passion, however, came out in his repeated invocations of the Bill of Rights. Echoing ideas that he and his aides had been expressing over the past few years, both his statement of August 8 and his veto message decry "police state measures" and the dangers posed by the legislation to the nation's basic freedoms. "Unwise or excessive security measures," the president insisted in the earlier statement, "can strike at the freedom and dignity of the individual which are the very foundation of our society—and the defense of which is the whole purpose of our security measures."[54] Similar language suffuses the September 22 veto message. Ever the history buff, Truman described how the McCarran Act's registration provisions "can be the greatest danger to freedom of speech, press, and assembly, since the Alien and Sedition Laws of 1798," since they could

> open a Pandora's box of opportunities for official condemnation of organizations and individuals for perfectly honest opinions which happen to be stated also by Communists.
>
> The basic error of these sections is that they move in the direction of suppressing opinion and belief. This would be a very dangerous course to take . . . because any government stifling of the free expression of opinion is a long step toward totalitarianism.[55]

53. Truman, press release, August 8, 1950, Box 881, Official File 263, Truman Papers.
54. Ibid.
55. Internal Security Act, 1950, Veto Message from the President of the United States, September 22, 1950, in *Public Papers of the Presidents of the United States: Harry S. Truman 1945–1953*, 8 vols. (Washington, D.C.: U.S. Government Printing Office, 1961–1966), 6 (1950): 645–53.

The president, however, was whistling in the wind. Only ten senators and forty-eight representatives voted to sustain his veto. Six weeks later, the Democrats' midterm election losses seemed to reinforce the power of McCarthyism.

Nonetheless, despite what was clearly a major defeat for the administration, Truman and his aides did not abandon the quest for a way to mitigate the witch hunt. For some time, they had been considering the appointment of a special panel to look into the workings of the loyalty-security program. The Tydings subcommittee had suggested creating such a body to investigate the federal employees McCarthy had named. The administration considered the project again when it sought an alternative to the McCarran Act. Although the Democratic leadership liked the idea, its members thought it premature. Once the elections were over, however, Truman decided to act. He would appoint a commission of eminent individuals who would study the internal security situation, head off further congressional investigations, reform the loyalty-security program, and come up with suggestions for amending the McCarran Act.[56]

The commission never got off the ground. To begin with, some of the more eminent individuals whom the administration was eager to enlist—like the jurist Learned Hand and former President Herbert Hoover—refused to serve. When it was finally formed with the World War II naval hero Chester Nimitz as its chair, its members were second-tier eminences—a former senator from Connecticut, an Episcopal bishop, a midwestern industrialist, and a Wall Street banker, among others. Although the opposition of Senator McCarran was to abort the panel's mission, it is unlikely that it would have lived up to Truman's libertarian hopes. In their informal correspondence, the panel's members did not seem to share the president's sensitivity to the rights of individuals. "I am also of the opinion." one of them explained, "that at all times we must keep in mind that doubts in the nature of things must be resolved in favor of the Government." Another commissioner was equally resolute. "Employee tenure, and civil rights generally," he explained to Truman, "will have to be subordinated to the right of the nation to defend itself against Russia, which is the enemy of all civil rights and all the freedoms. Freedom of speech and freedom of thought do not include freedom for those who have surrendered their freedom of thought and of speech to the Kremlin, to parrot

56. Spingarn, Memorandum for Mr. Clifford, May 5, 1949, Box 35, Internal Security File/Loyalty Program [3 of 4], and Murphy, draft memo for the President, November 16, 1950, Box 36, Internal Security File/Loyalty, Communism and Civil Rights [1 of 3], Spingarn Papers; Harper, *Politics of Loyalty*, 164–87.

the teachings of the Kremlin in our schools and colleges and newspapers and over the air."[57]

Perhaps it was fortunate, therefore, that Pat McCarran scuttled the commission before it had a chance to do its work. He and his colleagues on the Senate Judiciary Committee refused to pass on a routine measure waiving the conflict-of-interest regulations for the commission. The Nevada senator might have approved the measure if the commissioners had been willing to give him access to the administration's loyalty-security records. Nimitz, however, rejected McCarran's "squeeze play to get something our friends on the Hill had been unable to get by direct request or appeal"; thus, by the middle of 1951, the commission was dead in the water. Rather than prolong the agony, its members resigned en masse, leaving the lame-duck administration unable to mitigate the excesses of the anti-Communist hysteria that it had, unwittingly, helped bring about.[58]

One of the reasons behind McCarran's hostility to the Nimitz commission was that his own Senate Internal Security Subcommittee (SISS) was about to begin its investigations.[59] With the help of the China lobby and the FBI, the SISS took off from McCarthy's initial charges to carry out a major investigation of the "loss of China" scenario. The hearings, which lasted for months, focused on an East Asian–oriented think tank called the Institute of Pacific Relations (IPR). Owen Lattimore, one of McCarthy's prime targets, had been associated with the IPR, as had almost everybody in the government or elsewhere who had anything to do with East Asian affairs. So, too, had a few members of the Communist Party. The connections were obvious. McCarran subpoenaed Lattimore and the State Department's leading China experts, exposed their links to the IPR, and highlighted their supposedly biased policy recommendations during the Chinese civil war. McCarran's power and thoroughness were devastating. Truman was horrified but impotent. He could not even prevent McCarran from forcing the newly appointed attorney general, James McGranery, to indict Lattimore for perjury as the price for the

57. Chas. H. Silver to Admiral Chester Nimitz, February 26, 1951, Official File, Presidential Commission on Internal Security and Individual Rights, January–November 1951, Box 2, Danaher, Sen. John, Truman Papers; Russell Leffingwell to Truman, August 20, 1951, Box 1716, Official File 2750-A (October 1951–1953), Truman Papers.

58. McCarran to Nimitz, February 21, 1951, Nimitz to John A. Danaher, March 8, 1951, Danaher to Russell C. Leffingwell, April 7, 1951, Box 1716, Official File 2750-A (1945–July 1951), Presidential Commission on Internal Security and Individual Rights, Box 2, Nimitz, Personal, Truman Papers.

59. Danaher to Nimitz, March 19, 1951, Box 1716, Official File 2750-A (1945–July 1951), President's Commission on Internal Security and Individual Rights, Box 2, Nimitz, Personal, Truman Library.

Judiciary Committee's confirmation of his appointment.[60] And the State Department, the true target of McCarran's investigation, responded by turning inward and stifling its own best and brightest.

Our story has a strange coda, one that might well be entitled "J. Edgar Hoover's Revenge." For the Communists-in-government issue returned to plague Harry Truman a few months after he had left the White House. Combing through a batch of FBI reports, Richard Olney, an assistant attorney general in the Eisenhower administration, noticed that J. Edgar Hoover had sent several warnings about Harry Dexter White to high-level officials just at the time the government was about to nominate him as the first executive director of the International Monetary Fund. The documentation clearly showed that the Truman administration was aware of the charges against White and yet appointed him anyhow.[61] In fact, the attorney general had discussed the problem with the president, the secretary of state, and the secretary of the treasury. Although Hoover had pressed the administration to rescind the appointment, he could not prevent it. The bureau did not want to produce Bentley in public, since its investigation into her charges was still ongoing. And whatever other evidence against White that was available in February 1946, Hoover explained to his aides, "was circumstantial." Moreover, any refusal to appoint White would have led to an outcry. Without stronger proof of wrongdoing, Truman and his advisers felt they had no alternative but to go ahead with the appointment.[62] Olney showed this evidence to his chief, Attorney General Herbert Brownell, who broke the story in a speech on November 6, 1953. The Truman administration, Brownell implied, had, indeed, been coddling Communists, just as the Republicans had been saying all along.[63]

Truman, of course, responded, trying to set the record straight by denying

60. Robert P. Newman, *Owen Lattimore and the "Loss" of China* (Berkeley: University of California Press, 1992).

61. White's FBI file contains a summary report, dated February 11, 1953, that describes the FBI's attempts to "disseminate" information about White to the Truman administration. A section of the document entitled "Purpose" is entirely blacked out, which might indicate that Olney did not pick up on this issue by himself, as he claimed in a later interview, but was alerted by the FBI.

62. Hoover to Attorney General, February 4, 1946, H. D. White file, #8; Hoover to Tolson, Tamm, Ladd, February 21, 1946, H. D. White file, #100; W. A. Branigan to Belmont, February 11, 1953, H. D. White file, #27; Hoover memo to Tolson, Nichols, Ladd, November 14, 1953, H. D. White file, #75; Hoover to Tolson, Tamm, Ladd, February 25, 1946, H. D. White file, #825

63. Warren Olney III, Oral History, March 25, 1974, Earl Warren Oral History Project, Bancroft Library, University of California–Berkeley, 373–74.

(incorrectly) that he had been warned in advance and explaining that the FBI had wanted to avoid publicity so it could keep White under surveillance. Brownell, who apparently did not realize what a can of worms he had opened, suddenly seemed vindictive and narrowly partisan. Worse yet, at least for the Eisenhower White House, HUAC was on the verge of precipitating an embarrassing jurisdictional crisis by seeking to subpoena the ex-president and thus raising the issue of executive privilege. But J. Edgar Hoover had the last word. Although he rarely went before Congress, he testified before the Senate Internal Security Subcommittee on November 17. Flaunting his reputation for probity and professionalism, he explained that he had issued repeated warnings about White's espionage connections, but that the Truman administration had ignored them. It was a particularly delicious moment for the FBI director. As he responded to the congratulatory letters and telegrams that poured into bureau headquarters, he could congratulate himself on having scored a major coup.[64]

Some years later, in response to an interviewer's question about the greatest mistake of his presidency, Truman replied, "Tom Clark . . . it isn't so much that he's a *bad* man. It's just that he's such a dumb son of a bitch. He's about the dumbest man I think I've ever run across."[65] There's something pathetic about that comment. Truman was, I think, on the right track, his instinctual libertarianism helping him recognize that something had gone seriously wrong with civil liberties during his watch. Yet he picked the wrong target. Tom Clark was an undistinguished attorney general and an even worse Supreme Court justice, but appointing him was hardly Harry Truman's worst mistake. In a way, however, this assessment reflects his administration's record with regard to the Red Scare: Truman knew that it was a disaster, but he did not understand why it was so bad, and he could not do anything about it.

64. M. A. Jones to Nichols, December 4, 1953, H. D. White file, #918.
65. Merle Miller, *Plain Speaking: An Oral Biography of Harry S. Truman* (New York: G. P. Putnam's Sons, 1974).

Apartment 15-A
29 Washington Square, West
New York City 11

November 13, 1947

Dear Mr. President,

I have wanted to write you for a long
time as I have been getting from all of my
friends, Republicans and Democratics alike,
such violent reactions to the Loyalty Tests.
And now, after the dismissal of the ten people
from the State Department, and the article in
the Herald Tribune, I feel I must write you.

I do not feel that Dr. MetaGlass should be
the only woman on the Committee for Review as
she is not a strong enough person. I feel more
people, not lawyers, should be on and another
woman might well be appointed. Perhaps Mrs.
Lewis Thompson of Red Bank, New Jersey, who is
a strong Republican but also a liberal, might
help to interpret the work of this Committee
to the public. Certain things need to be interpreted to the public. My own reaction is
anything but happy. I feel we have capitulated
to our fear of Communism, and instead of fighting to improve Democracy, we are doing what the
Soviets would do in trying to repress anything
which we are afraid might not command public
support, in order to insure acceptance of our
own actions.

I am sorry that I cannot see you before

(over)

I go to Geneva to the Human Rights Commission
meetings and since this session of the General
Assembly is drawing to an end, I want to thank
you for your kindness in appointing me. It has
been interesting work and I hope that I have
been helpful. When I return from Geneva and
the holidays are over, I will try to come to
Washington in order to see you again.

   With best wishes to Mrs. Truman and
Margaret, and congratulations to her on her
successes, and wishing you all a Happy Thanks-
giving and Christmas season, I am,

   Very sincerely yours,

   Eleanor Roosevelt

November 26, 1947

Dear Mrs. Roosevelt:

Your letter of November thirteenth was of great personal
interest to me, and I have read it with sympathetic reactions to the
ideas you express. I can well understand that you may be disturbed
by some of the articles and summaries that have been published about   x144-A
the loyalty review of the present incumbents and new employees of the
civil service posts.

I have told the Civil Service Commission, the members of the
Loyalty Review Board, and the Press that I did not wish this inquiry to
become a "witch hunt", but rather to establish what I think is the
truth, that the overwhelming number of civil servants in the United   x252-K
States are not only faithful and loyal, but devoted patriots. It is,
of course, contrary to American tradition to inquire into the political
or philosophical views of anyone, and I think that is why all of us
feel a certain repugnance to this program, but I became convinced that
it was necessary, not because, as you say, "we were trying to repress
anything we were afraid might not command public support", but because
there were certain indications of a small infiltration of seriously
disloyal people into certain sensitive parts of the Government. The   x48-73
disclosures of the Canadian Government, and in particular the report
of the Canadian Civil Service Commission as to the way in which previously quite innocent and simple people had been trapped and led into
a situation of securing and revealing information to agents of another   x562
government — contrary to all instructions and policies of Government
service — were sufficient to convince me that we had to make some
positive and constructive inquiry into the state of affairs in our own
civil service.

The Civil Service Commission, into whose hands I placed most
of the development of the program, is cautious and fully aware of the
Constitutional rights of human beings that need to be protected. We   x252
all must remind ourselves that no one has a Constitutional right to   xPP7465
work for the Government. He has a Constitutional right to express him-   x274
self and his opinions any way he chooses, and to associate himself with   xPP71729
organizations that are quite opposed to the Government, or even to
attempt to alter the Constitution, but it is not appropriate that he
xPP7452 should carry on such activities while working for the Government of the
x285   United States.

255

The <u>Loyalty Review Board</u> which is made up of distinguished persons outside the Government is, I think, going to prove not only an aid in distinguishing the true from the false and in uncovering actual disloyalty, but it will also serve to protect the civil liberties of individuals in this new and unusual field.

I am interested in your reaction to the Board, and I do want to tell you of a very great difficulty which we experienced in finding enough of the right kind of people to serve. There are a good many lawyers on the Board, I agree. The reason for having so many lawyers is that it is hoped that the Board will sit in panels of three on the cases, and that at least one lawyer will be a member of each panel. A legal mind, while it may be narrow in some instances, is, as I think you know, very strong on the right and proper procedures for the handling of witnesses and the establishing of true evidence as against rumor and slander, before making a conclusion of fact that the individual charged with an offense is guilty. I really believe that a sound, conservative, legal mind will be of great assistance in establishing a proper method of carrying on this inquiry.

However, there are still several posts to be filled on the Loyalty Review Board, and we are attempting to secure a number of other persons of broad public interests who are not lawyers. I have noted with interest your recommendation of <u>Mrs. Lewis Thompson</u> of Red Bank, New Jersey, and I will send her name to the Civil Service Commission with the suggestion that they look into that possibility.

I am grateful for your letter because I am always glad to have your views.

Thank you very much for your good wishes and your congratulations to Margaret on her successes as a singer.

I hope that you will come to see me when you return from Geneva.

Very sincerely yours,

(Sgd) HARRY S. TRUMAN

Mrs. Franklin D. Roosevelt, x280
Apartment 15-A, x pp 7460
29 Washington Square, West,
New York 11, N. Y.

x pp 73 Radio & concert appearances "R"
x 2-E Endorsements Thompson

Behind the Silences

Challenges to the Gender Status Quo during the Truman Years

Susan M. Hartmann

Reading Harry S. Truman's Farewell Address, we conclude that his presidency dealt with nothing of any importance relating to women's status. Even his memoirs, whose thousand pages afforded plenty of space, are silent on the subject of women as political actors and on women's place in postwar America. More than once during his presidency, Truman indicated how trivial he considered issues about women's status. After he met with a delegation of women pushing a constitutional amendment guaranteeing equal rights for women, he commented on his appointment calendar, "A lot of hoey [*sic*] about equal rights."[1] Truman's impulsive, private jottings by no means tell the whole story of his position on equal rights for women, but they do reflect the insignificance of that issue in comparison to his momentous decisions relating to the Cold War, civil rights, and the economy.

Why then should we bother to examine policies and politics concerning women's roles and gender relations during the Truman years? Can the silences

I wish to thank Jackie Della-Rosa, Stephanie Gilmore, Audra Jennings, Kathleen Laughlin, and Caryn Neumann for their helpful comments and the staff at the Truman Library for their expert and generous service. Research funding was provided by the CDW–Coca Cola Fund for Women's Studies Scholars at Ohio State University.

1. The President's Appointments, Friday, September 21, 1945, Box 82, President's Secretary's Files, Truman Library.

tell us anything? What might Truman have referred to if he had thought more broadly and deeply about the era of his presidency? What might his Farewell Address have included if he had shared our benefit of hindsight along with three decades of women's history research? What can we learn from probing behind the silences?

The absence of women—whether as voters, officeholders, politicians, or the objects of policy—from Truman's accounts of his presidency did not mean that gender was absent from politics in the 1940s. In fact it was everywhere. Few noticed the deeply gendered nature of politics, because male control of the public sphere seemed to represent the natural order. No woman sat on the Supreme Court or in the Cabinet; only seven women served among the 425 members of the House of Representatives. This pattern was part of a larger gender system in which men were breadwinners and participants in the public sphere and women were responsible for keeping house and tending children. In this gender system, few doors were entirely closed to women, and some women could do almost anything, but men occupied the most powerful and visible public positions, and it was assumed that those belonged to men by right. Embedded in law and policy, popular values, and practice, this gender structure disadvantaged women yet seemed fair to most people. In fact, it seemed so natural to men and women alike that it was invisible to all but a few.

For the most part, gender became manifest only when women's traditional roles offered political capital or when the occasional female politician appeared on stage. Although Bess Truman—unlike Eleanor Roosevelt—pursued no public purposes of her own and did not relish political campaigning, she and Margaret played important roles in Truman's 1948 campaign. According to one aide, "Mrs. Truman and Margaret certainly stole the hearts of the people as we went along," and *Newsweek* reported that the "Truman ladies" became "a Presidential trademark." The family appearances, according to *Newsweek*, "put the nation's First family on a comfortable footing with millions of Americans whose own home life they saw reflected there." People saw the conventional gender system embodied in Bess Truman's life. As a feature in *Look* magazine put it approvingly in 1949, "She doesn't try to save the world, nor to look like a Powers model. She's the very opposite of the brittle career woman."[2]

Truman also recognized the political capital of women as voters, especially

---

2. *Newsweek* and *Look* quoted in Gil Troy, *Mr. and Mrs. President: From the Trumans to the Clintons* (Lawrence: University Press of Kansas, 2000), 43–45.

in the months leading up to national elections. In September 1948, for example, he acknowledged that the Democratic Party "has relied on you women." Noting that women had "a million and a half more potential votes than men," he reminded them that they "hold the balance of power in this election." Similarly, in September 1950, he decried the low voter turnout in 1946 and 1948, told women that "the future of your jobs and your homes depends on the kind of government you have," and insisted that "women will bear a great share of the responsibility for the kind of Congress we elect."[3]

Gender also became transparent in American politics when candidates or officials were women, for the very reason that they upset what was considered the natural order. It was not unusual for a female candidate to be challenged simply on the basis of her sex. For example, when Congresswoman Margaret Chase Smith threw her hat into the ring for a Senate seat, one Maine Republican leader declared, "The little lady has simply stepped out of her class." And the wife of one of Smith's opponents asked, "Why take a woman to Washington when you can get a man?"[4] Dorothy McCullough Lee, a veteran of the Oregon house and senate, lost her bid for reelection as mayor of Portland to a challenger whose slogan was "a man for a man's job."[5] While not all female candidates faced such blatant sex-biased challenges to their aspirations for public office, they uniformly found themselves presented by the press in photographs and text that accentuated their traditional roles. Few escaped references to a husband, children, kitchen, and domestic skills. Margaret Chase Smith was one of those few, because she was widowed and without children and because she refused to pose cooking. Still, as her biographer tells us, "the press took considerable pains to note Mrs. Smith's youth, petite stature, and 'attractiveness.'"

Such assumptions about women's place in the gender system were also reflected in law and policy. Gender inequality was written into national policies, including the federal tax code, Social Security, and unemployment

3. Remarks Recorded for Broadcast on Democratic Women's Day, September 17, 1948, *Public Papers of the Presidents of the United States: Harry S. Truman, 1945–1953,* 8 vols. (Washington, D.C.: U.S. Government Printing Office, 1961–1966), 4 (1948): 580; Recorded Address for Broadcast on Democratic Women's Day, September 17, 1950, *Public Papers: Truman, 1950,* 654.

4. Quoted in Hope Chamberlin, *A Minority of Members: Women in the U.S. Congress* (New York: New American Library, 1974), 146–49. See also Janann Sherman, *No Place for A Woman: A Life of Senator Margaret Chase Smith* (New Brunswick: Rutgers University Press, 2000), 73–89.

5. Quoted in Jane S. Jacquette, ed., *Women in Politics* (New York: John Wiley and Sons, 1974), 201–18.

insurance,[6] and women's disadvantaged position under the law was declared to be perfectly constitutional by the Supreme Court. In 1948, for example, the Court heard a case, *Goesaert v. Cleary,* initiated by two women who owned taverns and their daughters whom they employed. The plaintiffs argued that a Michigan law that prohibited the licensing of a female bartender unless she was the wife or daughter of the male owner of the establishment deprived them of their livelihood and violated the equal protection clause of the Fourteenth Amendment. Ostensibly, the Michigan legislature had sought to protect women from the hazards of bartending. Yet women were not barred from being waitresses in liquor establishments—jobs that paid less than bartending and in which there was no protective barrier separating them from male patrons. This, however, did not concern the justices, nor did it matter that the legislation had been initiated by a male bartenders union, part of a national effort to exclude women from bartending. "We cannot give ear to the suggestion that the real impulse behind this legislation was an unchivalrous desire of male bartenders to try to monopolize the calling," Justice Felix Frankfurter declared for the court, which upheld the Michigan law.[7]

Although the *Goesaert* decision reflected the prevailing judicial reluctance to scrutinize economic regulation or to substitute the courts' opinion for that of the legislatures, it is not likely that the Supreme Court would have upheld a law that discriminated against white male breadwinners. The decision in this case illustrated the tenacious assumption that women, as women, needed special protection and supervision and that this need for protection abrogated their right to have the same access to jobs as did men. The tendency of most Americans to think of men, but not women, as breadwinners made a decision like the one in *Goesaert* seem perfectly reasonable.

Congressional debate over the Employment Act of 1946 provides another example of how firmly entrenched were what Alice Kessler-Harris calls these "gendered habits of the mind."[8] This so-called full employment bill, origi-

---

6. See Alice Kessler-Harris, *In Pursuit of Equity: Women, Men, and the Quest for Economic Citizenship in Twentieth-Century America* (New York: Oxford University Press, 2001), chaps. 2–4

7. Christopher A. Anzalone, ed., *Supreme Court Cases on Gender and Sexual Equality, 1878–2001* (Armonk, N.Y.: M. E. Sharpe, 2002), 111–12. See also Barbara Allen Babcock, Ann E. Freedman, Eleanor Holmes Norton, and Susan C. Ross, *Sex Discrimination and the Law: Causes and Remedies* (Boston: Little, Brown and Co., 1975), 93–96; Judith A. Baer, *The Chains of Protection: The Judicial Response to Women's Labor Legislation* (Westport, Conn.: Greenwood Press, 1978), 116–21; Leo Kanowitz, *Women and the Law: An Unfinished Revolution* (Albuquerque: University of New Mexico Press, 1969), 37–41, 94–95.

8. Kessler-Harris, *In Pursuit of Equity,* 5.

nally proposed in 1944 and part of Truman's liberal postwar agenda, required the government to undertake economic policies that would ensure a job for everyone. Conservatives in Congress weakened the bill by eliminating a provision that would have specified the right to work. But the debate over that provision illuminates official thinking about gender, as legislators addressed the question of which Americans have the right to work.

The original provision in the draft bill established that "all Americans able to work and seeking work have the right to useful, remunerative, regular, and full-time employment," but then went on to enumerate two exceptions to this right: students and those with "full-time housekeeping responsibilities." When questioned about these exceptions, one of the measure's sponsors, James Murray of Montana, responded that the legislation "was not intended to maintain at Government expense employment for people who ought to be in school or who ought to be at home helping to raise families." Any right to work was secondary to maintaining what lay at the core of the gender system, he implied when he insisted that the bill's drafters wanted "to make sure that we were not undertaking by a Government program to break up the family." At one point Truman, when asked by the National Federation of Business and Professional Women's Clubs (NFBPW) for a statement to kick off its National Business Women's Week, declared that "full employment means work opportunity for every man or woman who wants to work." But Secretary of Labor Louis Schwellenbach, testifying before Congress on the full employment bill, stated the administration's position to be that a woman "who does not have the necessity of working, but is just working because of the fact that she had gotten in the practice of it and likes it, . . . should stay home."[9]

Gendered habits of the mind were also revealed in public opinion polls about whether women should hold high political office. In 1945, just 37 percent of women and 29 percent of men indicated that they would vote for a woman for president. Only slightly more, and still a minority, favored women for a cabinet post—43 percent of women and 33 percent of men.[10] Having worked nearly exclusively with men throughout his political career, Truman had little reason to feel differently. In fact, he was not comfortable with women, believing that they inhibited free discussion among men. He did not want a woman in his Cabinet and refused to appoint one to the Supreme Court. As he explained to an aide, "The Justices don't want a woman. They

9. Murray and Schwellenbach quoted in ibid., 19–21, 62; Truman to Margaret A. Hickey, September 10, 1945, Box 536, President's Personal File 1900, Truman Papers.

10. George H. Gallup, *The Gallup Poll: Public Opinion, 1935–1971*, 3 vols. (New York: Random House, 1972), 1:548.

say they couldn't sit around with their robes off and their feet up and discuss their problems."[11]

That Truman even contemplated the idea of a female Supreme Court justice suggests that the customary gender order did not have an iron grip on the political imagination. Moreover, the efforts to link public women to domestic responsibilities, visible both in the media treatment of women in politics and in the assumptions about full employment, reveal a certain defensiveness growing out of perceptions that the older gender order was being gently shaken. Thus, an examination of what Truman left out of his Farewell Address reveals undercurrents swirling below the seemingly natural arrangement of male and female roles. Recognizing these undercurrents, in turn, helps us to understand the eventual revolution in women's status, gender roles, and public policy that occurred in the 1960s and 1970s.

The disruptions to the traditional gender system in the late 1940s were rooted in important material changes in women's lives. Responding to the demands and opportunities of World War II, six million additional women had joined the labor force between 1940 and 1945. Although reconversion and the return of veterans sent women's labor force participation plummeting after a high of 36 percent during the war, by the end of the 1940s women's employment outside the home was on the rise again. In 1950, close to 29 percent of all women were in the labor force, and they constituted 30 percent of all workers, testifying to the importance of women workers both to the economy and to the material well-being of their families.[12]

As the service sector of the American economy grew in the years after World War II, demand accelerated for workers in positions traditionally associated with female skills, such as clerical work, record keeping, retail sales, teaching, and the like. Moreover, as Truman noted in his Farewell Address, the postwar economy provided Americans with "more of the good things of life than ever before in the history of the world." Americans beheld a dazzling array of new products, and aggressive marketing encouraged their desire for these goods. Wishing to provide some of this new abundance for their families—television sets and other appliances, college education for their children, new homes in the suburbs—married women increasingly sought a second family paycheck. As paid employment became even more common

11. Alonzo L. Hamby, *Man of the People: A Life of Harry S. Truman* (New York: Oxford University Press, 1995), 307; Truman quoted in Cynthia Harrison, *On Account of Sex: The Politics of Women's Issues, 1945–1968* (Berkeley: University of California Press, 1988), 57.

12. Bureau of the Census, *Statistical Abstracts of the United States: 1952* (Washington, D.C.: U.S. Government Printing Office, 1952), 177–79.

among women, and especially married women, the idea that home was women's primary responsibility and breadwinning that of men increasingly clashed with reality.

Also drawing women out of the home was their growing involvement in higher education. The efforts of colleges and universities to sustain enrollments despite the absence of men during World War II had benefited women, whose share of college enrollments reached nearly 50 percent during the war years. As had been true in the case of women's employment, the return of veterans had negative implications for women's educational status. With help from the GI Bill, veterans flooded college campuses, comprising nearly half of all students in 1947; institutions gave preference to veterans, and women's share of enrollments dropped to just one-third. Even as returning veterans completed their education, the proportion of women students remained below the prewar high of 40 percent.[13]

Yet there is another side to this picture. Although women's share of college enrollments declined relative to that of men, their absolute numbers increased steadily in the Truman years and beyond. The "democratization of higher education"—the ever expanding accessibility of college to young Americans—that the GI Bill fueled ultimately benefited women as well as men. And higher education eventually led large numbers of women to challenge traditional assumptions of what women should be and do. Even some of those who attended college while Truman was president expressed frustrations about the abrupt transition they had to make from college or paid employment to domesticity. One woman reported, "Some of my interests and attitudes were so very academic that I didn't take to the routine of a homemaker for quite a while." Another also pointed to the discontinuity between college and full-time homemaking: "I would much prefer to play a Bach fugue than . . . scrub the kitchen floor. I have needed all my philosophy courses to reconcile myself to accepting the monotony of household chores."[14]

These changes in women's employment and education, then, put more and more distance between women's actual experiences and the gender ideal

13. Susan M. Hartmann, *The Home Front and Beyond: American Women in the 1940s* (Boston: Twayne, 1982), 103–8. Because African American women had already surpassed African American men in college enrollments before the war, the effect of the GI Bill was to bring black men and women closer to parity in terms of undergraduate degrees.

14. Mirra Komarovsky, *Women in the Modern World: Their Education and Their Dilemmas* (Boston: Little, Brown and Co., 1953), 100–165; Ernest Havemann and Patricia Salter West, *They Went to College: The College Graduate in America Today* (New York: Harcourt Brace and Co., 1952), 64–68.

that assigned breadwinning and public life to men and domesticity to women. Some women—like those bartenders in Michigan—were already challenging the legal obstacles that put women at a disadvantage in the labor market. What had once seemed fair, given the presumed devotion of women to the home and family, gradually came to be seen by more and more people as unjust.

Truman himself acknowledged the fluid state of the gender order as well as his own attachment to tradition when he addressed a Women's Bureau conference marking the centennial of the Seneca Falls women's rights conference. The Women's Bureau had adopted the title "The American Woman, Her Changing Role: Worker, Homemaker, Citizen." When Truman gave his remarks he insisted on reversing the order, placing "homemaker" first. His attempt at humor and flattery also trivialized women as serious political actors; he remarked to his audience that when he told aides that he was going "to address a conference of good-looking women, you should have seen them run to get into the car." At the same time, however, he acknowledged the "unfinished tasks" regarding women's rights, including equal pay legislation, and encouraged women to "make your goals known and persist in demanding action."[15]

Women as public actors were most visible to Truman and his advisers just before elections, not only as voters but also because they performed indispensable, if mundane, work for the parties at the grassroots level. That labor, in fact, increased in the post–World War II era. With the passage of the Hatch Act in 1940, less patronage was available to attract men, and parties turned to a still substantial pool of middle-class married women who did not hold jobs, encouraging them to volunteer as canvassers, office staff, and poll workers, under the direction of male professionals. Women constituted substantial majorities of these grassroots volunteers, and they filled seats on state and national party committees, but they had no voice in any key decisions. At a time when party conventions still controlled the nominating process, women constituted less than 15 percent of the delegates.[16]

For most of Truman's presidency, these women were represented by India Edwards, who chaired the Women's Division of the Democratic National

15. Remarks at the Opening Session of the Women's Bureau Conference, February 17, 1948, *Public Papers: Truman, 1948*, 142.

16. Paula Baker, "'She Is the Best Man on the Ward Committee': Women in Grassroots Party Organizations, 1930s–1950s," in *We Have Come to Stay: American Women and Political Parties, 1880–1950*, ed. Melanie Gustafson, Kristie Miller, and Elisabeth Israels Perry (Albuquerque: University of New Mexico Press, 1999), 151–60.

Committee. Although never a part of Truman's inner circle, Edwards gained his respect for her ability to mobilize women, her keen political skills, and her unwavering support. While some of his associates found her "unladylike" and called her a "battle-ax," Truman gave Edwards the dubious compliment of acting like a man. Edwards served as the conduit to Truman for a collective effort by leaders of seventy-five women's organizations, begun in 1944, to win political appointments for women. In response to her urging, Truman bested Franklin Roosevelt's record in female appointments, naming eighteen women to posts requiring Senate confirmation and adding two hundred women to significant federal positions. Among the "firsts" during his administration were the appointment of Eugenie Anderson as ambassador to Denmark and of Georgia Neese Clark as treasurer of the United States.[17]

"Begging that one woman be included in the twenty-seven new judges whom you will nominate soon," Edwards warned Truman, "there will be a bad reaction to the naming of so many new judges and not one woman among them." In response, the president appointed Burnita Matthews as federal district court judge. Yet, as we have seen, he stopped short of insisting that the Supreme Court justices conduct their deliberations in the presence of a female; and he rejected another woman for a federal judgeship because "her husband is already a Judge in the New York Courts and it seems to me that one Judge in the family is enough."[18] Here again he expressed accord with traditional notions about the appropriate relations between husbands and wives.

Advocates on behalf of women were not the only Americans who wrote passionate letters to the president about his female appointments. His selection of Anna M. Rosenberg for assistant secretary of defense in 1950 immediately got caught up in the politics of anti-Communism, when arch-conservative radio commentator Fulton Lewis Jr. assailed her foreign birth and connections to members of left-wing organizations. Yet it was not just her "questionable loyalty" that inflamed those who urged Truman to drop her nomination. They routinely pointed as well to the fact that she was a woman and a Jew. Robert Herndon could not understand why Truman "could not have picked out some *American* male, who had been born in America and fought through the wars." Paul H. Hines, a decorated veteran who had observed Rosenberg's

17. Harrison, *On Account of Sex,* 54–56. For a description of Edwards's efforts to mobilize women, see Report Made by Mrs. India Edwards, October 20, 1948, Box 2, Edwards Papers, Truman Library.

18. Edwards to Truman, October 14, 1949, Box 2, Edwards Papers; Truman quoted in Harrison, *On Account of Sex,* 57.

World War II service chairing the War Manpower Commission in New York, found her "totally unfit . . . for the handling of men . . . not only tactless but arrogant and domineering." Conveniently ignoring the fact that women, too, served in the military, other writers also linked fitness for a high position in Defense with the male obligation of military service. Mrs. Ralph Stewart expressed shock at Truman's decision because "the draft is a matter which affects men *only,* and by no stretch of the imagination can we see how a woman, any woman, could be better qualified to handle it than a man." These and other correspondents not only chafed at how women supervising men defied the natural order of things, but they also revealed how the obligation of military service endowed men with certain "rights" not deserved by women. Truman nonetheless held his ground on Rosenberg's nomination, and the coalition for women's appointments chalked up another victory.[19]

Edith Sampson is yet another example of the pressures on the president from women's organizations to name women to important posts, but her appointment also served Truman's purposes in another way. Named alternate delegate to the UN General Assembly in 1950, Sampson became the first African American emissary to the United Nations. Her presence there helped to counter foreign critics of the racism embedded in American law and practice, criticism that came from leaders of Third World countries as well as those from Communist nations that sought to use U.S. racial practices as a propaganda weapon in the Cold War.[20] Of course, an African American man could have served this purpose just as well, and India Edwards feared as much in 1951 when she heard that Sampson might be replaced "just because she got in the hair of some of the State Department boys who think they know it all and never want anyone with an idea or any initiative on the Delegation." Edwards urged Truman to reappoint her, and he did.[21]

Organized women did not stop with the goal of getting women appointed to policy-making posts, though it was the objective that most firmly united a diverse range of women's groups. Truman had also to contend with women's

19. W. H. Whittekin to Mr. Secretary, December 8, 1950; Robert Herndon to Truman, November 14, 1950; M. H. Rothbert to Truman, November 22, 1950; Paul H. Hines to Truman, January 12, 1951; Mrs. Ralph Stewart to Truman, January 29, 1951; Byrnina Garrity to Truman, February 14, 1951, Box 1060, Official File 385, Truman Papers. For the links between obligations and rights, see Linda K. Kerber, *No Constitutional Right to Be Ladies: Women and the Obligations of Citizenship* (New York: Hill and Wang, 1998).

20. Thomas Borstelmann, *The Cold War and the Color Line: American Race Relations in the Global Arena* (Cambridge: Harvard University Press, 2001), 74–78.

21. India Edwards to The Chairman, April 20, 1951, India Edwards to Mr. President, July 12, 1951, Box 2, Edwards Papers.

demands for actions in the policy arena. From the 1940s to the 1960s, politically active women—in women's organizations and in the fringes of party politics—worked on three policy objectives to widen women's opportunities and diminish sex discrimination: a national equal pay law; an equal rights amendment to the Constitution (ERA); and a federal commission to investigate the status of women and recommend policy changes.

Braced by women's performance in defense jobs during the war and encouraged by National War Labor Board rulings against wage discrimination, a number of women's organizations coalesced behind a federal bill to prohibit wage discrimination by private employers in interstate commerce. Labor unions joined the coalition in an effort to maintain prevailing wages and to prevent employers from displacing men with cheaper female labor. Truman himself endorsed the principle of equal pay, and the secretary of labor testified in favor of the bill. Yet, although committees in both chambers reported the bill favorably in 1946 and in subsequent years, and while twelve states had equal pay laws by 1950, Congress failed to act on national legislation.[22]

Several factors contributed to its defeat. Not surprisingly, employers' organizations fought the bill. Moreover, the postwar wave of strikes and the election of more conservative members to Congress reduced legislative sympathy for organized labor, a development manifested in the antilabor Taft-Hartley Act of 1947. Democrat Mary Norton from New Jersey, who headed the House Labor Committee, warned the bill's supporters that only if women's organizations, labor unions, and the administration expressed "intense interest" in the bill would it succeed. Yet, equal pay was only one of many issues that engaged women's groups in the postwar period, the administration had more pressing priorities, and the American Federation of Labor itself failed to testify for the bill in 1948 and 1950, preferring to achieve the goal of equal pay through collective bargaining.[23] The equal pay coalition itself survived the defeat, however, laying the groundwork for its ultimate success when Congress passed the Equal Pay Act of 1963.

Instead of a national sense of urgency occasioned by the need for defense production, which had evaporated with the end of the war, equal pay advocates now faced, as veterans returned to civilian life, a national concern about whether the economy could provide sufficient jobs for all who needed work. In the context of such concern, the possibility that higher wages might draw even more women into the labor force was not a welcome one. Even after

22. Hartmann, *Home Front and Beyond,* 134.
23. Harrison, *On Account of Sex,* 39–45.

North Korean soldiers crossed the thirty-eighth parallel in 1950 and prompted a renewed war mobilization effort, administration officials looked benignly on sex discrimination in employment. Responding to India Edwards's protest that the Departments of Defense and State were requesting only males in positions as analysts, political scientists, and historians, Donald Dawson, Truman's administrative assistant, wrote that 31 percent of those requests did not specify sex at all, and 5 percent called for women. For Dawson, that apparently settled the matter of sex discrimination.[24]

The proposed equal rights amendment to the Constitution met a fate similar to that of the proposed equal pay legislation, though for somewhat different reasons. The administration's lack of enthusiasm contributed to the defeat of both measures. As a senator, Truman had endorsed the ERA, and that endorsement became known to friend and foe of the proposed amendment early in his presidency. How seriously he took the issue was another matter. When prominent Democratic National Committee member Emma Guffey Miller pressed Truman to support the ERA again in 1950, his condescending response indicated how free he was to blow off challenges to the gender status quo. "It has been my experience there is no equality," he wrote, "men are just slaves and I suppose they will continue to be." A stunned Miller wrote India Edwards that Truman's words came as "a solar plexus blow," expressing her disbelief that he had even read the letter over his signature.[25]

Deep divisions among politically engaged women over the proposed ERA and the relatively small numbers of feminist activists enabled—even required—Truman to dismiss Miller's appeal. As his administrative assistant, David K. Niles, declared in 1946, "This Equal Rights thing is dynamite which ever way you place it," urging that it was best to keep the president out of it.[26] Initially proposed in 1923 by Alice Paul of the feminist National Woman's Party as the follow-up to the suffrage amendment, the ERA met passionate opposition from key elements of the Democratic Party. The chief objection of liberal Democrats, most women's organizations, and organized labor was that the ERA would nullify protective labor laws for women. These state laws, strenuously fought for in an era when the Supreme Court rou-

24. Donald S. Dawson to India Edwards, Box 654, Official File 120-A, Truman Papers.
25. Grace E. Blackett et al. to Truman, April 20, 1945, Florence L.C. Kitchelt to Truman, May 21, 1945, Truman to Miller, August 12, 1950, Box 534, Official File 120-A, Truman Papers; Miller to Edwards, August 17, 1950, Box 2, Edwards Papers.
26. Niles to William Hassett, February 18, 1946, Box 534, Official File 120A, Truman Papers.

tinely struck down measures regulating the working conditions of men, imposed minimum wage and maximum hours standards, prohibited night work, required such provisions as seats, rest periods, and restroom facilities, and absolutely banned women from jobs deemed hazardous to them. ERA advocates objected that such measures operated to discriminate against women in employment, while supporters of protective legislation fought the constitutional amendment on the grounds that women's maternal roles and weaker physical constitutions required special protections. Bowing to his most important political constituents, Truman abandoned his initial support of the ERA and ducked the issue for the remainder of his presidency. Although the Senate considered the amendment in 1946, the 38–35 vote did not meet the two-thirds majority needed to submit a constitutional amendment to the states.[27]

The broad range of women's organizations that opposed the ERA—including the Women's Bureau of the Department of Labor, the American Association of University Women, and the National League of Women Voters—sought to eliminate what they considered the most glaring discriminations against women and to head off the amendment with an alternative measure. In part borrowing from the idea behind Truman's Commission on Civil Rights, they proposed legislation to establish a national commission on the legal status of women to "make a full and complete study . . . of the economic, civil, social and political status of women, and the nature and extent of discriminations based on sex."[28] While the bill went nowhere in the 1940s, as was the case with equal pay legislation and the ERA, its proponents laid the groundwork for eventual success (though, in the case of the ERA, passage by Congress was not followed by ratification by the required number of states) when, in 1961, President John F. Kennedy created the President's Commission on the Status of Women.

Women's activism on behalf of government appointments, equal pay, the ERA, and the status of women bill reflected how much the wartime need for women's labor had caused at least some Americans to think more critically about the traditional gender system. Day care for the children of employed mothers, another issue growing out of the wartime mobilization of women, remained on the national agenda for a brief time in the postwar period and likewise indicated slight shifts in notions about women's appropriate place and responsibilities. Under the Lanham Act during World War II, the federal

27. Hartmann, *Home Front and Beyond,* 129–30.
28. Quoted in Harrison, *On Account of Sex,* 27–28.

government had provided funds to states and localities to establish child care centers in areas where large numbers of women workers were needed in war production. When those funds expired with the end of the war, employed mothers and their advocates urged that public provision for child care continue, meeting with success in New York City, Philadelphia, and the state of California.[29] Because Congress controlled appropriations for the District of Columbia, the issue came to Truman's desk in 1946 in the form of a bill providing $500,000 for the continuation of day care centers that had been established in the district during the war.

The D.C. commissioners urged Truman to veto the bill, citing financial reasons and the undesirability of providing "free education" to just one special group. They noted that the original justification for the centers, to further the war effort, no longer operated, and they objected that the bill would be "an inducement to parents to transfer to the municipal government their responsibility for the training and rearing of their children." Both the Department of Labor, which housed the Children's Bureau, and the Federal Security Agency, which housed the Office of Education, however, recommended approval, and Truman agreed.[30]

Truman decided to extend the government's support for day care centers on the narrowest of grounds, believing that they should be "tapered off for the use of servicemen's wives" and thus rationalizing their temporary continuation on the basis of the nation's obligation to the men who had won the war. Officials of the Department of Labor and the Federal Security Agency supported the bill on grounds of children's welfare. Women who used the centers, however, implicitly expressed a changing notion of women's roles and responsibilities. While not directly insisting on the right of mothers to work, they provided a new definition of maternal responsibilities. Two mothers, for example, wired Truman that the centers were "not just a convenience but an absolutely [sic] necessity. . . . We want to raise our children properly, and we want to earn our living and theirs in self-respect." Daisy Peck, another employed mother, insisted, "As long as we are able to work . . . why should we not be permitted to do so instead of going on relief, losing our self respect."[31] These and other women linked the public provision of child care to their financial distress and did not suggest that society owed such provi-

29. Elizabeth Rose, *A Mother's Job: The History of Day Care, 1890–1960* (New York: Oxford University Press, 1999), 182; Sonya Michel, *Children's Interests/Mother's Rights: The Shaping of America's Child Care Policy* (New Haven: Yale University Press, 1999), 150–54.
30. Paul H. Appleby to M. C. Latta, July 16, 1946, White House Bill File, Truman Papers.
31. Samuel I. Rosenman to Maj. Gen. Philip B. Fleming, August 24, 1945; Telegram to the President, July 5, 1946; Mrs. Daisy Peck to the Secretary to the President, July 6, 1946, White

sion to all women, but they did assert a conception of mothers' obligations that extended beyond the home. And they grasped for at least some women a right traditionally associated with men—the right to respect that grew out of the ability to support one's family.

Just as World War II had called into question older notions about women's roles, the Cold War and the nation's new international responsibilities encouraged the development of expanded visions of women's place in the world outside the home. Of all the wartime challenges to the traditional gender system, the most dramatic had been the incorporation of women into military service. More than 350,000 women served in all branches of the military, and they were utilized in nearly every activity short of combat. On the whole, of course, gender norms largely withstood this breach of the last male bastion. The great majority of servicewomen, for example, performed clerical, communications, or health care work, mirroring the character of women's work in the prewar civilian labor force. (In fact, because of the great need for defense industry workers, women in the civilian labor force actually had more opportunities to perform nontraditional work during the war than did servicewomen.) Recruitment materials and propaganda similarly upheld the traditional gender order by stressing the "femininity" of female soldiers and portraying their service in terms of how it benefited their sweethearts and husbands.[32]

The contributions of women's service to the nation as a whole secured their permanent participation in the military as a new crisis—the Cold War—posed another challenge to traditional gender arrangements. Facing an immediate shortage of personnel and convinced that "the most economical use of all personnel" could be advanced "by the utilization of women in positions where their special aptitudes best fill army requirements," the military asked Congress to give women permanent regular status in the defense establishment. To be sure, the request was couched in terms that assured legislators and the public that women's primary interests remained rooted in the home. Gen. Dwight D. Eisenhower, one of the Women's Army Corps's most enthusiastic supporters, predicted that "after an enlistment or two enlistments women will ordinarily—and thank God—they will get married."[33] Although the Women's Armed Services Integration Act of 1948 limited women to 2

House Bill File, Truman Papers. See also Emilie Stoltzfus, *Citizen, Mother, Worker: Debating Public Responsibility for Child Care after the Second World War* (Chapel Hill: University of North Carolina Press, 2003).

32. Hartmann, *Home Front and Beyond*, 31–42.

33. Press Release, Public Information Division, War Department, April 16, 1947, Box 5, Westray Battle Boyce Long Papers, Truman Library; Eisenhower quoted in *New York Times*, February 19, 1948.

percent of total personnel, restricted their advancement, barred them from combat, and banned married women entirely unless they were veterans, it further unsettled the traditional order. Women gained a new avenue for individual development and self-fulfillment and won important rights linked to military service such as those provided by the GI Bill, while redefining the presumed "natural" roles and responsibilities of men and women.

Once engaged in the Korean War, Truman himself drew public attention to an expanded concept of women's place. His manpower mobilization policy announced in January 1951 called for "full use of women, handicapped workers, and minority groups." Reflecting the power of tradition, Truman did qualify that appeal by focusing "major emphasis" on the training and recruitment of single women and married women without children. But he also called for support for "nursery schools as an aid to mothers who want jobs." Moreover, he devoted more than half of his radio address on Armistice Day, November 1951, to the need for women "in every part of our national effort," focusing on their military service. Calling for 72,000 women to join the 40,000 already on active duty, he stressed both "their opportunity to make a vital contribution to our national security" and their "opportunity to learn new skills that will help them advance in their chosen fields of work." And he once more hailed the variety of women's military contributions in 1952 when he spoke at the ceremony for a new postage stamp commemorating women in the armed services.[34]

Just as the Truman administration was moved by international developments to advance a new vision of what was appropriate to women, women activists used the nation's new international position to advocate for their own goal of breaking down the disparate treatment of men and women. The creation of the United Nations provided one such opportunity when, in a pathbreaking move, officials signing the UN Charter in 1945 affirmed "the equal rights of men and women" and "fundamental freedoms for all without distinction as to race, sex, language or religion." Two years later, the United Nations established the Commission on the Status of Women, creating a

34. Memorandum Establishing a National Manpower Mobilization Policy, January 17, 1951; Annual Message to Congress, The President's Economic Report, January 12, 1951; Radio Address to the American People on Armistice Day, November 11, 1951, *Public Papers: Truman, 1951,* 109, 39, 627–28. Remarks at a Ceremony Marking the Issuance of the "Women in the Armed Services" Commemorative Stamp, September 11, 1952, *Public Papers: Truman, 1952–1953,* 569–70. Truman could not refrain from the timeworn practice of making reference to women's physical appearance when it had nothing to do with the subject at hand, declaring "that there are a lot of good places for good-looking young ladies, and good-looking middle-aged ladies, who can help the welfare of this country now as never before."

forum for women from around the globe to meet and be heard; and in 1948 it adopted the Universal Declaration of Human Rights, which enumerated an extensive set of rights and explicitly rejected sex discrimination. These principles, of course, went far beyond those rights women currently enjoyed in the United States. Women pressed hard for such guarantees—including Eleanor Roosevelt, U.S. delegate to the United Nations, who chaired the commission that drafted the declaration; Hansa Mehta, legislator and women's rights advocate from India; and Minerva Bernardino of the Dominican Republic.[35]

Consequently, when Emma Guffey Miller wrote Truman urging his support of the ERA and claiming that "all we want is equality of opportunity and the right to control our own actions the same as men," she pointed to the "solemn assurances in the Charter of the United Nations which in five different articles equality is promised all citizens regardless of sex." Although the League of Women Voters disagreed about the desirability of a constitutional amendment, that organization, too, appealed to the UN precedent in advocating the elimination of unwarranted discrimination against women. "Because of our commitment to the U.N. it is a fitting time to review the question of the status of women in the United States," the league insisted. "It is, therefore, our duty to bring our laws . . . into harmony with these principles."[36]

Although Truman devoted attention to the United Nations in both his Farewell Address and his memoirs, he made no mention of its unprecedented consideration of and commitment to women's rights. These silences illustrate the firm hold of the traditional gender structure on the president and on most Americans. Looking beneath these silences, however, reveals challenges to older gender norms that were emerging in the 1940s and helps explain the more sweeping changes in policies and practices that occurred in the 1960s and 1970s.

Ignored by Truman as he retrospectively surveyed his presidency, women's participation in government, equal pay legislation, an equal rights amendment to the constitution, official investigation of women's status, public provision of child care services for employed mothers, and women's military service—all of these issues claimed some part of the public's attention and

---

35. Mary Ann Glendon, *A World Made New: Eleanor Roosevelt and the Declaration of Human Rights* (New York: Random House, 2001), xx, 90–92, 162, 164.

36. Miller to Truman, August 9, 1950, Box 654, Official File 120-A, Truman Papers; League of Women Voters, "Brief for Action," Publication No. 91, April 1, 1947, Box 2, Edwards Papers.

from time to time that of Truman himself. Because his entire political career was shaped in an era when women were largely absent from politics and when policies and practices that viewed women primarily as wives and mothers were deemed perfectly natural, it is not surprising that he marshaled so little of his power against inequities based on sex. Truman attended to women's issues when forced to do so, as was the case with his response to India Edwards and the campaign for women's appointments to government positions. And he supported the expansion of public opportunities for women when such initiatives accomplished larger purposes, as was the case with women's permanent military status. Truman sometimes paid lip service to gender justice, for example voicing support for equal pay or for the need to investigate women's status; but no strong political movement existed to require action beyond perfunctory mention.

If the Truman *presidency* holds little historical significance in the area of state action on gender issues, the Truman *years* saw the gathering of critical forces that would eventually compel a reconsideration of older gender ideas and adoption of new laws and policies that would transform gender relations. The 1940s were in this case a time of transition, giving rise to international developments that created new national imperatives and changes in the ways in which more and more women *actually* lived their lives as they increasingly deviated from prevailing notions about *how* they should live them.

Imperatives related to the nation's security from international threats and a growing, increasingly service- and consumption-oriented postwar economy drew more women into the labor force and higher education. The inequities embedded in the gender system that had once seemed fair and natural began to seem unjust and out of step with reality, at least to politically active women who wanted to eliminate barriers to women's participation in the public arena and to ensure their equal treatment there. Unlike organized labor or civil rights activists and their white liberal allies, these women's rights advocates were not substantial enough to constitute a political threat to Truman and his party. Yet they were energized by the contributions women had made to the World War II effort and were being called upon to make to the waging of the Cold War; and they forced new issues onto the president's desk, onto the legislative agenda, and into public discourse. Although most of the goals of organized women did not move beyond discussion (slightly more women appointed to government positions and permanent military status were exceptions), their activism laid foundations for policy changes that would reach fruition in the 1960s and beyond. And the international and economic revolutions that had inspired and undergirded their demands on government would continue to effect a transformation in relationships between men and women and between women and policy that lay far beyond the imagination of Truman and most of his contemporaries. Given Truman's deep roots in the older gender order, it was no doubt a blessing to his peace of mind that he was able to contemplate the history of his presidency without giving women a thought.

10.00 - Congressman Hatton W. Sumners, Texas (Re legislation)
Veto of specific items. Limit Pres. tenure & majority for
10.15 - Congressman Reid F. Murray, Wis. (Rep.) *veto.*
(Reconversion as affects agriculture - He wrote the
President on this and the President said he would
be glad see him CORRESPONDENCE ATTACHED)

10.30 - Congressman Albert Gore, Tenn. *Gave me a nugget of old*
30th Secrets.
(Bringing package to the President, corn mash, pre-
Prohibition, which a doctor in Nashville promised
to give the President when he was a Senator)
(OFF RECORD OF COURSE)

10.45 - Senator Burton K. Wheeler *Discussed PM in Butte*
Federal Trade Com etc.
(Among other things, to discuss Mr. Lowell Mason for
Federal Trade Commission)

11.00 - Mr. Max Lowenthal. *Worried about demobilization.*

11.15 - Congressman Pat Cannon, Fla. *Hurrican damage*
(Re hurricane damage)

11.30 - Hon. Charles Harwood, Governor of the Virgin Islands
Wants another job. Talked of Sec
11.45 - Hon. David Sholtz *Promoting International Fair.*
(Thinks he has some idea which will save the President some worries)

12.00 - Hon. and Mrs. Hubert Humphrey *Politics. Quote me on*
Mr. Arthur Naftalin *Shipstead.*
Mr. E. M. Kirkpatrick
(Hubert Humphrey is Mayor of Minneapolis - made at
suggestion of Oscar Ewing)

12.15 - Mrs. Emma Guffey Miller *A lot of hooey about*
Miss Ella Sherwin
Dr. Mary Sinclair Crawford *equal rights.*
Mrs. Harvey Wiley
Dr. Alma Jane Speer
Mrs. U. S. Guyer
(These women represent group sponsoring Equal Rights
Amendment - have tried for good while to arrange this
through Senator Radcliffe)

12.30 - Miss Maycie K. Southall, President, Assn. for Childhood
Education
Mrs. Harriet A. Houdlette, American Assn. of University
Women
Miss Lelia Massey, American Home Economics Assn. et al
(Miss Southall and representatives of eleven organiza-
tions such as above, who are joining in conference on
long-term planning for the needs of young children,
meeting here Sept. 19-21 - Dr. Studebaker, Commissioner
U.S. Office of Education was asked about these people
and thought might be good idea for them to be allowed
to see the President.)

*Gave me a great song & dance on
education.*

12.45 - Mrs. Dorothy K. Roosevelt
         Miss Diana Roosevelt
           (Divorced wife of late Hall Roosevelt, brother of
            Mrs. Franklin D. Roosevelt - to pay call. Have
            been in Hyde Park and New York)

1.00 - (LUNCH) *Just came in. Don't know why.*

1.45 - The President will present D.S.M. to Hon. Henry
         L. Stimson *a nice ceremony.*

2.00 - Cabinet

*Cabinet meeting discussed
Atomic Bomb. Most interesting.*

8.15 - Movies ("The House on Ninety-second Street" and
              Signal Corps pictures of Potsdam Conference)

OCTOBER 8, 1947

CONFIDENTIAL: The following address of the President to be broadcast as part of a program by the Women's Division of the Democratic National Committee on Democratic Women's Day, October 8, 1947, MUST BE HELD IN CONFIDENCE until released.

NOTE: Release is automatic at 1:30 P.M., E.S.T., Wednesday, October 8, 1947. The same release applies to all newspapers and broadcasting stations.

PLEASE GUARD AGAINST PREMATURE PUBLICATION OR RADIO ANNOUNCEMENT.

CHARLES G. ROSS
Secretary to the President

- -

I speak today to you -- the women of the United States -- in order to emphasize the need for greater participation by women in the affairs of our country. Our nation, at this time, must have responsible citizens, thoughtful citizens, earnest citizens, who will work to solve the difficult problems confronting us.

The women of this country, by recognizing their responsibility to take an active part in the determination of the grave issues of the day, can furnish this type of citizenship.

Women can provide immediate leadership in dealing with one of these great issues. Women can make an invaluable contribution to the welfare of our nation -- and of the world -- by lending their wholehearted support to our food-saving program. Indeed, the responsibility for the success of that program rests very largely with the American housewife. She is an indispensable fighter in our war against hunger. The American housewife has never failed her country when she has been called upon to sacrifice in its interest. I know that she will not fail in the great task now before us.

I know, too, that if the women of our nation exert the tremendous moral force for good which they possess, we shall make greater and more lasting progress in overcoming the other difficulties that concern us and the world.

As a nation we stand now on the threshold of a wonderful opportunity, unique in history. We are a thriving country. The facts of our high employment and our great farm and industrial production speak for themselves. We are a strong and peace-loving nation.

The United States, more than any other nation, is in a position to give reality to the Four Freedoms. The United States should and can be the first nation in which the people -- all the people -- are free from want and free from fear, free to speak and to write as their hearts dictate, and free to worship as they will.

This is no idle dream. It is a goal well within the power of this mighty nation of ours to achieve.

The actions of our government to improve social security, public health and education, and to develop and conserve our national resources, must not be allowed to lag behind the needs of the people. Nor can we falter in our unceasing quest for a just, permanent peace in the world. The need is for us, the people, to summon the will to achieve these goals, and to translate that will into positive action.

In this undertaking, the women of the United States have a great opportunity and a great responsibility to play the decisive part. Women in this country won the right to vote only after a long, hard struggle. Now, over one million more women than men are eligible to vote in the United States. Thus, the power lies in the hands of American women -- in your hands -- to shape the destiny of America. And yet when the time comes to register and the opportunity comes to vote, many of our women neglect this responsibility of citizenship.

Foreign nations are deeply interested in the size of our vote. The reason is clear. The United States is the foremost example of democratic government in the world. Men and women in other lands are comparing the operation of our democratic system with other forms of government. We do not want them to conclude that we are not interested

(OVER)

in the vigor of our government, or that we are indifferent to the issues
before us! We must prove to them that we take our democracy seriously.
They must understand that we accept the responsibilities of our form of
democracy as well as its privileges.

When you, the women of America, make your will felt at the
polls, you make an invaluable contribution to this democratic system.
The moral force of women has always had a wholesome influence upon
the character of our civilization. They are deeply responsive to the
fundamental human values. Women care more for people than for dollars,
more for healthy children than fat dividends. Women want a society
in which we build schools instead of prisons. Women want a world in
which we sow and harvest the seeds of a good life instead of the seeds
of war.

You now have a great opportunity to make this wholesome influence
increasingly effective by the full use of your power at the ballot box.

Your vote is your insurance that the American people will always
be free members of a democratic society; your insurance that we shall
continue to live in a democracy where men can worship God in their own
fashion, can speak and write as they please, and have equal justice under
law.

Your vote is your investment in the future of the United States,
your investment to insure a country where your children will have
opportunities for decent homes, good health, good jobs and adequate
education.

Your vote is a down payment on the kind of world in which
nations respect one another, a world in which nations are good neighbors
because they know that good neighborliness offers the only hope of
lasting peace.

Your vote is your best way of getting the kind of country —
and the kind of world — you want.

- - - - -

279

Harry Truman, Immigration, and Ethnicity at an Imperial Moment

Rachel Ida Buff

I. Introduction: Cold War and Culture War

As we reflect on Harry S. Truman's Farewell Address, we note the areas of public policy he emphasized, those he minimized, and those he left out entirely. Truman said little in the address about the initiatives on civil rights with which he has historically been associated. As Richard Kirkendall notes in his Introduction, "What seems clear is that he was not nearly as pleased with what he had accomplished in this area as he was with what he had done in international relations."

I have been charged with reflecting specifically on immigration and ethnicity, two issues in many ways related to civil rights but not specifically mentioned in the Farewell Address. I will do this by looking at Truman era public policy in relation to issues of immigration and ethnicity. But in order to understand what these areas of public policy might have to do with "Harry's Farewell," I want to suggest some connections between the seemingly disparate areas of civil rights, immigration and ethnicity, and international relations.

It has recently been well established, for example, that the prevailing international Cold War order influenced federal policy on civil rights.[1] Concerned

1. See Mary L. Dudziak, *Cold War Civil Rights: Race and the Image of American Democracy* (Princeton: Princeton University Press, 2002); Brenda Plummer, *Rising Wind: Black Americans and U.S. Foreign Affairs, 1935–1960* (Chapel Hill: University of North Carolina Press, 1996);

with promoting democracy around the world, Cold War politicians such as Truman focused on some of the impediments to domestic democracy. They did this in part because of concerns about the international image of the United States as the "leader of the free world," something often parodied in the Soviet press by reference to the history of African Americans. Civil rights leaders, in turn, pressed this advantage. At the same time, they drew parallels between their struggle for full citizenship in the United States and the freedom struggles of decolonizing nations in Africa, Asia, and the Caribbean. Truman's overarching concern was for the Cold War: what he called in his farewell "the conflict between those who love freedom and those who would lead the world back into slavery and darkness." But this focus on the international balance of power led also to engagement with domestic affairs, specifically the politics of racial inequality.

Historians have made similar arguments about other aspects of Truman's foreign policy, in particular his deployment of atomic energy, first in dropping the bombs at Hiroshima and Nagasaki and later in the way he guided national nuclear policy to favor atomic secrecy rather than international cooperation. Historian John Dower has persuasively demonstrated that the decision to "end the war" by dropping nuclear bombs on Japan was premised as much on cultural attitudes toward Asian peoples as on strategic considerations.[2] Japanese Americans were interned during the war under a rubric of security. The federal government was able to disregard the claims of Issei, Nisei, and third-generation Japanese Americans to citizenship because of their status as a racial minority, on the West Coast and in the national imagination. Similarly, the decision to drop the bomb was informed by racial ideas of the Japanese as less than human combatants in the Pacific Theater. Domestic matters, in this case racial inequality and its relationship to national identity, overlap importantly with international relations.

Truman presided over the inauguration of the nuclear age, also known as the era of atomic secrecy. The sole sentence referring to this in the address occupies its own paragraph and rings loudly despite its brevity: "Meanwhile, the first atomic explosion took place out in the New Mexico desert." This lonely spectacle had great implications for the immediate postwar period and for the Truman presidency. From the emergence of the Truman Doctrine of

---

Penny Von Eschen, *Race Against Empire: Black Americans and Anti-Colonialism, 1937–1957* (Ithaca: Cornell University Press, 1997); Nikhil Pal Singh, "Culture/Wars: Recoding Empire in an Age of Democracy," *American Quarterly* 50 (September 1998): 471–522.

2. Dower, *War without Mercy: Race and Power in the Pacific War* (New York: Pantheon, 1986).

containing Communism, to the increasing power of a Red Scare promising to purge the nation of threats from within, atomic secrecy linked domestic and international security concerns. The resulting political ideology, as well as the public policies it informed, linked the ideas of domestic harmony with a safe and united international order.

For example, the crucial internal memorandum, National Security Council document number 68 (NSC-68), established the principle of strategic containment of the Soviet Union in 1950. The centrality of this doctrine permeates Truman's address and largely explains his focus on international stability. But, as political scientist David Campbell argues, this focus on international security paralleled and was informed by particular notions of national identity and domestic stability. Campbell cites Truman foreign policy adviser George Kennan, who said in 1950 that Communism "had to be viewed as a crisis of our own civilization, and the principal antidote lay in overcoming the weakness of our own institutions." In explaining this, Campbell asserts that "the texts which guided national security policy did more than simply offer the 'reality' they confronted: they actively concerned themselves with the scripting of a particular American identity."[3]

How did this "scripting" of national identity operate to influence public policy? It linked the international security of the nation to specific domestic conditions. Consider three examples that, geographically and sociologically, span early nuclear America.

First, testing the effects of radiation on civilian populations, military scientists conducted secret experiments on working-class communities in Minneapolis and East St. Louis during the 1950s.[4] These experiments were intentionally conducted in poor and minority neighborhoods, because the denizens of such places lacked access to established channels of political protest. Because this program sheltered under the nuclear secrecy associated with containment, those suffering the resulting, often grave, health problems had little recourse. Here we see the exigencies of national security dictating a public policy deeply based on existing social inequalities.

Second, Jewish Communists Julius and Ethel Rosenberg were executed

3. Campbell, *Writing Security: United States Foreign Policy and the Politics of Identity* (Minneapolis: University of Minnesota Press, 1992), 28, 38, 33; "Draft memorandum by the counsellor (Kennan) to the secretary of state," February 17, 1950, in U.S. Department of State, *Foreign Relations of the United States, 1950* (Washington, D.C.: U.S. Government Printing Office, 1951), 1:164.

4. Leonard Cole, *Clouds of Secrecy: The Army's Germ Warfare Tests over Populated Areas* (Totowa, N.J.: Rowman and Littlefield, 1988).

for atomic espionage in 1953, after repeatedly being denied stays of execution. Historians such as Virginia Carmichael and Andrew Ross have argued that the thin sinew of evidence connecting the Rosenbergs to this treasonous act—in sentencing them, Judge Irving Kaufman asserted their responsibility for national losses in the Korean War—was further strengthened by their status as political and cultural outsiders: Communists, Jews, urban dwellers in a nation rapidly moving to the new suburbs created by the dual forces of the GI Bill and real estate and insurance redlining. In a January 1953 memo, the CIA proposed a deal: if the Rosenbergs would agree to "appeal to all Jews in all countries to get out of the communist movement and seek to destroy it," they would be saved.[5] Here again, national security policy purportedly based on international concerns drew on categories of domestic social identity—in this case, anti-Semitism. The Rosenberg trial and execution dramatized the high seriousness of the new atomic order and drew boundaries between appropriate and inappropriate conduct and associations for citizens.

Finally, consider the source of the atomic age: uranium. Uranium miners in the southwestern United States were primarily Navajo and Latino. Mining for uranium, often found on tribal lands, became a significant source of employment for these ethnic minority groups in the 1940s and 1950s.[6] Because uranium mining represented a key component of atomic national security, the Atomic Energy Commission controlled dissemination of information about the health risks of exposure to uranium and miners were consistently denied access to health information and safety gear. Published reports of cancer deaths in association with such exposure did not emerge until the 1960s.[7] Here again, we see categories of national identity in dialogue with the seemingly pragmatic dictates of national security policy. So, perhaps, Truman's emphasis on international policy in his Farewell Address has much to say about domestic politics after all.

As president, Harry Truman was particularly concerned to remedy the nation's legacy of social inequality for African Americans by addressing civil rights. Just as African Americans had waged a "double V" campaign during

5. Carmichael, *Framing History: The Rosenberg Story and the Cold War* (Minneapolis: University of Minnesota Press, 1995); Blanche Wiesen Cook, "The Rosenbergs and the Crime of the Century," in *Secret Agents: The Rosenberg Case, McCarthyism and Fifties America,* ed. Rebecca L. Walkowitz and Marjorie Garber (New York: Routledge, 1995), 25.

6. Ward Churchill and Winona LaDuke, "Native North America: The Political Economy of Radioactive Colonialism," in *The State of Native America: Genocide, Colonization and Resistance,* ed. M. Annette Jaimes (Boston: South End Press, 1992), 241–66.

7. Robert N. Proctor, "Censorship of American Uranium Mine Epidemiology in the 1950s," in *Secret Agents,* ed. Walkowitz and Garber, 64–65.

the war for victory over fascism abroad and victory over racism and white supremacy at home, Truman drew parallels between these struggles for democracy. He wrote to the American Veterans' Committee in 1946: "We have only recently completed a long and bitter war against intolerance and hatred in other lands. A cruel price in blood and suffering was paid by the American people in bringing that war to a successful conclusion. Yet, in this country today there exists a disturbing evidence of intolerance and prejudice similar in kind, though perhaps not in degree, to that against which we fought the war."[8]

In both his administrations, Truman cautiously raised civil rights issues, through the Fair Deal and other policies designed to sustain African American faith in the Democratic Party without alienating the crucial, traditional southern white constituency.[9] His support for civil rights indicates his awareness of both domestic and international pressure. However, in his Farewell Address his concerns for international relations overshadowed his attention to civil rights and domestic inequality. This ambivalence toward social equality came from his personal attitudes, as well as the political impediment of a Republican Congress. But the ambivalence is also very much part of Truman's historical moment: a moment marked by imperial expansion.

At the imperial moment of the Truman administration, the United States consolidated a global empire of political and economic alliances as well as social and cultural influence. Seen through the prism of the Truman Doctrine, the world was a turbulent and menacing place, fraught with expansionist Soviet totalitarianism and a newly decolonizing Third World likely to fall prey to it. Consequently, Cold War politicians tended to view the world in terms of black-and-white distinctions: good and evil, freedom and slavery, democracy and totalitarianism, and capitalism and socialism. These distinctions, in turn, read both domestic and international politics through a particular ideological prism, characterized by a very specific definition of the kind of citizenship and rights that could be extended to minority populations. Just as the Truman Doctrine dictated intervening in the politics of sovereign nations in the name of democracy, domestic policy advanced specific and limited notions of enfranchisement and full participation.

8. Truman, "Letter to the Chairman, American Veterans' Committee, Concerning Discrimination on Campus," September 4, 1946, *Public Papers of the Presidents of the United States: Harry Truman, 1945–1953*, 8 vols. (Washington, D.C.: U.S. Government Printing Office, 1961–1966), 2 (1946): 423.

9. Harold Gosnell, *Truman's Crises: A Political Biography of Harry S. Truman* (Westport, Conn.: Greenwood Press, 1980), 275. See also Alonzo L. Hamby, *Man of the People: A Life of Harry S. Truman* (New York: Oxford University Press, 1995), 272.

This imperial public policy had specific implications for immigrants and ethnic minorities. Domestic policy toward Indian nations, "the nations within," as Vine Deloria has called them,[10] paralleled immigration and foreign policy in important ways. Indian peoples were rediscovered as a national problem in the wake of their heroic and disproportionate service in World War II, represented most vividly in the popular imagination by the story of Ira Hayes, who after participating in the flag-raising on Iwo Jima returned to life on the reservation. Communalist Indian nations, however, were viewed as antagonistic to the project of Cold War democracy. To marry into the national family, to be eligible for the benefits as well as the depredations of citizenship, immigrants, Indians, and other internal aliens had to change.

While foreign policy and immigration had long been entwined prior to the Cold War, the regulation of aliens entering the civic body became something of a political obsession in the post–World War II period, in light of contemporary concerns for subversion and infiltration. The transformation of aliens into citizens was a central issue in public policy. Whether they were domestic dissenters, native "communalists," or immigrants at specific risk for being foreign agents, aliens to the social body needed transformation. A gendered ideology of a national family helped to organize social politics in this period. Threatening aliens could become cheerful citizen-family members by passing through state-mediated rituals of naturalization. And, in the prevailing patriarchal order of the day, those allowed into the family, as wives, children, and stepchildren, were compelled to adopt its ways. As anthropologist Ann Stoler has noted, managing the "conjugal relations of empire" has always entailed the regulation of citizen and foreign bodies, and any possible relations between them.[11]

In what follows, I will look specifically at two arenas of Truman-era public policy to document the effects of this Cold War imperial moment on ethnicity and immigration. First, I will examine Indian policy under Truman, arguing that Truman's general support for civil rights and his Cold War assumption that societies were either democratic or undemocratic informed his support for a policy of termination—terminating the trust relationship between Indian nations and the federal government—that came into conflict with most contemporary Indian ideas about democratic reform. Then, I will look at his immigration and refugee policy, which, of course, was a component of a more

10. See Vine Deloria and Clifford Lytle, *The Nations Within: The Past and Future of American Indian Sovereignty* (New York: Pantheon Books, 1984).

11. Stoler, "Making Empire Respectable: The Politics of Race and Sexual Morality in Twentieth-Century Colonial Cultures," *American Ethnologist* 6:4 (1989): 77.

general policy toward the ethnic composition of the nation as a whole. Throughout, I argue that public policy on immigration and ethnicity was profoundly entwined with international relations.

II. Truman and Indian Policy:
Termination and Individual Rights

Historian Donald Fixico asserts that Truman was "an assimilationist who believed that all Americans should enjoy the constitutional rights that the United States guaranteed, although he realized that the dominant society excluded Native American people from exercising their citizenship rights." Truman supported what he considered the full enfranchisement of American Indians and thought of the reservation system and federal land trust as a "special handicap or special advantage" impeding the equality of Indian people.[12] Federal Indian policy under Truman attempted to advocate for Indian people, but it did so with the intent of assimilating them into a specific kind of democratic citizenship, one that often contradicted indigenous ideas as well as long-standing claims to a land base guaranteed by the federal trust relationship.

This contradiction was evident from the outset of Truman's Indian policy. The creation of the Indian Claims Commission in 1946 responded to a demand from Indian people for federal action to adjudicate claims for illegally seized property. The new commission investigated all Indian claims that contested federal or private title, attempting to define the lands in question precisely and to figure out whether the lands had been illegally taken from Indian people. In cases where the commission found in favor of Indian claims, it was responsible for establishing compensation, in terms of market value at the time the land was taken. Truman said, upon signing the bill creating the commission: "I am glad to sign my name to a measure which removes a lingering discrimination against our First Americans and gives them the same opportunity that our laws extend to all other American citizens to vindicate their property rights and contracts in the courts against violations by the Federal Government itself."[13]

12. Fixico, *Termination and Relocation: Federal Indian Policy, 1945–1960* (Albuquerque: University of New Mexico Press, 1986), 18; "Statement by the President upon Signing Bill Creating the Indian Claims Commission," August 13, 1946, *Public Papers: Truman, 1946,* 414.
13. Ward Churchill, "The Earth Is Our Mother: Struggles for American Indian Land and Liberation in the Contemporary United States," in *The State of Native North America,* ed.

Indian people seized on the Indian Claims Commission as a means for adjudicating long-term injustices, and by the end of 1951 more than six hundred cases had been filed. Some were awarded monetary compensation for lost lands; others, like many Indian nations on the East Coast who had been militarily defeated before the American Revolution, used the commission to establish land claims and work for federal recognition in the 1970s.[14]

While Indian people saw and used the Indian Claims Commission as a place to advance their struggles to maintain a sovereign land base, the Termination Policy gained support in Congress under a quite different rubric. Truman saw the inauguration of the commission as removing "lingering discrimination" against Indians and any "special handicap or special advantage." In his interpretation, land claims impeded Indians from becoming ordinary democratic citizens, holding them back in an antiquated, and possibly anti-American, communalism.[15] Similarly, many in Congress saw the commission as the first step to absolving any Indian claims to tribal lands. Support for the commission in Congress was part of a broader effort to clear out the bureaucracy of the Interior Department and Bureau of Indian Affairs, reduce spending, and, ultimately, terminate the federal trust relationship between Indian nations and the government.

Advocates of Termination Policy sought to end the trust relationship between Indians and the federal government. Under termination, land claims would be individualized. Indians would, in the language of the time, become citizens, even though they had legally become citizens under the Snyder Act of 1924, and reservations would disappear into local counties. The dual claims of Indians to citizenship in the United States and in their own Indian nations had been a crucial component of federal jurisprudence since Justice John Marshall deemed Indian peoples "domestic, dependent nations" in 1831. But Termination Policy twisted the rhetoric of the African American civil rights movement to argue that the loyalty of Indian people to tribal nations impeded their access to full citizenship. Thus, the "nations within" were also subject to the project of regulating "the conjugal relations of empire."

Truman was not a hard-core terminationist. He saw the importance of Indians becoming "independent, self-supporting citizens of this Nation." Like many of the architects of Termination Policy in Congress, he also recognized

---

Jaimes, 144–46; "Statement by the President upon Signing Bill Creating the Indian Claims Commission."

14. Churchill, "Earth Is Our Mother," 147.

15. See Michael Rogin, *Ronald Reagan, the Movie: And Other Episodes in Political Demonology* (Berkeley: University of California Press, 1988).

that Indian lands were often "rich in timber, oil, gas, and other materials, the conservation and development of which should be related to programs affecting similar lands."[16] Many in Congress, particularly those from the western states, saw the absorption of tribal lands into federal and private hands as crucial to developing the resource-rich West and making the United States economically independent. Republican senator Patrick McCarran of Nevada, for example, wrote, "The West today is a land of empire, of opportunity, of destiny. Today, more than ever, the West is plain every day American for 'opportunity.'" The West had water and uranium to support growing urban populations and an emerging nuclear state; in addition, the West has long had tremendous ideological capital in the national imagining of freedom and destiny.[17]

Truman supported termination because, in his interpretation of civil rights, bringing Indians into a life of citizenship and individual property ownership would be beneficial both to them and to the nation. Unlike the most extreme supporters in Congress, he tried to execute the termination project slowly, in ways that would be most beneficial to the Indians involved. In 1948, he vetoed a measure for the disposal of some submarginal lands on reservations in the West, cautioning against a too-rapid sell-off that would further impoverish already struggling tribes.[18] He also expressed fatherly concern about the ability of Indians to manage their finances after termination, sternly cautioning one of the first nations to exchange its lands for one-time cash allotments under Termination Policy: "I urge the Klamath Indians to give deep thought to the use of their resources, both individual and tribal, in ways that will insure their future security and progress. I say this because it will not be possible for them to recover these resources if they are once lost through unwise transactions."[19]

Termination was to complete the "break up of the tribal land mass" begun by the Dawes Allotment Act in the late nineteenth century. In addition, the termination project included a relocation program, which was to bring Indians

16. "Annual Message to the Congress: Fiscal Year 1953," January 21, 1952, *Public Papers: Truman, 1952,* 90; "Annual Message to the Congress; Fiscal Year 1951," January 9, 1950, *Public Papers: Truman, 1950,* 91.

17. McCarran quoted in Gerald D. Nash, *The American West Transformed: The Impact of the Second World War* (Bloomington: Indiana University Press, 1985), 187; Rachel Buff, *Immigration and the Political Economy of Home: West Indian Brooklyn and American Indian Minneapolis, 1945–1992* (Berkeley: University of California Press, 2001), 53.

18. "Veto of Bill for the Disposal of Submarginal Lands within Indian Reservations," February 10, 1948, *Public Papers: Truman, 1948,* 134.

19. Quoted in Fixico, *Termination and Relocation,* 41.

off reservations, relocate them into cities, and, it was hoped, naturalize them into life as American consumer-citizens. In their attempts to forcibly assimilate Indians to mainstream American life, these programs failed, engendering instead a revived, pan-Indian political identity on reservations and in cities. Truman's likely genuine concern for the rights of Indian people was hostage to the larger historical moment of atomic secrecy and the profound narrowing of definitions of citizenship during the Cold War.

III. Immigration and Refugee Policy in the New Global Order

In many ways, Truman's immigration policy was impelled by the same political exigencies as was his Indian policy. Just as Indian policy mediated an internal frontier, between semi-sovereign nations and the federal government, immigration and refugee policy regulated external boundaries, controlling the demographic homeostasis of the nation. Which immigrants and refugees, and how many, to allow into the country was an extremely important question for Cold War politicians across the political spectrum. While immigration policy had historically been deeply entwined with international relations, this connection took on renewed significance in a divided world fraught with the potential for military hostilities abroad or infiltration at home.

Like civil rights policy, Truman-era immigration and refugee policy attempted to balance the new status of the United States as the "leader of the free world" with concerns about the potential for immigrants and ethnic groups to be fifth-column infiltrators. Central to immigration policy in the postwar imperial moment were issues such as the controversy over how many refugees to allow in from Europe, devastated from war and segregated by the Iron Curtain; the slow easing of long-standing barriers to the naturalization of Asian immigrants; the importance of agricultural labor and concurrent concerns with "illegal" immigration from Mexico and the South; and a renewed pressure for immigration quotas, to maintain the cultural balance that was, in the eyes of hard-line Cold Warriors, so precious to national security.

Truman struggled mightily with a reluctant Congress to argue for the admission of greater numbers of refugees, as well as the lifting of restrictions admitting refugees based on their national origins and religious faith. Signing the Displaced Persons Act of 1948, he excoriated the legislature: "The bad points of the bill are numerous. Together they form a pattern of discrimination and intolerance wholly inconsistent with the American sense of

justice." Along with a coalition of church and ethnic groups, Truman worked
to found and support the International Relief Organization. He made reform
of the flawed Displaced Persons Act a priority, emphasizing that many refugees were fleeing Iron Curtain regimes. In 1950, Truman signed an amendment to the 1948 act, approving a larger number of refugee admissions, as
well as "correcting the discrimination inherent in the previous act."[20]

Truman described himself as a humanist, concerned with freedom rather
than national origins, race, or religion. Speaking to a group of refugees in 1952,
he asserted: "I am not an ancestor hunter. I am a man who believes in doing
things today that will make the world a better place to live in." Yet in his
struggle to liberalize refugee admissions, Truman focused almost entirely on
European refugees and immigrants, emphasizing in particular the "problems
of these fugitives from Soviet terror." As historian Matthew Frye Jacobson
points out, Truman's advocacy of equality among Europeans was consonant
with the processes of racial and ethnic formation in the postwar period.
Whereas distinctions among Europeans had been important to previous racial
thinking, postwar racial ideology tended to recognize distinctions based on
the color line between black and white.[21] Like many of those favoring liber-
alized admissions of refugees and immigrants in this period, Truman expected that Europeans fleeing Communism would make ideal U.S. citizens.
There was no racial division between them and the American people, and
their status as refugees from totalitarian governments would enable them to
assimilate into democratic life easily and gratefully.

In the postwar period, national origins were perceived less as a racial and
more as an ethnic matter. This shift was of great consequence to many groups,
such as Italians and Jews, previously not considered entirely white and,
hence, not American. Historian David Roediger has called these groups the
"not-yet-white ethnics." As a humanist, Truman campaigned against anti-
Semitism and anti-Catholicism. At the National Cemetery at Arlington, he
commented: "No American knows, no real American cares, whether that
man was a Catholic, a Jew, or a Protestant, or what his origin and color were.

20. "Statement by the President upon Signing the Displaced Persons Act," June 25, 1948,
Public Papers: Truman, 1948, 382–83; "Statement by the President upon Signing Bill
Amending the Displaced Persons Act," June 16, 1950, *Public Papers: Truman, 1950,* 483–84.
21. "Remarks to a Group of Displaced Persons," April 14, 1952, *Public Papers: Truman,
1952,* 264; "Special Message to the Congress on Aid for Refugees and Displaced Persons,"
March 24, 1952, *Public Papers: Truman, 1952,* 211; Jacobson, *Whiteness of a Different Color:
European Immigrants and the Alchemy of Race* (Cambridge: Harvard University Press, 1998),
256–60.

That grave—the grave of the Unknown Soldier—symbolizes our faith in unity."[22]

But this unity broke down when Truman confronted barriers against immigrants still perceived to be racially distinct from white Americans. This contradiction is exemplified in his implementation of the Bracero Program, which brought braceros, or "hired hands," into the U.S. from Mexico, starting in 1942. Reflecting steady pressure from agricultural regions, where labor shortages were impeding production and driving wages up, Truman supported the importation of Mexican workers at the same time he proclaimed the need to deal with "the pressing problem of illegal immigration." Much like nineteenth-century ideas of the Chinese as temporary contract laborers, the Bracero Program assumed that Mexican workers could contribute to the national economy but were unassimilable into the national culture. If these workers overstayed their work permits, or attempted to bring family members across the border, they became "illegal immigrants." These "illegal immigrants," in turn, were responsible for eroding living conditions for real Americans: "The standards of living and job opportunities of American farm workers are under constant downward pressure. Thousands of our own citizens, particularly those of Latin descent, are displaced from employment or forced to work under substandard conditions because of the competition of illegal immigrants."[23]

Truman advocated a few different solutions to the concurrent shortage of agricultural workers. (Despite the alleged loss of jobs caused by the "crisis" of "illegal immigration," even restrictionists like Patrick McCarran were authoring exceptions to allow for the importation of workers to their constituencies. In McCarran's case, this meant a special clause in the 1952 Immigration and Nationality Act allowing for the immigration of Basque shepherds to Nevada.) First, Truman saw an expansion of immigration from Europe as being able to provide the agricultural workers necessary to the national economy. Second, he encouraged the Department of Labor to help "improve the utilization of our own citizens in the farm labor force, and reduce to a minimum our dependence on foreign sources."[24] Finally, consistent with federal policy into the twenty-first century, he proposed making the Immigration and Naturalization Service more efficient, beefing up border patrols, and

22. Roediger, *Wages of Whiteness* (New York: Verso, 1991); "Address at a Luncheon of the National Conference of Christians and Jews," November 11, 1949, *Public Papers: Truman, 1949*, 561.

23. "Special Message to Congress on the Employment of Agricultural Workers from Mexico," July 13, 1951, *Public Papers: Truman, 1951*, 389, 390.

24. Ibid., 392.

encouraging employers not to hire undocumented workers through sanctions against them. Nowhere did he recommend giving agricultural laborers the rights of collective bargaining granted to other workers in 1935.

Unlike European immigrants and refugees, then, Mexican immigrants were, in the eyes of Cold War immigration policy, unassimilable. The Bracero Program made national dependence on Mexican labor a feature of the economy until immigration law was reformed to allow for dramatic increases of legal immigration from the Western Hemisphere, Africa, and Asia. But crucial as these workers were to the functioning of agriculture, their presence was not welcome under the Cold War order. Unlike Europeans, who were seen as political refugees coming to the United States to seek democratic freedoms, Mexicans coming across the border were deemed mere "economic" migrants, drawn only by the lure of the dollar. Ironically, the Immigration and Nationality Act of 1952, also known as the McCarran-Walter Act, which Truman had strenuously opposed and twice vetoed, made this distinction between economic and political migrants a permanent feature of federal policy.

Here again, Truman was very much compelled by the imperial moment: the entwining of federal policies on immigration and ethnicity with the international exigencies of the Cold War. He vociferously opposed the changes embodied by McCarran-Walter, in particular the renewing of very limited national-origin quotas for the admission of immigrants. He exclaimed: "Today we are 'protecting' ourselves, as we were in 1924, against being flooded by immigrants from Eastern Europe. This is fantastic. . . . We do not need to be protected against immigrants from these countries."[25] Truman also objected to the scrutiny the legislation provided of immigrant loyalties, the ability to strip citizenship from native-born Americans holding dual citizenship as well as those in violation of a wide range of laws, and the possibility of deportation of resident aliens. Like Ashcroft-era immigration and civil liberties legislation, McCarran-Walter provided little in the way of judicial, or even executive, review.

Both Truman and his congressional opponents advocated the extension of naturalization to Asians. The abolition of long-standing impediments to Asian naturalization was a component of the international Cold War order, as Truman explained in 1950: "At a time when the United Nations Forces are fighting gallantly to uphold the principles of freedom and democracy in Korea, it would be unworthy of our tradition if we continue now to deny the

25. "Veto of Bill to Revise the Laws Relating to Immigration, Naturalization, and Nationality," June 25, 1952, *Public Papers: Truman, 1952*, 443.

right of citizenship to American residents of Asian origin."[26] What Truman objected to in the legislation that eventually passed Congress, overriding his vetoes, were the small numbers for admission of Asians, as well as the tendency of the legislation, as written, to ancestor hunt. The admission of any person of Asian descent, from anywhere in the world, was charged against the tiny quotas for Asian countries. Truman saw this as unfair and possibly offensive to crucial U.S. allies on the Pacific Rim.

Truman's position on immigration in some ways anticipated the transition from a policy based on national origin to the one focusing on work preference and family unification implemented in 1965, a year after the end of the Bracero Program. In other ways, however, his position was consistent with the Cold War racial order proposed by his adversaries in Congress. His overriding concern for immigrants fleeing Communism and his awareness of immigration as foreign policy were very consistent with the legislation that eventually passed as the McCarran-Walter Act.

Truman-era immigration policy was part of a general transition from the racialized national-origin quotas of 1924 and 1952 to the civil rights–inspired Immigration and Nationality Act of 1965. This "liberalization" of immigration policy, including the gradual abolition of Asian exclusion and the transition from national-origin quotas to family unity and work preferences, was as much a component of the Cold War order of U.S. imperialism as it was of the civil rights–inspired moment. During this period, immigration policy screened new immigrants for their assimilability and whether they deserved admission to democracy. In addition, immigration policy, like federal Indian policy, sought to administer the "conjugal relations" of empire, bringing a select few Asian immigrants from new allies in the Pacific Rim into the nation, thus promoting an ideology of democratic inclusion. While Truman consistently opposed the scourge of national-origin quotas, his general position on immigration supported the needs of his time.

IV. Conclusion

As historian Nikhil Singh has observed, the Cold War also occasioned a culture war.[27] Truman and his advisers, the architects of national security policy, worked from an assumption that they were fighting in the international

---

26. Ibid., 625.
27. Singh, "Culture/Wars," 510.

arena to defend everything America stood for in the "all-embracing struggle" between democracy and totalitarianism. The distinction between these two forms of state was, of necessity, a cultural one that was easily mobilized to determine domestic policy and to script a national identity premised, in large part, on social inequality.

While Truman was concerned with equal rights, the dawning international order, as his Farewell Address demonstrated, weighed much more heavily on him. As the United States consolidated its position as leader of the free world, Truman pursued the abundant opportunities for international political and economic power. Just as the Truman Doctrine was foundational to the Cold War international order, the implications of it for public policy regarding immigration and ethnicity within the nation were also large. At this imperial moment in history, international and domestic policies on citizenship, democracy, and rights were deeply entwined.

Informal Remarks of the President at the
Nisei Regiment Ceremonies on the Ellipse

It is a very great pleasure to me today to be able to put the seventh Regimental Citation on your banners.

You are to be congratulated on what you have done for this great country of ours. I think it was my predecessor who said that Americanism is not a matter of race or creed, it is a matter of the heart.

You fought for the free nations of the world along with the rest of us. I congratulate you on that, and I can't tell you how very much I appreciate the privilege of being able to show you just how much the United States of America thinks of what you have done.

You are now on your/home. You fought not only the enemy, but you fought prejudice -- and you have won. Keep up that fight, and we will continue to win -- to make this great Republic stand for just what the Constitution says it stands for: the welfare of all the people all the time.

Bring forward the Colors.

- - - - - - - - - -

June 21, 1952

MEMORANDUM FOR: Mr. Charles S. Murphy,
                    The White House.

I am attaching a letter from Mr. Harriman
to the President recommending veto of the McCarran-
Walter bill.

The first draft of this letter was discussed
by Mr. Harriman in detail with his staff before his
departure from Washington, and this final draft was
read to him in Des Moines, Iowa, this morning and approved by him. He requested that I sign his name to
the letter and deliver it to you today, in order that
it might be in the President's hands while he is considering his action on the bill.

GEORGE M. ELSEY
Assistant to the Director

June 21, 1952

Dear Mr. President:

Although the McCarran-Walter bill (H.R. 5678) will not materially affect our various mutual security programs, I personally feel very strongly that it does such violence to the traditions and heritage of this nation that I am compelled to urge you to veto it.

The bill represents the first major revision of our immigration laws since 1924. As such I think it should make a contribution to the solution of some of the problems we face in the world; it should be in harmony with the spirit which animates our foreign policy and our relations with other countries; and it should strengthen our claim to leadership of the free world. Measured by these standards, it is a thoroughly bad bill.

Except for two liberalizing provisions -- the naturalization of Japanese and other Asiatics and the establishment of quotas for certain Asiatic countries hitherto barred -- and some minor improvements, the bill retains most of the bad or outmoded features of our present laws, and then goes on to add a whole series of new provisions which in many ways will give us an even worse statute than what we now have. I particularly wish to point out that it reenacts provisions of the Internal Security Act of 1950, which you so vigorously denounced at the time you vetoed it.

The legislation looks upon immigrants and aliens with suspicion and hostility. It establishes unjustifiably restrictive principles of selection. It erects new and even more arbitrary barriers to entry. It transforms naturalized citizens into an inferior class and makes them subject to denaturalization on new grounds of uncertain effect. The bill retroactively subjects aliens to deportation for acts which were not grounds for deportation when committed. It curtails and, in some cases, removes the right of appeal and abolishes the statute of limitations. References in the bill to persons whose ancestory is one-half Asiatic is more in keeping with the Nuremberg laws than with American conceptions. It establishes grounds for exclusion, denaturalization and deportation which are unreasonable and unwarranted. It provides a basis for unreasonable search and interrogation of American citizens lawfully returning to this country.

It does nothing to give us a fairer and more up-to-date quota system that takes into account our new responsibilities in the world and the new relationship we are trying to develop with other countries.

This bill is another manifestation of that ugly trend among certain elements in our national life, which I can only characterize as mean, short-sighted, fearful and bigoted. I fervently hope that you can see your way to reject it in the most vigorous terms.

Respectfully yours,

W. A. Harriman
Director for Mutual Security

A Legacy in Concrete

The Truman Presidency Transforms America's Environment

Karl Brooks

As he bade them farewell in January 1953, President Harry S. Truman told the American people the essence of his job was "to make decisions—big ones and small ones." In eight postwar years, Truman and his appointees made big and small decisions about using nature, in America and across the globe, to meet human demands. So consequential was the combined effect of his actions that we inhabit a disordered natural world today. During his presidency, federal agencies rerouted rivers, laid low forests, and killed animals by the millions, fish by the billions, and insects in quantities beyond reckoning. His decisions encouraged the application of chemicals and the explosion of weapons with biological and ecological consequences still unknown today.

Not only did the Truman administration disorder the natural world during

I much appreciate the many helpful comments and thoughtful criticism this article generated when I presented it as a paper at the Truman Library conference. I especially thank William Stueck for correcting an embarrassing factual error and Richard Kirkendall for putting in clearer context the New Deal hydropower dams in our shared homeland, the Northwest. All conference participants sharpened my thinking about Truman and his presidential times. Dale E. Nimz and Jeffrey P. Moran made helpful comments on an early version of this paper. Nimz's careful studies of Truman administration environmental policy and our conversations during the past four years have stimulated my interest in the postwar era as a crucial, little-understood "seed-time" for environmental law and politics.

its years in power, the president's decisions also constrained those, both big and small, which his successors had to make during the next two decades. A proper appreciation of Truman's impact on nature thus requires consideration of choices made and forgone during his presidency as well as those denied us today.

The Truman presidency transformed American nature. Part of its environmental legacy endures, a visible heritage of concrete and steel throughout the nation: McNary and Oahe Dams blocking the Columbia and Missouri Rivers, the Central-South Florida Conservation Project choking the Everglades, suburbs sprawling miles into Kansas City's hinterland. Proving less durable, however, were the concepts his administration tried to implant within the American legal system. Laws empowering federal agencies to alter ecosystems, almost at will, actually stimulated two decades of popular protest and legal innovation to limit government's power. Frustrated, even horrified, by the scale and speed of nature's manipulation, citizens provoked political reform that triggered a revolution in legal thought. By the early 1970s, the environmental movement was dismantling the legal edifice that subjected nature to federal authority. Disassembling the postwar concrete and steel, though, remains beyond our capacity even if we desired to do so.

Truman's environmental heritage thus presents a double-sided aspect. Permanent ecosystem disruptions matched profound shifts in American thought caused by those very disruptions. With the tenacity of a Missouri mule, Truman hauled New Deal models for controlling nature into the postwar era. He stubbornly ignored mounting evidence about environmental damage caused by the New Deal and World War II. By defending the "destiny of free men" with armed might and ceaseless economic growth, he suppressed criticism about the environmental consequences of Cold War militarization and pell-mell prosperity. Nevertheless, by extending the welfare state and national-security establishment, his presidency ultimately compelled Americans to consider the catastrophic ecological impacts of federal natural-resources policy. His presidency wreaked profound damage on the earth but ignited the constructive creativity that finally forced a reckoning of the costs. His years in power thus fashioned an environmental legacy in American life as important as those his presidency bequeathed to global politics and civil rights.[1]

1. Among the few interpretive studies of the Truman presidency's environmental policies, the best are Elmo Richardson, *Dams, Parks, and Politics: Resource Development and Preservation in the Truman-Eisenhower Era* (Lexington: University Press of Kentucky, 1973), and Samuel P. Hays, *Beauty, Health, and Permanence: Environmental Politics in the United States, 1955–1985* (New York: Cambridge University Press, 1987) and *A History of Environmental Politics since*

This assessment of the Truman presidency's effect on our earth's history begins at the apex of his power and popularity. His characteristic words and deeds illuminate personal convictions and political calculations that shaped his environmental legacy.

An excited crowd of thirty-five hundred buzzed in anticipation on May 10, 1950. Two bright yellow Union Pacific engines were gently nudging backward three great dark-green passenger cars and one Union Pacific baggage car. Bunting draped the rear platform of the last car, the *Ferdinand Magellan,* above a large ceramic Great Seal of the United States. The car touched the hognose barrier at the siding's end, and the train stopped. A massed band of high school students and military reservists struck up "Here We Have Idaho," the state song, and then swung into a patriotic medley. In just minutes, they would blare "Ruffles and Flourishes," followed somewhat uncertainly by "Hail to the Chief." Five years into his presidency, Harry S. Truman strode to the *Magellan*'s microphone. As he had at other stops on this "nonpolitical" journey across the West, he intended to tell the trackside audience in Boise, Idaho, that relentless pursuit of economic security and world power required further disordering of the natural world.[2]

Brisk wind rolled south down the forest-fringed mountains above town, snapping dozens of American and Idaho flags that encircled the graceful Spanish Revival Union Pacific depot. Late-morning sunshine, bright with the promise of spring in the northern Rockies, splashed the little capital city. Spectators gazing north from the depot saw the tree-lined Boise River sliding through the city halfway between the depot and the state capitol. Its banks still braided with cottonwoods, the Boise curled out of the mountains onto its last reach. It would run nearly fifty miles due west across what was once sagebrush-speckled high desert before reaching the Snake River, the largest tributary of the West's biggest waterway, the Columbia. From atop the high bench of land crowned by the depot, observers who glanced northward, away from the pageant unfolding on the siding, could plainly see the statehouse dome glistening gray below the tan foothills of the Boise Front.[3]

1945 (Pittsburgh: University of Pittsburgh Press, 2000). Hal K. Rothman, *The Greening of America? Environmentalism in the United States since 1945* (Fort Worth: Harcourt Brace, 1998), skims the period. Karl Brooks, "Illuminating the Postwar Northwest: Private Power and Public Law in Hells Canyon, 1950–57," *Western Legal History* 12 (Winter/Spring 1999): 49–75, compares Truman's and Eisenhower's approaches to river policy during the fifties.

2. *Idaho Statesman,* May 11, 1950, 1.

3. A native of Boise, I am relying on my memory and my reading of numerous photographic images to describe the prospect from the depot across the Boise River and into the mountains above my hometown.

A few drifts of snow still mantled Shaffer Butte and Deer Point five thousand feet above the city. As they melted, their runoff mingled with snowmelt tumbling down the four hundred and fifty miles of granite peaks that formed the west slope of the Continental Divide. These mountains, ranging north from Boise to the Canadian border, defined the eastern boundary of the Snake-Columbia Basin. Its waters nursed the world's largest anadromous (migratory) fishery, birthplace of the salmon and steelhead trout that had been coursing between the Divide and the Pacific for ten millennia. These same waters, pooled behind dams great and small, also irrigated thousands of acres of crops in Idaho, Oregon, and Washington: alfalfa hay that fed beef and dairy cattle, sugar beets and potatoes that had fueled Allied armed forces in World War II, fruit trees and honeybees. And from these same waters, spun through turbines encased in the same dams that governed the irrigation supply, flowed the world's greatest concentration of hydroelectricity.[4]

In addition to thousands of Boiseans who came to see and hear President Truman, hundreds traveled from small farm towns downstream. Their rural landscape, which proud boosters called the "Treasure Valley," depended utterly on irrigation projects built by the federal government.[5] In the biggest city between Salt Lake City, Utah, and Portland, Oregon—a nerve center for federal irrigation, forestry, and dam-building efforts across the Snake Basin since Progressive and New Deal days—President Truman outlined his plans for exploiting the Northwest's water and land for its people's material prosperity.

Truman intended his Boise speech—like others in Twin Falls, Idaho; Baker, Oregon; and Pasco and Seattle, Washington—to mobilize opinion behind a federal direction of comprehensive, intensive water use. He had carried Idaho and Washington in the 1948 presidential election, won nine other western states, and nearly broken the century-old Republican hammerlock on Oregon. Northwestern congressional Democrats, liberals from the industrial Midwest and Northeast, the biggest trade unions, and farm groups rooted in the

4. Anthony Netboy, *The Columbia River Salmon and Steelhead Trout: Their Fight for Survival* (Seattle: University of Washington Press, 1980); Joseph Cone and Sandy Ridlington, eds., *The Northwest Salmon Crisis: A Documentary History* (Corvallis: Oregon State University Press, 1996); Mark Fiege, *Irrigated Eden: The Making of an Agricultural Landscape in the American West* (Seattle: University of Washington Press, 1999); Gus Norwood, *Columbia River Power for the People: A History of the Policies of the Bonneville Power Administration* (Portland: Bonneville Power Administration, 1980).

5. Susan M. Stacy, *Legacy of Light: A History of Idaho Power Company* (Boise: Idaho Power Co., 1991); Tim Palmer, *The Snake River: Window to the West* (Washington: Island Press, 1991); Todd Shallat, ed., *Snake: The Plain and Its People* (Boise: Boise State University Press, 1994).

Populist legacy all favored Truman's ambitious natural-resources program. A dedicated partisan, who believed he understood the American majority's craving for economic security, Truman sought to rally his victorious coalition behind his commitment to cheap public hydroelectric power. As his great idol, Franklin Roosevelt, had done so thoroughly during the New Deal and war, the president wanted his own stamp on aggressive federal exploitation of nature. He belittled opponents who doubted the wisdom of spending federal money to extend the national direction of resource use as selfish corporate apologists and obstructionist Republicans.[6]

The 1950 congressional elections, barely six months off, shaped the trip's itinerary. In two weeks of hard traveling, Truman crisscrossed the High Plains, Intermountain West, and Pacific Northwest. Nature in these regions now reflected the unprecedented exertion of federal power that today remains the New Deal's most durable heritage. Truman explicitly tied his liberal postwar agenda, dubbed the Fair Deal, to FDR's vision of planned development of nature for human betterment. Federal agency strategists in the Northwest, like their counterparts from the Missouri and Colorado Basins to South Florida, envisioned using money and technology to remodel economies and societies.[7] As the president told the Boise crowd, "We have done a great deal of good pioneering work in resource development, but we need more power dams to develop mineral resources, and to bring cheap power to all the communities of this area."[8]

Back in Washington, the Eighty-first Congress, elected along with Truman in 1948, had approved a water-management strategy breathtaking in scope and size. The most Democratic Congress since the New Deal's heyday in 1935–1936 passed a Rivers and Harbors Act authorizing nearly all new dams and irrigation projects the president had sought since his first State of the Union Address in 1946. In all, Congress committed the nation to spending

6. Samuel Lubell, *The Future of American Politics*, rev. 2d ed. (Garden City: Doubleday, 1956), chaps. 2, 8; David McCullough, *Truman* (New York: Simon and Schuster, 1992), chaps. 15, 16; Alonzo L. Hamby, *Beyond the New Deal: Harry S. Truman and American Liberalism* (New York: Columbia University Press, 1973) and *Harry S. Truman and the Fair Deal* (Lexington, Mass.: D. C. Heath and Co., 1974).

7. John Gunther, *Inside U.S.A.* (New York: Harper and Bros., 1947), chap. 43 (southern public power) and chap. 8 (northwestern public power); Marc Reisner, *Cadillac Desert: The American West and Its Disappearing Water* (New York: Penguin, 1986) (Southwest); Michael Grunwald, "Everglades Restoration Plan," *Washington Post*, June 23–27, 2002, A1 (series on Everglades ecosystem restoration).

8. *Public Papers of the Presidents: Harry S. Truman, 1945–1953*, 8 vols. (Washington, D.C.: U.S. Government Printing Office, 1961–1966), 6 (1950): 344–46.

a record $1.5 billion to build more than one hundred and fifty new water projects across the country. Parceled between the Army Corps of Engineers and the Interior Department's Bureau of Reclamation, the water-control blueprint envisioned decades of earthmoving to serve the president's goals of power generation, flood control, and irrigation of desert lands.[9]

While generally satisfied with Congress's work, Truman expressed pique that disputes between the Army Engineers and the Reclamation Bureau were impeding authorization of what would have been the world's largest hydroelectric dam, Hells Canyon High Dam on the Snake River between Idaho and Oregon, some seventy-five miles northwest of Boise. The High Dam would have funded a massive desert irrigation scheme to re-create in the Boise-Snake Basin a postwar version of the New Deal's Grand Coulee Project.[10] Bold and costly, Hells Canyon and the Mountain Home Project demonstrated "the kind of comprehensive planning and action that is required if we are to conserve, develop and use our natural resources so that they will be increasingly useful to us as the years go by," the president proclaimed. He vowed to press Congress again to authorize them in his fiscal 1952 budget.[11]

The nation was marking the fifth anniversary of VE-Day, so FDR's successor hailed the New Deal's great dams in the Columbia, Colorado, and Tennessee Basins as powerful patriotic symbols. He reminded listeners of recent sacrifice and triumph, exhorting them to new endeavors necessary to defend American values in the Cold War. "I want to say to you," Truman told the Boise audience, "that if we hadn't had the power projects in the Tennessee Valley, if we hadn't had the Bonneville and Grand Coulee Dams and the other power projects, it would have taken us much longer to win the war. . . . Now I want to see a Northwest power development. . . . I want to say to you that if we get that done, nothing in the world can prevent this country from accomplishing its purpose. It will mean an economic development that will keep us the most powerful nation in the world." Americans by 1950 had grown accustomed to their president linking nature's subjugation to Communism's defeat. "This is what I want you to understand," Truman concluded, "that I am working for world peace on a basis that will make our eco-

9. Congressional Quarterly, *Congress and the Nation: A Review of Government and Politics in the Postwar Years, 1945–1964* (Washington, D.C.: Congressional Quarterly, 1966), 823.

10. Karl Brooks, "Unplugging the New Deal: Hells Canyon High Dam and the Postwar Northwest" (Ph.D. diss., University of Kansas, 2000; forthcoming from the University of Washington Press).

11. *Public Papers: Truman, 1950,* 427–30.

nomic setup the greatest in the history of the world, as it is right now. I want to keep it that way. I want to keep on developing it."[12]

Later that afternoon, trackside in Baker, Oregon, the president insisted "there must be continued development of the natural resources of the Northwest" if the region was to "keep right on growing." Big federal dams like High Hells Canyon, driving vast federal reclamation systems like the Mountain Home Project, promised "full, unified and coordinated development of the rich natural resources of the Northwest." The High Dam "will add close to a million kilowatts of power to this section of the country. It will help control flood waters, it will help bring a higher standard of living to this entire region." Across the Columbia, in Pasco, Washington, the next day, Truman accused his foes of small thinking and pinched vision. "They do not understand the greatness of our goals. They fear some impairment of their selfish interests."[13]

Sweeping rhetoric befitted the time and place of Truman's characteristic defense of federal mastery over nature. From the Continental Divide to the Pacific Coast, between 1933 and 1945, government actions to combat the Depression and wage war had fashioned something resembling an irrigation and hydroelectric empire.[14] Northwestern land and water, the teeming nonhuman life they supported, and the people living beside them all depended on federal law and policy for their fate. And the Northwest was not unique. During the fifteen years before 1950 the national government had redirected natural forces and rearranged earth's landscape first to revive the economy and then to win the war.[15] As a United States senator from 1935 to 1945 and

12. Ibid.
13. Ibid., 351–52 (Baker), 373 (Pasco); "President Dedicates Grand Coulee," *Public Power* 8 (June 1950): 12.
14. Vera Springer, *Power and the Pacific Northwest: A History of the Bonneville Power Administration* (Portland: Bonneville Power Administration, 1976); Richard Lowitt, *The New Deal in the West* (Bloomington: Indiana University Press, 1984); Carlos A. Schwantes, *The Pacific Northwest: An Interpretive History* (Lincoln: University of Nebraska Press, 1989); T. H. Watkins, *Righteous Pilgrim: The Life and Times of Harold L. Ickes, 1874–1952* (New York: Henry Holt and Co., 1990); Paul C. Pitzer, *Grand Coulee: Harnessing a Dream* (Pullman: Washington State University Press, 1994); Richard White, *The Organic Machine: The Remaking of the Columbia River* (New York: Hill and Wang, 1995); Jeanne Nienaber Clarke, *Roosevelt's Warrior: Harold L. Ickes and the New Deal* (Baltimore: Johns Hopkins University Press, 1996); William G. Robbins, *Landscapes of Promise: The Oregon Story, 1800–1940* (Seattle: University of Washington Press, 1997).
15. Brooks, "Illuminating the Postwar Northwest"; Michael C. Blumm, "The Northwest's Hydroelectric Heritage: Prologue to the Northwest Power Planning and Conservation Act," *Washington Law Review* 58 (1983): 175–244; Gerald D. Nash, *The American West Trans-*

then as Franklin D. Roosevelt's vice president, Harry Truman had enthusiastically endorsed federal exertion of power over nature.[16]

The question of how to use federal power over water, land, and life inspired and divided Americans in the decade following World War II. What
the federal government ultimately did during the Truman presidency, from
1945 to 1953, shaped for another half century the places where fish, animals,
and people lived. In the Columbia and Snake Basins, and in other great river
basins—the Mississippi, Tennessee, and Colorado—the Truman years cast a
legacy in concrete. Around America's cities, sprawling suburbs stitched together by asphalt reflected the president's drive to secure economic opportunity for ordinary people. From Los Angeles to Philadelphia, polluted skies,
poisoned waters, and toxic dump sites testified to the president's passion for
undergirding Cold War military power with postwar economic abundance.[17]

From the first summer he took office, Truman aggressively deployed federal power against natural systems. He imagined nature as both an untapped
warehouse of useful products and an unruly menace. In whatever guise, nature needed a strong hand guided by human skill and knowledge to manage,
control, harness, and tame it. His passion for prosperity and security, heightened by fears that peacetime reconversion would trigger another depression,
mobilized the federal government's campaign to remodel nature. After Japan
surrendered, the new president presented Congress in September 1945 with
a comprehensive plan to "reestablish an expanded peacetime industry, trade,
and agriculture, and to do it as quickly as possible." Recalling the New Deal's
objective of planned development to maximize the economic potential of
natural resources, President Truman linked a time-honored American dream—
conquering a frontier—with a modern technique, "conservation and development . . . according to an intelligent and coordinated design." Only national

formed: The Impact of the Second World War (Bloomington: Indiana University Press, 1985);
Dale E. Nimz, "Damming the Kaw: The Kiro Controversy and Flood Control in the Great
Depression," *Kansas History* 26 (Spring 2003): 14–31; Paul Hirt, *A Conspiracy of Optimism:
The United States Forest Service in the Inland Northwest, 1945–1975* (Lincoln: University of
Nebraska Press, 1996).

16. Donald R. McCoy, *The Presidency of Harry S. Truman* (Lawrence: University Press of
Kansas, 1984); McCullough, *Truman;* Richardson, *Dams, Parks, and Politics.*

17. Charles McKinley, *Uncle Sam in the Pacific Northwest: Federal Management of Natural
Resources in the Columbia River Valley* (Berkeley: University of California Press, 1952), should
be read in conjunction with three fine recent collections: Kevin J. Fernlund, ed., *The Cold War
American West, 1945–1989* (Albuquerque: University of New Mexico Press, 1998); Bruce
Hevly and John M. Findlay, eds., *The Atomic West* (Seattle: University of Washington Press,
1998); and Dale D. Goble and Paul W. Hirt, eds., *Northwest Lands, Northwest Peoples: Read-
ings in Environmental History* (Seattle: University of Washington Press, 1999).

efforts, directed by comprehensive river-basin plans, could "harness the waters of our great rivers so that they may become vehicles of commerce, beneficent producers of cheap electrical power, and servants of the nation instead of instruments of destruction."[18]

Truman's first State of the Union message in January 1946 urged Congress to unleash weapons that had won the war—technology, management expertise, and the federal purse—on water- and land-development projects intended to secure the peace. He had been president for little more than a year when, in the summer of 1946, he gladly signed legislation authorizing construction of nearly two billion dollars worth of new federal dams, locks, and irrigation canals.[19]

New interventions into natural systems aroused some citizens and scientists to challenge the president's insistence that even more needed to be done. Doubts surfaced about damming rivers and draining wetlands. A new, more activist national conservation movement signaled an upwelling current of dissent in the immediate postwar years. Conservationists, backed by state and federal government scientists, urged Americans to appreciate rivers and wetlands as complex, vibrant biotic systems instead of mere pollution sinks, transport corridors, or power sources. Conditioned by depression and war to think mainly about national strengths, conservationists began stretching customary definitions of "natural resources" to argue that water's quality, as well as its quantity, measured national prosperity.

In the summer of 1945, the influential chair of the House of Representatives Select Committee on Wildlife Conservation, Democrat A. Willis Robertson of Virginia, had launched yearlong, broad-ranging hearings into the state of America's environment. Biologists from federal and state agencies, wildlife managers, and outdoor sports activists detailed the damages done to American ecosystems by fifteen years of economic pump priming and war production. Worried, often passionate, critics detailed the impacts of war and economic stimulus on waters, forests, and wildlife.[20]

Outside Washington, conservationists contended that peace and victory gave the nation breathing room to consider both past mistakes and future opportunities to safeguard environmental values. The editor of Missouri's

18. This argument reflects points made by Dale E. Nimz, "Rivers That Work: Environment, Engineering, and Policy Change in the Kansas River Basin" (Ph.D. diss., University of Kansas, 2003), chap. 5. Truman's messages are discussed on 206–8.

19. Ibid.

20. U.S. House of Representatives, Select Committee on Conservation of Wildlife Resources, *Hearings under H. Res. 75*, 79th Cong., 2d Sess. (1946).

state conservation magazine, Charles H. Callison, wrote in autumn 1945 that "nothing strips a man's thinking down to fundamentals like fighting a war." He detected Americans starting "a drastic reappraisal of values which should point the way toward more intelligent living and, therefore, a stronger democracy." Foremost in this calculus was "a new conception of the function of wildlife in a modern civilization." "Millions of people who live and work in the complex society of modern America," Callison believed, saw "wild creatures and the environment in which they live [as] essential to the very health and morale of the nation."[21]

The House Conservation Committee and National Research Council published in January 1946 a study of peacetime priorities for restoring damaged ecosystems and preventing further losses. *Some Wildlife Jobs Awaiting Attention* argued that "the improved standards of living, the augmented security we all crave, are dependent on the proper rehabilitation and management of our basic natural resources." "Most leaders in high places, whether in the Army, Navy, or civil government, show little appreciation of these problems," the study asserted. Therefore, "prompt and drastic change . . . should be the responsibility of each informed and interested citizen, and especially of scientific and conservation organizations, [to] bring the national and local needs in the field to the attention of lawmakers."[22]

The previous autumn, *Sports Afield,* one of the country's three big outdoor-recreation magazines, had editorialized about "the crisis" Truman's water-construction plans posed to wildlife habitat. Michael Hudoba, the magazine's capital correspondent, privately pleaded for the president to "calm the trepidation in the minds of sportsmen who are concerned about this program in various river basins." He suggested issuing a presidential statement "of assurance that fish and wildlife resources would not be overlooked or needlessly destroyed in water-use programs as developed and administered by federal construction agencies, and if destroyed to be replaced if possible." Truman blandly replied that "there can be no objection to the viewpoint that the development of river basins should not impair the existing values and resources, including fish and wildlife, where it is humanly possible to avoid such impairment." That same week, on Interior Secretary Harold Ickes's advice, the president provided quite a different "statement of assurance," telling the National Reclamation Association "you should think of the Federal Gov-

21. Charles H. Callison, "The Real Value of Wildlife," *Missouri Conservationist* 6 (November 1945): 4, 10–11.
22. Reprinted in *Hearings under H. Res. 75*, 112–23.

ernment as your strong right arm doing for you collectively what none can do for himself alone."[23]

Congress's aggressive response in 1946 to the president's call for intensified federal water control alarmed conservationists. Reviewing legislation passed by the Seventy-ninth Congress, the House Select Committee on Wildlife Conservation in early 1947 warned that "over 600 reservoir projects alone have been proposed for construction by the Federal Government [that] will have important effects on the fish and wildlife resources of the Nation." With too little yet known about the environmental damage already caused by federal projects between 1933 and 1945, "your committee cannot stress too strongly that the fish and game resources of this country will be facing critical times in the years immediately ahead."[24]

Conservationists in and out of government echoed the House committee's concern about the accelerating pace of federal intervention into natural systems. The director of the Missouri Conservation Department, I. T. Bode, warned his state's anglers and hunters in autumn 1945 that New Deal and war-mobilization water projects had reduced ecological values to "an afterthought, giving to these the crumbs that are left if public indignation forces the issue." Despite apparently persuasive cost-benefit calculations favoring new dams, "we think there has been much distorted conclusion with regard to the benefits to be derived."[25] Just days after the Seventy-ninth Congress sent its water-project bills to the White House for Truman's signature, the executive director of the Izaak Walton League, Kenneth Reid, called the Army Engineers and Reclamation Bureau "a swarm of locusts scouring the country trying to find every possible site for a dam." He warned a Senate committee in July 1946, "All over the country the destruction is going to be terrific. . . . I just want to put in a word of warning here. Unless we do something to curb the unbridled dam-building proclivities of two of our Government agencies, you are going to destroy the salmon runs on the Pacific Coast."[26]

23. U.S. House of Representatives, Agriculture Committee, 79th Cong., 2d Sess. H. Rpt. 1944 (April 17, 1946), 26–27 (*Sports Afield* reprint). Michael Hudoba to Truman October 25, 1945, and Truman to Hudoba, November 13, 1945, Box 1057, Official File 378–1945; Harold L. Ickes to Truman, November 9, 1945, and Truman to National Reclamation Association, November 10, 1945, Box 69, Official File 6-E, Truman Papers, Truman Library.

24. U.S. House of Representatives, Select Committee on Conservation of Wildlife Resources, *Report on Conservation of Wildlife*, 79th Cong., 2d Sess. H. Rpt. 2743 (January 2, 1947), 1–3, 96–97.

25. Bode, "Wildlife Stake in Flood Control Planning," *Missouri Conservationist* 6 (September 1945): 1–3.

26. Senate Agriculture and Forestry Committee, *Hearings on H.R. 6097*, 79th Cong., 2d Sess., July 19, 1946, 52–53.

In late 1946, the United States Fish and Wildlife Service's Portland, Oregon, office and the Oregon Fish Commission both concluded that new dams on northwestern rivers "would literally destroy the valuable Columbia River salmon fishery." Oregon's chief fishery manager advised his state "that we are witnessing the most crucial period in the history of our fisheries." Should Truman and the Congress decide to fund five new dams on the Columbia and Snake, "complete development of those plans . . . can only lead to the virtual extinction of our great fishery resources, particularly the salmon."[27]

Between 1947 and 1950, the Truman administration ignored conservationists' criticism. The president had grounds for ordering federal agencies to accelerate research into fish losses and water pollution. He might have encouraged local citizens and state-agency managers to challenge federal engineers and planners.[28] Yet the president drove water-management policy further along directions he had outlined since 1945. The Reclamation Bureau and Army Engineers filled shelves with reports and studies extolling the virtues of comprehensive river development under federal direction. A special presidential message to Congress in July 1947 declared, "The major opportunity of our generation to increase the wealth of the nation lies in the development of our great river systems." The State of the Union and Economic Report of 1948 proposed "multiple-purpose dams on our great rivers—not only to reclaim land, but also to prevent floods, to extend our inland waterways, and provide hydroelectric power."[29] A special presidential Water Resources Policy Commission released in 1950 a three-volume study dedicated to the proposition that the main task of the federal government was accelerating the pace of dam-building and desert irrigation. Dale E. Nimz has found that natural resources development provided the president with one of his most popular, and ultimately effective, campaign slogans in the dramatic 1948 presidential election. "This repeated

27. Netboy, *Columbia River Salmon*, 78–79; Oregon Fish *Commission Biennial Report: 1947*, 3–6, Oregon Department of Fish and Wildlife Archives, Clackamas, Ore.

28. The president could have claimed bipartisan political support for postwar conservation initiatives. The Democratic Seventh-ninth Congress enacted the Wildlife Coordination Act in 1946, 60 Stat. 1080, directing state and federal wildlife experts to prepare biological surveys about proposed water projects' environmental impacts. The Republican Eightieth Congress passed the first Water Pollution Control Act in 1948, 62 Stat. 1155, authorizing scientific research into pollution's health effects.

29. Special message cited in Lewis W. Koenig, ed., *The Truman Administration: Its Principles and Practices* (New York: New York University Press, 1956), 140–44; *Public Papers: Truman, 1948*, 4–5 (State of the Union), 66–67 (Economic Report).

theme," Nimz concludes, "helped him carry ten out of eleven western states and win the presidency."[30]

A shrewd and opportunistic campaigner, the president several times between 1947 and 1951 hurried to flood-damaged regions to reaffirm his commitment to "harnessing" and "taming" rivers. After Mississippi River floods in 1947 and again in 1948, when Columbia Basin floods drowned more than fifty Oregonians, the White House capitalized on regional trauma. To press his case for more federal spending on multipurpose water projects that would safeguard lives and property while fueling continued economic growth, the president blamed floods on undammed, unplanned watersheds. In Portland, Oregon, he linked New Deal power dams, wartime triumph, and Fair Deal economic policy: "I hope we can pass a program under which these disastrous floods will never happen again. . . . There is a plan for a Columbia river development program and I hope to see it outlined and completed. Had it not been for the immense power dams on the river, it would have been much more difficult for us to win the last war." He accused congressional Republicans of letting citizens suffer from floods because of their misguided support for smaller private dams. "Had we had some of these projects which have been pending for several years," he claimed in Pocatello, Idaho, in the spring of 1948, "we might to some extent have alleviated the Columbia flood which caused so much damage."[31] Nimz found that Truman "used the public reaction to the 1951 Kansas River flood disaster to unify support for building, first, Tuttle Creek [Dam], and then the entire system of multiple-purpose dams and reservoirs in the Missouri River Basin. . . . Truman's determination led to the construction of a water infrastructure that prepared the region for modern development."[32]

One feature of modern development triggered environmental changes as multiform and intractable as any in the twentieth century, the postwar proliferation of suburbs. America today is a distinctively suburban nation. While Americans since the mid-nineteenth century had been relocating their residences outside central cities, between 1945 and 1960 the outward flow became a torrent. Kenneth T. Jackson, the preeminent historian of the suburban experience, located the impulse for suburbs in a complex blend of cultural values, economic advantages, and government policies. During the Truman

30. Nimz, "Rivers That Work," 209, bases his conclusion on Richardson, *Dams, Parks, and Politics*, 26–28. The Democrats barely lost Oregon.

31. Nimz, "Rivers That Work," 208; *Oregonian*, June 8, 1948, 1, and June 11, 1948, 1; "Truman Mans Reclamation Pumps," *Public Utilities Fortnightly* 42 (July 1, 1948): 37–38.

32. Nimz, "Rivers That Work," 239–40.

presidency, federal policy subsidized suburbanization. Postwar suburbs grew so quickly after 1945 because the federal government encouraged citizens to buy homes, underwrote the easy credit needed to finance the purchases, facilitated provision of the cheap energy required to fuel expansion, and helped state and local governments build the highways essential to speed the depopulation of city cores.[33]

Kansas City, home to Harry Truman nearly all his life, changed its shape as much as any other metropolitan area. Of course, the president did not himself cause suburbanization there or in any other city. In many ways, in and out of office, he remained a proud booster of rural small towns and the Kansas City of his young manhood. Nevertheless, policies he promoted and executed while president forever shattered old categories marking rural from urban. He applauded the very forces—prosperity, mobility, opportunity— that did so much to obliterate the Kansas City that had shaped his life.[34]

During his presidency, Kansas City's municipal area nearly doubled, yet its population remained roughly the same. Within two decades after he left office, the city would double in area again, but within its postwar boundaries population had actually declined. By 1963, Kansas City was the third largest American city in terms of geographic size with only the twenty-sixth largest population. And a startling, ominous demographic trend had become apparent: almost one hundred thousand fewer white people lived within the old boundaries in 1970 than in 1960. The Kansas City metropolitan area had bifurcated, like so many other great American urban complexes between 1945 and 1970. New houses and inhabitants poured into the suburbs, which were now overwhelmingly white, while African Americans increasingly lived in the center city, where jobs, new housing, and private investment were all withering.[35]

Suburbanization happened in the decade after World War II because American prosperity and national values encouraged citizens to leave farms and small rural towns as well as central cities. Their mass migration to the suburbs ultimately transformed the shape of every American metropolitan area. Far more people settled into suburban residential neighborhoods be-

33. Jackson, *Crabgrass Frontier: The Suburbanization of the United States* (New York: Oxford University Press, 1985).

34. McCullough, *Truman.*

35. Sherry Lamb Schirmer and Richard D. McKinzie, *At the River's Bend: An Illustrated History of Kansas City* (Woodland Hills, Calif.: Windsor, 1982), 201; Rick Montgomery and Shirl Kasper, *Kansas City: An American Story* (Kansas City: Kansas City Star Books, 1999), 285–87.

tween 1945 and 1955 than migrated overland across the Oregon and California Trails between 1845 and 1865. Federal housing, transportation, veterans, and educational policies during the Truman administration encouraged suburbanization. By housing these migrating millions in areas that had previously been agricultural, land developers and home builders "were free to cause a variety of environmental problems," according to Adam Rome's history of America's postwar suburban transformation. "The construction of tract-house subdivisions after World War II changed the nature of millions of acres of land," Rome found. Builders polluted surface water and groundwater with septic tanks. They leveled hills, filled wetlands, and packed floodplains with houses, stores, and parking lots. They cleared vegetation from millions of acres, altering and often destroying wildlife habitat. And to heat and cool suburban single-family homes, they installed inefficient furnaces and air-conditioners within structures only minimally insulated, requiring generation of far more electricity and the burning of tons of coal.[36]

A quarter century after the suburban exodus began, a presidential commission on population concluded in 1972, "During the rapid expansion of suburban areas since World War II, we failed to plan for anticipated growth; instead, we allowed it to spread at will. . . . Without proper efforts to plan where and how future urban growth should occur, and without strong governmental leadership to implement the plans, the problems of sprawl, congestion, inadequate open space, and environmental deterioration will grow at an ever-increasing scale."[37]

Federal lending and housing policies, endorsed by President Truman to house returning veterans and relocated war workers and to stimulate continued national economic expansion, fueled staggering rates of suburban home building after 1945. By the 1950s, suburban expansion consumed more than a million acres per year—a territory larger than Rhode Island. Between 1950 and 1959, builders erected more than fifteen million homes, most located at the edges of cities. Between 1940 and 1949, about seven million new homes had been built, nearly all after 1945. By contrast, during the 1930s, builders completed barely two million new homes. A decade after the war had ended, 60 percent of Americans owned their homes. In 1930, the figure was about 40 percent.[38]

Land use in the new suburbs was, of course, primarily a matter of local

---

36. Rome, *The Bulldozer in the Countryside: Suburban Sprawl and the Rise of American Environmentalism* (New York: Cambridge University Press, 2001), xi, 256.

37. Ibid., 143.

38. Ibid., 35 (ownership), 120 (Rhode Island).

politics and policy. Yet local and state governments were essentially managing a land rush caused by federal actions, coping at the grass roots with national policies enforced by presidential and congressional choices. In the aftermath of World War II, the Truman administration decided to both solve the shortage of housing and allay fears of a new economic depression by encouraging suburban home building and the road building that supported it. "The federal government," Rome argues, "had played a key role in the housing revolution" that ignited a record number of home starts in the late 1940s. In 1949, builders finished more than one million new homes for the first time in American history. The next year, two million went up. Fueling the surge in home building were federal grants and loan guarantees to mass-production builders, such as William Levitt; cheap mortgage insurance to stimulate borrowing; and inexpensive credit targeted to demobilized veterans.[39]

Optimistic, hopeful suburbanites moved into their new homes under a cloud of nuclear anxiety. President Truman's contributions to the proliferation of nuclear weapons are beyond the scope of this essay. Undoubtedly, though, his presidency's pursuit of nuclear supremacy during the Cold War made the natural world a different, more forbidding place after 1953. Weapons production and testing during the postwar years led the government to sacrifice both human health and environmental quality. Even today, the extent of pollution attributable to military activities during the Cold War is unknown.[40] At just one nuclear-weapons research and production facility, the Hanford site in southeastern Washington State, more than two hundred billion gallons of waste were discharged into the air, water, and land between 1945 and 1985. Bordering the Columbia River, Hanford is, by all definitions, the most heavily contaminated of all the nuclear weapons sites scattered coast to coast. On this one small outpost of the nuclear establishment created by Truman Cold War strategy, covering barely more land than Jackson County, Missouri, and Wyandotte County, Kansas, the federal government's "sole mission is now waste management and cleanup."[41]

39. Ibid., 15–16.
40. Disposition of land in Johnson County, Kansas, once occupied by the Sunflower Army Ammunition Plant continues to be complicated by ignorance about the quantity, location, and toxicity of buried waste materials (*Kansas City Star*, May 22, 2003, B-2; *Lawrence Journal-World*, February 6, 2003, 1B). Toxic materials discharged by the U.S. Department of Energy nuclear-bomb component plant, which has operated for a half century on Bannister Road in southern Kansas City, Missouri, still pollute the lower Blue River watershed (*Kansas City Star*, February 15, 2003, B-2).
41. Donald G. Kaufman and Cecilia M. Franz, *Biosphere 2000: Protecting Our Global Environment* (New York: HarperCollins, 1993), 390–93.

The globe itself bears the scars of the Cold War. Not only Americans suffered and died because of governments' frantic pursuit of security through nuclear might. Russians and Eastern Europeans, disgusted by the environmental destruction inflicted on them and their landscapes by the Soviet system, challenged Communist dictatorships in the late 1980s. Citizen demands for truth telling and environmental protection proved one of the most corrosive acids that ultimately ate away Communism's legitimacy in the former Eastern Bloc.[42] In the United States, though, people in the West may have paid the highest price for President Truman's determination to build a nuclear arsenal capable of protecting not only the United States but all of its Cold War allies as well. "The race for nuclear superiority against the Soviets took precedence over the safety of Americans," concludes a recent survey of American history, while the "Atomic West" paid the price for preeminence "with serious environmental costs."[43]

In his January 1953 farewell to the nation, Truman "dream[ed] out loud just a little." Any listener surprised by his "dream of the future" must have been sleeping during the previous eight years. As he had since taking office in 1945, the president linked national security in a dangerous, wartorn world to economic security at home. In fact, although the main thrust of his Farewell Address dealt with foreign and military policies he had pursued to wage the Cold War, his other major topic was purely economic. He restated two principles that had shaped his natural-resources policy since becoming president: controlling nature with technology to serve material prosperity and guaranteeing national security by stimulating permanent economic expansion. "We can use the peaceful tools that science has forged for us to do away with poverty and human misery everywhere on earth," he urged. From the Tigris and Euphrates basins in the Mideast to northeast Africa to South America, the president imagined "developments [that] will come so fast we will not recognize the world in which we now live." At home, "we . . . have learned how to attain real prosperity for our people . . . [and] all have better incomes and more of the good things of life than ever before in the history of the world."

The Truman era's environmental history transformed his and our world. Writing the history of the postwar years requires new scrutiny of environmental changes. We need to reassess the cultural values—mastery of nature,

42. Douglas R. Weiner, *A Little Corner of Freedom: Russian Nature Protection from Stalin to Gorbachev* (Berkeley: University of California Press, 1999).

43. Paul S. Boyer et al., *The Enduring Vision: A History of the American People* (Boston: Houghton Mifflin, 2000), 2:797a–b.

technological worship, boundless optimism—that sanctioned them. Environmental history remains a subject too little understood by Cold War era historians. Truman surely refashioned world politics, American race relations, and the citizen's relationship to the federal government. Just as profoundly, his decisions remade and damaged the natural systems on which all life depends. To attain his goals of material prosperity, national security, and global influence, Truman's administration commanded natural forces and resources to serve the single-minded cause of economic growth. A half century after he left office, the destructive power Truman's presidency unleashed on American nature reminds us that choices have lasting consequences.[44]

History happened to Harry Truman. A president as well as the most ordinary citizen must respond to past events that constrain options and force actions. But we also, presidents and citizens alike, make our own history. From this blend of momentum and choice emerged President Truman's distinctive contribution to environmental history. Of great moment to the president were resource policies his predecessor, Franklin Roosevelt, established during the Great Depression and World War II. With hardly any of them did Truman disagree. As president, he persistently pursued what he believed was the general goal of both the New Deal and Roosevelt's war-mobilization strategy: to put nature to work in the quest for the individual citizen's economic security and the nation's material prosperity. As the leader of the Democratic Party after 1945, Truman committed the majority party to his postwar version of FDR's liberalism. The Fair Deal linked the principles of economic growth and broadly distributed prosperity to widespread, intensive development of natural resources. In some measure, therefore, the Truman presidency merely extended into the postwar era environmental policies at the core of the New Deal. Roosevelt's political legacy thus determined Truman's environmental history.[45]

Like the second Roosevelt, as well as the first, Harry Truman called his policy "conservation." In his hands, though, that well-worn doctrine came to

44. Mark W. T. Harvey, *A Symbol of Wilderness: Echo Park and the American Conservation Movement* (Albuquerque: University of New Mexico Press, 1994); Richardson, *Dams, Parks, and Politics*.

45. Anthony J. Badger, *The New Deal: The Depression Years, 1933–1940* (New York: Hill and Wang, 1989); A. L. Riesch Owen, *Conservation Under F.D.R.* (Baltimore: Praeger Special Studies, 1983). Neal M. Maher, "A New Deal Body Politic: Landscape, Labor, and the Civilian Conservation Corps," *Environmental History* 7 (July 2002): 435–61, and Paul S. Sutter, *Driven Wild: How the Fight against Automobiles Launched the Modern Wilderness Movement* (Seattle: University of Washington Press, 2002), offer a fresh look at New Deal resource policies.

emphasize permanent prosperity based on planned development of nature's bounty. Neglected, even denied, was conservation's promise of limiting human wants according to nature's sovereign imperatives. Theodore Roosevelt's Progressive conservation implied restraint, at times even commanded responsibility as the duty development owed to the future. Truman's view of conservation, by contrast, reflected two epochal events unknown to the first Roosevelt: national economic collapse and global struggle for national survival. These searing experiences, intensified by the Cold War anxiety he both incited and tried to allay, fired the president's determination, once in power, to make nature serve human needs.[46]

Truman's actions, between 1945 and 1953, were not all foreordained. He could have chosen to reexamine New Deal assumptions about comprehensive, planned exploitation of river basins. He could have encouraged the kind of scientific research and popular protest that were, at the postwar's outset, potentially capable of infusing conservation with restraint and humility.[47] As he challenged the southern congressional barons and courthouse politicians of his party on race relations, he could have stubbornly insisted that federal biologists' and grassroots activists' concerns about environmental damage deserved a fair hearing.[48] He did none of these things, instead insisting that the federal government's highest duty was to secure the nation against another economic collapse and new foreign adversaries. By defining the postwar's environmental agenda solely in terms of prosperity and security, Truman delayed for two decades Americans' reckoning with the disastrous implications for the earth of full employment and national defense.

Not far from the Truman Presidential Library, the Missouri River slides eastward past Independence. Inhabitants of the Missouri Basin are trying to make sense of what the Truman administration did to their river, struggling often loudly and rancorously to make the Army Engineers' and Reclamation Bureau's dams serve purposes other than flood control and subsidized barge traffic. Half a continent east, in Florida, citizens are slowly struggling to undo grave damage done to the Everglades by drainage channels carved during Truman's presidency. And out West, in the vast Snake-Columbia Basin,

---

46. Theodore Roosevelt offered one of the best distillations of his conservation philosophy in his opening address to the first presidential conservation conference, held in the White House in May 1908. *Proceedings of a Conference of Governors in the White House, 1908* (Washington, D.C.: U.S. Government Printing Office, 1909), 3–11.

47. Karl Brooks, "'Powerless' No More: Postwar Judges and Pacific Northwest Hydroelectrification, 1946–1967," *Idaho Yesterdays* 45 (Winter 2001–2002): 11–26.

48. Donald R. McCoy and Richard T. Ruetten, *Quest and Response: Minority Rights and the Truman Administration* (Lawrence: University Press of Kansas, 1973).

biologists desperately debate economists in hopes of salvaging some pale remnant of the silver-bright river of fish nearly extinguished by Truman's dams and locks.[49] In all these places in our American landscape, we are trying to find our way through and around the dense, permanent bulk of the Truman environmental legacy.

Like history itself, the natural world both remakes itself and is being remade, a work in time and space forever undone and largely beyond human capacity to direct for long. Some thoughtful Americans who watched the Berlin Wall fall in November 1989 quite rightly reflected that, more than three decades earlier, Harry Truman predicted Soviet-style Communism's demise at the hands of free people. Democracy in Eastern Europe is thus part of Truman's legacy, a prediction foretold in his 1953 Farewell Address. Other thoughtful Americans gaze with barely suppressed rage at a concrete monument still standing implacably, McNary Dam on the mid-Columbia River. This dam hastened the probable destruction of the world's greatest salmon fishery. As much a part of Truman's contemporary legacy as the section of Berlin Wall now standing in the Truman Presidential Museum, McNary poses a question unanswered yet: how and when shall free people, working in concert with nature's own unquenchable power, force a reckoning with this concrete symbol of the Truman presidency's environmental history?

49. Thorson, *River of Promise;* "Big Muddy Blues," *Kansas City Star,* November 9–11, 1997, A-1 (series on Missouri River); October 5, 2000, B-12 (Stephen Ambrose column); June 5, 2003, B-4 (Missouri River Conference); "Everglades Restoration Plan," *Washington Post,* June 23–27, 2002, A1 (series on Everglades restoration); Keith Petersen, *River of Life/Channel of Death* (Lewiston, Idaho: Confluence Press, 1995); Joseph E. Taylor III, *Making Salmon: An Environmental History of the Northwest Fisheries Crisis* (Seattle: University of Washington Press, 1999).

·' DECEMBER 5, 1947 ·

CONFIDENTIAL: ·The following address of the President to be delivered
at the dedication ·of Everglades National Park, Everglades City, Florida,
MUST BE HELD. IN CONFIDENCE UNTIL RELEASED. ·

NOTE: Release is automatic at 2:50 P.M., E.S.T., Saturday,·
December 6, 1947, or when delivery begins, if earlier. The same release applies to all newspapers, radio announcers and news broadcasters.

            Please guard against premature publication or radio
announcement.

                        CHARLES G. ROSS
                        Secretary to the President

- -

            Not often in these demanding days are we able to lay
aside the problems of the times, and turn to a project whose great
value lies in the enrichment of the human spirit. Today we mark
the achievement of another great conservation victory. We have
permanently safeguarded an irreplaceable primitive area. We have
assembled to dedicate to the use of all the people for all time,
the Everglades National Park.

            Here in Everglades City we can savor the atmosphere of
this beautiful tropical area. Southeast of us lies the coast of
the Everglades Park, ·ut by islands and estuaries of the Gulf of
Mexico. Here are deep rivers, giant groves of colorful mangrove
trees, prairie marshes and innumerable lakes and streams.

            In this Park we shall preserve tarpon, trout and pompano,
bear, deer and crocodiles -- and rare birds of great beauty. We
shall protect hundreds of kinds of wildlife which might otherwise
soon be extinct.

            The benefits our Nation will derive from this dedication
will outlast the youngest of us. They will increase with the passage
of the years. Few actions could make a more lasting contribution to
the enjoyment of the American people than the establishment of the
Everglades National Park.

            Our national park system is a clear expression of the
idealism of the American people. Without regard for sectional
rivalries or for party politics, the Nation has advanced constantly ·
in the last 75 years in the protection of its natural beauties
and wonders.

            The success of our efforts to conserve the scenery and
wildlife of the country can be measured in popular use. The
national park system covers but a fraction of one per cent of the
area of the United States, but over 25 million of our fellow
countrymen have visited our national parks within the past year.
Each citizen returned to his home with a refreshed spirit and a
greater appreciation of the majesty and beauty of our country.

            These are the people's parks, owned by young and old,
by those in the cities and those on the farms. Most of them are
ours today because there were Americans many years ago who
exercised vision, patience, and unselfish devotion in the battle
for conservation.

                                                    (OVER)

320

Each national park possesses qualities distinctive enough to make its preservation a matter of concern to the whole Nation. Certainly, this Everglades area has more than its share of features unique to these United States. Here are no lofty peaks seeking the sky, no mighty glaciers or rushing streams wearing away the uplifted land. Here is land, tranquil in its quiet beauty, serving not as the source of water but as the last receiver of it. To its natural abundance we owe the spectacular plant and animal life that distinguishes this place from all others in our country.

Our park system also embraces such national shrines as Jamestown Island, the Statue of Liberty, and the battlefields of Yorktown and Gettysburg. These historic places — as much as the scenic areas — also need to be protected with all the devotion at our command in these days when we are learning again the importance of an understanding loyalty to our national heritage.

Our parks are but one part of the national effort to conserve our natural resources. Upon these resources our life as a nation depends. Our high level of employment and our extraordinary production are being limited by scarcities in some items of our natural wealth. This is the time to develop and replenish our basic resources.

Conservation has been practiced for many decades and preached for many more, yet only in recent years has it become plain that we cannot afford to conserve in a haphazard or piecemeal manner. No part of our conservation program can be slighted if we want to make full use of our resources and have full protection against future emergencies.

If we waste our minerals by careless mining and processing, we shall not be able to build the machinery to till the land. If we waste the forests by careless lumbering, we shall lack housing and construction materials for factory, farm, and mine. If we waste the water through failure to build hydroelectric plants, we shall burn our reserves of coal and oil needlessly. If we waste our soil through erosion and failure to replenish our fields, we shall destroy the source of our people's food.

Each conservation need is dependent on the others. A slashed and burned forest brings erosion of uplands and fills downstream reservoirs with silt so that water power is lessened and irrigated farms lose their water supplies. Eroded farmlands contribute to devastating floods. Uncontrolled rivers mean lost electricity, farms without water, and perennial and increasing flood danger.

To maintain our natural wealth we must engage in full and complete conservation of all our resources.

Full conservation of our energy resources can be accomplished by continued construction of dams, hydroelectric plants and transmission lines; by greater use of natural gas, by research for more efficient methods of extraction of coal and oil, and by exploration for new reserves.

In forests, conservation can be achieved by adhering to the principle of sustained yield and forest management so that timber is harvested each year just as other crops are. This should be true for both privately owned and publicly owned forest lands.

In farmland, conservation can be achieved by expanding and intensifying the many soil conservation practices developed by our agricultural technicians to sustain productivity. The area of irrigated land can be expanded materially with new reclamation projects. Range lands in the West can be protected by the control of erosion and by the enforcement of safe limits on the number of grazing stock.

In minerals, we can come closer to the proper balance with increased efficiency in extraction and with scientific exploration for new reserves. When ores contain several minerals, we should extract all the useful products and waste none. Despite a bounteous nature, this country has never been self sufficient in all minerals. We have always imported minerals to meet these deficiencies and we must continue to do so.

In water, we need to prevent further dropping of the water table, which in many areas is dangerously low. Surface water must be stored, and ground water used in such a way as to cause the least depletion. Although the water level is high now here in the Everglades, there has been damage from a lowered fresh-water table, and, during the war, fires raged through the glades -- fires fed by dry grass which should have been covered by water.

The battle for conservation cannot be limited to the winning of new conquests. Like liberty itself, conservation must be fought for unceasingly to protect earlier victories.

Public lands and parks, our forests and our mineral reserves, are subject to many destructive influences. We have to remain constantly vigilant to prevent raids by those who would selfishly exploit our common heritage for their private gain. Such raids on our natural resources are not examples of enterprise and initiative. They are attempts to take from all the people for the benefit of a few.

As always in the past when the people's property has been threatened, men and women whose primary concern has been their country's welfare have risen to oppose these selfish attacks. We can be thankful for their efforts, as we can be grateful for the efforts of citizens, private groups, local governments, and the State of Florida which, joined in common purpose, have made possible the establishment of the Everglades National Park.

The establishment of this Park is an object lesson and an example to the entire Nation that sound conservation depends upon the joint endeavors of the people and their several governments. Responsibility is shared by the town, the state, and the Federal Government; by societies and legislatures and all lovers of nature.

No man can know every element that makes a nation great. Certainly the lofty spirit of its people, the daily cooperation, the helpfulness of one citizen to another are elements. A nation's ability to provide a good living for its people in industry, business, and on the farm is another. The intelligent recognition by its citizens of a nation's responsibility for world order, world peace, and world recovery is still another.

The wise use of our natural resources is the foundation of our effectiveness in all these efforts.

The problems of peace, like those of war, require courage and sustained effort. If we wish this Nation to remain prosperous, if we wish it still to be "the home of the free," we can have it so. But, if we fail to heed the lesson of other nations which have permitted their natural resources to be wasted and destroyed, then we shall reap a sorry harvest.

And for conservation of the human spirit, we need places such as Everglades National Park where we may be more keenly aware of our Creator's infinitely varied, infinitely beautiful, and infinitely bountiful handiwork. Here we may draw strength and peace of mind from our surroundings.

Here we can truly understand what the Psalmist meant when he sang: "He maketh me to lie down in green pastures, He leadeth me beside the still waters; He restoreth my soul."

Using the Farewell Address to Teach the Truman Presidency

Jeff Gall

A Unique Historical Conference

During the week of July 14, 2003, two worlds that rarely converse came together for an extraordinary conference at the Harry S. Truman Presidential Museum and Library in Independence, Missouri. These two worlds were the world of higher education and academic research and the world of secondary education and the day-to-day teaching of junior high and high school students. The conference showed conclusively that these two worlds have a great deal to offer one another.

Unlike most historical conferences in which historians talk to one another, this conference brought together fourteen Truman scholars and thirty high school and junior high teachers from the Midwest. Most came from urban schools. The objective of Richard Kirkendall, the conference organizer, was to provide an experience that would be beneficial to both groups.

I came to the conference with perhaps a unique perspective on its goals. I have lived in both of the worlds represented. I was a high school history teacher for fourteen years before becoming a history professor at Truman State University, where I have taught for the last six. Both worlds have their models for professional growth, and over the years I have found both to be lacking.

As a high school teacher, professional growth opportunities were offered under the banner of "in service." I know very few teachers who ever found such "opportunities" very relevant or meaningful. Typically, the administration brought in an educational "expert," who was not from my school and who was not in my field, to offer suggestions on how to better reach kids. Sometimes I picked up a new idea, but rarely were these sessions *memorable.*

As a historian, I attend historical conferences where scholars *read* papers to their peers. The word *read* needs to be taken literally. They typically sit before their small audience and actually read their work, often centered on topics that lack meaning or relevance to a broader audience outside the historical profession. This format also never struck me as particularly engaging or *memorable.*

The conference at the Truman Library on "Harry's Farewell" improved on both of these models in remarkable ways by building meaningful bridges between the worlds of academia and of public education. It began with scholars writing provocative, accessible papers on important, relevant topics. It continued with talented teachers, who were all clearly committed to the young people they teach, focusing on how to take the issues raised in the papers into their classrooms. The final component of the conference, and in fact the "glue" that held it together, was the Truman Library's educational staff, which made many of the library and museum's resources that related to the conference topics available to both groups. The educational staff also worked throughout the week to provide "hands-on" teaching examples from the library's web site (www.trumanlibrary.org) and numerous educational initiatives. In the minds of all who were involved, this conference provided a professional development opportunity that was *memorable* indeed.

It was memorable because public school teachers and university scholars thrived on the chance to talk about historically significant topics and big ideas. Such topics included: Truman and his view of "the people," the atomic bomb, Korea, Truman and civil rights, Truman and the economy, Truman's "prophecy," and Truman's foreign policy. Also discussed were topics Truman did not broach in his farewell, such as the Red Scare, women's rights, immigration, and the environment. Following each scholar's presentation, a panel of teachers took charge of critiquing the paper and sharing teaching ideas they drew from the content presented.

The scholars and teachers went even deeper into the prescribed topics by analyzing primary sources from the varied archives housed at the Truman Library. Each scholar's paper was accompanied by artifacts or archival material assembled by the library's staff. In some cases this meant a Truman diary entry, in others a political cartoon, or even a sound recording from a Truman speech. And of course the teachers had an opportunity to frequently move from the conference presentations to see for themselves the rich materials on display in the Truman Museum. In all cases, teachers focused on how such sources can be used in classrooms to help students learn critical thinking skills (analysis and evaluation), and more important learn to "do" history for themselves. When students personalize history and enter the world of historical figures by reading the papers they wrote and listening to the words they uttered, the process of self-discovery takes history from the pages of a dull textbook and makes it real and engaging.

Throughout the week, one could not help but notice how empowering it was for the two worlds to come together in the conference room, on breaks, and over meals. I am confident that the classrooms these teachers lead will be enriched by the deep content and pedagogical discussions they shared throughout the week.

Teaching Ideas

As the conference went through the papers, discussions flowed as to how to *teach* the topic presented in the paper. In the rest of this chapter I will try to encapsulate some of the ideas that flowed from those discussions. They represent the collected offerings of the scholars and teachers present at the conference.

Alonzo Hamby's paper, "The Politics of Democracy: Harry S. Truman and the American People," set a tone for the conference. With the discussion of this paper, a consensus emerged among the teachers and scholars. That consensus was the importance of taking the Farewell Address, learning the "facts" about Harry S. Truman, and then tying those facts to *universal themes* that will engage students and spark their interest in history. For example, Hamby discusses charisma and Truman's lack thereof. This should help students focus on the importance of this attribute in a candidate. What are its plusses and its minuses? Could Truman be elected today with his lack of charisma? If not, what has changed about our society, our electoral process, and our ways of assessing candidates? Relating to his lack of charisma, Hamby contrasts Truman with Franklin Roosevelt and Eisenhower, noting that Truman tried to use his "ordinary" status as a way to connect with the people. Students might analyze the risks of such an approach to leadership. To continue this evaluation of leadership traits, students could brainstorm a list of characteristics of a great president, assess whether Truman possessed those attributes, and compare Truman with another president based on the same list.

Another theme in Hamby's paper that could be helpful to students is Truman's growth in his vision of "the people." Hamby told the conference that, by and large, Truman had an "open and tolerant personality." This is shown in his paper as Truman's view of the people expands from rural, white, Protestant people to include urban dwellers, Irish Catholics, Jews, small businessmen, and blacks. This transition from a provincial to a more open-minded view can be used in the area of character education as students compare their own journey toward acceptance of diversity with that of Truman's.

Finally, Hamby's paper generated a great deal of discussion among the assembled teachers about ways to teach the political process. Like all politicians, Truman had to negotiate the needs of multiple interest groups to get elected and stay in office. One classroom activity that could illustrate this would be a mock election in which a student could role-play Truman meeting with and speaking to several interest groups in 1948. He would have to listen to each group's demands and then adapt his speech to appeal to each group's core constituency. This also relates to a key point in Hamby's paper, the tension Truman faced between idealism and pragmatism. This is certainly a universal dilemma faced by any person entering politics. Truman's experience can be used to illuminate this for students, and contemporary examples can make the quandary faced by today's political leaders relevant to young people.

In his paper on claims Truman made in his farewell address about economic achievements, Robert Collins analyzes the degree to which Truman was right in claiming success for prosperity, economic security, and what he believed to be the fairest distribution of income in recent history. Collins concludes Truman did have some reason to claim credit in all three areas. Teachers at the conference believed the paper would be an effective tool for teaching important vocabulary terms, such as *Gross National Product*. But once again, it was the more universal themes students can draw from these factual issues that they believed would be most engaging. Truman's definition of prosperity and a "fair" distribution of income might lead students to evaluate what *is* prosperity and what is a *fair* distribution of income? By comparing concepts of prosperity and income distribution in the United States with the same concepts in different regions of the world, teachers believed they could develop effective interdisciplinary lessons (history, geography, economics). Even within our own nation, students can see trends toward certain aspects of prosperity beginning during the Truman years and continuing to our present day. Examples include the growth of suburbia and the Sun Belt and the corresponding deterioration of urban areas and the industrial heartland.

Students can also discuss American income distribution in 1952 and compare it to that of today. If Truman believed the distribution in his era was moving toward fairness, what would he say about today? Can we as a society ever decide what constitutes a fair distribution of income?

Carol Anderson's reappraisal of the Truman civil rights legacy stimulated a great deal of discussion among the teachers gathered at the conference about teaching approaches to this crucial topic. Whereas a great deal of Truman historiography lauds his desegregation of the armed forces, his inclusion of a civil rights plank in the 1948 Democratic platform, his willingness to speak to African American groups, and, perhaps most of all, his ability to grow beyond his racist upbringing, Anderson strongly criticizes the Truman administration for failing to address key civil rights crises in the areas of voting, housing, and lynching. From the platform, she argued that saying "at least he tried" seems to be acceptable only when talking about civil rights. She went on to say that the standard should be what did he actually *do* in the areas where he could have done *something*. Teachers saw many aspects of this paper that would be fruitful for classroom use. Beginning with a look at rhetoric versus reality, students can examine the often stark difference between what our leaders say and what actually follows. There are certainly limits to what a president can do. Even a president with a clear vision of justice can be limited by staff members who are more interested in placating key members of Congress (like southern Democrats in the late 1940s) and maintaining the status quo. Students can take this idea and compare it to what citizens can accomplish by working together. Real change in the civil rights movement came not from the actions of presidents or political leaders, but as a result of people taking collective action themselves. This provides a meaningful lesson for students on the importance of civic engagement. Teachers at the conference also recommended that Anderson's paper be used as a way to stimulate student research into local history. Was there redlining in their city? What about voting patterns? Last, teachers believed that the horrific stories of civil rights atrocities described in Anderson's paper were important for students to examine. The conference discussed the fact that these incidents were occurring at the same time the Nuremberg Trials were shedding light on the horrors of the holocaust. The irony of this is certainly something students can analyze.

Needless to say, Richard Frank's paper on Truman and the atomic bomb elicited a number of classroom suggestions from the teachers in attendance. Teachers find that this rich topic nearly never fails to engage students. Frank's paper helps frame some of the issues involved in new ways. One of his key points is that to fully understand any historical decision, one must (as much as possible) view the decision as decision makers did *at the time* the decision was made. This will help students understand how "presentism" often colors our view of the past in ways that are at times unfair to historical actors. This is a topic for which students can do their own primary source investigation, just as Frank did and just as other historians do. The ample primary resources relating to this topic available at www.trumanlibrary.org are an outstanding place to begin. Such primary source analysis will go a long way to help students enter the world of the past. This topic also provides a prime opportunity to introduce students to the concept of shifting historiography, something the teachers at the conference believed is lacking in most curriculums. One can quite easily find articles from revisionist historians to contrast with Frank's paper and thus illustrate to students the interpretive nature of dealing with historical evidence. Teachers at the conference also believed this topic was ideal for the discussion of the place of ethics and morality in decision making. A lesson might begin with a discussion of the evolving Western notion of "just war" theory. They then envisioned a student panel assessing Truman's decision to use atomic weapons, made up of students role-playing veterans, religious leaders, military leaders, Japanese survivors, and newspaper editors. Each of these roles could also be used to illustrate how people of different perspectives can read the same primary sources with very different eyes.

This topic is also ideal for helping students "personalize" the past. Students can put themselves in Truman's shoes by having him defend his decision at a "press conference." Students can tap into the sentiment of the times by writing a newspaper editorial either defending or criticizing Truman. They can enter the past by writing a journal entry from the perspective of Truman, an American soldier in the Pacific, or a Japanese witness to Hiroshima or Nagasaki. Finally, students can explore the dynamics of decision making by looking at key historical decisions like the one to use the bomb and employing a framework like the one used in the Truman Museum's own "Decision Theaters." Those theaters encourage visitors to enter Truman's decision making process by considering public opinion at the time of the decision, what Truman's advisers were telling him, what the national interest dictated, and how his personal values colored his thinking. All of these exercises will go a long way toward helping students do something critically important in a history classroom—learn to make a historical argument based on evidence.

Mary Ann Heiss's analysis of Truman's foreign policy illuminates another rich topic to teach historiography and to generate student connections between historical events and today's world. To begin with, her paper can be used to show students how historical interpretation is not black and white. Each topic Heiss addresses illustrates the nuances of historical points of view. Her footnotes alone can be used to show students how divergent historical interpretation can be on any given topic. Her analysis also reminds us of the importance of introducing students to historical complexity. The values embedded in the Truman Doctrine reflect the very best American traditions. Yet the regimes supported under the banner of the policy did not always reflect those values (the Greek military government, for instance). The teachers at the conference noted that when teaching these historical principles, Truman's view of foreign policy can also be used to discuss how leaders use and misuse history. Heiss points out that Truman frequently drew on historical lessons when explaining his decisions. He certainly did so in his Farewell Address. Students can delve into historical theory as they discuss whether history can indeed be used as a predictor of the future, as Truman clearly believed. How *should* our leaders use history to evaluate the present?

As a vehicle for teaching historical facts that are clearly relevant to today's world, the gathered teachers believed Heiss's paper was laden with information that students will find relevant. The United Nations and NATO are just two examples of organizations dating to the Truman era that students can investigate to discover their contemporary functions. But beyond these facts, the teachers believed a discussion of Truman's foreign policy is a logical place to help students begin to think critically about our nation's role in the world today. As Heiss points out, the Truman administration ushered in a revolution in foreign policy. With new alliances and a new global involvement, the United States began to assert itself in unprecedented ways. Again using the Truman era to give students the opportunity to evaluate large, universal themes, this seemed to the teachers to be an ideal time to lead students in a discussion of the proper role of America on the world stage both then and now. In addition, how did Truman use our opponent then (the USSR) to help define who we are? How do we use our opponent today (international terrorism) to do the same?

William Stueck's paper on Truman and Korea brought forth a frank discussion among the teachers and scholars on how Korea truly is a "forgotten war" in many of our classrooms. At this point in the conference, the Truman Library's educational staff sent the teachers to explore the museum's recently opened exhibit on the Korean War. That was followed by a forum among the educators on how to make classroom use of historical artifacts like those on display. Teachers discussed how the students could be given many of the dramatic photographs in the exhibit and asked to provide captions or to write before-and-after stories, based on their knowledge of the history of the conflict. The flags of North Korea and South Korea could be analyzed for symbolism. An M-1 rifle could be used to illustrate evolving military technology between then and now. Psychological warfare pamphlets could be used to teach students a military strategy they rarely consider. Even MacArthur's rumpled hat could be used to teach students some of the personality conflicts that led to tension between the general and his commander in chief. One of the most dramatic artifacts the teachers discussed was a Purple Heart on display that was found in Truman's desk at the library soon after he died in 1972. With it was a letter from a father whose son died in Korea. The letter asked Truman to take back the award and expressed the sentiment that the president's daughter, rather than the man's son, should have been sent to die. What a powerful way to illustrate the personal impact of war on both presidents and ordinary people.

Stueck's analysis of Truman's handling of the Korean conflict provided the teachers at the conference with the opportunity to discuss the many important concepts that can be illustrated to students by exploring this war. Many see the "imperial presidency" as taking shape in a war that was never officially declared by Congress. Investigating how Truman handled his relations with the general public as the war became unpopular is an excellent way for students to see the challenges facing leaders in difficult times. The teachers believed that the reasons nations go to war when a threat is not clearly direct and imminent could be explored by studying the origins of wars from Korea to Iraq. Students can also be challenged to think critically by contrasting Truman's use of the United Nations as he led the nation to war to President Bush's hesitancy to do so in our present conflict. What has changed? Which approach was most in line with our national interests? Were Truman's actions in Korea justified when viewing them through the lens of the UN Charter? Were Bush's? On the deepest level, the teachers concluded that the Korean War could be used to challenge students to assess why nations go to war at all. Once again using the facts of the Truman era to open up big ideas and universal themes, a class could consider what makes a war the only option for our nation—direct military threat, perceived aggression, injustice, a threat to needed resources, spreading ideologies that run counter to our values, or as a way to deter our enemies in other regions of the world? Our entry into the Korean War can be used to help students focus on today's discussion of the doctrine of preemption as a justification for war. As students study the current status of South Korea and the state of tension between our nation and North Korea, this once again brings extreme relevance to the classroom.

Randall Woods's paper on Truman's "prophecy" serves as an excellent overview of Cold War policy shifts for any class studying recent U.S. history. It also provides the opportunity to encourage students to look deep into the forces that led to the Cold War. Teachers at the conference thought that students need to understand Truman's vision of containment and why he believed it would triumph. This begins with his belief that the Soviet model was flawed and did not account for basic human nature. Was he correct? Students can read Truman's prediction about victory in the Cold War, then study the end of the Cold War. Was Truman indeed prophetic? In his Farewell Address, Truman has a utopian dream of what the post–Cold War world might be like, especially with the harnessing of atomic energy. Now that we are more than a decade beyond the end of the Cold War, students can assess what aspects of today's world square with Truman's dream and what aspects do not. What has kept his dream from becoming a reality? The prophecy section of the Farewell Address clearly reveals Truman's worldview—his view of America and his view of the Soviet Union. Students should be able to clearly see how that worldview impacted Truman's key Cold War policy decisions.

One interesting teaching suggestion coming out of the conference relating to Truman's prophecy was a panel discussion in which students choose to award a grand prize for efforts leading to the end of the Cold War. Students could work in teams researching "their" candidate, and each team could send forth a member who would role-play that person, making a persuasive argument for his selection. The class could then vote. Candidates might include Harry Truman, Dwight Eisenhower, John Kennedy, Richard Nixon, Ronald Reagan, Lech Walesa, Mikhail Gorbachev, and Pope John Paul II.

After the Woods paper, the conference moved in an interesting direction. It moved from issues Truman raised in his Farewell Address to consider issues he did *not* broach. That question in itself, the teachers and scholars decided, is a good place to begin with students. Why was there no mention of the McCarthy hearings? Why were issues we consider crucial today (women's issues, ethnicity, the environment) not included in Truman's Farewell Address? What does this say about the man and about his era? Students have a tendency to assume issues people are passionate about today have always been the focus of attention. It is important to help them see otherwise.

Ellen Schrecker's paper on the Red Scare led to a discussion among the teachers and scholars about the dichotomy between Truman's civil rights instincts and his administration's inability to control a situation that clearly infringed on the basic liberties of countless Americans. Why didn't he do more to stop this? Students can learn a great deal about the inability of even the "world's most powerful leader" to impact events in his own backyard. Teachers can help students see the crucial connection between foreign and domestic policies. Some have argued that the Truman administration had to overplay the Communist threat abroad to gain support for foreign policy initiatives. This certainly had an impact on the fear of subversives at home. Students also need to understand that a president has to work with people in Congress who may not share his philosophy. In Truman's case that meant Republicans and conservative southern Democrats. Students learn a great deal about legislative processes when they see the compromises that take place on both sides of issues. A president often gives up on an issue he is passionate about to build support for another issue. And, of course, the teachers believed that a discussion of civil liberties in our own era and during the war on terrorism needs to be brought to class in light of what happened during the Truman era. Are there parallels? Finally, of the four topics discussed at the conference that were not included in the Farewell Address, McCarthyism was the one that had appeared in early drafts of the speech. Students need to consider reasons it was scratched from the speech.

Susan Hartmann's paper on gender issues during the Truman years gives teachers a great deal to consider. When analyzing primary sources, in this case Truman's Farewell Address, how often do we ask students to consider what is *not* there? Or as Hartmann says, to "probe behind the silences." Hartmann argues that in the 1940s women were asking for every issue that became very public in the 1960s and 1970s: equal pay, a commission on women's rights, and an equal rights amendment. Why were these appeals very public then, yet not in the 1940s? Hartmann encouraged teachers to use this question to get students thinking about long-term change and citizenship. The story of how women mobilized to pressure their government is a lesson for students that should motivate and inspire them toward civic engagement.

The world of Truman and the world of our students are dramatically different where gender roles are concerned. Hartmann's use of the phrase *gendered habits of the mind* seems a great way to get students thinking about the way different generations view the world. The teachers at the conference believed students need to be shown that most people in the 1940s, male and female, saw male dominance as natural and the only way to order things. This was reflected in the law and in the structure of virtually all social connections. The conference looked at a primary source from the Truman archives. On September 21, 1945, Truman's typed daily calendar lists all of his meetings. Just after noon, he met with six women who were seeking support for an equal rights amendment to the Constitution. One can assume Truman met with them and graciously heard their concern. Yet at the end of the day when he added handwritten notes to the calendar, he inscribed next to this meeting: "A whole lot of hoey about equal rights." The teachers believed students would be engaged by a discussion of what attitudes were behind Truman's entry. Last, to make these gender issues more personal, the teachers believed students might explore gender roles of the women in Truman's life—Bess and Margaret. How did their lives differ from those of women today? Students could also look at gender roles of women in their own family who lived in the Truman era and compare and contrast those roles with the women in their lives today.

Like Ellen Schrecker's paper discussed earlier, Rachel Buff's analysis of the Truman era illustrates the effect the Cold War had on all aspects of American life. Getting students to understand how America's new relationship to the world after World War II had a deep impact on domestic culture is a challenge for teachers. Buff addresses two areas rarely dealt with in depth at the secondary level—Indian policy and immigration policy. She makes the case that Cold War national security interests led to a cultural battle over what it meant to be an American and how citizenship was defined. Teachers at the conference concluded that, once again, a study of the Truman administration gives students a chance to explore larger, more universal themes. Students can compare the Truman administration's Indian policy ("termination" of tribal and land bases) with policies of other eras up to the present. As they see shifting policies, from assimilation to acceptance of tribal entities, they can begin to appreciate what an unsolved challenge America's Indian policy has been. Likewise, they can compare Truman's attitude toward immigration (he was open to expanding immigration—especially from East Europe) to our policy today. How do we judge which immigrants are *desirable* and which are not? As students research different eras, from open immigration, to the quotas of the 1920s, to our current struggle with how to handle immigration from the south, they will come to see that deciding how open we are to outsiders is a work in progress. Most important, Buff's contention that Americans' fear of subversives abroad colored their conception of who should be called an American at home struck the teachers as a timely topic in light of current events and tensions around the globe.

The fourth topic not covered in Truman's Farewell Address but explored at the conference was Truman and the environment. Environmental history is now common on college campuses but rarely appears in high school history textbooks or curriculums. Teachers at the conference appeared eager to accept Karl Brooks's challenge to bring an environmental awareness into their classrooms, and the Truman administration appeared to them to be a good place to begin. They believed one might start by challenging students to define "conservation." Brooks argues that conservation meant something different to early-twentieth-century leaders of the movement than it did to Truman and his cabinet. He also believes the post–World War II economic expansion made Truman's administration one of the most environmentally consequential administrations in history. He concludes that Truman's policies were devastating to the natural world, but also that they ironically helped lead to a movement that began to assess the costs of such policies. Brooks encouraged teachers to help students understand that environmentalism did not begin with Rachel Carson in 1962 or with Earth Day in 1970.

Brooks casts Truman as a president who when making a choice between protecting the environment and promoting economic development was prone to choose the latter course. Brooks challenged the teachers to evaluate this choice with their students. What other options were there for Truman? How do we face similar decisions today? What do Americans mean by progress? How are environmental issues factored into our notion of progress? These are *big* issues, and again, teachers can use the Truman era to get students thinking critically about them. Several of the teachers could envision developing geography skills by having students study city maps from 1950 and today to chart the growth of cities and, more particularly, the explosion of suburbs. What has been the cost to the environment? Most students who live in suburbs cannot even begin to imagine what existed (or what did *not* exist) only fifty years ago where they live. Getting them to see the past in such a way can help them begin to see dramatic historical change and begin to consider its impact. Brooks argued at the conference that students should be challenged to read their daily newspaper with an environmental consciousness. Having them do so will help them begin to consider consequences of societal decisions both in Truman's time and today.

Conclusions

In summation, the conference accomplished two important things. First, by bringing in noted Truman scholars to work with the assembled teachers and ask for their input, it gave *dignity* to what those "in the trenches" of public education do on a daily basis. Frankly, I have found that many in higher education do not really care about what goes on in our nation's schools. They just want to complain about how woefully unprepared students are when they reach their university. Second, the teachers challenged the scholars to think about how complex ideas can be broken down and placed within the reach of younger students. They also made it clear that teaching requires one to constantly reassess how one presents material to students—a fact that is too rarely discussed in university settings. In short, the conference provided meaningful and memorable professional growth for both the teachers and the scholars.

On a personal note, I believe the conference clearly demonstrated the power of grounding professional development for teachers in their *content* area. Too often teacher educators divorce teacher training from content. One of my frustrations as a high school history teacher (a job I deeply loved, by the way), was that the system almost never gave me time to talk to my peers about the subject I have a passion for—history. Such conversations almost never took place because either there simply was not enough time in the day or administrators never saw the importance of such talk. It is my contention that teachers who develop a rich content knowledge deepen their passion for their subject—a reality that students are bound to see. Teachers must be models of curious, lifetime learners. Unfortunately, many history teachers never take or are never given an opportunity to get beyond their assigned textbook.

But perhaps the highlight of the conference was the fact that those of us from both the world of public schools and the world of higher education were reminded of the power of *one* document, in this case Harry S. Truman's Farewell Address, to provide a window to a man, a leader, and a critical time in world history. The scholars and teachers used the facts surrounding the Truman era to open up discussions about truly big questions that are bound to inspire students to learn about the man from Independence. What is the importance of "charisma"? What is a *fair* distribution of income? Is *trying* to establish racial justice enough to merit greatness? Do morality and ethics have a place in modern technological war? What is the proper role of the U.S. in the world (then and now)? How do evolving gender roles change our politics? How are civil liberties protected in times of fear? All of these provocative questions (and many others) spring from Truman's Farewell Address! They should provide material for rich and deep learning in all of the classrooms of the teachers involved, and for those who read this book.

Harry Truman

A Biographer's Perspective I

Robert H. Ferrell

A biographer becomes familiar with aspects of a presidency that are not evident from the public speeches. Sometimes the least noticed parts of a presidency turn out to be more important than the spectacular, the newsworthy. In the case of Truman, the president's accomplishments as an administrator were more important than many of his decisions.

The need was to control the federal bureaucracy; it goes almost without saying that if Truman could not have gotten the bureaucracy to do his bidding, he would have become only another actor in the pageant of the presidency, something other than the head of the government of the United States. The bureaucracy had grown enormously under Truman's predecessor, Franklin D. Roosevelt, who needed large government for the New Deal programs and then for the war. Truman likewise needed a government of size in order to continue the social and economic policies to which Americans had become accustomed and to carry out his foreign and military policies. The size of the federal government increased from 600,000 civilian employees in 1933 to 2,600,000 twenty years later, with 4,000 in the judicial branch, 22,500 in the legislative, and 2,570,000 in the executive (500,000 in the post office and 1,300,000 civilian workers in defense).

To keep such an organization moving in the same direction was a herculean task. By and large Truman managed it. On April 12, 1945, few of the new president's fellow Americans had any idea that they were receiving as their new president a man who had made his mark as an administrator. Harry S. Truman had spent ten years as administrator of Jackson County, Missouri, the county that in its western half contained Kansas City. This rather large job offered substantial learning opportunities.

Truman's first years as a member of the three-person county court, as it was known in Missouri, offered little evidence of what he would become. Elected in 1922 to a two-year term as eastern judge, meaning that he was elected from the county's eastern half, which included the town of Independence and its rural hinterland, he chose—as perhaps he had to, considering that he had the support of the political boss of Kansas City, Thomas J. Pendergast—to side with the western judge, Pendergast's man, Henry F. McElroy, against the presiding judge, Elihu W. Hayes, a supporter of Boss Tom's rival in Kansas City, Joseph B. Shannon. The years when Truman was eastern judge were the epitome of bad county administration, in which he and McElroy (who claimed to have learned administration from his "old Presbyterian mother") created fourteen-month fiscal years and gave undue attention to the Miles Bulger Home for Negro Boys, named for the previous presiding judge, who had turned on Pendergast and hence needed to be driven into a political wilderness. The two conniving judges, Truman and McElroy, pointed out the huge brass plaque in the home that dedicated it to Bulger, the ornate drinking fountains, and other irrelevancies. For their labors, they both lost reelection. Truman was defeated by an Independence harness maker, Henry W. Rummell, who had been put into the race so that he could resign in favor of a more appropriate candidate, but then refused to resign and obtained the endorsement of Shannon, who had gone over to the Republicans.

Although Truman in this initial foray into politics displayed little achievement as an administrator, in his second, after he was elected presiding judge of Jackson County in 1926, he made a remarkable record. Again he was elected with Boss Tom's support; the support was crucial because the presiding judge was elected at large and needed the votes of Kansas City, not just those of Independence and the farmers. Truman thereupon turned the county into one of the three best-run counties in the United States in terms of what administratively counted at the time, which was a good road system. The other outstanding counties were Wayne County, the county of Detroit, and Westchester County, next to New York City.

As the junior senator from Missouri beginning in 1935, Truman learned another aspect of administration, which is getting along with people. He of course had to do that in Jackson County, but now he was one of a group of ninety-six individuals who were, he liked to say, either show horses or work horses. He needed to handle the other ninety-five carefully, for upon their goodwill rested any success he might achieve in the Upper House. He followed the initial rule of Senate good behavior, which was that junior senators were to be seen, not heard. To gain respect, but especially to make his judgment worthy of respect, he chose to become a specialist in transportation—in part because of what he had accomplished in Missouri. He easily saw that the organization of the country's transportation systems—railroads, waterways, the new airlines—was in disarray. He beheld especially the woeful condition of the railroads, which had been subject to raiding from their financiers and lawyers, with the result that they were unable to compete with the rising trucking industry that was using taxpayer-financed (mostly local, some state and federal) roads. Meanwhile, the nation's waterways had become objects of much congressional pork-barrel legislation. The Mississippi served parts of the Middle West, and Truman thought it would be possible to develop the Missouri River as a regional waterway as well. The prospect moved him to become a member of the Senate's Interstate Commerce Committee, ordinarily a committee that attracted few members of the Upper House.

The senators who were "work horses" rather than "show horses" had respect for his judgment. By not catering to the show horses but avoiding behavior that would turn them against him, he became a Senate leader. The result was two major pieces of legislation in his first term, 1935–1940, the Civil Aeronautics Act of 1938 and the Wheeler-Truman Transportation Act of 1940.

In his second Senate term, abbreviated by his selection as President Roosevelt's running mate in the presidential campaign of 1944, he spent most of his time investigating the war effort, which when he took interest in the subject early in 1941 was sprawling in administrative disorder. He managed a special Senate investigating committee with extraordinary adroitness, obtaining members who were work horses while avoiding antagonizing the president, who was sensitive to supervision from the Senate. This required skill of a high order. At the outset the president gave the committee little support. Through the Senate's leader, James F. Byrnes, Roosevelt gave the committee fifteen thousand dollars, an insignificant amount to investigate the expenditure of billions; the hand of Byrnes was in evidence, but behind it was the hand of the president, who wanted no one looking into his administrative sloppiness.

As preparation for administering the presidency, the chairmanship of the special committee could not have been better. The separate investigations and their reports went to the center of wartime production and displayed how the Roosevelt administration assisted it or in some cases hindered it. By supervising this vast searching out of the workings of labor and industry with government, Truman could see for himself what to do, and what not to do, when opportunity might permit—although he had no inkling that the presidency might come to him until just before the Chicago convention of the Democratic Party in the summer of 1944, when because of the obvious illness of President Roosevelt he knew that if FDR survived the campaign he, Truman, would likely become president in succession to him.

Truman's vice presidency early in 1945 lasted a few weeks, and then he was president. His first administrative move was to replace most of Roosevelt's cabinet. He decided that he would control the government's vast bureaucracy through the cabinet departments.

The president's decision to use the cabinet as his leading device for controlling the bureaucracy was crucial, at the center of his administrative procedures. In addition to the cabinet he employed two other administrative devices, of lesser importance. One was to organize the White House staff with an efficient, highly talented group of administrative assistants, whom he saw for a half hour every morning, including Saturdays. His procedure with them was to go around the table at which the dozen assistants sat, apportioning work and calling for new business. At the same time, he made careful use of the executive office staff, created by Roosevelt in the Reorganization Act of 1939. When Truman took office it comprised mostly the Bureau of the Budget, to which Congress added, not much to the president's initial liking, the Council of Economic Advisers in 1946. Truman felt that he did not need a three-person committee to advise him on how to achieve full employment, the purpose of the committee as mandated by Congress. His first appointee as committee chairman, Edwin A. Nourse, was too conservative for the president's taste, and also had a habit of lecturing the nation's chief executive. Nourse's replacement in 1949, Leon Keyserling, proved much more helpful, and his prediction of an expanding national economy was of great value during the Korean War. In the National Security Act of 1947 the president received another advisory body, the National Security Council. At first he largely ignored the NSC, but after the opening of the Korean War he found it useful as a resource for joining military and foreign policy issues. When Congress began to force more of its ideas on him, beginning with the Eightieth Congress in 1947 in which the Republican Party had a majority of both Houses, he enlisted the prodigious energy of former president Herbert Hoover, an impeccable Republican, who chaired a commission that rearranged parts of the administration. Truman managed this by making the commission an adjunct of the executive office staff.

But Truman's principal device for managing the federal bureaucracy was his cabinet. Here, in the changes he made during his administration (he had twenty-four cabinet members during his virtually two terms, for ten cabinet posts), he depended primarily on his appointments to the office of secretary of state and to the secretaryships of war and of the navy and, beginning with the Defense Act of 1947 and the reorganization of the military services into the army, navy, and air force, the secretaryship of defense.

The first cabinet change the president had in mind, and he arranged it during the course of the San Francisco Conference in the spring and early summer of 1945 to organize the United Nations, was to give the secretaryship of state to his once fellow senator, Byrnes. During the war Byrnes had been successively associate justice of the Supreme Court and Roosevelt's right-hand man in the White House with the title awarded by the president of "assistant president." When Truman assumed the presidency, Byrnes was without appointment, having retired to Spartanburg, South Carolina, when Roosevelt tired of his presence.

Byrnes was an obvious appointment to the Department of State, for two reasons. One was the sheer inability of the then secretary, Edward R. Stettinius Jr., who looked like a secretary of state, with his handsome countenance, suave manner, and prematurely white hair. His father had been a Morgan partner and considerable figure in the Woodrow Wilson administration during World War I. The son had enjoyed, as one might have expected, a meteoric career and while in his thirties was president of the United States Steel Corporation. But at the state department he was a figurehead, to allow President Roosevelt to dominate foreign policy. Truman so regarded him and believed rightly that he could not have a cipher as his adviser on foreign relations, a subject of nearly overwhelming importance as World War II drew to a close. Stettinius therefore had to be eased out of office, one way or another.

As incompetent as Stettinius was, a second reason for his replacement was that, lacking a vice president, Truman if assassinated or otherwise incapacitated would give way, by the 1886 law of presidential succession, to whoever was secretary of state.

The manner in which Stettinius left the secretaryship must be described as one of the least ceremonial, close to being cruel, administrative arrangements of Truman's presidency. The president deputized his friend George E. Allen, a roly-poly man about Washington who was secretary of the Democratic Party, to go out to San Francisco and get Stettinius out of office. It was a bizarre way of dismissing a secretary of state. But then Stettinius departed with a bizarre series of requests. He was willing to become the first permanent U.S. delegate to the United Nations, with the rank of ambassador. For this he asked a four-motor airplane, an office and secretary in the White

House, and the use of White House stationery. When he arrived back in Washington after his labors at San Francisco he spoke privately with the president. An account of the conversation is in Stettinius's papers at the University of Virginia. It was an incredible conversation, in which he referred to his own defenestration as "a kick in the pants." The president assured "Ed" that his departure to the United Nations would not look like a kick in the pants. Stettinius asked for his special arrangement. "Ed," the president said, perhaps with as much seriousness as he could muster, "I had already planned on it and thought about it, so why do you bring it up?"

Byrnes took office on July 1, 1945, and did better—how could he have done worse?—than his predecessor, but gradually revealed awkwardnesses. In the White House as Roosevelt's assistant he had shown ability to negotiate, and Truman hoped to use that ability in relations with the Soviets. But Byrnes proved more of a maneuverer than an inventor of solutions to problems. As time passed, he took positions without consulting the president, which was not a wise thing to do. He was a poor administrator of the State Department, which needed organization. Byrnes had to negotiate the peace treaties with the former German satellites, now Russian satellites, in Eastern Europe, and was largely unsuccessful in guaranteeing free elections in those countries. The strain of this affected his ability to administer the State Department; it was said that "the department fiddles while Byrnes roams." When his sister fell dead in the Washington railroad station he feared that he too might suffer a heart attack. These were the reasons for his departure. Later, in 1948, when during the election of that year Byrnes went over to Truman's enemies in the South, the Dixiecrats, the two men fell out, and remained that way until both died in 1972.

One could argue that Truman did not display good judgment in choosing Byrnes as secretary. But at the time he seemed the best individual available. He had national visibility. He had attended the Yalta Conference with President Roosevelt and there taken stenographic notes—in his early years he had been a court reporter—of the discussions and decisions.

Byrnes's replacement, Gen. George C. Marshall, saw immediately that the United States would have to support Western Europe, including Great Britain, all dramatically weakened by World War II, with a declaration of policy (the Truman Doctrine), economic policy (the Marshall Plan), and military assistance (the North Atlantic Treaty Organization). He was not in the best of health and for that reason resigned at the end of 1948. The Atlantic Treaty was signed by his successor, Dean Acheson, whom he had relied on to reorganize the department's offices and bureaus before Acheson left his position as undersecretary in mid-1947.

What Acheson accomplished in reorganizing the department made it a bulwark of the Truman administration, and the department's influence was mightily increased by the friendship that developed between the two men when Acheson took Marshall's place as secretary. On the surface they seemed so different, Truman the graduate of Independence High School, Acheson the product of Groton, Yale, and Harvard Law. All that mattered for nought, for they both were direct in conversation and possessed the same purpose, which was to stabilize American-Soviet relations. The fortunate linking of the two during the Truman era produced a unity in foreign policy that the American nation perhaps never had before nor has had since.

In making appointments to the military departments—combined in 1947 into the single Department of Defense—President Truman displayed the same generally good judgment he showed with the Department of State. In the first years, with Secretary of War Henry L. Stimson, who soon resigned because of his age, and his successor, the Wall Street lawyer Robert P. Patterson, there were no problems. Nor were there any with the secretary of the navy, James V. Forrestal, although Forrestal resisted the unification of the military departments. When the military reorganization act of 1947 called for appointment of a secretary of defense, Truman calculated that by appointing Forrestal he could control the navy, which did not like amalgamation. In this he soon saw he was wrong, for Forrestal was a psychological case, unable to control himself, a poor administrator who took every issue, large and small, to the president, and confused them with his increasing certainty that the Russians were coming—that the United States would be attacked. The president had to wait out the year 1948, for his election was so uncertain he could not afford a resignation at Defense, which Forrestal was unwilling to offer. After the campaign he took Forrestal's resignation, a sad task, made worse by the former secretary's suicide a few weeks later while a patient at the naval hospital in Bethesda.

The feuding services, led by a "revolt of the admirals" in 1949, were not brought into order by the talented but insensitive Louis A. Johnson, who served as secretary of defense in 1949–1950. He infuriated the navy by canceling construction of a large carrier. He undercut Secretary of State Acheson on policy toward China. Truman was forced to take his resignation with almost as little diplomacy as in the case of Stettinius. "Lou," he said one day, "I have to ask you to quit." Johnson wept, refused to sign, and then was told by his undersecretary, Stephen T. Early, Roosevelt's former press secretary whom Truman had installed at defense to hold Johnson down, to sign—it was a messy denouement. Johnson was followed by the superb Marshall and then

Marshall's undersecretary, the equally competent Wall Street financier Robert A. Lovett.

As for the other cabinet departments, when Truman took over from Roosevelt in April 1945, he determined to have strong personalities in control, willing to carry out his directives. In 1945 the president expelled from the cabinet the secretary of labor, Frances Perkins, an attractive woman who possessed good judgment but was so devoted to President Roosevelt, whom she had known since the early years of the century when FDR was in the Albany legislature, that she allowed him to push her around and remove virtually all of her department's bureaus. He took the resignation of Attorney General Francis Biddle, who had as little respect for the new president as had Byrnes, and who was a blueblood from Philadelphia and in his memoirs displayed his family's lineage in a genealogical table on both of the flyleaves. He took the resignation of Secretary of Agriculture Claude R. Wickard. Secretary of the Treasury Henry Morgenthau Jr., whom Truman considered "a blockhead, nut" ("I don't know how Roosevelt kept him around"), insisted on going to the Potsdam Conference in July–August 1945. He already had attended the Quebec Conference of 1944, where he muddied the waters by introducing the Morgenthau Plan that would have turned postwar Germany, the industrial heart of Europe, into farmland. As head of the treasury, Morgenthau would have been an important figure at Potsdam. Truman could not allow such undercutting of his foreign policy and dismissed him out of hand. Roosevelt's postmaster general, a former chairman of the Democratic Party, Frank C. Walker, left the cabinet because his successor as chairman, Robert E. Hannegan, aspired to the conventional place for party chairmen, the post-office department. Perkins was replaced by one of President Truman's closest friends in the Senate, Lewis B. Schwellenbach of Washington; Biddle by a department officer, the able Tom C. Clark; Wickard by Clinton P. Anderson; and Morgenthau by the canny Kentucky politico Fred M. Vinson. When Vinson became chief justice of the Supreme Court, he was replaced by St. Louis banker John W. Snyder, a Reserve officer and friend of Truman's.

Two remaining Roosevelt cabinet members roiled the political waters in 1946. Their departures were messy not only privately but also publicly, the worst of all administrative worlds. The president obtained supporters in their places, essential to control of their cabinet departments.

The first of the disorderly resignations—cabinet members are supposed to resign with great goodwill for the president, and the president in a bouquet of words accepts their resignations with deepest regret—was Secretary of the Interior Harold L. Ickes. His name was then a household word, as he had held office since 1933 and been a figure in the New Deal. Fortunately for Truman, after the resignation his reputation diminished and disappeared into one of the back corridors of history.

Ickes had been known as a maverick and during the Roosevelt years threatened to resign on numerous occasions. With Truman he threatened once. Roosevelt had nominated the California oilman Edwin W. Pauley as undersecretary of the navy, and the nomination languished after the president's death. Truman revived it, for Pauley had proved to be an able executive with his oil properties. He had also been the principal mover and shaker in dissuading Truman's predecessor from keeping Vice President Henry A. Wallace as the president's running mate in 1944; Truman may not have known that when he revived Pauley's nomination in 1946—he did not learn much about how he himself became the vice presidential nominee until 1950, when the former postmaster general, Walker, told him. Another reason for Pauley's nomination was that the new president did not know many "big people," as he told a friend. He knew the little people of Missouri and a few solid Democrats such as members or former members of the Senate or House of Representatives, but that was it. Pauley seemed ideal for the Navy Department, and it is possible that the president had him in mind as secretary of defense when that office obtained legislative approval.

Ickes behaved badly over the Pauley nomination, but it is not clear why. He told Truman that he might be asked by the pertinent Senate committee to say something about Pauley, which was hardly the way to inform the president that he, the secretary of the interior, might testify against a presidential nomination. Ickes so testified, saying Pauley was unfit. He followed with another piece of disloyalty, telling the reporter Edwin A. Harris of the *St. Louis Post-Dispatch* that the committee should ask him to read from his diary. Harris acted on the information and received a Pulitzer Prize for his labors. Ickes returned to the committee to read a passage relating that Pauley in 1944 had said he could raise $300,000—he then was party treasurer—among California oilmen for the Democratic Party if the oilmen had assurance that the federal government would not try to claim that offshore oil—oil beyond the continental shelf—was subject to federal regulation, presumably taxation. This, Ickes said, was "the rawest proposition that has ever been made to me." With that he finished off Pauley.

All sorts of things were wrong with this testimony, the principal one being disloyalty to the president. An interesting point was why Ickes waited a year and a half to relate the rawest proposition ever made to him.

Truman took Ickes's resignation and in a letter that he did not write—an exchange of complimentary letters was pro forma—said that the secretary's services would end in all matters connected with the government. It was a piece of epistolary fluff, and Ickes must have known that. He sputtered instead in an announcement of his own that he wanted nothing to do with the Truman administration.

What does the Ickes resignation say about Truman as an administrator? It says that when a cabinet member presented him with complicated reasons for the member's dismissal, the president did not hesitate to act. Ickes had a large public reputation and thought he could rely on it. The president refused to give reasons for Ickes's dismissal and let the secretary's overweening confidence speak for itself.

Ickes, one must conclude, was an ingrate, but that did not make the lot of the thirty-third president easier. The Ickes resignation and the one that followed later that year were no easy occasions. They came when postwar strikes in major industries were riling the economy, threatening inflation. Relations with the Soviet Union were rapidly deteriorating; it was the year of former prime minister Winston Churchill's speech at Westminster College, the Missouri institution to which Truman footloosely invited him, and the Russians claimed to be badly treated by the American president's sponsorship of such an address. Then there was Ickes's almost open assumption, altogether unkind of him, indeed downright wrong, that Truman was a worse administrator than Roosevelt.

Months later, in September, in a much worse administrative imbroglio, Truman had to deal with the resignation of Henry Wallace as secretary of commerce. Unlike Ickes the ingrate, Wallace was an impossible combination of idealism and opportunism. Like Ickes, he was a part of the Roosevelt heritage, which was disorder in the cabinet.

Roosevelt had made Wallace secretary of commerce as a consolation prize instead of the vice presidency (and presidency). The former vice president, before that secretary of agriculture, had no general knowledge of commerce. The Wallace family had published a farm journal known as *Wallaces' Farmer*. He himself was an agricultural economist and had helped develop a remarkably successful business in seed corn.

Unsatisfied with his post at commerce, Wallace had in mind making pronouncements about foreign affairs, especially Soviet-American relations, getting into the domain of Secretary of State Byrnes. One day he came in to see the president for a short, fifteen-minute visit and produced a speech he proposed to make two days later at Madison Square Garden in New York. Truman riffled the speech and pronounced it fine. Wallace gave it and said the president approved it, and it stood against the policy that Byrnes, then in Paris negotiating the East European peace treaties with the Russians, had been following, which was to prevent the Soviets from dominating elections in the East European nations. In the speech Wallace addressed the feelings of many Americans that the Russians, who had sacrificed so much during the war, needed more careful treatment. "The tougher we get," he said, "the tougher the Russians get."

It is impossible not to think that he knew what he was doing—he was nominating himself as a better foreign policy expert than Truman and Byrnes. One can only conclude that in 1946 he was attempting to force the president's hand on foreign policy and stood ready, in case the tactic did not work, to oppose him in the election of 1948, which he did.

The Truman cabinet was no kaleidoscope, in which the picture changed month by month, even though at one time or another twenty-four different individuals sat around the large table. For some of the lesser departments the names were difficult to hold in mind, creating the appearance of constant change. When Tom Clark went to the Supreme Court, he was succeeded as attorney general by J. Howard McGrath, then James P. McGranery. Hannegan resigned as postmaster general, and the president appointed a career member of that department, Jesse M. Donaldson. Ickes was followed by Julius A. Krug and, as in the case of Donaldson in the Post Office Department, another department careerist (Truman rightly liked people who knew the work), Oscar L. Chapman. Wallace's successor as secretary of commerce, Averell Harriman, was followed by Charles Sawyer. When Secretary of Labor Schwellenbach died, he was succeeded by Maurice J. Tobin. Truman greatly admired—along with Acheson he denominated him his best cabinet appointment—Charles F. Brannan, who succeeded Anderson. Brannan was the author of the Brannan Plan, which proposed a limit to support programs for rich farmers; the program was admirable, going to the center of the troubles in the support programs, but too honest for the big agricultural lobbies such as the Farm Bureau, and lost out for that reason.

With his cabinet appointees the president managed what he was supposed to do, which was to preside in such a manner as to control. It is not too much to say that this activity, prosaic as it seemed, was the essence of his presidency. Without it he would not have been equal to his tasks. It was necessary to announce policies and give the impression they were about to be carried out. The president of 1945–1953, who was not adept at public speaking, as he well knew, did the best he could in that regard, and sought to make his administration newsworthy. But for the day-to-day administration, so important, he brought together in the cabinet room every Friday morning ten individuals, with only one or two visitors, who could sit around the large, glossy table. He followed the same procedure each session, going around and assigning tasks, then calling for new business. He never asked the others to decide on something; the decisions were his. There was none of the Roosevelt time-serving whereby the president told stories and afterward received individual cabinet members who presented their causes privately—the advantage to Roosevelt being that in case of later trouble the president could deny any agreement he had made.

Given the importance of Truman's administrative acumen to the accomplishments of his administration, one might properly inquire why the president and his staff, bringing together points of achievement for the Farewell Address, did not include the management of the bureaucracy. To that question, the present biographer has no answer.

Harry Truman

A Biographer's Perspective II

Alonzo L. Hamby

Harry Truman's Farewell Address appears at first reading to be the vale-dictory of a leader delivering a final report to his people, speaking of his ac-complishments with pride, confident in the ultimate judgment of history. But of course "history" makes no judgments. *Historians* do. When they grap-ple with presidential history, they inevitably act also as biographers, taking the measure of the man with whom they are engaged. More than fifty years after the Farewell Address, the actions Truman recounted as signal achieve-ments remain hotly contested by scholars. Estimates of the man vary accord-ingly. It is safe to say, however, that virtually no one accepts the serene, above-the-fray sense of his personality suggested by this one speech.

Almost all historian-biographers of the Truman presidency agree that they have dealt with a far-from-commanding personality—often insecure, anger-prone, and not always possessing a firm grasp of the issues he attempted to manage. What they have made of this is another matter. Some do not go be-yond simple description. Others proclaim these characteristics as proof of a fundamental inadequacy. Still others find them amusing and shrug them off. My own sense is that in his weaknesses as well as his strengths, Harry Tru-man was a prototypical representative of American democracy.

Biographical Genesis

I was five years old on April 12, 1945, the day Franklin Roosevelt died and Harry Truman became president. I remember hearing it announced on the radio that President Roosevelt had died and going to tell my mother. This is literally my first historical memory. From that point on, Harry Truman was part of my life.

I was born and raised in Humansville, Missouri, a small town just off State Route 13 about fifty miles north of Springfield. It's not much different now than it was then, except in those days a much more meandering Highway 13 ran right through town. Politically, it was then, and remains now, strongly Republican. Harry Truman didn't have a lot of fans there, but my parents were among the minority who liked him. So I was *very* conscious of Truman throughout my grade school years. The fact that he was president of the United States no doubt helped me develop an interest in politics that was odd, if not downright unhealthy, for a preadolescent.

I might as well admit that I did so without a lot of perspective. It seemed perfectly natural to me that a Missourian should be president. And I couldn't understand why national newspaper and magazine writers thought he was a mediocre speaker with some kind of a "twang" in his voice. He sounded just like about everyone I knew and seemed to make a better speech than most of them were capable of making.

Although Truman was a person who always interested me, when I went to college, decided on a major in history, and got admitted to graduate school for a Ph.D., I did so without any idea that I would be a Truman biographer and a historian of his presidency. I knew I wanted to do twentieth-century U.S. history and that I wanted to concentrate on politics. But in the early 1960s, the "progressive era," the age of Theodore Roosevelt and Woodrow Wilson, seemed to be a hot topic, and I was well on the way to picking out some obscure progressive who had not been written up and building a dissertation around him.

I was rescued from that dire fate by Richard Kirkendall, who had the enterprise to develop a school of Truman graduate students at the University of Missouri *and* to secure National Defense Education Act fellowships to support them. My long interest in Truman suddenly became a valuable professional opportunity. The Truman Library was just beginning to attract scholars who would write the first generation of Truman history, and I had the good fortune to be among them. Kirkendall also had the tolerance to let me take on a bigger dissertation topic than any graduate student should attack.

The eventual result was a book called *Beyond the New Deal: Harry S. Truman and American Liberalism* (1973), which was not a biography but more an interpretation of the Truman presidency. After it was published, I decided that some day, when enough sources were available, I would attempt a full-scale one-volume biography. By the mid-1980s, after the deaths of Harry and Bess Truman, the time was ripe. Truman's personal White House papers, left to the library at his death, were there. So was a lot in the way of family papers, including the "Dear Bess" correspondence. (Robert Ferrell, by the way, gave us two very good and very useful edited works based on those collections. And by then he was researching his own Truman biography. We would encounter each other from time to time in the research room of the Truman Library. I would ask, "What are you working on now, Bob?" He would reply, "Just keeping up with the new sources." He didn't fool me.)

After about a decade of work, *Man of the People: A Life of Harry S. Truman* (1995) finally hit the market. It says pretty much what I have to say about Harry Truman. I will try to highlight some salient points.

American Democrat

Before I talk about Truman the president, I want to talk about Truman the man. His presidency was an important one, but his appeal as a historical figure of mythic proportions rests as much on *who* we think he was as on *what* he did. In the American historical imagination, he was an ordinary man who displayed the greatness of our democracy by assuming leadership of it and seeing it through difficult times. Truman himself liked the image and promoted it throughout his career.

It is easy enough to punch holes in what was to some extent a self-made myth. Truman's cultural tastes—his love of classical music, his fascination with history and biography—were not exactly ordinary, for example. Nor was the drive and ambition that ultimately led him to the presidency. But there is a larger truth to it. In most nations—even democratic nations, even in today's world—national leaders are products of elite leadership classes. This has always been somewhat less true of the United States, but as a matter of degree rather than kind. In the Europe of the early twentieth century, Truman would have been dismissed as someone who had "no family"—that is, no family of importance. The United States of those years seemed to many people to be converging with Europe on the matter of leadership. Let us recall that the presidents of Truman's early adulthood were Theodore Roosevelt (old family, wealth, Harvard), William Howard Taft (old family, upper middle class, Yale), and Woodrow Wilson (high-status family of Presbyterian church leaders, Princeton), that few Cabinet members were from society's lower half, that well-off and educated classes were increasingly represented in a growing professional bureaucracy, and that the U.S. Senate was often called a millionaire's club. Let us remember also that, perhaps not surprisingly, this was a time of increasing anxiety about the future of American democracy.

Finally, let us contrast Truman's career trajectory with that of his immediate predecessor, Franklin Delano Roosevelt—the product of one of America's oldest families, a wealthy Harvard graduate, extremely well connected. When Roosevelt became the number-two man in the Navy Department in 1913, Harry Truman, just two years his junior, was still, as he put it, trying "to dig a living out of the ground" on the family farm at Grandview, fearing that it might be lost in a family lawsuit, and contemplating resettlement as a homesteader in Montana. Roosevelt had money, status, and confidence. By contrast, Truman was indeed an ordinary American striving, as he put it, to "make good." Unlike Roosevelt, he lived in a world of stress and insecurity for most of his prepresidential life.

Harry Truman was an interesting person simply in himself and in the details of his life, but a biographer should search for larger meanings in the lives of his subjects. Truman struck me as a compelling case study of democratic (small "d") man in the first half of the twentieth century. Like the vast majority of Americans, he came from a middling family of no particular distinction or social recognition. Like the vast majority, he had to attempt to establish an identity and find his level in a mobile society. His ambitions were large, his resources few, the resulting stress great. Let's begin with ten years of work on a farm that in the beginning was owned, not by his parents, but by his grandmother and uncle. Then the largest portion of it became a disputed inheritance that might be lost altogether and a sure generator of big legal bills. Finally, with the settlement of the lawsuit, it was his mother's, not his, and it provided a way of life with which he was thoroughly dissatisfied.

At age thirty-two, Franklin Roosevelt was an increasingly visible assistant secretary of the navy; at age thirty-two, Harry Truman was starting over again as a small businessman, drawing on his share of the farm for capital. The results were disastrous. His business career displays a genius for buying high and selling low. First, a speculative mining enterprise in Commerce, Oklahoma, ended as a total wipeout. Then, a speculative oil business did no more than return his original investment, if that. Then, the Twelfth Street haberdashery was ill conceived and destined to fail from the beginning. Truman also acquired a heavily mortgaged farm in Johnson County, Kansas, that would wind up being sold for unpaid taxes. All these ventures, save the real estate speculation, had one thing in common. They were efforts of a little guy with skimpy resources to compete with big boys who had deep pockets. They represented an obsolete dream of nineteenth-century entrepreneurship that already had been pretty well smashed by Rockefeller, Carnegie, and other master organizers of American business. They not only tell us something about Truman's business aptitude but also help explain his visceral hostility as a politician toward Wall Street and big business as more than just a matter of abstract conviction.

There is no way to sugarcoat Truman's early business career. It was one of consistent failure that must have exacted a high psychological toll. (Only his military career, brief and without career prospects, was satisfying and successful.) It was not just that he never owned a home of his own, or that, after his marriage in 1919, he surely felt he was letting his wife down. The simple social toll of frustrated hopes must have been equally high. He had hoped to be a civic leader in Kansas City, had been sponsored by some prominent figures, accepted for membership in the Kansas City Club and the Lakewood Country Club, then forced to resign from both for lack of funds to cover his dues. (Remarks about the Kansas City Club that find their way into the record in later years are seldom complimentary.) Harry Truman had always been interested in politics, but when he made his first serious campaign for office as Eastern District county judge in 1922, he did so because he had to. Having been unable to make it in business, he had to turn to politics as a profession in a renewed quest for success and a respected identity.

Truman's political skills were of a much higher order than his business sense, but at the age of thirty-eight he launched himself into one of the most insecure and least respected of American careers. Alexis de Tocqueville had bluntly stated the case nearly a century earlier:

> In nations where the principle of election extends to everything, no political career can, properly speaking, be said to exist. Men arrive as if by chance at the post which they hold, and they are by no means sure of retaining it. . . . The consequence is that in tranquil times public functions offer but few lures to ambition. In the United States those who engage in the perplexities of political life are persons of very moderate pretensions. . . . it frequently happens that a man does not undertake to direct the fortunes of the state until he has shown himself incompetent to conduct his own.[1]

1. De Tocqueville, *Democracy in America,* trans. Henry Reeve and Francis Bowen, ed. Phillips Bradley (New York: Vintage, 1945), 1:216.

The prospect of facing the electorate every two or four years was daunting enough, but the terms of a political career in Jackson County were unsatisfactory in other ways. Truman privately described himself from the beginning as an idealist in politics and was, I believe, sincerely committed to the ideal of politics as public service. But the real world in which he lived was one of spoils politics, less about issues and disinterested administration than about who got the jobs and public contracts. (It tells us much that the dominant Democratic Party factions called themselves the Goats and the Rabbits. Try to find content in those labels.) Through a ten-year career on the county court, Truman did his best to modify the rules of the game and took some real risks in the process, but he rightly understood that he could not rewrite the rule book. As he himself in one of his bitter moods put it, he had to hire a lot of no-account sons-of-bitches for jobs that were at best half done and turn a blind eye to the theft of hundreds of thousands of dollars in order to save millions. Still, it was psychologically important for him to be loyal to his patron, Boss Tom Pendergast, who made it possible for him to hold office in the first place and who, after refusing to support him for governor or congressman, would send him to the Senate. In such circumstances, frustration was part of the job description.[2]

Truman loved the U.S. Senate, but his first term was difficult. The job security was tenuous, and his reputation as a boss-sponsored candidate damaged him with progressive leaders he greatly admired. He got next to no respect and precious few patronage appointments from the Roosevelt White House. Nevertheless, he established an identity as a hard-working New Deal senator, attracted attention by taking over a high-profile investigation of the railroad industry, and won many friends. Winning a close, hard-fought battle for a second term after the downfall of the Pendergast machine, he moved toward a position of leadership and prominence in the upper house as the chairman of another investigating committee—this one with a broad mandate to investigate World War II economic mobilization. By 1944, the work of "the Truman Committee" had brought his name into every household in America that subscribed to a newspaper or listened to news on the radio.

How then did this man's so-called early life—his first sixty years!—determine his character and personality? I have not discussed his childhood. We all know that the thick eyeglasses, the piano lessons, and the bookishness set him apart from other boys. The experience may have precipitated some inner

2. See the diary memorandums intermittently written by Truman during his second term as county judge on Pickwick Hotel stationery and informally known to scholars as his "Pickwick Papers." The best copies are in the President's Secretary's File, Truman Papers, Truman Library.

doubts about his masculinity. But he seems to have dealt with it all pretty well. Certainly his war experience, which exhibited courage and devotion to duty, must have put an end to any questions he had about how much of a man he was. I have found myself less concerned with whatever impact his childhood had upon him than with the precarious adult experiences involved in establishing a career and an identity. The failures, the frustrations, the insecurities brought out traits that did not always serve him well: combativeness, a consistent sense that he did not get the respect and recognition he deserved, and above all a seething anger he never quite brought under control. Let us be clear that he was a man of principle and a person who combined talent with hard work. His temperament had certain qualities that served him well, especially his insistence that presidents had to make firm decisions and live with them, but it also had its defects. At times, these could cast a large shadow over a remarkable career. A Roosevelt by contrast—either Theodore or Franklin—knew who he was from birth, accepted leadership as natural, and by and large never had to deal with such issues.

Struggle for Greatness: The Presidency

I have talked about Truman's defects of temperament because they too often adversely affected his presidency. It is never good to appear erratic and cranky in public; he too often did. One need only recall the Pulitzer Prize–winning cartoon of an angry Truman confronting a group of newsmen and telling them: "Your editors ought to have better sense than to print what I say!" And, of course, everyone knows about the letter to the music critic Paul Hume. Truman at his best, we should add, could be an attractive personality, and everyone who worked for him in the White House to whom I have spoken remembered him as a kind and considerate boss. Nevertheless, political command at this level did not come naturally to him. At times this showed—never to his advantage.

Substantively, academic debate on the Truman administration has focused on two large issues: (1) the Cold War and (2) the problem of social reform along the lines of the extension of the New Deal in postwar America. The Cold War debate has also produced as sort of a prologue a rather intense controversy on the use of the atomic bomb and a large literature on McCarthyism and the related matter of Soviet espionage. The social reform/New Deal debate has evinced a special interest in the development of the civil rights movement. For organizational reasons, I have separated these, but the fact is that, rare exceptions aside, the same historians can be found on the same sides in all these debates. They illustrate what strikes me as a singularly unhealthy aspect of contemporary academic life: centrists and those moderately left of center are "conservatives" in academia; those farther to the left, including a significant number of Marxists and a few unrepentant Stalinists, are "liberals." Their positions on a large range of issues are fixed and predictable. As for real conservatives, forget about them; their representation is too small and scattered to make an impression. There is a fundamental ideological divide here. It began to appear in the early 1960s, was intensified by Vietnam, and has hardened ever since. At times, I despair of ever getting beyond it; there are other directions, less susceptible to personal ideology, that discussion on the Truman era might take. At other times, I simply tell myself that, well, there are real, living, fundamental matters of contention we must live with.

I have written on all these matters. Time does not permit me an extended discussion of any of them. So I am going to give you my short conclusions on each of them:

The Cold War was the result of an altogether merited response by largely free societies to an expansionist Stalinist totalitarianism, fully as loathsome as the Nazi totalitarianism that World War II was fought to defeat. Revisionists ask us to assume that Joseph Stalin had no designs on Western Europe; that it would have made no difference if Communist regimes had come to power in Greece, Italy, and France. Such scholars are neither realists nor idealists. At best, they are wishful thinkers who assume that international conflict can be avoided by policies of passivity and appeasement. It was a strategic imperative for the United States to work for a democratic and friendly Western Europe after having fought a long war to defeat Nazi despotism. It was a moral imperative to defend liberal governments based on principles of individual freedom against an equally evil Stalinist despotism. Reams of documentation from the former Soviet Union have demonstrated that foreign Communist Parties were funded and controlled from Moscow, were participants in Soviet espionage, and, especially at the leadership levels, were thoroughly disloyal to their countries.[3]

The atomic bomb was not the first shot in the Cold War; it was the last shot in the worst war in human history and was deployed to end that war as

3. On this point, see Harvey Klehr, John Earl Haynes, and Kyrill M. Anderson, eds., *The Soviet World of American Communism* (New Haven: Yale University Press, 1998), as well as numerous other works edited by Klehr and Haynes. See also their *In Denial: Historians, Communism, and Espionage* (San Francisco: Encounter Books, 2003).

quickly as possible. Japan displayed no evidence that it was "ready to surrender" before bombs were dropped on both Hiroshima and Nagasaki. To the contrary, code-breakers intercepted one diplomatic and military message after another indicating that the Japanese government was determined to fight a final decisive battle that would inflict intolerable casualties upon the American invaders and compel a negotiated peace.

Revisionist historians have charged that "McCarthyism" was the logical and inevitable outcome of Truman's needless Cold War policies. The effect of their writings has been to blur a fair and indeed necessary distinction between McCarthyism and a responsible anti-Communism. The Truman administration's record in combating Communism at home was not perfect. The federal loyalty program unjustly deprived some government employees of their jobs, but it was far from the reign of terror some historians depict. The Smith Act prosecutions of the leaders of the Communist Party of the United States were unwise, although what we know now would have merited prosecution of them on more serious charges. Nonetheless, McCarthyism (or the Second Red Scare) was not the creation of the Truman administration or such supporting forces as the original Americans for Democratic Action (ADA). Truman, the ADA, and other Fair Deal Democrats were guilty of some lapses, but in general they practiced a sane and merited anti-Communism. McCarthy and his fellow travelers were irresponsible liars; the difference was evident to most observers at the time.

Truman was a committed liberal; this is clear to anyone who reads his private utterances. His Fair Deal, however, faced what Richard H. Pells has described as the difficulties of liberalism in a conservative age.[4] So most of the elements of Truman's Fair Deal program—civil rights legislation, ambitious income supports for farm families, federal aid to education, national health insurance, repeal of the Taft-Hartley Act, new river valley authorities—never made it through the legislative mill. His relatively few successes were incremental—a very significant enlargement of the social security program, for example. He also could sometimes break new ground by using his executive authority, especially in the area of civil rights. By and large a prospering America was unreceptive to new departures, although happy enough to see the consolidation and enlargement of such established programs. Franklin D. Roosevelt likely would have enjoyed no more legislative successes, although he probably would have looked better in failing to achieve his objectives.

---

4. Pells, *The Liberal Mind in a Conservative Age: American Intellectuals in the 1940s and 1950s* (New York: Harper and Row, 1985).

Truman, as the product of a southern culture, had conflicted attitudes about blacks. But he also believed in equal opportunity and had political respect for all voting groups. It is understandable that one might look back and think that such progress as he achieved was glacial at best. Nonetheless it is well to remember that he faced three hundred years of mass indifference to the problems of blacks. His rhetoric, his establishment of policies and precedents—however halting and uneven their implementation and enforcement—made real differences in the lives of some people and established a foundation for the greater endeavors that followed. What preceding chief executive had accomplished as much? It may be remarkable that he supported civil rights at all. It is hard to deny that he did more for the advancement of African Americans than any president before him.

I have been asked how I might best describe Harry Truman in a phrase or short sentence. The title of my book, *Man of the People,* is a good indication. The working title, changed at the inspired behest of my editor, Nancy Lane, was "American Democrat," implying not simply a leader of the Democratic Party but a product of small-"d" democracy. Truman, I have suggested, was right to depict himself as an ordinary American, and it tells us much that he gloried in the image. He was also, I have suggested, a man of genuinely liberal values, the two most important of which were individual freedom and the furtherance of individual opportunity through public policy. So let's combine these two elements and conclude that, at least as much as any American president of the twentieth century, Harry Truman was the living representation of the ideal of a vigorous liberal democracy.

Appendix A

The Authors

Carol Anderson, a Ford and American Council of Learned Societies Fellow, is Associate Professor of History at the University of Missouri–Columbia. She is the author of *Eyes Off the Prize: The United Nations and the African American Struggle for Human Rights, 1944–1955* as well as numerous articles. Professor Anderson is the recipient of the Provost's Teaching Award for Outstanding Junior Faculty, the Gold Chalk Award for Graduate Teaching, and the William T. Kemper Fellowship for Excellence in Teaching.

Karl Brooks, an Idaho native, has taught American environmental and legal history and environmental law at the University of Kansas in Lawrence since earning his doctorate in 2000. After completing law school at Harvard, he was a trial and appellate attorney for a decade in Idaho, then worked three years for his home state's biggest grassroots environmental group. Between 1986 and 1992, he represented a Boise district in the Idaho State Senate. His study of the postwar Hells Canyon Dam controversy is forthcoming, and he is at work on another book about the emergence of American environmental law between 1945 and 1980. During 2001–2002, he worked in Washington, D.C., as a Supreme Court Fellow, helping write a history of federal criminal sentencing practices.

Rachel Ida Buff is Associate Professor of History and Director of the Ethnic Studies Program at the University of Wisconsin, Milwaukee. The author of *The Political Economy of Home: Caribbean Brooklyn and American Indian Minneapolis, 1945–1992,* she is currently working on a manuscript about immigration policy, gender, and empire from 1945 to 1975, as well as a project on Brooklyn, New York, and the Model Cities Program.

Robert M. Collins received his Ph.D. from Johns Hopkins University. He specializes in the history of political economy and business-government relations and is the author most recently of *More: The Politics of Economic Growth in Postwar America.* His articles have appeared in the *Journal of American History* and the *American Historical Review.* He currently teaches modern U.S. history at the University of Missouri–Columbia.

Robert H. Ferrell is Professor Emeritus of History at Indiana University in Bloomington. He is a student of American foreign policy and a scholar of the American presidency. He came to Indiana University in 1953 and became a full professor in 1961. He has authored or edited a total of twelve books on Harry Truman, including *Truman and Pendergast, Harry S. Truman and the Modern American Presidency,* and *Harry S. Truman: A Life.*

Richard B. Frank was born in Kansas in 1947. Upon graduation from the University of Missouri in 1969, he was commissioned in the U.S. Army, in which he served four years, including a tour of duty in Vietnam as an aerorifle platoon leader in the 101st Airborne Division. In 1976, he completed study at the Georgetown University Law Center in Washington, D.C. He retired as a member of the Board of Veterans Appeals in 2003. His first book, *Guadalcanal,* won the General William Greene Award from the Marine Corps. His second work, *Downfall: The End of the Imperial Japanese Empire,* won The Harry S. Truman Book Award. Both books became main selections of the History Book Club. He contributed a chapter to *What If? 2* entitled "No Bomb; No End." He was a consultant to Dr. Robert Ballard for the documentary and book *The Lost Ships of Guadalcanal* and has appeared frequently on the History Channel.

Jeff Gall is Associate Professor of History at Truman State University, teaching courses in U.S. and Missouri history. He also works in the area of teacher preparation, teaching a history classroom methods course and supervising teaching interns each semester. Before coming to Truman State, Gall taught high school history for fourteen years in Lee's Summit, Missouri. He is a native of Independence, Missouri.

Alonzo L. Hamby is Distinguished Professor of History at Ohio University. His works on Harry Truman include *Beyond the New Deal: Harry S. Truman and American Liberalism* and *Man of the People: A Life of Harry S. Truman.* His most recent book is *For the Survival of Democracy: Franklin Roosevelt and the World Crisis of the 1930s.*

Susan M. Hartmann teaches modern U.S. history and women's history at Ohio State University. She has written several books on women's history and political history since 1940, including *Truman and the 80th Congress* and *The Home Front and Beyond: American Women in the 1940s.* Her most recent book is *The Other Feminists: Activists in the Liberal Establishment,* and she is co-author of the U.S. history textbook *The American Promise.*

Mary Ann Heiss received her Ph.D. from Ohio State University and is currently Associate Professor of History at Kent State University. A specialist in the history of U.S. foreign relations, she is the author of *Empire and Nationhood: The United States, Great Britain, and Iranian Oil, 1950–1954* and coeditor of books on the future of NATO and U.S. relations with the Third World. She is a former associate editor of *Diplomatic History* and a current member of the journal's editorial board and is at work on a study currently entitled "Transatlantic Communion? Anglo-American Visions of Empire, 1945–1956."

Richard S. Kirkendall is the Scott and Dorothy Bullitt Professor Emeritus at the University of Washington. A native of Spokane, he was educated at Gonzaga University and the University of Wisconsin. His contributions to Truman historiography include three books—*The Truman Period as a Research Field, The Truman Period as a Research Field: A Reappraisal 1972,* and *The Truman Encyclopedia*—and his work with a talented and productive group of doctoral students. A researcher in the Truman Library since its early years, he has participated in most of the conferences sponsored by the Truman Library Institute and has long been an active member of its Board of Directors.

Ellen Schrecker received her Ph.D. from Harvard University and is Professor of History at Yeshiva University, where she has taught since 1987. Widely recognized as a leading expert on McCarthyism, she has published many books and articles on the subject, including *Many Are the Crimes: McCarthyism in America* and *No Ivory Tower: McCarthyism and the Universities,* which won the History of Education Society's Outstanding Book Award for 1987. The recipient of fellowships from the Bunting Institute and the National Humanities Center, she has taught at Harvard, Columbia, New York University, and Princeton. Schrecker has also written about contemporary academic freedom and, from 1998 to 2002, was the editor of *Academe,* the magazine of the American Association of University Professors.

William Stueck is Distinguished Research Professor of History at the University of Georgia. His books include *The Korean War: An International History* and *Rethinking the Korean War: A New Diplomatic and Strategic History.* During 1995 he was a Senior Fulbright Scholar at Hankuk University of Foreign Studies, Seoul, Korea.

Randall B. Woods is Cooper Distinguished Professor of History at the University of Arkansas. Among his publications are *The Dawning of the Cold War* with Howard Jones, *A Changing of the Guard,* and *Fulbright: A Biography.* He is currently writing a history of the life and times of Lyndon Baines Johnson.

Appendix B

The Participants in the Planning and Development of the Conference

Members of the Harry S. Truman Library Institute's Committee on Research, Scholarship, and Academic Relations

Carol Anderson	University of Missouri–Columbia
Jeff Gall	Truman State University
Alonzo L. Hamby	Ohio University
Susan M. Hartmann	Ohio State University
Mary Ann Heiss	Kent State University
R. Crosby Kemper, III	UMB Bank, N.A.
Richard S. Kirkendall	University of Washington
Michelle A. Mart	Pennsylvania State University
Dennis J. Merrill	University of Missouri–Kansas City
Steve Neal	*Chicago Sun-Times*
Ellen W. Schrecker	Yeshiva University
Randall B. Woods	University of Arkansas

Staff of the Truman Presidential Museum and Library and the Harry S. Truman Library Institute

Mark P. Adams	Education Coordinator
Michael J. Devine	Library Director and Institute President
Raymond H. Geselbracht	Education and Academic Outreach Coordinator
Thomas M. Heuertz	Associate Education Coordinator
Kathryn A. Knotts	Vice President for Advancement and Public Affairs

Judith A. O'Neill	Education Outreach Coordinator
Scott E. Roley	Deputy Director
Randy Sowell	Archivist
Lisa A. Sullivan	Office Manager

Appendix C
The Teachers

Center District (Missouri)
Johnna Fraise, Center High School
Erik Swanstrom, Center High School
Kathy Unger, Center High School
Claudette Williams, Center High School

Grandview District (Missouri)
Eric Reid, Martin City Middle School

Hickman Mills District (Missouri)
Donald Frazier, Ruskin High School
Chad Ryerson, Ruskin High School

Independence District (Missouri)
Karen Roberts, Bridger Eighth Grade Center

Kansas City, Kansas, District
Kim Buck, Argentine Middle School
Mark Daniels, Argentine Middle School
Ed Michalski, Rosedale Middle School
Charisse Morgan, Washington High School
Steve Smith, Sumner Academy of Arts and Science
Darwyn Thomlinson, Washington High School
Marilyn Vest, Northwest Middle School
John West, Argentine Middle School
Ethel Winston, Northwest Middle School

Kansas City, Missouri, District
Lisa Bankston, Hogan Preparatory Academy
Greg Cox, Van Horn High School
Dale Kindred, Paseo High School
Kim Miles, Hogan Preparatory Academy
Louis Read, Hogan Preparatory Academy
John Schmiedeler, Hogan Preparatory Academy
Rosemary Schmiedeler, Hogan Preparatory Academy
Michael Somodi, Van Horn High School
Travis Stevens, Hogan Preparatory Academy

Omaha District (Nebraska)
Holly Glade, Monroe Middle School
Lisa Krieser, Monroe Middle School

Saint Louis, Missouri (Parochial)
Timothy O'Neil, St. Louis University High School

Shawnee Mission District (Kansas)
Martha Howard, Indian Hills Middle School

Index